One Day in May – Bleiburg 1945

One Day in May – Bleiburg 1945

Jean Lunt Marinović

Copyright © 2016 Jean Lunt Marinovic

All rights are reserved. The material contained within this book is protected by copyright law, no part may be copied, reproduced, presented, stored, communicated or transmitted in any form by any means without prior written permission.

Disclaimer

Although the author has made every effort to ensure that the information in this book was correct at press time, the author does not assume and hereby disclaim any liability to any party for any loss, damage, or disruption caused by errors or omissions, whether such errors or omissions result from negligence, accident, or any other cause.

Typeset by BookPOD Pty Ltd

ISBN: 978-0-646-96374-7

National Library of Australia Cataloguing-in-Publication entry

Photo credits:

p. xvi   Photo by Modzzak - Own work, Public Domain, https://commons.wikimedia.org/w/index.php?curid=2765617

For my husband Ante
and our children and grandchildren

This book is dedicated to the memory of
Croatian civilians and unarmed soldiers
who were force-marched by Tito's communist Yugoslav Armies
on "Death Marches", slaughtered and
thrown into mass graves after the Second World War

Acknowledgments

I first began writing this book while in Croatia two years ago although the 'Bleiburg Tragedy' has held my interest for several decades. I wouldn't even have known about the 'Bleiburg Tragedy' if not for some individuals in the Croatian community who never lost hope, and who gave me books, in English, on the topic. The assistance, encouragement, and moral support of my husband Ante and our five children made it easier for me to get through the marathon task of researching and writing this book. It took us a few months to sort through dozens of musty boxes containing collections of newspapers, journals, printed internet articles and books. Because most of the material is in the Croatian language the challenge was to spot the word "Bleiburg" in the text or heading. My husband helped with translations, family members helped with constructive criticism and reading drafts, and our daughter Jenny Marinović edited my photographs in the book and for the montage and cover design. A thank you to Sylvie at BookPOD Pty Ltd for producing the four maps from my rough sketches. And a thank you also to the critics who seek to deny to Croatian people their very existence, their identity, and their basic human rights, for inspiring me to continue my research.

Jean Lunt Marinović
May 2016

About The Author

Jean Lunt Marinovic was born in Ottawa Canada during the Second World War. She has a Bachelor of Arts degree with a major in Communist politics and the political history of the former Yugoslavia. In over 100 published articles in the Australian/Croatian media Jean has commented on many historical events including the creation of the Kingdom of Serbs Croats and Slovenes and the inevitable collapse of Communist Yugoslavia. Jean represented Australian/Croatian parents on the School Council of the 'Saturday School of Modern Languages' in Melbourne during the 1980s. At Melbourne's new Immigration Museum Jean was the co-founder and co-ordinator of the Australian Croatian World Congress's 'Croatian Exhibit' in 1999. Together with her husband Ante, in 2005 Jean created and maintains the 'Croatian Viewpoint' website which features Croatian historical events in the English language. Ante and Jean married in Melbourne and have five children, and they often visit Croatia since its independence.

Contents

PREFACE
One Day in May – Bleiburg 1945 xv

PART 1
Introduction 1
Chapter 1: The Croatian Surrender to Yugoslavs at Bleiburg 5
Chapter 2: Southern Carinthia – Recent History 27
Chapter 3: Southern Carinthia – Post-WWII History 33
Chapter 4: The Croatian Retreat Routes 43

PART 2
Introduction 51
Chapter 5: 1970s 55
Chapter 6: 1980s 67
Chapter 7: 1990s 115
Chapter 8: 2000s 169
Chapter 9: 2010s 221
Chapter 10: Conclusions 259

APPENDIX I: The Creation of first Yugoslav Dictatorship 277
APPENDIX II: Who Created The First Yugoslav State? 281
Bibliography & Further Reading 289
Index 305

Genocide means any of the following acts committed with intent to destroy in whole or in part, a national, ethnic, racial or religious group, as such,

a. killing members of the group
b. causing serious bodily or mental harm to members of the group
c. deliberately inflicting on the group conditions of life calculated to bring about its physical destruction in whole or in part
d. imposing measures intended to prevent births within the group
e. forcibly transferring children of the group to another group

Article 2, United Nations
'Convention on the Prevention and
Punishment of the Crime of Genocide (1948)'

"Power is not a means, it is an end. One does not establish a dictatorship in order to safeguard a revolution; one makes the revolution in order to establish the dictatorship."

George Orwell
"Nineteen Eighty Four"
1949

PREFACE

ONE DAY IN MAY – BLEIBURG 1945

"Why Another Book about Bleiburg?"

When I decided to write a book about the "Bleiburg Tragedy" I collected all the information I could find. A lot of information is available, if you know what you are looking for, but a museum exhibit or an 'interpretive centre' do not exist anywhere as far as I know. A monument in Zagreb's Mirogoj national cemetery does exist, along with a memorial site at the Bleiburg field, but these memorials do not explain what the Bleiburg Tragedy means to non-Croatian visitors. There is no defining statement. There are few genuine photographs. I began to read the existing literature and documents and what I discovered surprised me!

The concrete memorial site and granite monument to Croatian victims at the Bleiburg field may survive the weather over time, but in contrast, the facts about the post-war events at Bleiburg Austria are gradually disappearing into the dustbin of history. Since the end of the Cold War people around the world are gradually becoming aware of Tito's genocide but the identity of his victims is rarely if ever mentioned. For this reason it's time for an objective narrative about the Bleiburg Tragedy, one which attributes total responsibility to Tito's communist Yugoslavia for the deliberate post-war genocide of unarmed Croatian victims.

I believe that this book is long overdue. The many conflicting inaccurate versions about the Bleiburg Tragedy left me wondering about what really happened! In this book I discuss what took place at the Bleiburg castle and the Bleiburg field on 15th May 1945 from autobiographical accounts and documents and also from the various perspectives of eye-witnesses. I interpret the events in the context of the recent history of Carinthia which explains why the Yugoslavs were occupying the region.

On my journey through the literature I soon discovered that many authors are trying to include several unrelated events in a single Bleiburg narrative. In this book I will argue that an inaccurate version of events on 15th May 1945 is counterproductive. Too many issues are left unresolved and pro-Yugoslav propaganda is winning the debate as a result. Dreams of justice and closure remain illusive.

"Hrvatskim zrtvama u Bleiburgu i na Kriznim Putovima 1945"
("Croatian victims at Bleiburg and the Way of the Cross 1945") [Monument, Mirogoj Cemetery Zagreb, Sculptor Augustin Filipovic, Erected by Croats 1994].

Many readers of this book may have already traveled to Austria to attend an annual commemoration at the site of the Bleiburg memorial to Croatian post-WWII victims. After visiting the Bleiburg memorial myself, in my book I re-visit Bleiburg by reviewing, comparing and contrasting the literature available to me. This has been a marathon task!

Today Bleiburg is a quaint tranquil setting with freshly rendered buildings but in my book we are transported to a post-WWII crisis which took place there on 15th May 1945. I was on a mission to discover exactly how the post-war events at Bleiburg fit into Tito's master plan to liquidate his Croatian opposition. Tito liquidated between 400,000 and 560,000 of his opposition after WWII to consolidate his power according to various sources such as the American President Truman. It was Croatian people who were the main victims of Tito's genocidal policies but this fact is barely known around the world.

Over the past decades I took everything I read about Bleiburg at face value. The problem was that my reading was more haphazard than thorough, and that is how misinterpretation overrides the facts. A lot of information has come to light in my research of various sources and mistakes and some themes have emerged which need to be addressed.

For example one of the themes which emerges is Tito's intentional lack of cooperation with the Allies in the months before the end of WWII and immediately afterwards. The Partisans were stockpiling Allied weapons for their occupation of Carinthia and after the war they were ordered to liquidate anyone who stood in their way.

This clandestine Partisan activity interested me because of my background. My father, born in England, was Assistant to the Financial Advisor for the Minister for Munitions and Supply in Canada during WWII. My mother, of Scottish ancestry, also worked in the same office where she met my father.

Many of the vehicles, munitions and supplies in southern Italy for the Eighth Army came from Canada, from Crown contracts and cheques signed by my

Win & Arthur D. Lunt, M.B.E.
Parliament, Ottawa in 1946

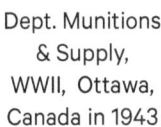

Dept. Munitions & Supply, WWII, Ottawa, Canada in 1943

Author Jean Lunt in 1959 at United Nations, New York

father. It's likely that some of these supplies were dropped to the Partisans in the Slovenian mountains in 1945 for use against the Nazis.

I have been writing about Croatian issues for decades yet my peers deem that I lack objectivity because my husband is Croatian. In 1970 I married a Croatian refugee from Yugoslavia, Ante Marinovic, born in Policnik, Zadar. On the other hand many Croatian people consider that I am biased because of my British background. Because of this dilemma my book about Bleiburg includes authors of many different perspectives and nationalities.

I believe I am qualified to comment on the Bleiburg issue because the major of my BA degree at La Trobe University (Melbourne) was revolutionary Communist politics. Although my Croatian language fluency is basic I did study a unit of Croatian language from Macquarie University as part of my degree. I also studied Political Geography and Economics at Ryerson University (Toronto). I have a long association with Croatian communities in Melbourne. Since the 1970s I have been involved in Croatian Community

Jean & Ante Marinovic, Geelong 1969

cultural events and I have witnessed first-hand the trauma experienced by Croatian refugees over several decades, up to the present day.

The mainstream public's lack of awareness about the Bleiburg Tragedy can be traced to the pro-Yugoslav propaganda which overshadows every attempt to expose their crimes against humanity. However, in "One Day in May – Bleiburg 1945" I offer some criticism regarding the existing Croatian interpretation of events. It's clear that Tito's "Death Marches" policy began 'before' the British repatriations of various ethnic groups, under the terms of the Yalta Conference, from more than one location across a wide front. Unfortunately many books or articles raise more questions than answers and as a result credibility has been lost. Because there are many issues to discuss regarding the events at Bleiburg this book will not go into any details about WWII, or any names, places, or battles, etc.

Jean & Ante Marinovic, at Brauhaus Breznik, Bleiburg 2014

I will attempt to answer the following questions in my book "One Day in May – Bleiburg 1945". Who did Croats negotiate with at Bleiburg and who did they surrender to? Is the Bleiburg Tragedy exclusively Croatian? How many British and Yugoslavs were in post-war Carinthia Austria? Are there any other factors which contributed to the crisis at Bleiburg? How many Croats went to the Bleiburg field, and how many were killed there? Why did Croats choose Bleiburg? Why do authors merge the Croatian surrender at Bleiburg to Yugoslavs, with the British repatriations at other locations as if all one event? Where does Bleiburg fit into this bigger picture of a Yugoslav planned and executed genocide? How many Croats were slaughtered after the Second World War and thrown into mass graves? Who is to blame for the "Death Marches" and massacres of Croatian people?

Jean & Ante Marinovic at Loibach Cemetery in 2014 at grave of Croats killed in May 1945 at Bleiburg

One Day in May – Bleiburg 1945

Ante, Ante Marinovic, Ilija at Bleiburg field 2014

I am grateful to many members of the Croatian communities around the world who have been kind and helpful over the past few decades. I'm also appreciative for the help of three Croatian men whose last names I have misplaced. Ante, Ilija and a third man also named Ante, all live in the town of Bleiburg. They help to maintain the Croatian memorial at the Bleiburg field, and regularly light candles for the victims. My husband Ante has shared with me a belief in this ambitious project and he has helped me with translations. Ante has patiently understood my frustration during the two years it has taken to write this book from the material I have collected over many decades. My five adult children have also assisted me with countless important practical needs. Without my family's support this book would never have been finished.

Jean Lunt Marinovic

May 2016

PART 1

INTRODUCTION

THE BLEIBURG TRAGEDY: AS IT HAPPENED

The first chapter of 'One Day in May – Bleiburg 1945' begins at the Bleiburg castle on 15th May 1945. It is devoted to eye-witness testimony of the tripartite surrender negotiations at Bleiburg, from all three perspectives: The Yugoslav, the British, and the Croatian. The book "Operation Slaughterhouse" and the contemporaneous Report of Brigadier Patrick Scott of the 38th Irish Brigade are my main sources.

The second and third chapters give a description of the situation in post-World War II Carinthia, and recent historical backdrop of the area. Chapter four is a chronology of the various Croatian retreat routes.

I acknowledge that, from a Croatian perspective, the term 'Bleiburg Tragedy' is symbolic of the "Death Marches" or "Way of the Cross" which followed various repatriations to Yugoslavia from Austria. However, throughout my book I distinguish between the surrender to the Yugoslavs at Bleiburg, and other British repatriations from other Austrian locations to Yugoslavia.

I do not focus on the deadly massacres which followed repatriations in this book except to establish the fact that they happened. Instead, in my book, my focus is on the 'responsibility' for those massacres, and in particular on Bleiburg. Tito's Bolshevik Yugoslav regime planned and executed the genocide of Croats in May 1945. There is no dispute that this genocide occurred because, since the collapse of the former Yugoslavia, hundreds of post-war mass graves have been discovered throughout Slovenia and Croatia.

In the second part of my book I introduce various perspectives of the events surrounding the Bleiburg Tragedy, from films, and from books and articles published over a fifty-year period. I compare and contrast the Croatian, British, or Yugoslav sources which I have been able to access over that period of time.

There is no scarcity of information about Bleiburg May 1945

Introduction

The Croatian Surrender to Yugoslavs at Bleiburg, 15 May 1945

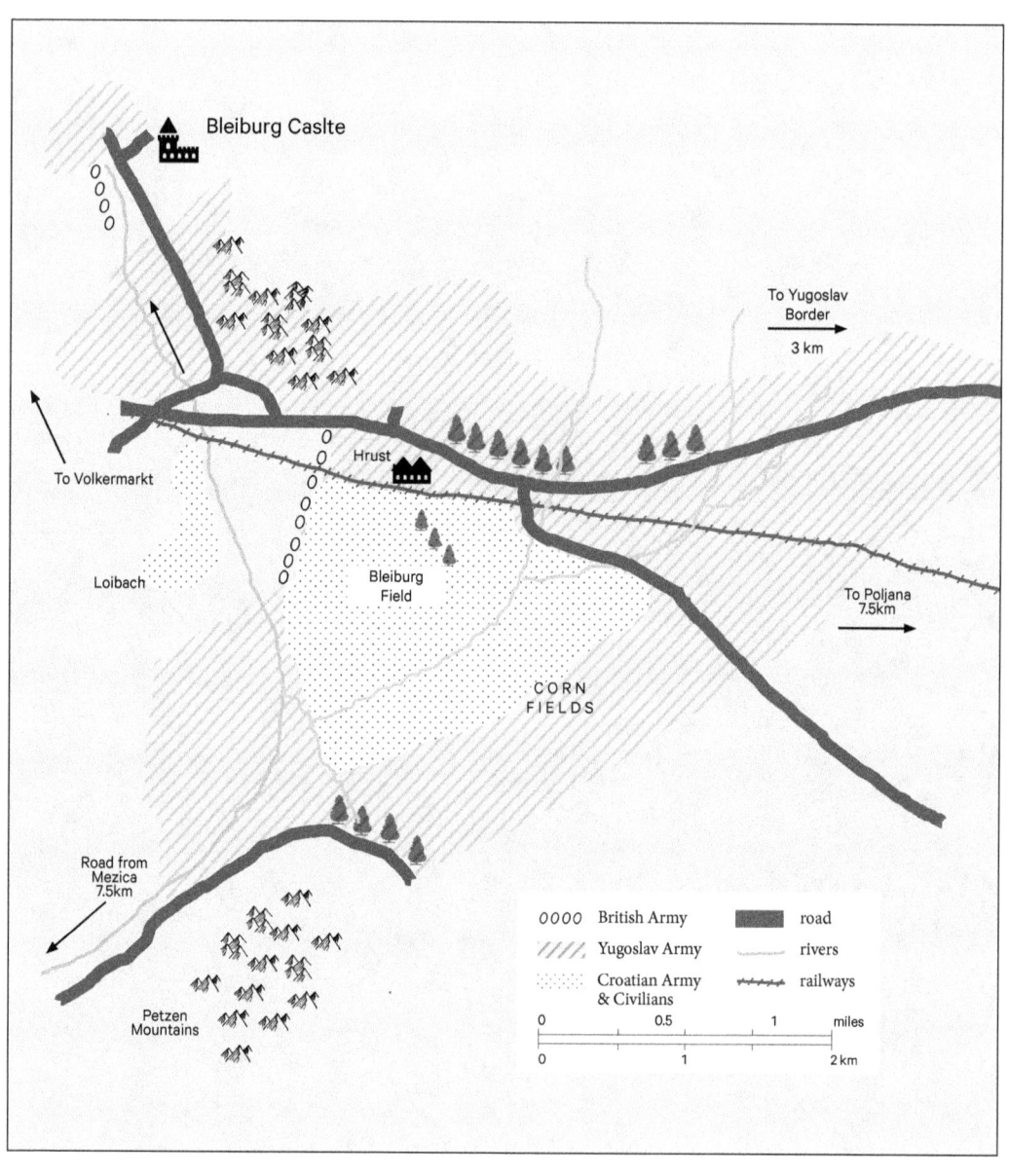

CHAPTER 1

THE CROATIAN SURRENDER TO YUGOSLAVS AT BLEIBURG

Three world mindsets met at the castle in Bleiburg to negotiate a surrender in post-WWII Austria: internationalist, imperialist, and nationalist. It was inevitable that their missions would be in conflict with each other. The war-weary British, who had just fought their way through northern Italy, were taken by surprise as a Communist-style revolution unfolded around them. Tension was increasing by the minute because the Yugoslav Bolshevik forces were intent on re-enforcing their occupation of Carinthia. This was the unexpected chaotic situation that the retreating Croatian army and civilians found themselves in at Bleiburg. By every definition and from every perspective this international crisis can be referred to as a tragedy.

The talks at the medieval Bleiburg castle occurred in three stages. The first and second stages were the negotiations between the British and the Yugoslavs, to be followed by separate negotiations between the British and the Croats. Finally all three groups came together in the same room and the only person present at all three talks, apart from the British officer, was the American-Croatian interpreter. There was a stark contrast between the orderly behaviour of the British and Croatian officers and the Yugoslav who dominated the room at all times with his disruptive behaviour. The Yugoslav left nothing to chance as he even interrupted the separate talks between the Croats and the British insisting that he would begin shooting the Croatian refugees at the nearby field if negotiations were not over in fifteen minutes.

The differences between the goals of the Yugoslavs, the British, and the Croats were clear very early in the negotiations. Judging by the terms of reference used by the Yugoslavs it is clear that the war was not yet over for them! The conflict between the Yugoslavs and the British at Trieste and Klagenfurt was coming to a climax at Bleiburg as the Yugoslav Armies were taking advantage of the chaos in the name of a peoples' revolution. In contrast to the Yugoslavs, the war was well and truly over for the battle-weary British Eighth Army whose orders were to maintain the uneasy peace and not to confront the Yugoslavs, and to ultimately to stick to the terms of the Yalta Agreement to return refugees to the Soviets and the Yugoslavs.

There are three eye-witness sources in writing about the exclusively Croatian surrender at the Bleiburg castle, namely of the Yugoslav Commissar, the commanding British officer, and of the Croatian political officer. The talks at the actual tripartite negotiations included two Yugoslav representatives, one a Croatian Serb and the other a Slovenian, and an interpreter, one British officer, and two Croatian representatives. No other army group was represented at the Bleiburg negotiations, in contrast to some insinuations that other nationalities were somehow represented there. According to the British author Nicholas Bethell, the British Brigadier, on arrival at Bleiburg, on 15th May drove his scout vehicle between the two armies at the field in order to locate and organise two groups of generals to drive up to his headquarters at the Bleiburg castle. Robert Plan, the interpreter present during the whole negotiation period, was also a witness to the negotiations.

Jean Lunt Marinovic at rear entrance to Bleiburg castle 2014

Basta's Report – Introduction

The Yugoslav officer's account of the surrender negotiations generally corresponds to the content of the Scott narrative, but he adds some additional information which is summarized herewith. We learn of the Yugoslav Commissar's name, Milan Basta, and the names of others at the negotiations. It would appear that Basta's Report was carefully written later in hindsight because it includes details not present in the British War Diaries.

This Yugoslav version of the surrender negotiations was published in the book "Operation Slaughterhouse" as Document II which uses as its source the book by Milan Basta entitled, "Rat Posle rata" (The war after the war), Zagreb, Stvarnost, 1963.

The Yugoslav representatives included the main spokesperson, Lt. Colonel Milan Basta, Political Commissar of the 51st Vojvodina Division of the Yugoslav Army, and one Slovenian Partisan from Slovenia (Ivan Kovacic). In Basta's account of the Bleiburg negotiations, he states that, much to his surprise, he saw four Ustasha generals, un-named by him, while on his way inside the Bleiburg castle which had made him feel nervous and restless. It was 15th May 1945 at 2 p.m. and Basta described his concerns at that time, which he kept to himself during the talks, of having no authority if the British were to offer protection to the Croatian generals. Basta also referred to the presence of five or six British officers though not by name.

Both the British Brigadier Scott and Basta did not name each other, and made no mention of names. Basta has identified the Croats present, suggesting that this report was made with information discovered later.

Basta's Report – first the Yugoslavs meet separately with the British

After exchanging introductory remarks, all translated by his un-named interpreter who he also described as a Liaison Officer, Basta was told that the British had called him to the meeting to respond to the Croatian wish to surrender to the British. Basta refers then to the British General's communication to him regarding the

> "300,000 enemy troops...before us"

who would continue to fight rather than surrender to the Yugoslavs. In writing this account in hindsight Basta admits he was surprised to learn at the time that there were about

"100,000 of Pavelic's soldiers around Bleiburg"

The Yugoslav Commissar informed the British officer that the Allies should not hinder the Yugoslavs in dealing with the enemy because the "prospective surrender" was a

"...purely Yugoslav affair..."

Basta must have written this account in hindsight with information known later, that Pavelic and his commanders had sought safety abroad. At this point in the initial discussions Basta informed the British General that the Croats had not all come to Austria and that

"...the majority of the Croatian forces were still on Yugoslav territory and had no great prospect of being able to cross the border".

Basta's orders, quite different to the British orders, were to

"compel the enemy troops to capitulate if they do not wish to do so willingly, and that it should happen in one hour...after the return of the enemy delegates to their camp..."

The British general had expressed doubt to Basta about the time frame (before nightfall) suggesting the capitulation would be better carried out the next morning, to which Basta, bragging about the Yugoslav strength in the area, emphasized that the time frame of one hour was the only option for the capitulation to begin, although the process could take "several days" if necessary.

Basta's Report – the Yugoslavs wait in the next room

The British general informed Basta that he would talk to the Croatian representatives. Basta thought to himself about why the British would even talk to the enemy representatives and wondered if the Englishman was contacting his superiors, or that he wanted to be an arbitrator.

The message from Basta that negotiations were taking too long, sent to the British commander when speaking separately to the Croats, is also mentioned in this account. What is new here is the fact that the Yugoslavs had seen, from the castle window, the approaching Yugoslav Army column of the 12th Proletarian Brigade from Dravograd. In this account of events the Yugoslav headquarters in the area, Hrust, is also mentioned by name.

From this Yugoslav vantage point, is the detail of Basta's mention of a second meeting with the British without any Croats present, where he was told by the British General that "definitive negotiations for the surrender would start at once". Once again Basta reminded the British commander that there was only half an hour left for the negotiations to finish.

It is becoming clear to all concerned just who was the most confident of their power on this day in Bleiburg once the Yugoslav reinforcements had arrived. Up to this point the only meetings between the Yugoslavs and the Croats had been settled by Yugoslav military attacks on the retreating columns in Slovenia.

Basta's Report – the final talks between the Yugoslavs, British & Croats

The two Croatian generals were brought into the room where the Yugoslavs had already been seated. The "Englishman" via the interpreter, immediately signalled to Basta to state the "capitulation" terms to the Croats. Basta was emboldened by this time by the fact that the Yugoslav 12th Brigade and its artillery had arrived. In his version of this opening statement Basta told the Croats they were encircled and surrounded on all sides by four Yugoslav armies and so, in other words, they were in a "dead-end street". This is the first mention of a name by Basta, namely he thought (incorrectly) the Croatian officer was Tomislav Sertic.

Basta demanded an unconditional Croatian surrender to the Yugoslavs by 4 p.m or they would be destroyed, to happen one hour after their return to their units. He said that civilians would be guaranteed a safe return home and could keep their belongings. The others would be escorted to P.O.W. camps according to international law, and that the generals could retain their valets and weapons. Once again Basta reiterated that any Croatian resistance would induce Yugoslav "liquidation" measures. Basta gives his threatening ultimatum.

> Basta: "I command you in the name of the Yugoslav Army to halt all attempts at resistance within one hour's time, to lay down your arms, and to carry out our orders…If you do not obey these orders, we will destroy you, and you will bear the responsibility for the fate of your troops and civilian population."

At this time Basta explained the surrender conditions that the civilians would be returned to their homes; that the military personnel would be escorted to P.O.W. camps provided they surrender unconditionally without resistance; and, members of the Croatian Armed Forces (HOS) would be treated in accordance with the stipulations of international law. Necessary belongings would be allowed and

Generals would be allowed their valets and personal weapons and that any resistance would be dealt with.

> "In such case we will treat you as rebels in whose liquidation our allies will assist us."

According to Basta the Ustasha chief repeated the capitulation conditions and understood them and that the only problem was the time limit. The Croatian general complained about the impossible time frame for him to be able to pass orders for capitulation and that it could lead to misunderstanding. Basta believes that Scott may well have been kept informed about the arrival of more Yugoslav troops in the area during a conversation between the British, which Basta could not hear, and it was probably in this context that the British General Scott stated that "my tanks are at your disposal". Basta thought to himself, as he wrote, that the British general's offer of help was his way of putting all responsibility onto the Partisans. But of course Basta was not aware of what was said previously between the others when he was not present. According to Basta, Sertic then asked that watches be synchronised.

After the Croats left, the British and Yugoslav officers synchronized their watches. Basta says that he thanked Scott for his "collaboration" and that they exchanged names in a memorandum, now lost. Basta also claims he gave orders to the 12th Slavonian Proletarian Division that after the Croats were disarmed, to conduct the escort back to Yugoslavia using strict discipline. The British were warned that their forces must not interfere with the surrender process, and that in that event, they would be advised of the decision reached at their command headquarters.

Basta's Report – in the Bleiburg Field

Basta is the only one to give an additional account of the Croatian General Stancer's attempt to conduct new negotiations at the Yugoslav headquarters, a short time after the negotiations at the castle. Named as Colonel General Slavko Stancer, the Commanding General of the regular army of the Independent State of Croatia (NDH), and General Tomasevic, Basta claims they came because they had not yet witnessed the return of the four Croatian generals from the castle negotiations.

> "From the generals who were brought to our quarters, we learned with great surprise that there were over 100,000 men of the Croatian Army in the immediate vicinity. There were many civilian refugees, also."

In the "garden house" Basta then explained to these Croats the decision at the castle and the "conditions of capitulation" under international law, and that white flags must immediately go up. The Croatian commanders were warned that any resistance would be crushed harshly but that they would be treated according to international law.

The surrender conditions described by Basta do not diverge from the terms and conditions described in Scott's Report. Finally Basta described the "dizzying pace" of the Croatian surrender to the Yugoslavs, and the column of Croats who were lined up on the "road in front of our headquarters" (presumably he means here 'Hrust', the garden house directly opposite to the Bleiburg field) between 4 and 4:30 p.m. on 15th May 1945. Here Basta refers to the numbers as a "multitude" of P.O.W.s and a "greater mass" of civilians. Once again Basta threatens to destroy them and that they would bear the responsibility for their fate. Finally the white flags were displayed "all over the nearby fields and surrounding hills" after which everything "went forward at a dizzying pace".

In the Reports by the British and Croatian representatives we will learn more names and about the Bulgarian blockade which Basta does not mention. Nevertheless the other versions of the castle negotiations do not greatly differ from each other.

Men standing beside memorial in Bleiburg field near former Hrust Tavern, in 2014, Memorial: "Vilim Cecelja 1909-1989, Salsburg, Dobrotvor Cuvar Bleiburske Uspomene" (Benefactor & Guard Bleiburg Memorial)

Scott's Report – Introduction

At the end of war in May 1945 the British Brigadier T.P.D. (Patrick) Scott commanded the 38th Irish Brigade which was slowly progressing eastwards from the Italian border through southern Austria. In post-WWII Austria the Zones of Occupation had not yet been officially defined.

Under the heading "Peacekeeping" the Report by Brigadier Scott appears under the sub-titles of "Into Austria – Settling Frontiers", and "Balkan Troubles" on the official website of the 38th Irish Brigade.

Scott's Report, which deals mostly with the Russians and Cossacks, details the logistics of the Carinthian region from Wolfsberg and St. Andre south of Wolfsberg, where he sent the "London Irish". He then sent his whole Regiment to Volkermarkt and "as far south as Bleiburg" due to having to deal with the unexpected Yugoslav attempts to set-up dual control in the region. By 12th May he had received word that the 1st Bulgarian Army (under Russian command) had set up headquarters in Lavamund, to where he sent the "Faughs" to "hold the fort". In addition the Hungarians had headquarters at Lavamund. On 12th May Scott ordered "13 Battery of 17 Field Regiment" to occupy the village of Bleiburg which was 20 miles west of Lavamund after which

> "17th Field Regiment really assumed responsibility for the area between Volkermarkt, Griffen and Bleiburg".

On 13th May the 38th Irish Brigade changed from being under the command of the 6th Armoured Division to the 46th Division. Also, in the 17th Field Regiment's area, on the 13th May, the German General Lohr had arrived at Bleiburg along with his one of his Divisions. The eventful 13th May finished with the capture of one of Croatia's government ministers by the "London Irish".

> "The German Puppet Minister to the Croat Republic was captured by the London Irish. He had a bag of 250 gold sovereigns with him amongst other things and a very fine car".

Meanwhile, according to Brigadier Scott, the total British resources at Bleiburg, at the time amounted to

> "Paul Lunn-Rockcliffe's Battery, a troop or two of 46 Reconnaissance Regiment, a couple of armoured cars of 27 Lancers and two or three tanks".

The Croatian Surrender to Yugoslavs at Bleiburg

Brigadier Scott reported that in the evening of 14th May 1945 a Croatian Liaison officer had arrived at the 17th Field Regiment outpost in the Bleiburg field to state the goal of the Croats approaching from the Yugoslav border. The still-armed Croats had been fighting with the Yugoslav Tito troops across the Yugoslav/Austrian border in an attempt to pass the established Bulgarian and Yugoslav outposts to cross the border.

The Croatian Liaison officer, not named in this original Report, referred to two groups of the still-armed Croatian army of 100,000 each coming from the south, and half a million civilians trailing behind, as well as some German divisions. The Croatian Liaison officer described how Croats had failed to get through the Bulgarian outposts. Instead, the Bulgarians had allowed the Croats to turn west towards Bleiburg "south of Lavamund" but that the Yugoslavs had then opened fire on the Croats with bazookas and shelling slowing down the Croat's progress.

At Bleiburg on 15th May 1945 there were three different sets of orders of the three different army representatives. The British officer refers to his orders early in his Report, regarding the approaching Croats, advising them that he had recently received new orders, and had been instructed by a "higher authority" not to "allow them (Croats) to surrender to us". The Croatian Liaison officer had however made his intentions clear that Croats would not surrender to the Yugoslavs; whilst the Yugoslavs were taking up "warlike positions" in the Bleiburg field to make sure that Croats would not "get out of their clutches", according to the British War Diaries.

At noon on 15th May 1945, Brigadier Scott arrived at Bleiburg and drove around to familiarize himself with the area where he "could not see anything except the Yugoslavs". Scott then drove up to the Bleiburg castle and sent for the Croatian and Yugoslav commanders who were already known to the 17th Field Regiment. During the morning of 15th May Scott organised for some "fighters" to fly around to "strike terror" into the Croats in the field, probably in an attempt to uphold his fresh orders not to allow anymore groups to surrender to the British.

At the end of the day on 15th May the 16 Durham Light Infantry Division was ordered to relieve the exhausted 13 Battery and 17 Field Regiment which would now remain north of the Drava River. In addition, at the end of the day further tanks were also called in if required.

SCOTT'S REPORT – FIRST SCOTT FIRST MEETS SEPARATELY WITH THE YUGOSLAVS

Brigadier Scott first met with the young Yugoslav Commissar who he had described as a "firebrand" in his Report. Scott does not mention the Yugoslav's name and wrote in his diary at the time that he thought that he was a 'Major General'. Accompanying the Yugoslavs was an interpreter of "Yugoslav" extraction, also not named. According to Brigadier Scott the Yugoslav's objective was to begin to

> "…defeat the Croat army in the field in battle…(in)…half an hour".

Scott continues in his Report that at this first meeting the Yugoslav officer did not request any assistance because his forces were already in the area and more Yugoslav troops were constantly arriving.

Since the war had ended a week earlier the new policy of the British Army was now to avert any fresh battles with the Yugoslavs. In this context, and carrying out his new order not to accept any more people behind British lines, Scott suggested, while in the presence of the Yugoslavs, that it would be easier if the Croats would lay "down their arms" and surrender to the Yugoslavs. The Yugoslav Commissar agreed but impatiently added that the "half hour" was almost over.

SCOTT'S REPORT – SECONDLY SCOTT MEETS SEPARATELY WITH THE CROATS

At this point the Yugoslavs withdrew and Brigadier Scott summoned the Croatian commanders from a group of about ten, who had been waiting in another room, to explain the proceedings to date with the aid of the interpreter who had remained in the room. The intention of the Croatian officers, it was emphasized to Scott, was that they did not want to surrender to the "Bolsheviks" and they described themselves as, "an emigration of the entire Croat nation". According to Scott's Report the Croats wished this "political" matter to be referred to Field Marshall Alexander.

In this separate discussion with the Croatian commanders Scott asked them where the Croats thought they would emigrate to, and how they would feed such a multitude. Scott made it clear that such an emigration was "out of the question" in war-torn Europe where food was already scarce.

During this private meeting between Scott and the Croatian generals the Yugoslav representative sent another urgent message to Scott

> "that he could not wait any longer, and that the battle must start".

Scott then entered directly into negotiation options with the Croatian officers. Brigadier Scott's Report details the alternatives given to the Croatian generals and with the ominous Yugoslav threat to begin shooting the Croats gathered at the field, he gave them five minutes to choose from the options.

1. The Croats could surrender to the Yugoslavs, after which Scott would attempt to use his influence to try and ensure they would be treated correctly.

2. Alternatively Croats could keep their arms and remain where they were, where they would most certainly be attacked by the Yugoslav Partisans surrounding them.

3. If the Croats attempted to go behind British lines the Yugoslavs and the British would probably react to prevent this with Allied Air and Land forces in which case they would unquestionably be annihilated.

Outnumbered and feeling pressured by serious Yugoslav threats to begin shooting within the hour, Brigadier Scott believed the first alternative he offered to the Croats would result in the least number of deaths, and he made his belief known to the Croatian representatives.

The Croat representative, who has not been named by Scott, chose the first option within five minutes, and the Yugoslavs were then brought back to join them in the room.

Scott's Report – at the final meeting the British, Yugoslavs & Croats sit together

Now together in the same room, the interpreter explained to all three parties the proceedings to date to everyone present. At this point, according to this official Report by Scott

> "An agreement was then made up on my presence and signed by the two armies".

Subsequently, on behalf of the surrendering Croats, Scott argued with the "firebrand" Yugoslav commander that the one hour period demanded by him was insufficient, but to no avail. Scott's careful response to this impasse was to tell the Croats that they were already over one week late in surrendering, and that their white flags should be up before the end of one hour and, that he would help enforce the agreement regarding the surrender to the Yugoslavs. Scott wrote in his Report that he had believed the least number of deaths would occur by the carrying out of the first surrender alternative. Scott promised his support to the Yugoslavs in reference to the first option which was that the Croatians would surrender to the Yugoslavs. This British offer of support was given with the awareness of the credible Yugoslav threats to begin shooting Croats within the hour with the intention to

> "...defeat the Croat Army in the (Bleiburg) field in battle".

Under the conditions of this agreement and openly expressed by the Yugoslavs, according to Scott's Report, the Croats were to be treated by the Yugoslavs as "Prisoners of War" as guaranteed by the Yugoslav Commander. In addition, any political criminals were to be tried by Allied courts, and that the civilians were to be fed and returned to Croatia by the shortest possible route.

Scott's Report – Croats surrender to Yugoslavs in the Bleiburg field

Close to the end of the elapsed hour the Croatian white flags were up, and handing in of arms to the Yugoslavs had commenced in the Bleiburg field. According to Brigadier Scott's narrative, to the best of his knowledge within the next 24 hours the surrender and evacuation was "carried out by the Yugoslavs efficiently".

Bleiburg castle in background and road junction near Bleiburg field, 2014

Crljen's Report – Introduction

The Croatian version of events is given by one of the spokesmen at the Bleiburg castle, Colonel Daniel Crljen, of the regular Croatian Army who was also in the Croatian Defence Ministry. Crljen's testimony is also available in the book "Operation Slaughterhouse" as Document III.

We have learned so far that the British were slowly making their way through southern Austria eastwards from Trieste, and that the Yugoslavs were also occupying the area and disrupting the peace. For the purpose of understanding the Bleiburg castle negotiations it is also important to understand why and how the Croats came to be in the same area at the same time. The Croatian retreat which started a week earlier will be described in a subsequent chapter in this book.

In his version of events Crljen refers to the Croatian military evacuation of Zagreb, on 6th May, and the miles and miles of columns of 200,000 officers and soldiers; and from 8th May 1945 that General Herencic of the Croatian Fifth Army Corps at Karlovac was commanding Crljen's "improvised officer" group. These numbers concur with Scott's Report of the approaching columns of Croats. Conditions were difficult as the weather was unusually hot in the daytime for that time of year but the temperature also plummeted at night.

Crljen writes that by 11th May the Croatian columns had begun to arrive at Slovenj Gradec in Slovenia which was on the road to Dravograd but that the Yugoslav Army and Bulgarian Army were blocking the bridge across the Drava River. According to Crljen this newly formed improvised Croatian army group under General Ivo Herencic held a "council of war" when it was decided that generals Crljen, Metikos and Servatski would meet the Bulgarians.

Crljen's Report – Croats meet with Bulgarians near Dravograd

The Croatian representatives met with a Bulgarian political commissar in a village "near Dravograd" in Yugoslavia. It was suggested that a meeting take place with the British, Russians, and Bulgarians the next day, but it was a meeting which did not happen because the British had not yet arrived. Crljen describes how the Yugoslavs occupied the terrain ahead of the Croats, and that skirmishes broke out, with the result that Croats decided it would be impossible to pursue any crossing of the Drava River. Therefore, instead of any crossing of the Drava, according to Crljen's account, the long Croatian columns turned towards the Miess River, two hours away.

Crljen's Report – The Arrival of Croats in the Bleiburg Field

Eight days after the evacuation of Zagreb, on 14th May, the Croats sent ahead one of their Liaison officers to contact the British near Bleiburg. Crljen claims that at this point British "military planes" hovered above which he suggests was done "to intimidate" the Croats. However Crljen is not specific about whether this occurred on 14th May or 15th May, or at what time of day, but at least it confirms what Scott said about sending up aeroplanes, although not on which day.

The Croatian generals were told, via their Liaison officer, to send delegates to the British "who had just arrived" from Klagenfurt. Generals Herencic, Servatski and Crljen, as a political negotiator, are mentioned in this report.

According to Crljen the route to the medieval castle at Bleiburg was lined with "British combat ready tanks", a claim very much at odds with the British report which said that additional tanks were called after negotiations had finished. Crljen had thought the British commanding officer was named Murray at the time, who was in attendance at the castle with a large group of officers. Crljen refers also to an American-Croatian interpreter, though not by name.

Crljen's Report – Croats Meet with the British

Crljen's account, like the other two versions, is about the exclusively Croatian negotiations at the Bleiburg castle with the British and Yugoslavs. No other nation or army was represented at this meeting according to these three original eye-witness accounts at the castle which at least do not conflict each other on this point.

General Herencic's instructions had been to offer a Croatian surrender to the western Allies and ask for political asylum, especially re the Croatian civilians. Crljen entered the discussion with the "Englishman" by explaining that they were "political exiles" who needed "protection". At the beginning however Scott, whose name Crljen did not know at the time, made it clear to the Croats that he had no political authority regarding this situation. It was on this basis that Scott refused to consider their demands, and stated that Field Marshall Alexander's orders were already made clear to him.

Crljen again referred to the hundreds of thousands of Croatian civilians who were trying to escape being massacred by the Yugoslavs. To this Croatian request, according to Crljen, Scott referred to claims by the Yugoslavs who had guaranteed that they would respect human rights and international conventions. Crljen kept thoughts to himself about the British officer's ignorance of Marxist intentions. In the crossfire of this discussion between the British and Croatian officers Crljen mentions that the interpreter was becoming bewildered. Crljen's version does not mention the options given to the Croats by Scott. On page 152 of "Operation Slaughterhouse" he claims that the conditions for surrender would be discussed in the presence of the Yugoslavs. He only mentions the alternatives later in connection with an alleged conversation with Metikos after Scott left.

Crljen's Report – the Yugoslavs, British & Croats meet together

It was then indicated by Scott that the Croatian generals should wait for the Yugoslav delegation and they agreed to wait in the anti-chamber. After a short while Herencic and Crljen left Generals Metikos and Servatski and entered a room where they sat across from two Yugoslav political commissars.

In the reports by both Scott and Basta we know that a separate meeting had also taken place between the other two without the Croats.

In his report written some time after the event, Crljen remarks on the fact that no record was being kept of the talks. On this point the reader might well ask themselves why the Croats themselves did not take notes, or request that a record be taken at the time. In any case a record of events does appear in the original British War Diaries written day by day.

According to Crljen, Basta asserted that the Croats were surrounded by Yugoslavs.

> "a number of communist (Yugoslav) divisions had encircled us...and that the Croatian General Sudar already surrendered".

Basta was probably referring here to the current situation and to a surrender which took place earlier inside Austria. At this point Basta insisted that the Croats had one hour to comply and that they would be taken to Maribor (Slovenia), and that civilians would be allowed to go home. Basta said that if they did not accept these surrender terms in "fifteen minutes" the Yugoslavs would begin attacking the Croats. Crljen replied that one hour was not enough time and proposed 24 hours, and at this point the British commander suggested (according to Crljen's account) that at least two hours should be granted, a request also refused by Basta.

I would suggest that it is possible that everyone was thinking about how many hours of daylight remained although no emphasis on this point is made by Crljen, Scott or Basta.

Crljen generalises that the British officer had made it clear to the Croats that British tanks were at the disposal of the Yugoslavs, and had offered to enforce the surrender process. According to Basta's account the British offer of help had been rejected in their first meeting apart from the Croatian generals. In any case Crljen does not make it clear that the British offer of help to the Yugoslavs would be forthcoming only in connection with the third option. The third option to try and go through the British lines was not taken up by the Croats however. In a reference to his own unspoken thoughts about alleged British responsibility written later, Crljen judges that this was a British "calculated atrocity" even though no atrocity had yet happened.

In Crljen's words, a strong division of opinion quickly emerged amongst the Croats at the field with some withdrawing to the surrounding forests, and some wanting to fight. Others, under General Stancer wanted to form a new delegation to negotiate with the Yugoslavs. The British refused to receive Stancer as negotiations had been completed, and he was then escorted to Partisan Headquarters, according to Crljen. In Crljen's words, General Herencic advised Crljen to inform the civilians about the surrender to Yugoslavs. Crljen himself headed for the "woods".

Synthesis – Negotiations and Surrender

In Crljen's report there is an acknowledgement that three options were offered to the Croatian generals by Brigadier Scott at the castle, namely to surrender to the Yugoslavs, to fight, or to flee. Crljen asked that the one hour time limit should begin upon arrival at the camp 20 minutes away. All of them agreed that the Croats would surrender to Yugoslavs and they synchronized their watches. No mention of any written or signed agreement seems to have survived, written at the time, other than in the British War Diaries or Scott's Report.

Another eye-witness to the 'surrender' was the American interpreter of a Croatian background who had been with the OSS and the Partisans in the Slovenian mountains during the war. After the war the American-Croatian interpreter Robert Plan returned to Slovenia to the location of his war-time service.

Franklin Lindsay's book, "Beacons in the Night: With the OSS and Tito's Partisans in Wartime Yugoslavia" tells how Bob Plan, an American who was born in Dalmatia, had arrived in Slovenia with the OSS and Captain Charles Fisher in September 1944. Robert Plan, known as 'Bob Perry' during the war was under the SI Austria section. Towards the end of the war OSS Captain Douglas Owen and Bob Plan were in the Partisan Fourth Zone.

In "Otvoreni dossier Bleiburg" we learn that many of the photographs of about 13 May 1945 around the Yugoslav/Austrian border were taken by Miroslav Lilik, aid to the British Major D. C. Owen. Douglas Owen had replaced the author Lindsay in early December in the Zone. It was Robert Plan who had survived who told Lindsay about the fate of their OSS group and about the Croatian regiments fighting with the Germans. Owen, Campbell, and Plan had eventually escaped at the end of December by crawling behind the hay stacks and to the forest. They remained in the high mountains until the end of the war.

Other Eye-Witness Accounts From 'Operation Slaughterhouse' Document IV – An Eye-Witness Account, J. Ursic, 1955

This Croatian civilian at the Bleiburg field on 15th May described seeing British tanks and vehicles lining up around the Croatian masses on the field. He remembers seeing twelve British planes flying low overhead. He describes the surrender following the negotiations at the castle, and witnessing Danijel Crljen and other Croatian officers as well as some Montenegrins, and learning that the surrender would be to the Yugoslavs.

> Ursic: "The multitude of Croatians assembled on the field were composed of a heterogeneous mass of officers, soldiers, women, and older people of both sexes. They were ordered to draw up in a column of fours and to be ready to leave at once... Partisan soldiers and officers...were trying to separate the officers and soldiers from the civilians...(and)...marched them off to an unknown destination."

According to this version by Ursic in "Operation Slaughterhouse" the British halted the surrender procedure at 6pm and that it would begin at 8am in the morning. By the morning the field was almost deserted however according to Ursic, and most munitions were gone. He and his group crossed a wooden bridge over the Drava and out of sight of any British. By 17th May they reached Dravograd.

Document V – An Eye-Witness Account, B. J., 1945

At Dravograd before entering Austria the eye-witness B.J. refers to the Croatian generals Herencic, Servatzi, Boban, Tomasevic, Metzger, Gustovic, Metikos and Stancer. Herencic had been unsuccessful at negotiations with the Bulgarians. At night on 13th May 1945 the Croatian retreat towards Bleiburg was subjected to attacks by Partisan units in spite of guarantees given the previous day. On 14th May the Bulgarians also supported the Partisans and several hundred Croats were lost in this battle. This group of Croats managed to reach the Bleiburg field by the evening of 14th May and joined other Croats already there. The Yugoslavs and the English were however blocking the entrance to the village of Bleiburg.

He writes that on 15th May the Croatian generals Herencic, Servatzi, Metikos and Colonel Crljen went to negotiations "with the British Commander" and that later these same officers returned and ordered us to "hoist white flags as signs of surrender" to the Communists. Some generals such as Boban and Colonel Sudar were returning to Croatia to fight. Others surrendered.

Document XI – an eye-witness account, I. S., 1956

This eye-witness I.S. accuses the Croatian General Herencic and other Croatian officers of deception, and of not telling their troops that they would be extradited to Yugoslavia. After describing the blockade across the Drava River by the Bulgarians, and subsequent unsuccessful talks, he described how the Croats had to go "around" Dravograd to reach the plain near Bleiburg in Austria on 14th May and 15th May 1945. At the field there were "great masses" of troops and "countless thousands of civilians". According to this source amongst the Croats were also a few Montenegrins and Chetniks and their families.

British planes overhead and some British tanks were in evidence inside this Austrian zone according to I.S. General Herencic was one of the spokesmen who contacted the British command, and who had returned from the talks and called together the Ustasha and Domobran officers. This eye-witness I.S., amongst about 200 officers assembled by Herencic, was standing only fifteen feet away and heard every word clearly.

> I.S.: "He told us that the only condition set for our surrender by the British Command was that we must lay down our arms. He did not utter one word intimating that we were in effect surrendering not to the British but to Tito's miserable Partisan bands. ... I do not know of anyone around me who had the slightest apprehension that the British had refused to accept our surrender themselves."

In the strongest words this eye-witness I. S. accuses General Herencic and other commanders for being responsible for the "disintegration and subsequent massacre of our Army" on 15th May 1945 which was still-armed and could have taken another course. He had not seen Partisans at the time, although of course it was later discovered that the Yugoslavs who were in the surrounding hills had them encircled.

The Croatian Surrender to Yugoslavs at Bleiburg

The Croats then surrendered their weapons at 4pm, and during the march back to Yugoslavia, following the course of the Drava River, he could not see either the beginning or the end of the column.

Document LV – an eye-witness account, L. J. Globan (no date)

After describing the retreat like other eye-witnesses at Bleiburg, Globan describes being re-routed at Dravograd by Bulgarians and following the bank of the Drava River until the field at Bleiburg on 15th May where they were ordered to "form up by unit". He was unsure if there may have been about 200,000 refugees of all categories there. Our commanding officer was General Herencic and Professor Daniel Crljen was the civilian representative of the Pavelic regime. They still anticipated that the surrender would be to the British at this time. At 4pm the Croats, unfurled their flags, put up white flags and stacked their weapons.

> Globan: "It was only when I noticed that it was not Englishmen, but men of the 16th Voyvodina Partisan Division, who were collecting our piled up arms that I began to feel uneasy."

He describes that it was the Yugoslav Communists which had them form into columns of eight and leave for Dravograd.

Summary

In a nutshell: Tripartite negotiations at the Bleiburg castle took place between two Yugoslav officers, a British officer, and two representatives of the Croatian Army and civilians in the absence of the Pavelic government leadership. A Croatian-American interpreter was present throughout. The Croatian Ustasha representatives at Bleiburg did not include anyone from Pavelic's group who were safely in north Austria by this time, having travelled via a totally different route. A new British order was handed down not to allow more refugees to cross the British lines. The 'option', one of three discussed with the British general, accepted by the Croatian commanders resulted in the Croatian surrender to Yugoslavs, who were already occupying the Bleiburg area. There were few surviving witnesses because the Yugoslavs had turned those surrendered Croats at Bleiburg back into Yugoslavia and massacred them along "Death Marches". Most of the hundreds of thousands of Croats had not come as far as Bleiburg and did not cross the border because they had been blocked by the occupying Yugoslavs and Bulgarians.

Not only were the British out-numbered at that time and place by the Yugoslavs, but the Yugoslavs had continually threatened that "the Croats were not going to get out of their clutches". If there had been as many British soldiers present on the day, or tanks, as was claimed later by some Croatian sources then it is certain that the Yugoslavs would not have behaved so brazenly and with such confidence.

These original testimonies do not basically differ. Of interest is how some authors incorrectly refer to an "English" officer or army rather than "British". Also I belive it's possible that some authors who refer to crossing the Drava River may be confusing this with the Meiss River (or Meza river), a tributary of the Drava. It is regrettable that many later accounts written about the events of 15th May contradict, omit, or misrepresent all three of these original eye-witness sources.

For example, some authors refer to subsequent Yugoslav gunfire against the disarmed Croats at the Bleiburg field, such as Tolstoy, but this claim was refuted by others. I will review important books by Lord Cowgill and Christopher Booker in another chapter of my book. In addition, assorted captions next to various photographs have been used to back-up widely diverging claims. For example, one photograph may have several different captions and time frame, depending on the author.

Why and how the retreating Croats came to Bleiburg and then surrendered to Yugoslavs instead of the British is the main focus of my book and to better understand the 'Bleiburg tragedy' it is helpful to have a look at recent history of the area.

Austrian Kingdom of Illyria 1822–1849

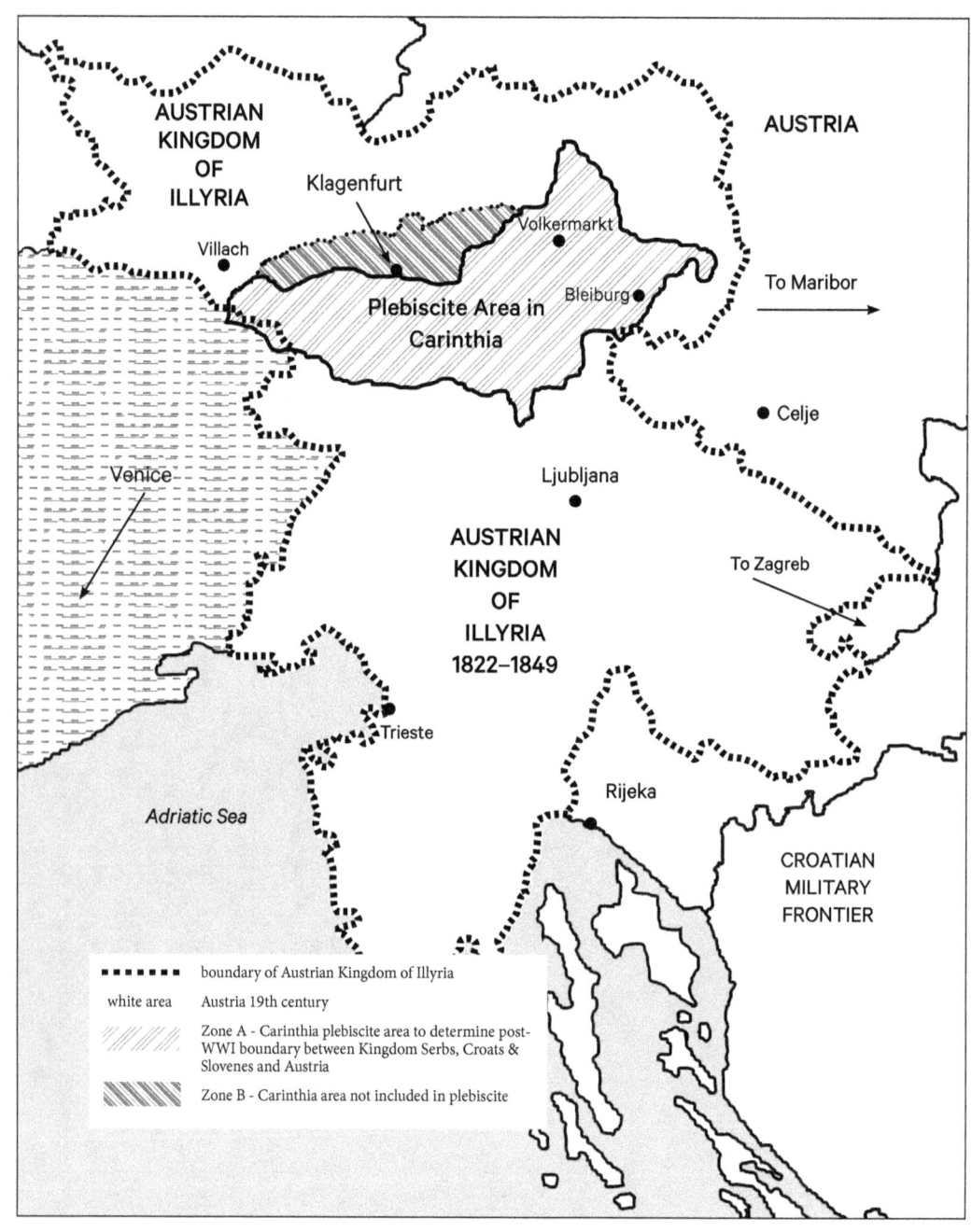

CHAPTER 2

SOUTHERN CARINTHIA – RECENT HISTORY

News from London about Tito's demands in Carinthia Austria on 15 May 1945 made headlines all around the world including Australia on 16th May and 17th May 1945. To understand why Yugoslavs were occupying and claiming southern Austria it is necessary to factor in 19th and 20th century events up to that point.

"Tito Grabs in Austria."
(The Daily News, Perth 16 May 45)

"Tito Defying Allied Request – Yugoslav Troops in Klagenfurt"
(The Canberra Times, ACT, 17 May 45)

"Trieste Not the Biggest Problem"
(The Age, Melbourne, 17 May 45)

"Storm Centres – Tito Makes New One –Moves in Austria – Land-grabbing Elsewhere"
(The West Australian, Perth, 17 May 45)

"Marshall Tito repeats his Trieste tactics in Klagenfurt."
(Queensland Times, Ipswich, 17 May 45)

"Tito Flouting Allies. – Seeking Control in Austria."
(Riverine Herald, Echuca, 17 May 45)

"Stand by Tito Forces New World Crisis."
(Northern Star, Lismore, 17 May 45)

"Yugoslavs Forming Own Military Government in Conflict With Allies. – British Ignored"
(Advocate, Burnie, 17 May 45)

"Tito's Forces Encroach in Austria. – Klagenfurt Entered. – British Troops Ignored by Partisans."
(Townsville Daily Bulletin, Qld, 17 May 45)

Napoleon Bonaparte: Commander of 'Army of Italy'

History was repeating itself. No one had anticipated this threat from the Yugoslavs after the war had ended! In recent history southern Carinthia in Austria has been subjected to various occupations, a national referendum or plebiscite in 1920, and international treaties.

Before WWI the wider Carinthian region and beyond was included in Napoleon's "Illyrian Province". Following Napoleon's defeat, until 1849, this area became known as the "Austrian Kingdom of Illyria". A south-Slav "National Council" was established in 1918 with headquarters in Zagreb Croatia. Up to this time a unified Slovenian nation still did not exist. Slovenia was created after the post-war collapse of Austria-Hungary when Slovenians and Croats co-founded the State of Slovenes Croats and Serbs. The proclamation by the "National Council" of the State of Slovenes Croats and Serbs in Ljubljana included territorial claims in Carinthia. A month later, in November 1918, this state became the "Kingdom of Serbs Croats and Slovenes" after joining with Serbia. The historical backdrop to the creation of the first Yugoslav state is described in the Appendix in this book.

After WWI southern Carinthia, including Bleiburg, was the scene of unsuccessful Slovenian territorial ambitions at Versailles, after the establishment of the State of Slovenes Croats and Serbs and unification with Serbia shortly after. The Plebiscite area included Rosegg, Ferlach, Volkermarkt, and Bleiburg. The administrative capital of Klagenfurt and surrounding area was automatically given to Austria.

In this south-Slav historical context, in post-WWII southern Carinthia, Communist ideological slogans were used to justify the Yugoslav National Army's "liberation" there. The Yugoslav proclamation was cited in many newspapers on 17th May 1945, one of them being The West Australian newspaper, Perth. In Klagenfurt, the capital of Carinthia, on 15 May 1945 the intention to include Carinthia in a greater Yugoslavia is clear.

> "The Yugoslav army has entered Carinthia to cleanse the land of Nazi criminals and guarantee for the entire Slovene and Austrian population true popular democracy, freedom and prosperity in a new, victorious and stronger Greater Yugoslavia...the Yugoslav commander has established a military government which the population must obey."

However, this Communist Yugoslav Army occupation in 1945 was not only an attempt to occupy Carinthia and widen Yugoslav territory. Royalist Yugoslavia had collapsed politically and militarily after a coup d'etat on 27th March 1941, and in this context, the Carinthian occupation was also part of an attempt to re-create a Yugoslav regime. At the beginning of the war the majority of Croats and Slovenes had withdrawn their support of Royalist Yugoslavia due to the cruel Serbian domination of the Royalist regime. In 1928 five Croatian front-bench politicians were shot at close range, by a Serbian politician, during a parliamentary session in Belgrade. These assassinations are described in the Appendix of this book.

In the wake of the coup d'etat in Belgrade and collapse of Royalist Yugoslavia a separate Croatian state was proclaimed. According to the American Consul, John J. Meily, in Zagreb at the time, this proclamation by the Ustase General Eugen (Dido) Kvaternik was made over the radio, in the name of Dr Ante Pavelic. Croatia was declared independent in a so-described "Ustase coup d'etat" according to Meily on 10 April 1941 on its historical territory. Meily's Report is contained in full in "Dramatis Personae and Finis of the Independent State of Croatia in American and British Documents", by Ivo Omrcanin. In Meily's own words in his Report to the American Secretary of State, on record in the Washington Archives, he wrote

> "The bloodless (one policeman was killed) severance of Croatia from the Yugoslav State was thus consummated."

This peaceful Croatian proclamation of independence was supported unanimously by Croatian people, and witnessed by the American Consul in Zagreb John J. Miely. Meily, who was killed in a plane crash in 1944, had a long career as an American Consul around the world. Those detractors today who try to argue, or believe, that Croatia was some sort of Nazi or Italian creation need to acknowledge the historical truth. Croatia had been a recognised ancient Kingdom from the year 925 AD until it joined Hungary in 1102 as part of a Dual Kingdom. Genuine 'original' historical maps do not lie and I am not being 'biased' for mentioning recognised history!

After WWII, on the 15th May 1945 the quaint Austrian town of Bleiburg was the scene of an exclusively Croatian surrender to the communist Yugoslav National Army (JNA). For me it has always been a mystery why Bleiburg was the scene of this Croatian tragedy and this was a puzzle I wanted to solve.

Bleiburg is situated in Carinthia close to the Austria/Yugoslavia border. Although Bleiburg may not have been the intended destination of the retreating Croats, at the end of WWII, the wider Carinthian region was. In a historical context Carinthia is more than just a random point on a map and, when the Croats tried to retreat through there, the occupation by the Yugoslav communists should not have been a big surprise! The Yugoslav National Army was there as part of their plan to occupy the area, claim it for Yugoslavia, and "liquidate" all opposition to the new Yugoslav regime. Today this would be called 'genocide' but after WWII the communists referred to it as "liberation".

Seventy years later in 2015 the freshly rendered buildings in old Bleiburg compliment its peaceful atmosphere and conceal its troubled past. Bleiburg's narrow winding hilly streets give us a picturesque snapshot of the old world and a church spire and an old castle distinguish its skyline. The name of the main street, 10 October Platz, in Bleiburg is reminiscent of the post-WWI Plebiscite in the region, held on the 10th October 1920. Looking up from 10 October Place the castle looks more like a stone fortress on top of a steep mountain. The Thurn-Valsassina castle appears inaccessible from the town below, but from the rear of the castle a steep road climbs upwards.

The open field south-east of the town of Bleiburg (also known as Loibach field) is surrounded by densely forested mountains which jut out from the valley on both sides and is about 3 kilometers from the Slovenian border. An old aerial photograph published, in the book "Operation Slaughterhouse", shows the scene after WWII with the train tracks and natural boundary formed by the Petzen Mountain. The Karawanken Mountains which separate Carinthia from Yugoslavia were described in an article from a London newspaper, and republished in The West Australian newspaper on 26 December 1946. Under the heading, "Slavs In Austria – Subject of Tito's Demands" the Karawanken Mountains are described as an

"Iron Curtain"... (and a)..."5000 foot wall of rock"

In the last months of WWII the Slovenian Partisans were already in the process of trying to occupy southern Carinthia, with the intention of joining the region to Yugoslavia. Irredentism was to repeat itself in Carinthia as the Slovenian ambitions resurfaced, similar to the WWI period, as described in Franklin Lindsay's book "Beacons in the Night".

The post-WWII situation was more chaotic than after WWI however because long columns of Croatian soldiers and civilians from Zagreb were making their way through eastern Slovenia towards the Austrian/Yugoslav border. In addition to the retreating German Army the retreating Croatian columns were moving north together from Celje with the intention to surrender to the western Allies in Austria.

Bleiburg was an outpost of the British V Corps in the early days of post-WWII Carinthia and the Allied Sectors were still not determined. It was here in Carinthia at the Bleiburg castle, and in these difficult circumstances, that the British Army, the 'revolutionary' Yugoslavs, and the military representatives of the former independent Croatian state met. In the next chapter I will discuss the immediate post-WWII circumstances of the three military groups.

East Carinthia and Yugoslav Frontier at 11 May 1945

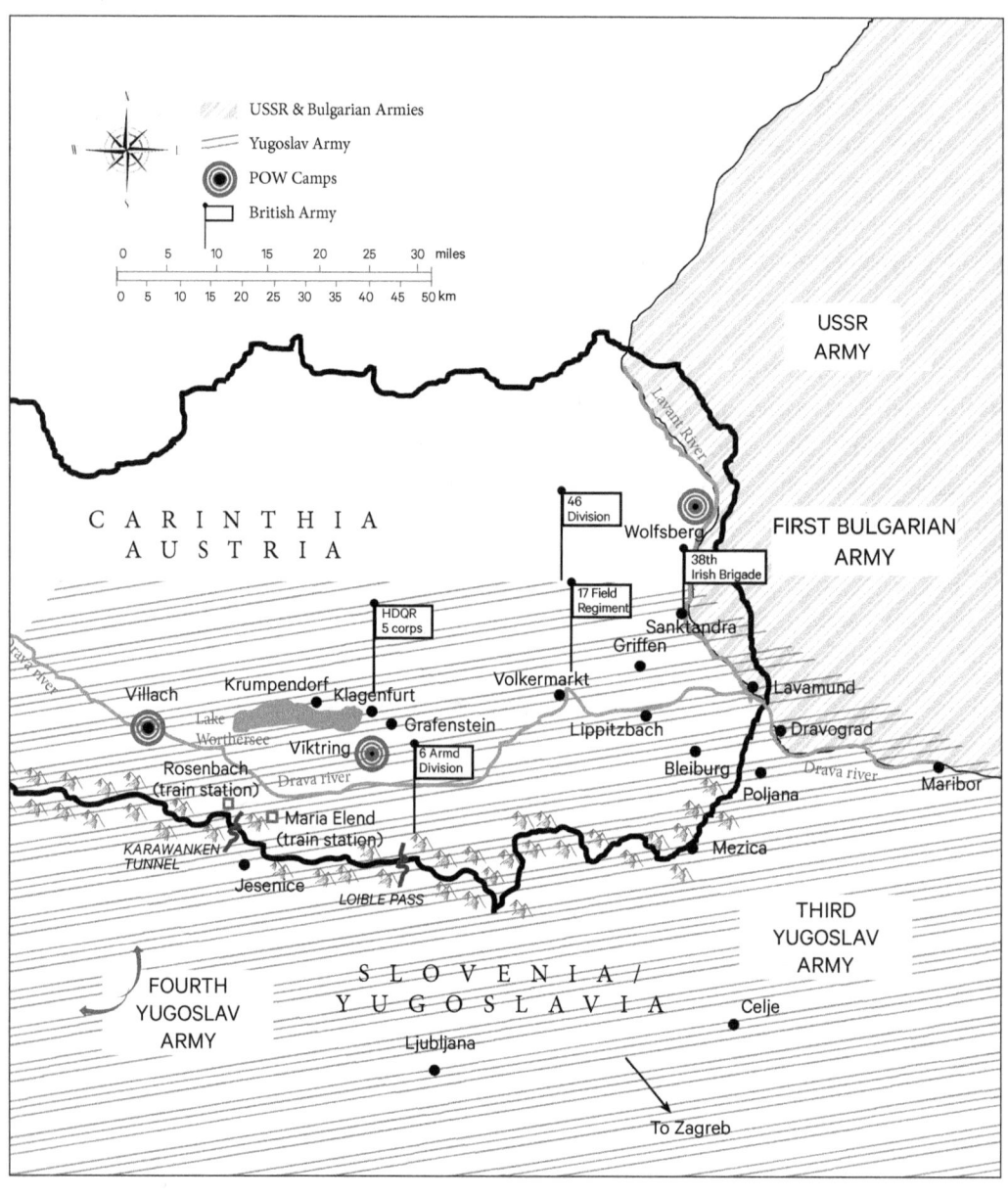

CHAPTER 3

SOUTHERN CARINTHIA – POST-WWII HISTORY

OVERVIEW

The German forces in northern Italy surrendered on 2nd May and, following the final Nazi unconditional surrender, V.E. Day was declared by the western Allies on 8th May 1945. Mussolini had already been executed on 28th April. Until the war's end Carinthia, Austria and Slovenia had been part of Hitler's Third Reich. General Alexander Lohr, Commander-in-Chief of the German Army Group E in south-east Europe, surrendered on 9th May near Velenje, Slovenia, and organized a German retreat. The command of the Croatian Army (HOS) was then transferred from General Lohr to the Croatian General Vjekoslav 'Maks' Luburic, and the Croats also began a retreat towards Austria. By 9th May only anti-Partisan forces had not surrendered, such as the Croats or Slovenes.

In early May a tense situation began to unfold in southern Carinthia as those anti-Partisan Axis forces were retreating towards Austria in addition to the British Army and additional Yugoslav forces. Those Axis forces mainly included members of the Slovenian Home Guards, Royalist Serbs, Montenegrin Serbs, Cossacks, White Russians, and various Croatian forces and government members. Civilians and 'camp followers' accompanied every group. This book is mainly concerned with the retreat and surrender of some of the main columns of Croats at Bleiburg.

Also relevant to what was happening in post-war Carinthia was the growing antagonism between the Soviet Union and the American and British Allies over occupation zones in post-war eastern Europe. The tension was evident at the United Nations Conference held in San Francisco on 25th April 1945, but at the same time the western Allies did not want to lose the Soviets as allies because the war was not over in the Pacific.

The Yugoslavs

The 'Yugoslavs' were composed of members of the various ethnic groups who had either joined or had been conscripted into the Communist Partisans under Tito. Josip Broz Tito had received Allied support since the Tehran Conference at the end of 1943. In spite of Allied support the main contributing factor to the post-war chaos in Carinthia and Trieste was the occupation and "liberation" by the Yugoslav National Army (JNA), and its policy of non-cooperation with the British Eighth Army. Tito made world headlines but not in a good way. Tito had no intention of sharing power in any democratic arrangement, under the Allied "Treaty of Vis", or the "Tito-Subasic Agreement" of June 1944. Trieste and the Adriatic Croatian coast had always been the object of Italian irredentism and was a big issue after WWI at Versailles. Another outstanding issue at Versailles had been the determination of the Carinthian borders. And after WWII in May 1945 the Yugoslavs were again reviving the unsuccessful post-WWI attempt to incorporate part of Austria into Slovenia.

Readers who want to learn more about the tense situation in Trieste can consult the books and articles in my bibliography or on the internet. In this book I will focus on the situation in post-WWII Carinthia, and in particular on the Croatian surrender to Yugoslavs at Bleiburg.

Before the end of the war the Yugoslav Partisans had been moving into Carinthia in early 1945, and their policy is well documented in Lindsay's book "Beacons in the Night: With the OSS and Tito's Partisans in Wartime Yugoslavia". Many other reliable sources on the topic of Yugoslav antagonism have come to light following the collapse of the Soviet Union and Yugoslavia. Franklin Lindsay's chapter entitled "The Cold War begins in Trieste" is particularly helpful on this topic. For example, Lindsay describes how the Allied command was caught unawares by the Communist Yugoslav behaviour immediately after the war.

> "(The Allies were)...unprepared for the political warfare unleased against them...
> (and the)...continuing battles with the Yugoslavs".

At the Yalta Conference in February 1945 the implementation of the "Tito-Subasic Agreement" was called for by the three powers. Lindsay discusses Yalta on pages 282 to 293 in "Beacons in the Night".

According to the author J.E. Lewis in his review entitled "Balkan Warfare" about "Beacons in the Night", Lindsay offers an important "counterbalance" to the previous British viewpoint of Fitzroy Maclean, Churhill's envoy to Tito between 1943 and 1945. Even in 1944 Lindsay had informed his command that the Partisans had intended to

Southern Carinthia – Post-WWII History

"annex the prewar Italian province of Venezia Giullia and Trieste".

In addition, the Partisans had continued to request and receive western Allied munitions and supplies, in spite of the information regarding Partisan intransigence in northern Slovenia. It is the particular issue of munitions and supplies that rekindled my interest in the ensuing Bleiburg tragedy after reading Lindsay's book.

The Yugoslav numbers were already strong around the Slovenian/Austrian border at Dravograd at the end of the war. The Yugoslavs in this area included the Slovenian Partisans and the Third Yugoslav Army. Christopher Booker's "A Looking-Glass Tragedy: The controversy over the repatriations from Austria in 1945" is informative on this issue. The retreating Croatian columns in this area reached a point of no return when they were faced with the Bulgarian Army. The Bulgarians were subsequently driven back by the Yugoslavs who then began to pursue the Croatian retreating columns. Accounts about how this and other subsequent incidents took place are supported by the Report of Brigadier Patrick Scott of the British 38th (Irish) Infantry Brigade, now available online, and by survivors' testimony in "Operation Slaughterhouse".

Elsewhere the Yugoslav troops had also followed the British Sixth Armoured Division into Klagenfurt and Villach which the Yugoslav Partisans intended to incorporate into Communist Yugoslavia. On 11th May after their occupation the Yugoslav Partisans had declared southern Carinthia including Klagenfurt as part of Yugoslavia.

Churchill, Roosevelt, Stalin at Yalta Conference 1945
A bronze sculpture unveiled at Yalta on 70th annversary of Conference

By 11th May the initial policy of Field Marshall Alexander was to keep the peace, not to eject the Yugoslavs but only to shoot in self-defence, due in part to the lack of available forces on the ground at the time. In other words, to maintain the 'status quo' was the initial British policy.

Meetings between the British and the Yugoslavs regarding the eventual Yugoslav withdrawal from Carinthia are mentioned in subsequent chapters in this book.

THE BRITISH

The chaotic situation on the ground was changing daily in post-war Austria. After the Allied offensive in northern Italy the war-weary British Eighth Army was slowly advancing eastwards through Carinthia from the Italian border. The Yugoslav Army, recently created from the Partisans, already occupied some parts of southern Austria and Slovenia, and it had also arrived in Trieste just before the Allies. In addition to the retreat of several different Axis ethnic groups and armies into Carinthia, Croatian soldiers and civilians were travelling north through eastern Slovenia, all with the goal of surrendering to the Western Allies.

Field Marshall Alexander of the British Eighth Army told American General Eisenhower on the 17th May that there were about 220,000 prisoners-of-war in the post-WWII British zone, and that number included the following groups.

> 100,000 Germans
> 46,000 Cossacks
> 15,000 Hungarians
> 25,000 Croats
> 24,000 Slovenes

And according to the author Nikolai Tolstoy in his book "The Minister and the Massacres" groups retreating towards the Western Allies also included about

> 12,000 Royalist Chetniks
> and White Russians

A brief mention of the prisoner-of-war camps where these other groups, including various isolated Croatian groups, were located can be found on page 80 of the book "Operation Slaughterhouse", namely, Klagenfurt, Krumpendorf, Toschling, Rosseg, Ferlach, Viktring, Maria Saal, Tamsweg, Grafenstein, Volkermarkt, Griffen, and Wolfsberg. The British extraditions to the Soviet Zone or back into Yugoslavia from these camps mentioned above occurred from the date 17th May 1945, in the days and weeks which followed the separate Yugoslav repatriation from Bleiburg to Yugoslavia. Some others refer to 19th May as the beginning of the extraditions.

By 15th May 1945 according to Field Marshall Alexander's report to the Combined Chiefs of Staff, 16,000 troops of the Yugoslav National Army had moved into southeast Carinthia. The same official UK history reported an additional 25,000 men just south of the Yugoslav border. In addition, the Yugoslav Fourth Army was pushing two or three Divisions towards Villach.

As a consequence of the advancing Yugoslav Armies, and the retreating Germans, and other groups blocking the roads, the advance unit of Leiutenant-General Keightly's V Corps from Trieste made slow progress on its way through Carinthia. The British arrived at Villach by 7th May, and a few days later the Main V Corps Headquarters was established at Klagenfurt but the British occupation of the area was not yet strong. Christopher Booker on page 167 in "A Looking-Glass Tragedy, The controversy over the repatriations from Austria in 1945" estimated that there were only 25,000 British stationed in the entire Carinthian area in the first post-war week. This was an area 100 miles long and 50 miles wide. After all, the Allied sectors of occupation were not officially decided until July 1945.

Yugoslav agitation was disrupting the peace at Klagenfurt, and in all parts of southern Carinthia, as noted in a BBC Timewatch documentary, "Betrayal", and in numerous other sources. At the end of April 1945 the British Eighth Army under General McCreery had arrived in Trieste one day after the Partisans, and the British V Corps arrived at Klagenfurt to find posters announcing the proclamation of the area for Yugoslavia, in violation of a treaty with Field Marshall Alexander in February 1945.

Further to the east the British outpost at the town of Sankt Andra (Saint Andra) had been set up by 11th May, according to British War Diaries of the 38th Irish Brigade. According to the book "Operation Slaughterhouse" and other sources, on 14th May on behalf of the retreating Croatian columns the Croatian Liaison Officer Deutsch-Maceljski had offered to surrender at Bleiburg.

A factor relevant to ensuing events was that the British orders were the same in Carinthia as in Trieste, basically to give-in rather than to confront the menacing communist Yugoslavs, to avoid risking the outbreak of another war. In Trieste Tito had accepted the creation of the "Morgan Line" on 23 May to determine, at a later date, the border between Italy and Yugoslavia. But the situation unfolding in Carinthia was more complex than in Trieste.

According to Lindsay on page 174-175 of "Beacons in the Night" and other sources the wartime Allies, including Stalin, did not support Tito's annexation of lands in Carinthia. The Yugoslav policy in Austria received no official Soviet support because Stalin's policy had been to include Austria into the eastern Soviet bloc. This territorial dispute was not only a precursor to the Iron Curtain, but laid a foundation for the later Stalin-Tito Split.

An official solution to disputed borders between Austria and Yugoslavia would be decided years later after the withdrawal of the Yugoslav Army from Carinthia in the last weeks of May 1945.

But in mid May, in response to the tense situation which was changing daily on the ground, British orders were also changing daily. New British orders had been issued regarding all the various already-surrendered groups now behind British lines, nowhere near Bleiburg. A new British order was the result of a brief visit to Klagenfurt by the British Minister Resident in the Mediterranean, Harold Macmillan, on Sunday 13th May, following his visit to Trieste. Amongst many other sources this visit is referred to in Tolstoy's "Minister and the Massacres" on pages 65 to 67. Macmillan's brief visit related to agreements reached by the Allies at Yalta in February 1945, namely that the existing surrendered groups would be extradited to their place of origin. Those extraditions were justified and carried out based on discussions and decisions reached by the big powers at Yalta. It was subsequent to the fresh orders by Macmillan that Brigadier Scott, as per British War Diaries, was told not to accept any more refugees, after he had already accepted a surrender of Cossacks near Lavamund.

The timing of the new order was important in relation to what was to happen next. Macmillan's new order had been issued just before the arrival of Croats at Bleiburg, and it was directly related to the British decision not to accept any more surrenders there or anywhere else.

As stated earlier the figures given by Alexander to Eisenhower on 17th May for already surrendered personnel in the area totalled about 220,000 which included 100,000 Germans, 46,000 Cossacks, 15,000 Hungarians, 25,000 Croats, and 24,000 Slovenes. These 220,000 surrendered personnel were distinct from those Croats described as "moving north to Austria from Yugoslavia".

The official UK perspective on the hand-overs of all groups was not only due to the terms of the Yalta Agreemnt but was also based on the logistical situation. For example, the decision to hand-over the already-surrendered Yugoslav POWs and others was an alleged direct response to the possible arrival in Austria of a mass exodus of Croats which was "moving north to Austria from Yugoslavia". Some authors refer to a meeting in Klagenfurt between Yugoslav and British officers in order to allege a link between the hand-overs and the Yugoslav withdrawal. Others refer to a more sinister alleged deal. They allege there was a trade made with Yugoslavia to hand-over the POWs to them in exchange for a Yugoslav withdrawal of troops. Some go so far as to say there was a 'British-Yugoslav conspiracy' to get rid of Croats! To that absurd suggestion I would say that post-war policies differ from wartime military objectives! Of course the British wanted to defeat the German Axis troops, but after the war it was the Yugoslavs who wished to get rid of the Croats, and they specifically said so!

THE CROATS

From eye-witness accounts we know that the small town Bleiburg was not the intended destination of the Croats who were retreating through Slovenia en masse from Croatia and Bosnia Hercegovina. It was merely their intention to cross the border into Austria and to surrender to western Allies. However after failed talks, and the Bulgarian refusal to allow the columns to pass through Dravograd, the Croatian plans collapsed. There was no 'plan B' so to speak. As ordered by Tito, throughout the Slovenian border region the Yugoslavs began surrounding the Croats to prevent them from entering Austria. Indeed, the Yugoslavs had already cut-off the retreat route at many points from Celje onwards. At Poljana, in the so-called last battle of WWII, the Croatian soldiers and civilians came under armed attack by the Yugoslav Army. Some of the Croatian columns, who were not turned back towards Maribor, were then able to enter Austria. According to various sources, some Croats crossed the Meza River at Mezica into Austria and others were able to cross the border between Poljana and Bleiburg after the attack.

It has been estimated that tens of thousands escaped into Austria but there they found themselves encircled in a field by Yugoslavs near Loibach which is three kilometers south of Bleiburg. The Loibach field has also been known therefore as the Bleiburg field.

It gradually became clear to the surrounded Croats in the retreating columns that the plan to retreat en masse in the north-east direction through Slovenia was the Croatian leadership's fatal mistake. The Croatian government's first major error was to quash the attempt to put Croatia on the Allied side, after the defeat of Mussolini. It remains a mystery just why a route through north-eastern Slovenia was chosen by the Croatian leadership, given the 'Yugoslav' history of the region, and the likelihood that Yugoslavs would be present in this no-man's-land.

Just to be clear those Croats who had already surrendered before 12th May, and were already in camps behind British lines, numbered about "25,000" according to most reputable sources. Their unfortunate fate was to be transported into the hands of Tito's executioners on trains, by the British. These 25,000 Croats were separate and distinct from the massive Croatian exodus which was trying to escape the Yugoslav Third Army and avoid being taken to Maribor east of Carinthia. In a publication published by Ante Beljo online, reviewed later in my book, Nikolai Tolstoy made an important statement about a distinction between the different groups of Croats. I will repeat it here because of its importance.

> "...an important matter needs to be emphasised. That is the distinction which should be drawn between the tragedy of the Croats driven back to Tito at Bleiburg...and the subsequent fate of the smaller body of Croats who remained in Austria following the Bleiburg tragedy..."

A figure of 500,000 people instead of 600,000 was reported by the Chief of Staff Army Group E, according to official UK history, who were approaching the Austrian border with Slovenia.

> "...estimated roughly at 300,000 Germans and 200,000 Croats, the troops had food for only two days...The Croats themselves claimed to represent 'a whole Croat nation' accompanied as they were by 500,000 women and children."

Bleiburg Castle with Petzen Mountain to the South, 1938

The details of all the movements towards the Austrian/Slovenian border in Carinthia, and the surrender, will be discussed in more detail in the following chapters from various perspectives. Many volumes have already been written about the subsequent massacres, and for this reason they are not the focus in this book. Those who want to know more about the massacres and the 'Death Marches' which constituted this genocide can consult the bibliography.

When the three opposing armies merged together in and around Bleiburg on one day in May, each with a mission, orders, and an ideology which contradicted the other's, just after the end of a world war, the tense situation ended in tragedy.

CROATIAN RETREAT ROUTES FROM ZAGREB IN MAY 1945

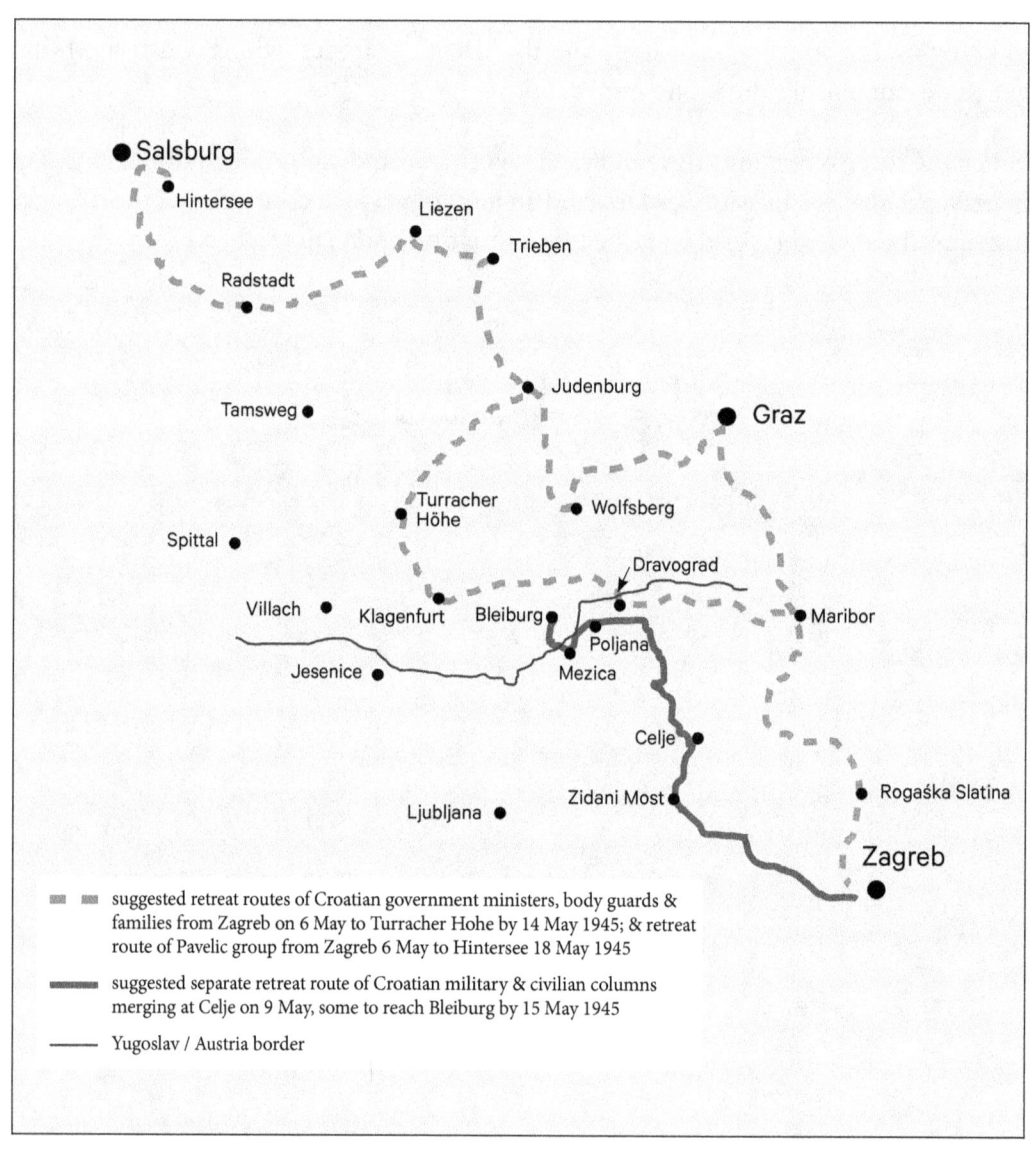

CHAPTER 4

THE CROATIAN RETREAT ROUTES

This chapter briefly discusses the Croatian decision to retreat, the time frames, and the various routes of the Croatian military personnel, the civilians, the government members, and Pavelic's elite group. This chapter gives a general description of the routes, and in Part II of the book I will introduce more details about the various routes as they appear in the reviewed material.

Croatia was the only nation in southern Europe which had not joined the Allies before the end of WWII. Therefore at the end of WWII the Croatian government ('sabor') decided to evacuate Zagreb before the arrival of the communist Yugoslav National Army. By 30th April 1945 it was determined that military operations in Croatia would cease. In early May Croatian soldiers and civilians proceeded through eastern Slovenia in order to surrender to the western Allies in Austria.

In the meantime, at the 'eleventh hour' a Croatian emissary was sent to Field Marshal Alexander to say that the Croats wanted to surrender and change sides, but this mission failed to reach its destination in time before the German unconditional surrender. It was too late.

The circumstances which led to the Croatian government's decision to evacuate Zagreb are well described in the book "Operation Slaughterhouse" in a chapter entitled "The End of the Croatian Army". The reasons for the evacuation decision are described in detail by the Croatian Ustashe commanding officer General Vjekoslav Luburic on pages 43 to 71. The Croatian General Vjekoslav Servatski was responsible for effecting an evacuation of Zagreb, according to the same source.

The decisions of the Croatian government and the orders of the Croatian General Military Headquarters were strictly followed by the retreating Croatian generals left in command. Any suggestion of fighting the Yugoslavs at the Croatian capital Zagreb, or to retreat in separate columns, was rejected outright by a majority vote of the Ustasha generals. The Catholic Archbishop Aloysius Stepinac had also expressed support for the injudicious decision not to defend Zagreb, on the rationale that there would be less destruction to Zagreb's infrastructure, according to Luburic.

The Ustasha General Ivo Herencic, writes Luburic, was retreating along with other Croatian generals at the head of a Croatian national exodus north of Zagreb into Slovenia. Ultimately it was Herencic who was one of the chief negotiators for surrender at the Bleiburg castle. One cannot fail to see the irony, that it was the same General Herencic who had prevented Croatia from joining the western Allies in 1944, when he foiled the pro-Allied "Lorkovic-Vokic Plot". Unfortunately the Minister of the Interior Mladen Lorkovic, and the Minister of the Armed Forces, General Ante Vokic were imprisoned, and both executed by the Ustasha just before the main retreat to Slovenia.

Another leading Croatian General Ante Moskov at the vanguard of this Croatian national retreat was charged with organising "receiving stations" for members of the Croatian government, throughout Austria and Germany, along different routes from the main columns of soldiers and civilians. In other words, although the decision was made that the main exodus columns were to retreat in a single column, the government group was to take a different route! The same chapter in "Operation Slaughterhouse" is the source of this eye-witness testimony.

As planned after 6th May 1945 all withdrawing Croatian military columns from Varazdin, Karlovac, Sisak and Bosnia merged at Zidani Most, Slovenia. As pre-arranged the Croatian mass exodus arrived at Celje, north of Zidani Most, on 9th May 1945 and proceeded towards the Karawanken Alps which formed a natural Austrian/Slovenian boundary. Hundreds of thousands of Croatian civilians from all over Croatia (which at the time included Bosnia and Hercegovina), had joined this national exodus.

It is easy to be critical in hindsight that a tragedy could have been prevented, if not for the decision to form a single exodus which stretched for tens of miles north of Zagreb. Many opinions on this controversial topic have been expressed verbally in the Croatian community, but very little in writing. In any case the decision had been made to evacuate Zagreb ahead of the advancing Yugoslav Army and the rest is history. Eventually the still-armed Croatian military columns and civilians reached as far as Dravograd in Slovenia in spite of constant attacks by Yugoslavs along the route.

It was at Dravograd that the Croats were first prevented from proceeding north towards Austrian territory. The Croats were met by the Communist Bulgarian Army just before Dravograd where they wished to negotiate to cross the Drava River. Further negotiations with the Bulgarians never happened however because the Yugoslav Army, jointly with the Bulgarians, managed to block the Croatian columns. After the successful blockade of the Croatian columns many Croats were herded back to Maribor on "Death Marches" and others were re-routed towards Poljana and along the Meza River. This was the beginning of the 'Death Marches'.

Pavelic's Separate Retreat Route

The Croatian political leader (Poglavnik), Ante Pavelic, together with his Croatian government members group, and bodyguards, left Zagreb on 6th May by a different route from the main Croatian columns. Perhaps a select elite group of Ustasha Generals knew that their leader and government members would be taking a different route but, judging from the plethora of eye-witness accounts in "Operation Slaughterhouse", the vast majority of Croats on retreat believed that their national leader was present.

Pavelic's group left Zagreb on the 6th May in a separate direction taken by the main columns and they arrived at Rogaska Slatina Slovenia on 7th May. The elite Pavelic group travelled from Rogaska Slatina to Maribor arriving on 8th May, crossed into north-east Austria and the temporary Russian zone and travelled towards Wolfsberg. By 10th May Pavelic's group made its way north towards Judenburg, Trieben, and eventually crossed the Enns River, and moved on towards Radstadt. Pavelic's plan was to join his family who had left Zagreb in December 1944 and were currently living at Hintersee south of Salzburg safely inside the American zone.

One of a few sources available which I will review in the following chapters, is "On the Concealment of Ante Pavelic in Austria in 1945-1946", by Ante Delic, published online. On page 299 readers will learn that the official date of arrival of Pavelic at Langreith-Hintersee, south of Salzburg was 18th May 1945. Other sources are reviewed in Part II of my book. One in particular, Z. Kruselj in Hrvatski Vjesnik (2001), mentions the escape of 34 Croatian government ministers into emigration.

Of course the escape of Pavelic and Croatian government ministers to the west is interpreted differently by authors such as Mark Aarons and John Loftus who wrote a book about the escape routes of former Nazi's in the book "Ratlines". Ivo Omrcanin also criticizes the decision to retreat on pages 176 to 177 of his book "Dramatis Personae and Finis of the Independent State of Croatia in American and British Documents".

In the meantime by 10th May the above-mentioned Pavelic group itself split into separate routes! It appears as though the retreat of the Croatian government group eventually travelled to Turracher Hohe, and by 14th May to Klagenfurt, after which some of them were discovered by the British Army. The experience of these Croatian government leaders was described in an article on 2nd November 2001 in the Australian-Croatian "Hrvatski Vjesnik". These Croatian government members were interned behind British lines, in contrast to what happened at Bleiburg.

Ultimately, many members of this separate NDH Croatian government group escaped the tragedy that awaited the retreating 'Croatian nation'. However the focus of my book is about the exclusive Croatian surrender to Yugoslavs of many Croatian columns at Bleiburg. By 14th May the vanguard of the main retreating columns of Croatian soldiers and civilians came to the realisation that they were surrounded by the Yugoslav National Army. The Yugoslavs had been in this whole area before the end of the war, as described in the preceding chapter in my book.

THE BULGARIAN AND YUGOSLAVS BLOCK CROATIAN EXODUS

The Bulgarian nation had strategically changed sides after the defeat of Mussolini's Fascists, and they were partly inside the Russian zone, and also had the support of the Yugoslav Army. On 11th May the retreating Cossacks successfully negotiated with the Bulgarians to cross the Drava River at Dravograd. Those Cossacks were ultimately successful in moving behind British lines, as described in British War Diaries. But the politico-military situation was changing daily.

A couple of days later a different Bulgarian approach was taken towards the retreating Croatian columns. Pending further negotiations with the Bulgarians the Croatian intention to escape to the Allied occupied area across the Drava River was unsuccessful. In contrast to the Cossacks, at Dravograd, after a brief meeting with the Croats on 13th May, the Bulgarians refused to accept the passage of columns of approaching Croats. A suggested meeting with Russian and British and Bulgarian leaders at Dravograd hadn't eventuated mainly because of Yugoslav Army intervention and attacks. A quick informal meeting between the Croats and the Bulgarians, described in "Operation Slaughterhouse" resulted in an agreement instead that the Croats

> "would direct columns to the Miess (River), a tributary of the Drava, south of Dravograd."

Eye-witness accounts in "Operation Slaughterhouse" confirm how, at this time, tens of thousands Croats never actually entered Austria.

> "...tens of thousands of other Croatian soldiers, surrendered to the Partisans at Dravograd. A portion of these captives were quickly marched to Maribor, while about 35,000 of them were marched towards Celje and further..."

On 13th May one eye-witness report on page 303 of "Operation Slaughterhouse" says that near Dravograd a Croatian officer suggested two options to the retreating columns. Croats could either surrender to the Bulgarians, or go into the woods in small units in order to reach the "English Army".

In addition, according to another eye-witness testimony, the Bulgarians had offered the Croats three options on 11th May or 12th May. First, the Croats could return home and take their chances with the Partisans. Or secondly, the Croats could hide in the forests and fight a guerrilla war with the Partisans. The third Bulgarian option to the Croats was that they could try to escape abroad. The Croats in this group, according to page 312 of "Operation Slaughterhouse", surrendered to the Bulgarians, a decision they would regret. The Bulgarians had promised to treat the Croats according to international law and to escort the Croatian columns to Maribor, but unfortunately international law was not respected. In the same book, another eye-witness describes the same surrender to Bulgarians at Dravograd.

> "The surrender occurred on either May 11 or 12. Our Bulgarian captors lined us up in column formation and started us off on foot towards Maribor ... The Bulgarians accompanied us only about seventeen miles out of Dravograd. Then a large number of very well-armed Yugoslav Partisans took charge of us...when the bulk of the column reached Maribor."

It is intriguing that in "The Minister and the Massacres" Tolstoy seems to misrepresent the eye-witness survivor's accounts in "Operation Slaughterhouse" about the Bulgarian refusal to allow the Croats to pass over the Drava River! On page 100 of Chapter five entitled, "Stratagems of Deception" Tolstoy incorrectly portrays the Croats' encounter with the Bulgarians.

> "... south of the Austrian frontier. There they (Croats) found their path blocked by Bulgarian troops ... Fighting not being the Bulgarians' forte, they consented after negotiations to permit the Croats to pass over the Drava into Austria during 14 and 15 May."

For his source regarding the Bulgarian encounter with the Croats Tolstoy refers to "Operation Slaughterhouse" on pages 149, 160, 196, 241-2, 253, and 303 in his endnotes. These pages do not confirm his allegation that the Bulgarians allowed the Croats to pass across the Drava River however. In "Operation Slaughterhouse" the Bulgarians are mentioned on page 312 where it is written that discussions there were unsuccessful, and that the Bulgarians escorted some Croats back to Maribor, while others were re-routed.

Over the decades many authors have ignored the issue of the Bulgarian blockade of the Croats at Dravograd, and the Bulgarian options to the Croats. A few high ranking Croatian generals and other important military representatives there, according to eye-witness reports in "Operation Slaughterhouse", included Generals Ivo Herencic, Vladimir Metikos, Vjekoslav Servatzi, Deutsch-Maceljski, Rafael Boban, Ivan Tomasevic, Josip Metzger, Artur Gustovic, Slavko Stancer, Franje Sudar, and the civilian representative Col. Danijel Crljen.

YUGOSLAVS ATTACK CROATIAN COLUMNS ADVANCE AT POLJANA

On the 13th May an order was issued by Tito to the Yugoslav Army.

> "...move your forces most urgently from the Celje area...in order to concentrate for an attack aimed at the annihilation of this column."

After the still-armed Croatian columns were re-routed west of Dravograd in Yugoslavia, they were attacked with cannons and bazookas by the Third Yugoslav Army, under Kosta Nadj. That conflict known as the last battle of WWII, the "Battle of Poljana", ended on 14th May, resulting in the deaths of a few hundred on either side, as Croats tried to defend themselves.

Thus on 13th or 14th May a proportion of the Croats who were not already turned back from Dravograd towards Celje or Maribor on the infamous "Death Marches", were able to cross the Austrian border. The Croats made their way along the Meza River (Meiss River) towards Mezica or via Poljana, or both, to Bleiburg. This is unclear in many sources. It was not just the British who awaited the Croats in Austria because the Yugoslavs were occupying the area also, and thus nothing went to plan for the Croats.

It is important to understand why and how Croatian troops and civilians were snared into such a Yugoslav ambush. It is no longer an historical secret, especially since the end of the Cold War, that the Yugoslav troops were occupying Carinthia. The broad Yugoslav front which surrounded the Croats is described, and applauded, on Exhibit Boards in Slovenia in part of an open-air Carinthian Regional Museum Exhibit.

The Croatian Retreat Routes

These Exhibit Boards can be seen on the side of a major road to Austria at Poljana. The sketched maps, diagrams and photographs on these Exhibit Boards, about events leading up to 15th May, are quite detailed. Unfortunately the opposite is true in this exhibit about what happened at Bleiburg. There is only a vague reference to surrender negotiations at Bleiburg and events afterwards. The content of this Exhibit is discussed in another chapter of this book. The title of this Exhibit gives away its ideological approach.

"And what is the price of freedom: at the end of the second world war in Carinthia."

Croatian Surrender To Yugoslavs At Bleiburg

As already described above and in my first chapter, following the Battle of Poljana many Croats were able to retreat towards the Bleiburg field on the night of 14th May and the morning of 15th May. At Bleiburg the Croatian leaders chose the option to surrender to Yugoslavs because of new British orders not to accept the surrender of any more refugees coming from Yugoslavia.

The new order to British V Corps involved the already-surrendered groups inside camps in Austria. As per the Yalta Agreement all of the already-surrendered ethnic groups in Austria would be repatriated to their place of origin. This new directive from higher Allied authorities was delivered by Macmillan on a quick visit to Klagenfurt a day before the Croatian columns crossed into Austria. In other words, the groups already inside the British POW camps would be repatriated, but further surrenders would not be accepted. This new order to refuse more surrenders applied to the approaching large Croatian group moving towards Austria. This tragic and untimely situation was complicated further by the presence of increasing numbers of the well-armed belligerent Yugoslav Army troops who had been in pursuit of those Croats. The negotiations at the Bleiburg castle, and the Croatian surrender to Yugoslavs in the Bleiburg field, have already been discussed in the first chapter of my book.

Since the publication of "Operation Slaughterhouse" in the 1970s many more books, journals, articles, online reports, films, and Youtube footage have been published. In Part II of my book I will review many of these sources, with a focus on what they have to say about the castle negotiations or the numbers of Croats at the Bleiburg field. The numbers on "Death Marches" and in mass graves throughout Slovenia and the rest of the former Yugoslavia are acknowledged but they are not the focus of my book.

PART 2

INTRODUCTION

PROPAGANDA AND INTERPRETATION

Propaganda, or ambiguous interpretation, about the Bleiburg surrender has left the majority of Croatian community members in limbo and without closure. Controversy persists regarding responsibility for the massacre of Croats when none should exist! It was the Yugoslavs in Tito's post-war Yugoslavia who planned and perpetrated genocide. It was not the fault of the Croatian victims for being in the wrong place at the wrong time, nor was it the fault of the British officers who did not have the benefit of foresight at the Bleiburg negotiations. It was the intention of the Croats and the western Allies to avoid another war, and it was the purpose of the Yugoslav revolutionaries to massacre their disarmed opposition once out of sight.

My goal in Part II is to identify the events and the numbers of Croats concerning the Croatian surrender to Yugoslavs at Bleiburg. I discuss the books, journals, essays, articles online or in print, and films on VHS, or DVD, or on Youtube in chronological order with a focus on 15th May 1945. I integrate the relevant material as I review it and try to avoid repetition as much as possible. I look for accuracy and consistency, or the absence of it, and identify various themes which emerge regarding the Bleiburg negotiations. Tragically, some themes and generalizations have overshadowed the original facts with the result that important information has faded into the background over the years.

For example, since a Croatian-American authored "Resolution" was created, many Croats have come to believe that all post-war British extraditions are associated with Bleiburg. Since the time of the Resolution a lot of misinformation has taken root in the Croatian collective memory. By innuendo, generalization, or confusing presentation, sometimes it appears as if there was only a single British extradition at Bleiburg. Although British documents, long available to the public, illustrate a distinction between events at Bleiburg and other British repatriations, this error has persisted in Croatian literature.

I include myself amongst readers who may have been misled by the misinterpretation of events at Bleiburg, that is, until I began to question what I was reading and seeing. A couple of years ago I was planning a trip to Bleiburg and therefore re-reading information about the 'Bleiburg Tragedy'. Due to ill health my trip was postponed and so I had more time to do further research about Bleiburg. My suspicions were raised when I discovered that many photographs in Croatian literature had differing captions. My awareness of the discrepancies in captions, and in texts, and on film was a turning point for me. I began to question whether the memory of Croatian victims was being best served, or sabotaged, by a blurring of the events.

For example, a single well known photograph of a signpost reading "Griffen 19 Km" and "Bleiburg 3 km" has had many different descriptions over the decades. Does this photograph show masses of Croats on their way to Bleiburg or does it depict Croats already at Bleiburg? Is this photograph taken at the Libuce crossroads, in Austria, or not? You cannot be on your way there if you are already there. For example, if you were disarmed at Bleiburg you cannot be on your way to Bleiburg. The most common caption for this location shows the other side of the signpost, allegedly at a junction of the Griffen, Volkermarkt and Unterdrauburg roads, and so this would perhaps be in Austria. Other captions over the decades indicate that the shot is taken in the Meze Valley, or near Mezica, both in Slovenia. Perhaps the authenticity of the caption is a moot point to some but serious historians or courts require authentic sources.

Introduction

Author looking at a signpost photograph, 2014 at Exhibit of Carinthian Regional Museum

I do not have any articles in my personal collection from the 1970s era although I am sure that many more exist in the Croatian emigration communities around the world. From memory, even the books I do have from the 1970s were not in my possession until the mid 1980s. In the 1970s and early 1980s I was juggling being a busy mother of a large family with working in an office and renovating an old Australian house. Not much reading material about Croatia came my way during those years and our connection with the Australian-Croatian community was mainly through the nearby Clifton Hill Catholic church, folklore dancing, or soccer. Indeed, in those days, a television was a luxury which we did not have for a couple of years. Bank loans for struggling Croatian refugees who came to Australia with a half-empty suitcase depended on careful saving in those early days. It was a struggle experienced by literally hundreds of thousands of Croatian refugees or migrants who settled around the world.

I am aware of a movie entitled, "Before Winter Comes" from 1969. Some older readers may remember this old film shown in an off-peak time slot one afternoon on television starring David Niven and Topol. There is nothing in this rather passé film about Croats but it is worth a quick mention because it is a dramatization about the British handover of Cossacks to the Soviets after World War Two under the terms of Yalta.

For those who want to know more about the "Death Marches" and massacres there are books on this topic mentioned in the Bibliography. According to eye-witnesses, these Yugoslav massacres began 'during' the post-war Croatian retreat, and continued 'after' the surrender to Yugoslavs at Bleiburg, and repatriations from other locations. All these Yugoslav-perpetrated atrocities are referred to by Croats as the "Bleiburg Tragedy" or the "Bleiburg Massacres".

CHAPTER 5

1970s

"OPERATION SLAUGHTERHOUSE: EYEWITNESS ACCOUNTS OF POST-WAR MASSACRES IN YUGOSLAVIA"
EDITORS, JOHN PRCELA & STANKO GULDESCU, PITTSBURG,
FIRST EDITION 1970, (SECOND EDITION 1995)

"Operation Slaughterhouse" is the original 'big book', in the English language, which presents eye-witness accounts of many various post-WWII surrenders in Carinthia, and various repatriations of Croatian soldiers and civilians to Yugoslavia. For me this book is indispensable because it provides key first-hand information about the negotiations at the Bleiburg castle which occurred on the 15th day in May. The testimonies about the negotiations at Bleiburg are followed by several hundred pages of survivor eye-witness accounts of "Death Marches" and mass grave sites. I have used "Operation Slaughterhouse" in the first part of my book as a starting point regarding the Bleiburg castle negotiations because it describes what happened at Bleiburg on 15th May 1945 from various perspectives. I won't repeat those negotiations again here.

The book is introduced by the two editors with a Foreward by one retired American Major General Charles A. Willoughby in 1968. In addition, one Dr David M. Baxter wrote an introductory chapter entitled the 'Serbo-Croatian Antagonism'. In "Operation Slaughterhouse" a summary and chronology of the Croatian surrender negotiations at Bleiburg is also given by the former Croatian General Vjekoslav Luburic in 1967.

The first edition of "Operation Slaughterhouse" has been written, seemingly before the release of 'all' British documents, so that the writers themselves may still be trying to piece together the whole situation. The Editors, with the knowledge to hand, have prepared this important volume, and published a 1960 Resolution in their Appendix B, which was presented to American politicians entitled,

> "Resolution: On the 15th Anniversary of the Croatian Genocide, The Bleiburg-Maribor Massacres".

In this 1960 Resolution we discover the infamous statement of Yugoslavia's notorious dissident Milovan Djilas.

> "Croatian soldiers must die in order that Yugoslavia may live".

Another more lengthy Resolution has been added in Appendix C of "Operation Slaughterhouse" in a later edition of the book. Whereas the 1960 Resolution refers to the "Bleiburg-Maribor" massacres, this second 1973 Resolution is now formally called the 'Bleiburg Tragedy' (published in the second edition) and it cites the number of 200,000 soldiers and "many thousands of civilians", thereby suggesting that this many people made it to Bleiburg. In this second 1973 Resolution it is incorrectly alleged that the Croatians are turned over by the British "en masse" to the Partisans for deportation and murder. The 1973 Resolution is known as,

> "Resolution of the Symposium on the Croatian Bleiburg Tragedy"

Both Resolutions, in addressing the United States government, ask for an end to support for Tito and help towards the restoration of an independent Croatia. In fact the Croatian people would not be able to benefit from any government intervention during those years due to the Cold War.

It is easy to be critical in hindsight, with the benefit of the internet, and many more released official documents and information. The authors and editors in "Operation Slaughterhouse" were working with the available information at the time. Some things are fair to say in hindsight however. I doubt it would have been helpful to introduce this serious book with a Foreward by the German-born retired American Major General Charles A. Willoughby. Apparently Willoughby was infamous for his extremist controversial right-wing opinions in addition to his allegedly violent anti-Communist position.

In his Foreward, Willoughby like many others in the following decades, has compared all repatriations from Austria to what happened at Bleiburg. To support his allegations Willoughby does not mention the negotiations at the Bleiburg castle, and instead incorrectly writes that it was the British military authorities who requested that the Croats at Bleiburg lay down their weapons. Willoughby intentionally over-simplifies and distorts his version of events at Bleiburg for readers in this way.

> "Once the British were sure that the Croats were disarmed, they began to herd the unarmed masses back across the border."

Willoughby poses the question whether or not there was an alleged agreement between the English commanders and the Partisan leaders. Then Willoughby, in reference to Bleiburg in his introduction, makes an allegation without a source.

> Willoughby: "Partisan units…opened fire on the refugees as the British forced them back over the frontier line…thousands of Croatians of all categories, but mostly unarmed soldiers, were shot down on that part of the Bleiburg field which lies within the frontiers of the Tito State."

Willoughby also describes the thousands of British handovers "elsewhere", and once again compares those other repatriations with Bleiburg, as if the same pattern of events was being taking place. The remaining part of his Foreward in "Operation Slaughterhouse" describes subsequent massacres. His whole summary of the event has been written, in English, in an anti-Anglo/American tone. Willoughby's errors have been repeated many times since by different authors, unfortunately without reference to the main content of the big book!

Another problem with "Operation Slaughterhouse" is the absence of complete maps. In "Operation Slaughterhouse" two maps focus on the "Death March" routes from both the Bleiburg region and Jesenice. The withdrawal routes from Croatia towards Austria illustrate only the route of the Croatian Armed Forces and civilians, and not route of the Croatian government groups. The map scales are in miles rather than in kilometres.

When I purchased a good map of Carinthia myself in 2014, and travelled through the region, I realized just how big the distances are, between various locations in Carinthia, and how far they are from the Yugoslav border. Just south of Klagenfurt, is Viktring which is about 60 Km from Bleiburg, and Villach which is approximately 90 Km from Bleiburg, via road. For Croats who want to imagine such a distance, it is 88 Km from Zadar to Sibenik, or 87 Km from Zagreb to Varazdin.

Our train journey from Zagreb to Bleiburg via Ljubljana in 2014, took us through the long tunnel to Villach and Klagenfurt. On the way back to Zagreb from Bleiburg the train followed the Drava River to Maribor, and then to Zidani Most. The scenery on the train route confirmed my judgments about the difficult mountainous terrain and river valleys.

"Operation Slaughterhouse" also has some aerial photographs which depict Bleiburg from all angles, and were probably taken after WWII. One photograph shows the field where the Croatian surrender to Yugoslavs took place. It shows the same pine trees that shelter the memorial to this day. Another photograph in this 'big book' shows

Loibach in the back left and the right side includes the Hrust Tavern where Partisans held talks with some of the Croatian officers, following the castle negotiations.

The Yugoslav's headquarters May 1945 beside Bleiburg field – Hrust Tavern, as it is today, 2014

Had there been other authentic photographs available I am sure that they would have been included when the second edition of "Operation Slaughterhouse" was published in 1995!

"Operation Slaughterhouse" gives eye-witness testimony regarding both Bleiburg and other repatriations. For example it mentions the separate fate of Croats at Wolfsburg, and on May 9 at Judenburg. These Croats had surrendered to the British days earlier, at the same time as the huge main Croatian columns of soldiers and civilians were just reaching Celje! Their fate and repatriation, at Lavamund, should not be confused with what happened at Bleiburg.

This Croatian group had left Zagreb on 6th May and by 8th May they were already in vicinity of Volkermarkt. The Yugoslavs had already penetrated Carinthia. This Croatian government group decided to go to Salzburg but had to go through Wolfsberg and Judenburg. British troops were encountered on 9th May for the first time by this Croatian group. These Croats proceeded to Judenburg, but on 19th May they were sent back to Wolfsberg. At Sankt Andrea the vehicles transporting them turned towards Slovenia rather than Klagenfurt. Trucks took these people to

Lavamund, and they numbered about 800 to 900, who were then extradited to the Yugoslavs under the watch of an unidentified Irish officer. According to "Operation Slaughterhouse" the British troops who escorted them had blue and violet feathers on their caps.

I mention this information because many authors have linked this separate repatriation to Bleiburg. This repatriation has also been the topic of the British War Diaries and a book written by an Irish officer to be reviewed later in my book.

In conclusion, this invaluable book has served as a milestone in the investigation of the whole issue in post-war Carinthia, especially with its first-hand accounts of the negotiations at the Bleiburg castle. I use information from it throughout this book. Unfortunately, at the same time, its introductory contributors have made some general conclusions and remarks which have confused the issue for decades to come. It is often the problem, with a lengthy book, that a reader will skim through the introduction and leave the rest for a later date. A later date could translate into decades later. I don't think I am alone in this practise.

For what ever reason, "Operation Slaughterhouse" was not a book often mentioned amongst the Croatian community at the time, perhaps because of the informative descriptions of the final days in Zagreb. During the 1970s and 1980s it was much more difficult to become aware of information, let alone access it. There was no internet and public libraries in Melbourne suburbs rarely if ever stocked books on Croatian history, in contrast to books on Yugoslavia.

"RISE AND FALL OF TITO", VLADIMIR VITEZ SENIOR, HISTORY AND LIFE PUBLICATION, MELBOURNE, 1972

Once again I am only looking for references to that 'one day in May' as I go through the books available to me. In a single paragraph on page 12 of this small book Vitez refers to 250,000 Croatian Armed Forces and civilians. On pages 11—12, Vitez writes that these Croats allegedly all reached Austria on 12th May 1945, where they surrendered to the British, who then handed them over to Tito's Communist guerrilla bands. Vitez then immediately refers to the "Maribor" Massacres of as many as half a million Croats who were killed by the Communist bands of Tito. Vitez has not used the information about the negotiations in "Operation Slaughterhouse", citing instead statements from its introductory sections.

In fairness it is thanks to the late Vladimir Vitez Senior that I had even heard of the book "Operation Slaughterhouse". Vitez generously lent his copy to me for a few years. Thankfully in the late 1980s I was able to refer to it in my university essays on the topic of the Communist Yugoslav dictatorship. I returned the book to his family after his untimely passing just before Croatian independence was internationally recognized in 1992.

"The Croats and the Cossacks" a chapter in "The Last Secret: The Delivery to Stalin of Over Two Million Russians by Britain and the United States", Nicholas Bethell, Basic Books Inc. New York, 1974

Nicholas Bethell, like the well-known author Nikolai Tolstoy, writes mostly about the repatriation of Cossacks rather than about Croats. But in "The Last Secret" Nicholas Bethell emphasised that,

> "...many other ordinary Croats, uninvolved in politics and innocent of any crime, suffered horribly during the years when Tito was consolidating his communist authority in Yugoslavia" ...(and that)...Tito was causing the Allies severe trouble, almost to the point of armed conflict".

Bethell does make a clear distinction between the exclusively Croatian surrender to Yugoslavs at Bleiburg, and earlier surrenders elsewhere to the British of various ethnic and Croatian groups. It is those other anti-Tito groups, described by Tolstoy and others, who were subsequently repatriated by the British, in the days 'after' the Bleiburg negotiations, from locations far away from Bleiburg.

It is true that, concerning the return of those above-mentioned other groups from different locations, the British did use deceit to facilitate the repatriations. But it is equally important to note that at Bleiburg the Yugoslav National Army used deceit to achieve its goal! This Yugoslav deception is clear in Bethell's account of what happened at Bleiburg.

The background to the British Brigadier Scott's handling of the situation at Bleiburg on 15th May was three-fold in Bethell's version of events, written in 1974. He obviously had access to Brigadier Scott's Report or British War Diaries.

Bethell notes that Keightley's order to Scott not to accept more surrenders came after Scott's assurances to the Cossacks that they would be safe behind British lines. Keightly, who was Scott's commander, had strongly expressed his alarm to Scott regarding the surrender of the Cossacks at Lavamund. Keightley further explained to Scott the rationale not to accept further surrenders under the terms of the Yalta Agreement.

Secondly, in Bethell's version, he writes that there were no provisions to feed and look after the "approaching" 200,000 Croatian army and 500,000 civilians escorting them.

Finally, Bethell writes that Scott, who had very little military presence at the time, was under duress created by Yugoslav threats to attack. Important to note at the time was the fact that the British were outnumbered by the Yugoslav National Army, which was occupying the area and threatening to attack the Croats. Bethell writes that the Yugoslav Commissar gave the following assurances.

> "…(the Yugoslav)promised that the civilians would be returned to Croatia and the soldiers treated as prisoners-of-war, 'with the exception of political criminals, who would be dealt with by Allied courts established to deal with this matter.'…'I (Scott) got an assurance (by the Yugoslav Commissar) that they would all be repatriated and looked after'…"

British-born Bethell is one of the few authors to mention details about the tri-partite negotiations at the Bleiburg castle, as we will discover in the following book reviews.

"Trial by Slander", Les Shaw, Harp Books, Canberra, 1973

Chapter twelve in this book, entitled "Bleiburg 1945" is devoted to Bleiburg, in the context of the background of Croatian settlers in Australia. In his book Shaw refers to the American Time magazine of 16 September 1946 entitled

> "The Nations: Proletarian Proconsul corroborates the liquidation of some 300,000 Croatians by the Partisans in the immediate post-war period".

Shaw briefly describes the exodus of Croatian soldiers and civilians from Zagreb on 6th May and 7th May, as numbering close to 500,000. Shaw claims that on 15th May there were over 100,000 Croatian soldiers and tens of thousands of Croatian civilians encamped at the Bleiburg field. He alleges that the British military authorities requested the Croats to lay down their arms and once disarmed they (the British) began to "herd the unarmed masses back across the border". He suggests that the Partisan units had come up in the night and began shooting the Croats.

Only at the end of his short five-page chapter does Shaw mention the British spokesman General Patrick Scott who, in this version of events, had allegedly

> "…informed the Croatian generals that all Croatian personnel, both military and civilian, were to be turned over to the communist partisans."

Like Vitez, Shaw seems to be taking his information mostly from Willoughby's introduction in "Operation Slaughterhouse". No distinction has been made between the method of operations at Bleiburg and the British extraditions out of Villach, Lawamund, Krumpendorf, Griffen, etc., where Shaw says that the Partisan adversaries were

> "a little more clever or discreet than those who had carried out the open massacre on the Bleiburg field."

Shaw then briefly refers to the extraditions "elsewhere" by trainload via a location distant from Bleiburg. But Shaw then jumps to the mass slaughters of "about 40,000" near Maribor by the "17th Partisan Assault Division", which is relevant to events after the Yugoslav evacuation Bleiburg. Shaw in succession then jumps again to describe the slaughter by the "11th Dalmatian Brigade" of "more than 30,000" Croats and Slovenes at Kocevski Rog, a slaughter which relates to other extraditions.

Like many Croatian authors Shaw, though not a Croat, uses the term Bleiburg as an umbrella name for several massacres and "Death Marches" in post-war Yugoslavia. The "Death Marches", Shaw continues, stretched all the way to the Romanian frontier. We learn that the locations and numbers of mass graves were well-known to Croats, even though the location of these mass graves only became open knowledge towards the end of the former Yugoslav state.

In hindsight it is obvious that Yugoslavia disintegrated, as it had been maintained, on the skeletons of its opponents, the vast majority of whom were Croats. I have referred also to the brazen shooting of five Croatian parliamentarians by a Serb in a Belgrade session of parliament in 1928 in my Appendix.

Importantly, Shaw also refers to other "butcheries" of those Croats who did not make it to the Austrian frontier at

> Dolensko, Ptuj, Celje and Krsko, Sestine (5,000), Vrgn-Most (7,000), Dubocac (3,000), Podravski Klostar (2,000), Virovitica (1,700), and also Bjelovar, Gracani, Sosice, Sisak, Butmir, Kasindol, Podgraci, and innumerable other places.

Like myself, Shaw has no Croatian background and so he is shocked and horrified when learning of these massacres. He quotes again from Willoughby in "Operation Slaughterhouse" about the nature of Tito's regime.

> Willoughby: "...concentration and slave labor camps throughout the country. Hundreds of thousands of citizens of all ages, sexes, and from every walk of life

were imprisoned, tortured, and finally liquidated. Croatia became an immense graveyard--her ditches, ravines, forests, and rivers all crowded with corpses".

"The pro-allied putsch in Croatia in 1944 and the Massacre of Croatians by Tito Communists in 1945", Ivo Omrcanin, Dorrance and Company, Philadelphia, 1975

This is probably the first, or one of the first, books by Ivo Omrcanin which mentions the Croatian surrender to Yugoslavs at Bleiburg. In the introduction chapters in Parts I and II Omrcanin writes a little about the Yalta Agreement and about an unsuccessful WWII Croatian government "pro-Allied putsch",which had failed due to Pavelic's strict domestic politics. The introductory part of Omrcanin's book finishes with the following criticism of the situation at the end of the war in Zagreb.

> Omrcanin: "The Croatian state authorities had many alternatives from which to choose. The first was to defend the fatherland to the last man and to the last drop of blood. They did not choose that alternative. For some arcane reason, they ordered retreat i.e., to leave national soil as an organized state power and organized army and take refuge on foreign soil with foreign authorities. They ordered the exodus of Croatians to Austria, to meet the Western Allies. The meeting was achieved in Bleiburg in Carinthia."

Immediately following the above paragraph, Part Two of the introduction begins with the title, "The Massacre of Croatians by Tito Communists in 1945". Here Omrcanin generalizes about what allegedly happened at Bleiburg.

> Omrcanin: "On May 15, 1945, the Croatian emissaries came to the commander of British troops in Bleiburg, Austria, Patrick Scott, to offer to the Western Allies the surrender of all Croatian troops and anti-Communist civilians...Croatian troops numbered about 300,000 and the number of civilians was about 250,000."

Omrcanin refers to the date that the Croatian government joined the "Geneva Convention" as being 20th January 1943. In the context of the Geneva Convention Omrcanin continues with his generalisation of the events at Bleiburg.

> Omrcanin: "General Patrick Scott refused to accept the surrender of Croatians and ordered them to surrender to Tito's Communists...a Commissar Milan Basta, answered: ...On behalf of the Command of the 51st Division of the Third Yugoslav Army, I demand your unconditional surrender. The time limit allowed for this surrender is one hour from the time of your return to your units, that is by 4. P.M. at the latest...your armed forces will be treated in accordance with the stipulations of International law provided for prisoners of war."

The next chapters I and II are still about the Geneva Convention and international law. Omrcanin continues in chapters III and IV about conspiracies, as quoted below. Omrcanin alleges, without evidence, that there was a reference to Croats at Yalta in the form of a list of names. In this way in the context of Yalta Omrcanin alleges that there was a conspiracy against Croats.

> Omrcanin: "There were two conspiracies which led Croatia into Communist slavery...and one is the Croatian conspiracy of those Croatians who were for a second Yugoslavia."

In chapter V, "The Widsom of the National Strategy" Omrcanin finally, for the first time, refers to the alleged "unconditional" surrender to Yugoslavs. Readers might wonder why Omrcanin did not consider the events as described by Crljen, Basta, and Scott themselves, as information was available by this time. Instead, Omrcanin is introducing the story in reverse chronology. Next Omrcanin alleges that after Scott refused to accept the surrender of Croats he then ordered the Croats to surrender to the Yugoslav Communists. In summary he then suggests that after the Croats had deposited their arms they gave themselves up to the Yugoslav Communists.

In subsequent chapters Omrcanin discusses "Operation Keelhaul", the handover of the Cossacks, and publishes some documents. Not one document refers directly to an alleged order by Scott for Croats to surrender to the Communists at Bleiburg!

However the reader is led to believe that the messages cited refer to Bleiburg in chapter IX, and he thus misrepresents the negotiations, the number of Croats who actually arrived at Bleiburg, and the order of events.

> Omrcanin: "1. On May 14, 1945, about 300,000 Croatian military personnel and about a quarter of a million Croatian civilians offered surrender to the British army in Bleiburg, Austria. The commanding general, Patrick Scott, delayed his decision until the next day...
>
> 2. On May 15, 1945, British General Patrick Scott ordered the Croatian army and the civilians to surrender to the Yugoslav Communist army. He promised help to the Communists if the Croatians refused to obey his orders, and he surrounded Croatian troops with tanks. British airplanes ready for action were flying over Croatians."

Finally Omrcanin presents many more messages, the majority of which are concerned with the later repatriations elsewhere, of several other groups which were far away from Bleiburg. I will discuss some of these messages further in other books written by Omrcanin. For example, the famous "ghastly mistake" quotation in reference to those 'other' repatriations was written by Addis on 14th August 1945, after the fact, and this message did not refer to Bleiburg.

Memorial Site at Bleiburg field 2014, photo taken from train on way to Maribor (front cover photograph)

Approaching Bleiburg field 2014, photo taken from train on way to Maribor

Leaving Bleiburg field towards Poljana 2014, photo taken from train on way to Maribor

CHAPTER 6

1980s

"The Death of a Greengrocer" in "That's Yugoslavia", Hanz P. Rullman, Ost-Dienst, Hamburg, 1981

This article under the sub-heading of "The Death of a Greengrocer" on pages 5—6 of the monthly "That's Yugoslavia", appears under the heading "Assassinations Commissioned by Belgrade: Documentation about the Yugoslav Murder Machine". This article in the above booklet is about the 1975 murder of Nikola Martinovic, a 65 year old man who lived in Klagenfurt and tended to the Bleiburg graves and the memorial. Rullman also refers to the murder of Ivo Bogdan in 1971 in Buenos Aires, a Croatian journalist who was writing about the Bleiburg Tragedy in the Croatian language. Rullman briefly mentions the attempted escape from the Yugoslav Communists of 400,000 Croatian people at the end of WW II. He repeats an often-told ambiguous version of events.

> Rullman: "...because in a similar way as the Britons mercilessly extradited the opponents of the Soviet Communism to the Russians—a fact that is today often deplored in London—the Western Allies handed over Tito's adversaries to the Communist partisans, who immediately carried out a massacre, in which according to an estimate, 300,000 people perished...approximately 200,000 Croats were killed and probably many more. The carnage at Bleiburg on the Austrian-Yugoslav border was the gravest war crime after the end of the war..."

Rullman then describes how bodies were thrown into caves or buried in open fields, quoting Milovan Djilas. I believe Rullman does get it right when he concludes that Yugoslavia fears the "Bleiburg dead".

> Rullman: "The Bleiburg dead unite the Croats above all ideological boundaries. They are not likely to be easily forgotten in the same way that the Poles never forgot the Katyn dead." The annual commemoration at Bleiburg continues.

"WORLD WAR II MASSACRE OF ANTI-COMMUNISTS HUSHED", HRVATSKI TJEDNIK, MELBOURNE, 29 SEPTEMBER 1981

This "Spotlight" article of 14th September 1981 was one of the first articles in the English language I had read about Bleiburg, and I took it at face value at the time. It was republished in Melbourne's Hrvatski Tjednik on page 8 in September 1981. I had not yet read the book "Operation Slaughterhouse" and I had no reason to question the validity of the article, because during the Cold War in Australia I often witnessed censorship about the former Yugoslavia.

I was acutely aware of the plight of Croatian refugees or Displaced Persons from the former Yugoslavia because I had personally listened to many shocking stories about that regime. Indeed my husband is a "UNHCR political refugee" from the former Yugoslavia and his document is published in this chapter.

I recently re-read many books about the Bleiburg tragedy for this book. After I reviewed those books and then looked at this 1981 "Spotlight" article I can recognize it as a piece of propaganda, but I didn't know that in 1981. The article has been republished from a controversial and now defunct newspaper Spotlight and it contains a number of falsehoods. In this article the Bleiburg-Maribor genocide is put into the context of anti-Bolshevism and the so-called "infamous Nuremberg trials". In reference to how

> "500,000 disarmed Croatian soldiers and refugee civilians"

were butchered by Tito's assassins, Spotlight alleges that the western Allies are partly to blame.

> "British and American governments were directly involved in this genocidal incident, it follows that both could have prevented this outrage.

To serve its main anti-American and anti-British argument the Spotlight article incorrectly asserts that months before the end of the Second World War the Croats had tried desperately to surrender to the British or Americans. The truth, not mentioned in the article, was that the Croatian attempt to change sides or surrender to the western Allies was stillborn, because it had been crushed by the Croatian government itself in 1944.

We also know that it was the decision of the Croatian government to retreat towards Austria at the end of the war. Thus the "Spotlight" article makes the preposterous suggestion that the Croats were lured into a trap which had been

> "...baited by the British military authorities stationed in the province of Carinthia in Austria".

It is absurdly inaccurate to state that "500,000" Croats escaped across the Austrian border "at the invitation of the British military authorities" who were encamped near Bleiburg, where the

> "...British disarmed over 100,000 Croatian soldiers...(and)... herded the refugees back across the Yugoslavian border and toward the line of ambush."

It is also falsely suggested by innuendo that what happened tens of kilometres away from Bleiburg also happened at Bleiburg, in reference to British deception that refugees were being transported to Italy.

In conclusion, I suggest that it is the readers who are unacquainted with the Bleiburg issue who are being deceived! Certainly I count myself amongst those who were duped by such tales. But I pose the question whether it is possible that even Spotlight was duped.

"Tihi Krivci" (Silent Culprits), Dinko Dedic, Hrvatski Tjednik, 29 September 1981

This article, in the Croatian language, is a brief synopsis of the "Spotlight" article reviewed above and makes no criticism of it.

"Dramatis Personae and Finis of the Independent State of Croatia in American and British Documents", Ivo Omrcanin, Dorrance & Company, Inc. Philadelphia, 1983

In order to discover anything about Bleiburg I had to read a lot of Omrcanin's text and often-cited British orders about other events. His whole book is written in a non-chronological order. But to his credit the book opens with a description of the peaceful and unanimous declaration of independence of Croatia in 1941, witnessed and described by the American Consul in Zagreb, John Meilly. Meilly's Report to the American Secretary of State entitled, "The Ustase Coup d'Etat in Croatia" on 13th June 1941 is quoted in full.

Early in his book Omrcanin quotes British messages of 24th May and after, which deal with other groups who were not in Bleiburg, and who were described as,

"...various groups of non-Partisan Yugoslavs likely to be found in Venezia Giulia and/or Carinthya and Styria".

By joining-the-dots, using maps and eye-witness testimony presented from many different viewpoints in Omrcanin's book, we begin to realise that these "non-Partisan Yugoslavs" have nothing to do with what happened at Bleiburg.

Initially, a non-Croatian reader like myself who was unfamiliar with the topic, and unfamiliar with the location, could be forgiven for believing these various British messages deal with exclusively with Croats at Bleiburg. This confusion occurs because one of Macmillan's documents refers to Croatian government leaders in a message. (F.O. 371-48919, R 9552/1728/92) Croatian government leaders of course were not close to Bleiburg, but this fact has not been clearly pointed out by Omrcanin. If all the dots are not there then the reader could be forgiven for making incorrect associations.

The key to unravelling the confusion is the fact that many Croatian government ministers had left Croatia before the general retreat from Zagreb. In my earlier chapter we have learned that the Croatian government had taken a different route, and some of them had entered southern Austria from a different point on the map, further north of Klagenfurt. Ironically, by this route some of the Croatian leaders thus found themselves amongst the "others" described above in British documents. From the list of Croatian leaders in Omrcanin's book, too long to mention here, and not relevant to my focus on 15th May at Bleiburg, one can also learn that many of these Croatian government ministers survived and emigrated.

Many of the subsequent pages in "Dramatis" deal with British documents which relate to the situation in April 1945 and other groups and other locations, such as those at Viktring Camp, as described in my book from different sources.

In chapter IV Omrcanin quotes the U.S. Ambassador Kirk in Caserta Italy on 23rd May 1945 who was not referring to Bleiburg, but to a previous order of 18 May regarding treatment of "enemy collaborators" who had been in camps behind British lines. We know from other authors that British and American policies differed at that time, and we know also on page 47 that,

> "Washington still did not know on May 18, 1945 of the extradition of Croatians to Yugoslav Communists".

The confusion continues. Without any source, and immediately after reference to this American document, Omrcanin jumps back in time to describe what happened at Bleiburg. Once again this would suggest to those unfamiliar with the topic that Kirk's message referred to Bleiburg when in fact it did not. At least Omrcanin does point to the different perspectives of British and American documents.

I was not able to access British or American Archives directly at the time, thus like many others I initially believed that these documents were all tied to what happened at Bleiburg.

Omrcanin then goes on to describe the decision to evacuate Croatia on 6th May, and that on 8th May 1945 the Communists took over Zagreb. Then on page 39 Omrcanin describes what happened when Croats arrived in Bleiburg.

> Omrcanin: "The Croatian army and civil refugees reached Austria on May 14, 1945, and in the small town of Bleiburg in Carinthia offered to surrender to the British Armed Forces. British officers informed Croatian military emissaries that they did not have the authority to accept the surrender and asked them to return the next day, saying they would ask their superior military authorities for a decision."

But then immediately after a few pages of documents which refer to 'other' locations and decisions, Omrcanin's next Chapter V is entitled, "Order of Surrender of the Croatian Army". We do know that Omrcanin already knew many more details than he gives here, from the books "Operation Slaughterhouse" and from Bethell's book "The Last Secret". Thus it is unclear whether Omrcanin is guessing and trying to put together documents new to him, or is he deliberately manipulating the order of the messages to appear that they relate to Bleiburg.

Up until now there has not been any sources provided by Omrcanin about the events of 15th May 1945. The sources he quotes in reference to Bleiburg, which were written in June and July 1945, refer to other repatriations elsewhere later than events in Bleiburg. Up to this point not one British message or source has been provided for Omrcanin's version of the surrender negotiations which he has inserted in between surrounding texts.

The following general statement about Bleiburg from Omrcanin does not accurately reflect the order of events which have been documented in both "The Last Secret" or in "Operation Slaughterhouse".

> Omrcanin: "At about 2 P.M. on May 15th, 1945, Croatian military emissaries General Ivo Herencic and Colonel Daniel Crljen arrived at the castle in Bleiburg, the headquarters of the British Army. Here the British Commanding General Patrick Scott, in the presence of the emissary of the Yugoslav Communists, Commissar Milan Basta, (Scott) gave the order to Croatians to surrender by 4 P.M. When

the Croatians protested, General Scott told the Commissar that the British Army would force the Croatians to surrender with their weapons and would give the Communists any help needed."

It is worth noting that Bleiburg was not the main "headquarters" of the V Corps, which was actually in Klagenfurt. It is also worth noting that the so-called "order" to surrender to the Yugoslavs was not a British "order". We know from original testimony that three options were suggested to the Croats, separately and in private, via an interpreter. Nevertheless confusing and contradictory accounts of events continue throughout Omrcanin's book.

After all the confusion and innuendo Omrcanin then refers to Alexander's message of 17th May, when he ultimately clarifies that this message actually refers to 220,000 people, who were located nowhere near to Bleiburg including

> Alexander: "109,000 Germans, 46,000 Cossacks, 15,000 Hungarians, 25,000 Croats, 24,000 Slovenes. Croat and Slovene refugees still pouring into my area number about 200,000."

On page 48 and 49 Omrcanin, for the first time, describes an important message of 19th May 1945 which does mention Bleiburg amongst other locations, a message (see below) which strangely begins with number "2". I cannot find number "1" in this reference. At least here we can get an idea about the Yugoslav strength in the region.

(F.O. 371-48817, R 8773 / 6 / 92):

> "Changes in military situation in Austria as reported by A.F.H.Q. today are as follows:
>
> 2. 3rd Yugoslav division has been newly identified in area Weitzendorf to south west of Klagenfurt. It is possible that this division is replacing 51st Yugoslav division which is reported to be moving eastwards through Bleiburg into Yugoslavia. 5th Yugoslav division has been identified in Bleiburg area and there are now a total of five Yugoslav divisions in Southern Austria or in frontier area.
>
> 3. 200,000 Croat troops have surrendered to Marshal Tito in Bleiburg area and a further 35,000 in Wildenstein area south east of Klagenfurt. These surrenders, together with 36,000 Quisling Yugoslavs already in British hands, should account for practically the whole Croat army and will accordingly release Yugoslav divisions for other tasks.

4. Headquarters 8th Army report that a Russian liaison officer informed British anti-tank regiment in area Wolfsburg that Marshal Tolbukhin has given permission for Tito's forces to enter that part of Austria now occupied by Bulgarian forces."

We can see clearly from the above message exactly what happened at Bleiburg, and what did 'not' happen at Bleiburg in areas farther west. Whilst Croats had surrendered to Tito in the Bleiburg area, there were others already in British hands in other locations. According to Omrcanin on page 169 Scott knew of the Croatian exodus of

> "...about 300,000 soldiers and about half a million people advancing towards the British in the valley of the Drava."

On 14th May, Omrcanin continues on page 169, the Croatian Lieutenant Deutsch-Macelski and a small group made up an advance Croatian group who located the British at 9pm in Hrust near Bleiburg. By 11pm Scott informed those Croats that the British

> "on no account would accept their surrender to them but that they must surrender to the Yugo-Communists."

"The Tragic Illegality of the Order to Surrender" is the title of Chapter VI. No other SACMED reference has been quoted about Bleiburg.

> Omrcanin: "As we have seen, on May 15, 1945 SACMED gave the order to General Patrick Scott in Bleiburg to force Croatians to surrender to Yugoslav Communist forces."

A SACMED order is then referred to on the same page 43 of "Dramatis" (F.O. 371 – 48825) dated 31 July 1945 which was about the groups repatriated from behind British lines elsewhere in the "latter part of May".

In a very short chapter VII entitled "Responsibility" the author repeats the words of Major General Charles A. Willoughby (USA Ret.) of 6 May 1968 who had written a Foreward to "Operation Slaughterhouse". Omrcanin has referred to just two of Willoughby's paragraphs.

My opinion is that some of Willoughby's observations are correct, but where he goes wrong is in his attribution of guilt. It is correct to state that Tito was responsible for labour camps set up all over Yugoslavia, and how hundreds of thousands of Croatian civilians were imprisoned, tortured, and finally liquidated, as Croatia became an immense graveyard.

But I disagree with Willoughby that some of the responsibility should go to the British for the fate of groups south-east of Klagenfurt. Just because the British were obligated by the terms of Yalta, which dealt with the post-War situation, it does not mean that they could see into the future! The British had no prior knowledge of the scale of Tito's intention to commit genocide! And, the Geneva Convention generally refers to the laws of war and not post-war situations. Omrcanin quotes Willoughby in "Dramatis" on page 59.

> Willoughby: "...hundreds of thousands of citizens of all ages, sexes, and from every walk of life...Although Tito and his aides actually carried out this "Operation Slaughterhouse," the British military authorities bear a moral responsibility ...The British were obligated by the Geneva Convention and by the laws of war to accept the Croatian surrender and to give the retreating Croat Army and civilian population sanctuary to protect them from Partisan vengeance."

The bias of Willoughby is uncovered when he links the massacre of Croats to "Partisan vengeance". At Bleiburg, after negotiations, the Yugoslav Commissar Basta had assured the British that international law would prevail. How would British officers and those who gave orders to them, believe in their wildest imagination, or know in advance, about the scale of atrocities and massacres that would happen in Yugoslavia afterwards between 1945 and 1948?

In hindsight it is easy to lay blame after the fact, but strange to do so in the case of the Bleiburg negotiations, which happened 'before' any other British repatriations! The agreements made at Yalta were for a post-war situation, and thus they superseded the Geneva Convention, a Convention which was actually meant to deal with prisoners-of-war captured 'in battle'. I have discussed the Geneva Convention articles in another chapter of my book.

In chapter IV, "Cover Up", the author refers to letters written 'after' the repatriations in the *London Times*, on 23 May 1945, and 24 May 1945, about the fanatical gangs of Tito in communist Yugoslavia! Of course this was after the events at Bleiburg, and also after many of the extraditions of Croats elsewhere by the British.

It needs to be stressed, because Omrcanin does not do so, that the British authorities and those involved have released documents, expressed regret, and granted permission for a monument in a public space regarding extraditions. In short the "ghastly mistake" has been uncovered. There was no "hush-up" in the west and never really has been! It was Yugoslavs who were covering-up their post-war crimes against humanity during the Cold War, and beyond.

Some may doubt that Omrcanin intentionally merged the evacuation by Yugoslavs at Bleiburg with other British extraditions. Croatian readers treat all repatriations under the umbrella name of the 'Bleiburg Massacres' anyways so they may not see a problem. But on page 99 of "Dramatis" Omrcanin adds to the confusion. In reference to Bethell's, "The Last Secret", Omrcanin quotes Scott's testimony that at Bleiburg Scott had only "...two men and a boy", and then he seems to suggest that all extraditions occurred at Bleiburg.

Omrcanin then deliberately puts the fate of Croats at Bleiburg together with other groups following an alleged quotation from Scott. It appears evident that this confusing detail is deliberate because Scott, in his original testimony, never mentioned dealing with any Montenegrins, Slovenians, or Serbians at Bleiburg. Omrcanin makes the following incorrect allegation!

> Omrcanin: "It is therefore evident that the British as late as 1972 and through authoritative spokesmen declare that the way they acted in Bleiburg — extraditing the Croatians (Montenegrins, Slovenians, and Serbians) — was the only right way to act."

But it is not "evident". To recapitulate, it should be obvious by now that at Bleiburg, on 15th May, the fate of other groups could not have been known because they had not yet been extradited!

Omrcanin also incorrectly discusses Scott in the context of an American telegram of 15th May yet we know from the above that the American policy differed from the British at this time.

Then once again readers are misinformed, that on 15th May at 2 P.M. Scott received the Croatian emissaries Herencic, Servatzy, and Crljen. Omrcanin incorrectly alleges that Scott gave them the order to surrender to the Yugo-Communists. He also incorrectly alleges that the Croatian accounts differed from Scott's Diary version.

> Omrcanin: "The descriptions of Croatians about the meeting with the British differ from those of Scott's diary...Two wrongs happened: the British order for surrender to the Communists, and the Croatian acceptance of the surrender."

In the next paragraph Omrcanin once again immediately jumps forward in time to the message of the end of July 1945!

In my reading of the various eye-witness versions of negotiations on 15th May I could not find any basic discrepancies. And so it appears, after nearly two hundred pages, that Omrcanin did see Scott's diary after all! The re-reading of this book "Dramatis" has been a very frustrating experience!

In the attribution of blame for Bleiburg there is an interesting comment by the author in "Dramatis". Omrcanin quotes the British Sir J. M. Addis remark about the British repatriations (elsewhere) as a "ghastly mistake", and he also criticizes NDH, the Croatian government leadership. Omrcanin remarks on the passivity, lack of political wisdom, and weakness of the Croatian leadership on pages 176 and 177. And Omrcanin also refers to four Croatian "capital errors". In so doing he attributes some blame (for the Bleiburg Tragedy) to the Croatian leadership for subsequent surrenders and repatriations.

Personally I would not attribute direct blame for anything to any victims, but would suggest instead that these leadership mistakes contributed to the presence of a Croatian 'national exodus' in a dangerous Yugoslav-occupied zone. But it's not even a 'grey' area: all blame should be attributed directly to the plan to liquidate Croats and get rid of opposition to Tito's power. I have paraphrased Omrcanin's analysis of "errors" below.

According to Omrcanin, firstly the Croats should not have left the "south flank" open to Yugoslavs who then entered Trieste on 1 May ahead of the Allies and in so doing could "encircle Croatia".

The decision to retreat is criticised as the second error, because it became clear later that Churchill expected and desired that Croatia could have given resistance to the Yugo-Communists.

The third error was the decision to retreat to Austria instead of to (northern) Italy because in that case there "would have been no extradition and so no Bleiburg tragedy or similar tragedy."

Omrcanin says that the decision to "surrender to the Yugo-Communists in Bleiburg was the fourth error". Here Omrcanin contradicts himself because up to this point he has referred to a British "order" to surrender rather than to a Croatian "decision" to surrender!

In addition Omrcanin harshly criticizes the earlier separate retreat of Croatia's Chief of State Dr Ante Pavelic.

> Omrcanin: "...(Pavelic)...left the whole group in exodus, the army and the people, to themselves...The government did the same. The army was left without a head, and

from Rogaska Slatina on, there was no supreme commander. The Chief of General Staff did not ever appear, and there was a vacuum in leadership and command... The whole Bleiburg tragedy could have been avoided if there had been competent, courageous, and wise leadership, far-seeing and ready to sacrifice. There was a total absence of wisdom: diplomatic, political, military, strategic, or any other kind."

In the map in my book I have deduced, from various sources, the route of the Croatian government members which is indicated separately from the main exodus retreat route.

In conclusion, I have covered the presentation of events in "Dramatis" in detail, and some themes will be referred to in later discussions in other books without repeating them in such detail again. It has been necessary for me to go into such repetitive detail initially because it has been difficult to separate information about Bleiburg from other repatriations in Omrcanin's "Dramatis".

"Enigma Tito: Documentary Expose of SOE and OSS Agents in Yugo-Communist State", Ivo Omrcanin, Samizdat, Washington, 1984

In reference to Bleiburg in this thick volume written in English only a couple of chapters are relevant, namely "Emptio-Venditio", "Klagenfurt Affair" and "Bleiburg's Smoking Gun". By 1984 we know that the author was familiar with many recently released British documents which he has referred to in earlier books!

The first chapter about Bleiburg is entitled "Emptio-Venditio". (The consensual contract between two parties for the purchase of something by one party and its sale by the other at an agreed price.) In this chapter Omrcanin is responding to a BBC history television program, and a 1983 article in the *London Observer* about that BBC program.

Chapter XI is about the "Klagenfurt Affair". Omrcanin mentions a 1984 article in the *London Times* which has referred to a Macmillan and Tito "Liaison in Tito's massacres". Omrcanin tries to lead readers to believe that the BBC Timewatch television program "The Klagenfurt Afair" was about Bleiburg, although in actual fact the BBC program was about the testimony of British officers who were in Klagenfurt and Viktring, etc.

The BBC program referred to orders of 14th May 1945 to return already surrendered refugees to Yugoslavia from Viktring and other camps, and this was the order which was referred to three months later by the British as a "ghastly mistake". The next order Omrcanin has mentioned, regarding the BBC program, was the order on 17th May 1945. Finally Omrcanin mentions a message of 19th May 1945, which was in response to the 17th May message, which mentioned that Partisans were to withdraw from around Klagenfurt and Villach.

In chapter XII, "Bleiburg's Smoking Gun", Omrcanin refers to Churchill's order of 1st April 1945 that "all supplies should be shut down" in reference to Tito's Partisans. The author then jumps to Field Marshall Alexander's telegram to Belgrade of 15th May 1945, regarding the "200,000 Yugoslav Nationals" who had surrendered to the British south of Klagenfurt, and that by the 17th May Tito had replied.

The above telegrams refer to an area south of Klagenfurt and other camps which held various ethnic groups of refugees who had already surrendered, and were behind British lines. Nevertheless Omrcanin leads readers to believe incorrectly that this particular situation refers to Bleiburg. In fact the negotiations at Bleiburg occurred far away and were not the subject of the orders and telegrams mentioned.

Thus, in yet another one of his books, Omrcanin does not correctly joint-the-dots for us. In his earlier book published in 1983 "Dramatis Personae and Finis of the Independent State of Croatia in American and British Documents" ("Dramatis") we have already learned that on 17th May (re 61179) the 220,000 number refers to groups not anywhere near Bleiburg. The order quoted by Omrcanin for example (WO 202/319 FX 75902) regarding a hand-over refers specifically to Villach. This number 220,000 refers to 109,000 Germans; 46,000 Cossacks; 15,000 Hungarians; 25,000 Croats; and 24,000 Slovenes.

In this chapter Omcranin is looking for a "Smoking Gun" amongst British orders for blame about what happened at Bleiburg, at a high level in the chain of command, when there is none. We already know from Bethell's book, published ten years earlier, that what happened at Bleiburg was separate from and entirely different to what happened elsewhere far to the west of Bleiburg.

Omrcanin acknowledges that Alexander's policy was to,

> "close the Austrian frontier to Tito's forces"...(but at the same time)...to avoid a clash with the Yugoslav forces except in self-defense...to hold the position without using force."

In summary I believe that Omrcanin is not wrong to say that Croats were handed over by the British, in the area referred to by the BBC Timewatch program in the above-mentioned messages and orders; but he does incorrectly allege that Alexander was talking about Bleiburg by referring only to "Death Marches"--"from Bleiburg to Belgrade on May 15 1945" in the context of orders above re Villach.

Finally, closer to the end of the chapter, Omrcanin actually refers to numbers regarding Villach.

> "... 26,000 persons, including many women and children, Croatians for the most part...".

Unfortunately, and not to his credit, Omrcanin lacks objectivity in his judgment when he blames the British of War Crimes and a "conspiracy" to commit genocide against Croats and others and inappropriately compares British political leaders to Nazi leaders!

To put such a slanderous accusation into 21st-century terms we know, from an ICTY Hague Court finding in 2015, that in order to prove genocide it is necessary to prove "intent". Omrcanin cannot prove any "intent" on the part of the British to commit genocide! There is however lots of proof that the Yugoslavs intended to commit genocide against the Croats in particular! The well-known Yugoslav dissident Milovan Djilas even admitted that "Croatian soldiers must die in order that Yugoslavia may live".

Omrcanin eventually acknowledges that 26,000 (not several hundred thousand) Croats were handed over at Rosenbach or Marie Elend train stations, and that they were deceived by the British about their destination. We know from other sources how difficult and stressful it was for the British soldiers to carry out their orders. But 'before the fact' there is no way those British soldiers could have fully comprehended the intention and colossal extent of Yugoslav-perpetrated massacres across such a wide front nor could they have known of this in advance.

In his Appendix V, Omrcanin publishes a chronology of the era from the "War Diary or Intelligence Summary" of Unit 3rd Bn Welsh Guards, Commanding Officer: Lt Col R.C. Rose Price, DSO...May 1945...Villach".

On the 15th May in a report from "Rosegg" it is written,

> "TITO tps become more active and more aggressive. Proclamation issued by TITO that CARINTHIA and GORITZA belonged to YUGOSLAVIA and that he claimed it on racial and martial grounds."

On 19th May 1945 around Maria Elend and Rosenbach stations the Croats are to be evacuated to the Yugoslavs.

> "Evacuation of Croats begin. Order of most sinister duplicity received i.e. to send Croats to their foes i.e. TITS to Yugoslavia under the impression that they were to go to ITALY. TIT guards on trains hidden in guards van."

"Military History of Croatia", Ivo Omrcanin, Dorance & Company, Inc., Bryn Mawr Pennsylvania, 1984

In this overview of all the battles in Croatia's history over two millennia two pages are devoted to Bleiburg. In "Military History of Croatia" we have an example 'in a nutshell' of an incomplete Bleiburg narrative. Omrcanin gives a brief timeframe for the retreat. On 4th May 1945 the Military and Civil Croatian leaders gave up a defence of Croatia and gave the order to troops to retreat to Carinthia. The 6th May is the date given that the Croatian government, with Pavelic retreated from Zagreb to arrive in Carinthia on 7th May 1945. The 8th May 1945 is given as the final evacuation date of Zagreb. After a brief background about the retreat towards Carinthia, Omrcanin first mentions the offer of surrender to the English command at Bleiburg on 14th May. But when Herencic and Crljen arrive on 15th May, according to Omrcanin, the British General Scott ordered the Croats

> "...to surrender to the Communist troops. Scott promised the Communist emissary, Commisar Milan Basta, there present, the help of the British Army if the Croatians refused to surrender. The British air force and armoured forces were put in motion to execute the order..."

'In a nutshell' Omrcanin leaves out vital facts in a brief generalisation of events which virtually changes the nature of what really happened.

There is no mention of the options given by the British general to the Croats, and there is no mention that the British had been given assurances by the Yugoslav Commissar that international laws would be respected! Also there is no information about the strong Yugoslav presence in the area and their confrontational behaviour. After all it could not be a coincidence that the three totally separate national representatives present at the surrender barely differed with each other on the description of events!

It is also incorrect to say that the "Death Marches" actually began at Bleiburg when only some tens of thousands made it that far. We know by eye-witness testimonies in "Operation Slaughterhouse" that large columns of Croats had already been re-routed on "Death Marches" days earlier, towards Maribor, or they had taken other totally different routes towards Carinthia. In other words, the "Death Marches" did not begin at Bleiburg.

> Omrcanin: "Almost all of the 300,000 military and 250,000 civilians were slaughtered on the "Death Marches" that began there in Bleiburg..."

By way of explanation, to help the unacquainted reader, I would stress again that the use of the term "Bleiburg" to describe the tragedy since the time of the "Resolutions" is symbolic and this was especially the case during the Cold War. I was one of those 'unacquainted' readers myself.

The Bleiburg field has been chosen as a symbolic place of commemoration because of the unique Croatian surrender to the Yugoslavs there after negotiations. Secondly, because commemoration of "Death Marches" or mass graves in Yugoslavia was forbidden before that regime's collapse, Bleiburg Austria was an alternative accessible location. The gradual uncovering of mass Croatian graves all around Yugoslavia in the late 1980s was a major factor in the demise of totalitarian Yugoslavia! I will briefly discuss the locations of the mass graves in subsequent chapters as they were reported on.

In conclusion, to Croatian communities around the world, Bleiburg represents Croatian surrenders and repatriations 'everywhere' according to a Croatian "Resolution". It is this inclusive meaning of the term Bleiburg which I believe is rather problematic. Although a commemoration needs to continue at Bleiburg, the narrative needs to be updated in accordance with the standards of international law.

"Ivan Mestrovic Centennial" in "A Journal of Croatian Studies: Annual Review 1983", Jerome Jareb & Karlo Mirth, Editors, Croatian Academy of America, Inc., New York, Volume XXIV, 1984

In "A Journal of Croatian Studies: Annual Review 1983" of the Croatian Academy of America Inc., written in English, 216 pages have been devoted to the life of Ivan Mestrovic. The world-famous sculptor is relevant to the issue of Bleiburg for a couple of reasons. On page 115 Ivan Mestrovic is acknowledged as one of the founders of Yugoslavia who later regretted it, in an entry by Christopher Spalatin entitled: "My Memories of Ivan Mestrovic".

> Spalatin: "founders of Yugoslavia" who in "1918 (they) brought about the dream of Gaj, Strossmayer, Racki and others... (Mestrovic was) convinced that the Yugoslav dream was a nightmare..."

In a chapter by Karlo Mirth entitled, "Mestrovic in America: Living from the Clod of Croatian Soil Attached to his Boots", on page 158 a meeting between Milovan

Djilas and Ivan Mestrovic is described. Djilas is famous for his reference to the trial, sentencing, and treatment of Cardinal Stepinac.

> Djilas: "...Stepinac is a man of integrity, of unwavering character. He really was sentenced as a righteous man, but how many times has it happened in history that just men were sentenced because of political necessity."

Also of relevance on page 185, one of Tito's remarks to Ivan Mestrovic is quoted by Karlo Mirth. Bleiburg is not mentioned, nor are numbers, so it is a general reference to the "Death Marches" or "massacres". Mestrovic, according to Mirth, also gives us a remarkable insight into Tito's refusal to take responsibility for post-war crimes against humanity! Tito blames the Serbs and not even the Partisans or the Yugoslav Army!

> "In his talks with Tito, Mestrovic raised the question of the massacre of the Croatian Army (domobrans and ustashas) and the civilians who were returned from Austria by the British after the end of World War II in May 1945. Tito answered that nothing could have been done to prevent the Serbs from venting their rage".

An entry in this volume about the life of Ivan Mestrovic is edited by Ivo Omrcanin under the heading "Ivan Subasic on his negotiations with Tito and Stalin during October and November 1944". On page 203, of relevance to post-war events is Tito's refusal before the end of the war to allow Anglo-American troops to land on the Dalmatian coast after a request from Churchill.

> Subasic: "Tito refused categorically to permit Anglo-American troops to land in Croatia ... Tito was nervous that the presence of Allied troops in Croatia and Dalmatia would jeopardize his position and would afford the Croatian nationalistic elements an opportunity to rally against the National Committee of Liberation."

"How Tito put down the Croatian Spring", Jure Lasic, Hrvatski Tjednik, Melbourne, 10 April 1984

There is only one sentence in this article in the Hrvatski Tjednik on page 13 about Bleiburg. Lasic incorrectly refers to how 300,000 Croats at Bleiburg

> "laid down their arms and surrendered to the British, were handed over to Tito's forces, only to be massacred."

We have learned from sources so far that a large proportion of the Croats failed to reach Bleiburg and that they surrendered to the Yugoslavs.

"The Bleiburg Connection", Jean Marinovic, Hrvatski Tjednik, Melbourne, 22 May 1984

In my poem I describe the events and locations, and call for Croatian people to never forget this tragedy known as 'Bleiburg'. I am not sure why I chose the title "The Bleiburg Connection" at the time but perhaps I meant it to signal how Bleiburg could unite Croatian people in their tragedy.

"In Bleiburg, Austria, valley of fear
Allied camp, the point of no return
Nineteen forty-five was the tragic year
Croatians had nowhere else to turn

Farewell dear Zagreb, old friend
With guns in their backs, evacuation
Croatian masses march to their end
Thousands walking in the same direction

To Bleiburg in Austria Croatians pour
Both soldiers and civilians knew not why
With new hopes in the aftermath of war
Surely not the time or place to die

Frightened children and old women too
Trudging on Croatian blood spilled underneath
Joining soldiers young and old, who knew
That to turn back would mean certain death

Naively, 150,000 lay their guns down
On May 15th, their day of arrival
Of conspiracy or betrayal there was no sound
Holding onto hopes for their survival

Croatian refugees, lost without a leader
In silence waited never questioning any order
Who were unwillingly forced by their deceiver
To Tito and his Serbian butchers at the border

Thousands massacred, fell to each others' feet
While at Maribor were slaughtered 40,000 more
Trainloads at Kocevje, victims of British deceit
Many thousands murdered, after the end of the war.

One Day in May – Bleiburg 1945

And on their 'March of Death' thousands went
Dropping dead in pain in the dirt along the way
And those not thrown into mass graves, were sent
To rot in concentration camps, that year, in May

From this genocide disappeared half a million
History shows us that this was just the start
In 4 decades Croatia has lost three more million
For them Croatia is real, only in their heart

The path away from tyranny for today's emigrants
Is not so blood stained as it used to be
The Croatian exodus from Yugoslavia never ends
In air-conditioned comfort with passports, free

But those who stay behind live in silent fear
As second-class citizens or cheap European labour
To be separated from their family, year after year
While imprisonment and assassination numbers soar

Would it be possible that from places near and far
Croatians who are able could return from everywhere
With those souls at Bleiburg as their guiding star
So relatives who still mourn need no longer despair

About the suffering at Bleiburg the world must hear
Of inhuman acts those responsible wish us to forget
Those of us, who can come, make 1985 the year
And the date May 15 for a Croatian pilgrimage set

Croatian brothers and sisters in Bleiburg, unite
Join, in strength, in remembrance of this tragedy
For our homeland we will not give up our right
To live as one nation, one people free

In this poem, written during the Cold War, I mention that "500,000" laid down their guns, and the disappearance of "half a million". I refer briefly to a potential conspiracy or betrayal and refer to British deceit. I mention thousands being massacred in a place other than the "40,000" victims at Maribor. I am possibly confusing the orders at Bleiburg with the orders at Villach—I don't remember. I wrote this poem after reading through the victims' testimonies about mass graves in the book "Operation Slaughterhouse". In this poem I am more emotional than factual about the events at

Bleiburg. Reference to a loss of "three more million" in the subsequent four decades, in hindsight, is an exaggerated figure.

"The 40th Anniversary of the Ambush at Bleiburg", Jean Marinovic, Hrvatski Tjednik, Melbourne, 21 May 1985

In this poem I am describing what I thought was the scene at "Bleiburg" and that it was an "ambush".

> I was born in nineteen hundred forty-five
> My parents and I were lucky to be alive
> Because in Croatia where I was born
> Every city and village was ravaged and torn
>
> For our people there was no tomorrow
> We were left with our dead and sorrow
> For the duration of forty-five and six
> Croatians were victims of Allied tricks
>
> On a mission of peace Croatians went ahead
> To a meeting with the British they were led
> But little did they know at that very time
> Tito had already arranged his bloody crime
>
> With the Soviets acting as his liberator
> And the Allies helping this Yugo dictator
> Croatian independence was to be crushed
> And this genocide to be carefully hushed
>
> For those Croatians who chose to remain
> In Zagreb, their life was to end in pain
> While the other hundreds of thousands fled
> From the Communists and their star of red
>
> Bleiburg for those who came was hell on earth
> Where they realized how little their worth
> As soon as their position became indefensible
> It was clear that Croatian life was expendable!
>
> This was the beginning of the end of fair play
> Now "divide and conquer" was the British way
> The human tidal wave at the Yugo border-line
> Had not been made aware of the Allies' design

One Day in May – Bleiburg 1945

The Croatians, army, priests, civilians alike
Across the Klagenfurt Valley were made to hike
They were bluffed into becoming a human cargo
On route to Italy—-with a short cut to Yugo!

The devil himself sealed the pact that day
When Yugoslav partisans got their own way
Screams echoed across the land, in vain
As Tito executed his merciless campaign

And in Carinthia in the dead of night
Unarmed Croatians were killed out of sight
The Allied forces pretended not to hear
As the shots rang out in May that year

Of course the British had no blood on their hands
Their only crime to send expatriots to their lands
Carrying out the order to prevent their surrender
Proving to be the world's greatest pretender

Once back across the Yugoslav-Austrian border
Murder was carried out with precision and order
Columns of hundreds and thousands of Croatians
Marched to their graves in unmarked locations!

Once peaceful valleys became mass graves
As the ground itself swelled up in waves
With one-sixth of their nation crucified
Croatians knew their salvation had been denied

Nineteen eighty-five is the anniversary year
For Croatians it marks forty years of fear
With half a million having died that way
It's the reason that Yugoslavia lives today!

"This year all European nations are holding memorial services in honour of those who died in the Holocaust of the 2nd World War, as a reminder to the new generations and students of today that such atrocities must never take place again. So, too, Croatians must never, never forget that Yugoslavia built their own 'Berlin Wall' between Austria and Slovenia from the skeletons of Croatians"

In this poem I mention that "hundreds of thousands fled" (Croats) and a "human tidal wave at the Jugo border-line". In this second poem I write more harshly against the British "tricks" ... "Allies helping this Jugo dictator" ..."the end of (British) fair play" ... "the Allies design" ... "The Allied forces pretended not to hear (shots)" ... "the world's greatest pretender".

It is clear to me, in hindsight, I was confused. Evidently I was thinking that the situation regarding the British sending Croats into trains to Yugoslavia was part of the Bleiburg tragedy, and when I mention hiking across the "Klagenfurt Valley" in the poem I am convinced about my confusion.

I am clear that 'inside' Yugoslavia "hundreds and thousands of Croats marched to their graves in unmarked locations". I write that "one-sixth of their nation (was) crucified". In another verse I mention how Croats were bluffed into "becoming a human cargo on route to Italy—with a short cut to Jugo". In this poem I am confused between what happened at Bleiburg and the train trips from Maria Elend and Rosenbach which were turned back into Yugoslavia. In this emotional poem I have tried to imagine myself in the position of how it felt to be a Croat in 1945.

"Tragedija se Dogodila u Svibnu" (Tragedy that happened in May), Vinko Nikolic, Knjiznica Hrvatske Revije, Barcelona, Part I 1984, Part II 1985

These two volumes which mention the Bleiburg Tragedy are in the Croatian language, and so much detail, and testimony, is contained in these 900 pages that it would be impossible for me to review. Nikolic has written these volumes whilst in refugee camps after WWII.

"Visitor recalls 'slaughter great powers would prefer forgotten'", John Jesser, The Canberra Times, Canberra, 9 May 1985

This article from the Canberra Times, was republished in Hrvatski Vjesnik on 21st May 1985, and it refers to the lecture of the visiting American "academic" from San Francisco, Michael McAdams. The Australian journalist takes McAdam's information at face value except for the numbers killed which he reduces. The article incorrectly alleges that the slaughter of "300,000" Croatians and other anti-communist minorities including Slovenians, Ukrainians and Cossacks happened after their surrender to British and American forces after the end of the war. Thus by this statement the journalist has merged what happened at Bleiburg with other British repatriations. The article states, according to McAdams, that Yalta has been hushed in relation to these repatriations. This article is one of the first in the 'mainstream' I have read which mistakenly ties the events at Bleiburg with the extraditions that happened elsewhere.

"Od Bleiburga do pobjede" (from Bleiburg to Victory), Dinko Dedic, Editor, Hrvatski Tjednik, Melbourne, 14 May 1985

A full-page photograph of the Bleiburg field appears on the front page of Hrvatski Tjednik with the headline "Od Bleiburga do pobjede" (from Bleiburg to Victory). No article about Bleiburg in this issue has survived in my collection.

The photograph of the pine trees is correctly described as: "borovi na Bleiburskom polju, gdje je pocelo klanje hrvarske vojske".(The pines at Bleiburg field where the slaughter of the Croatian army began.) Inset in the larger photograph of pine trees is an often-published photograph of a signpost which points to Volkermarkt in one direction and to Unterdrauburg (Dravograd) in the other direction. This signpost photograph is captioned: "jedan dio razoruzanih hrvatskih vojnika, kratko prije pokolja" (One part of Croatian soldiers disarmed shortly before slaughter). This photograph and others are discussed in a later chapter of my book under a review of Vukusic's "Bleiburg Memento fotomonografija" or under the "Carinthian Regional Museum" review.

"Visiting Historian Reveals Fats on the Bleiburg Massacres: Expert reveals unrecorded horror", F. Barbic, Hrvatski Vjesnik, Melbourne, 21 May 1985

This article on page 4 of the Hrvatski Vjesnik is about a public lecture on 13th May 1985 of the visit to Australia, from the United States, of Michael McAdams. Although McAdams is described as a "professor" it is my belief that he was working in Administration at a university. The spelling and grammar mistakes in the quotations are most likely those of the reporter or typewriting errors.

> Barbic: "He also reminded his audience of the British and Yugoslav contribution to VE Day at Bleiburg ... Croatians are reminded of 600,000 of their brethren tortured and killed at Bleiburg by those who brought victory to Europe...after the initial masqure of hundreds of thousands of Croatians, the Yugoslav liberators organized a death march..."

By his comments above and below it would seem that McAdams attributes blame to the British.

> McAdams: "Bleiburg must not be remembered in vengence of justice. It is too late for that ... Croatian people should never trust any great power but only the Croatian people."

Needless to say, today in 2015, I disagree with this interpretation of events at Bleiburg, the numbers given, and on the attribution of guilt to big powers. Such statements must be corrected wherever they appear. Yes, Yalta was the rationale for decisions made, but it was the Yugoslavs who deceived the British at Bleiburg and who were responsible for organising and executing the massacres of Croats in Yugoslavia.

Perhaps McAdams intended the term Bleiburg to symbolically cover all tortures and "Death Marches" which lasted over a two-year period. A map of the routes of various "Death Marches" accompanies the article with the caption "Routes of the numerous death marches in which hundreds of thousands of Croats were massacred".

"Hurford: Yalta Tragic Error Enslaved Millions: Yalta Condemned", Chris Hurford, speech reprinted on page 12 Hrvatski Vjesnik, Melbourne, 21 May 1985

Mr Hurford, then Australian Minister for Immigration and Ethnic Affairs, made a speech to a meeting organized by a "Renounce Yalta Committee" in a Polish Centre in Adelaide on 30th March 1985.

> Hurford: "What happened at the Yalta Conference was a tragic error that has deprived millions of the liberty we in the Western world enjoy"... "There is no equivalence between freedom and totalitarianism".

Hurford described the fate of many nationalities who were victims of Yalta in his anti-Communist, anti Soviet, anti-"others" speech. The Yalta agreement he said had affected countries in Central and Eastern Europe. Tragically no mention is made of either Yugoslavia or Croats.

"McAdams at Melb Uni: The Truth Emerges", L. Topic, Hrvatski Vjesnik, Melbourne 28 May 1985

This article on page 11 of the 'Croatian Students' pages in Hrvatski Vjesnik (the Croatian Students Association of Victoria) is about the lecture given by Michael McAdams. In his lecture Michael McAdams focussed on the role of the Yalta Treaty in the extradition or repatriation of 'Eastern Europeans', and their liquidation by "Soviet, Yugoslav, Bulgarian and other forces".

McAdams has mistakenly asserted in relation to Bleiburg that on 14th May and 15th May 1945 the Croats surrendered to the British at the Austrian border, and that then the British repatriated them. He does correctly refer to the subsequent deaths as the Bleiburg tragedy however as that term has a symbolic meaning for Croats for all "Death Marches". In reference to an alleged "trade-off" and to Macmillan, McAdams says that the truth is emerging. The lecture by McAdams at the university attracted some mainstream media attention.

In conclusion McAdams has put Bleiburg into the context of various other repatriations carried out by various armies in post-war Austria. He has incorrectly included Bleiburg with other surrenders to the British. In hindsight I don't mean to sound too critical of McAdams because I was making mistakes myself about the order of events in my own writing.

"HOLOCAUST OF CROATIANS", IVO OMRCANIN, SAMIZDAT, WASHINGTON DC, 1986

The disturbing anti-British theme of this book is set on the inside cover where an inappropriate caption of the cover-photographs (Macmillan & Alexander/Tito & Mihailovic) reads, "War Criminals Yugo and British Twins Who Ordered the Croatian Holocaust". In this book Omrcanin is following up the similar themes in his "Enigma Tito" book which essentially fall into the category of conspiracy theory.

The first part of this book is about the murdered Catholic clergy in Croatia by the "Chetniks". The rest of the book provides assorted correspondence about the post-war situation. Only the middle of this book, in the third chapter entitled "Holocaust", deals with repatriations and Bleiburg.

Essentially Omrcanin is reacting to a 1983 BBC program about Tito's massacres. An additional article is cited from *The Times* in London of 3rd January 1984 entitled "Macmillan and Alexander—liaison in Tito's Massacres". Omrcanin cites British correspondence about Tito, including from Churchill. On pages 74 and 75 the numbers of refugees in Austria are given, which is a direct quotation from his book, "Dramatis Personae and Finis of the Independent State of Croatia in American and British Documents".

In chapter Four the misleading title of "British Killing Papists in Croatia" more correspondence is provided, but most of it is dated in years after 1945. Omrcanin opens the chapter in a direct manner by asking a ridiculous question which embodies his own answer.

"Why did the British in World War II order the Holocaust of Croatians? Why did the British continue to kill Croatians even after the extradition of more than half a million Croatians on May 15 1945?"

Omrcanin begins his answer by philosophising about ethics, and then dives into 10,000 years of Croatian history. The typical often-heard argument that Croats never "waged aggressive wars" in their history is also given. The argument that Croats did not wage war outside their state territory is incorrect of course, if the Croatian presence at the Battle of Stalingrad in WWII is taken into consideration.

Typically he alleges on page 82 that on 15th May at Bleiburg 300,000 Croatian soldiers and 250,000 (or more) civilians surrendered to the Anglo-Americans. It is clear from many reliable sources however that only a proportion of that huge number were able to escape from the Yugoslavs, or Bulgarians, and were never able to cross the Austrian border! Even Omrcanin himself has asserted that the Croats did not surrender to the British at Bleiburg. Some few thousands of Croats did manage to surrender to the "Anglo-Americans" elsewhere of course. Omrcanin finishes by alleging that all that number were handed to Tito, which of course a deliberate lie. He refers to the British hatred of papists as if this motivated the British after WWII, when it is known that all big powers contributed to the chain of events following the end of the war. Religion just did not come into it! All powers were involved in a hunt for alleged "war criminals".

"The Minister and the Massacres", Nikolai Tolstoy, Century Hutchinson Ltd., London, 1986

Count Nikolai Tolstoy, whose real name is Tolstoy-Miloslavsky, is a distant cousin of the Russian novelist Leo Tolstoy. I have an autographed copy of his book "The Minister and the Massacres", signed at a public lecture given by him at the La Trobe University in Melbourne during his visit to Melbourne. This lecture, like most of his book, was devoted to the repatriation of the Cossacks. A few years later, after this book was published, Nikolai Tolstoy was indicted for libel in the British High Court for certain allegations in his book and for other distributed material about some of the forced repatriations.

Tolstoy's book is lengthy and deals almost exclusively with the repatriation of the Cossacks, his main reason for writing this book. Tolstoy's version of what happened to Croats and why is mostly in the chapter entitled, "Stratagems of Deception". The title of Tolstoy's book, mentions the "Minister" (Macmillan) because of Macmillan's brief visit with Keightly at Klagenfurt on the 13th May, a visit which resulted in a changed British policy. This visit is described on pages 65 to 67 by Tolstoy. For the purposes of my research in this book I am only interested in the parts of Tolstoy's "The Minister and the Massacres" which deal with the Croats.

When I finished reading the book after Tolstoy left Melbourne, I noticed that in his numerous descriptions of massacres that the Orthodox victims had "souls" and that the Croats had "bodies". It was too late to ask Tolstoy about that!

> Tolstoy: "Large numbers had evaded returning with those of their compatriots who had been turned back at Bleiburg, while others had swarmed across at different points along the frontier. Unknown numbers had gone to ground in the countryside, while the remainder were dispersed in prisoner-of-war camps at Griffen, Rosegg, Klagenfurt, Tamsweg and elsewhere."

Tolstoy separately deals with the negotiations at Bleiburg castle very briefly and readers are thus generally misled.

> "His (Scott's) next interview was with the unfortunate Croatian commander, General Herencic, whom Scott and Basta managed to cajole and bully into accepting these unequivocal terms. Deciding there was no alternative, Herencic capitulated. By 4.30 on 15 May the independent state of Croatia had ceased to exist. Hemmed in by Partisans, within twenty-four hours the would-be Croatian national emigration was to be herded back across the Drava."

Tolstoy then describes an alleged massacre at the Bleiburg field using unsourced testimony. The British High Court later successfully challenged the accuracy of some of Tolstoy's text in relation to Bleiburg, and this will be described in another chapter in a review of a book by Christopher Booker, "A Looking-Glass Tragedy: The controversy over the repatriations from Austria in 1945".

Of relevance is the fact that Tolstoy inserted Colin Gunner's testimony in his chapter about Bleiburg, even though Gunner together with one Lieutenant Hogan was never at Bleiburg. Gunner's testimony, without a name or source, was taken word for word by Tolstoy from Gunner's book. Gunner was probably referring to the fate of another group of 800 Croats being driven back across a "Drau bridge" near Lavamund later than 15th May. This Croatian group who had surrendered at Wolfsberg has already been mentioned in my review of "Operation Slaughterhouse". I will also review Colin Gunner's book separately.

In addition, Tolstoy's version of what happened when the Croats encountered the Bulgarians near Dravograd before crossing the Austrian border is different to what actually happened.

Tolstoy's accusations of conspiracy were dismissed at the British trial. Following that trial Tolstoy added the following sentence in a publication by Ante Beljo entitled, "An International Symposium "Southeastern Europe 1918–1995", which clarifies any previous ambiguity about Bleiburg in Tolstoy's book.

> Tolstoy: "…an important matter needs to be emphasised. That is the distinction which should be drawn between the tragedy of the Croats driven back to Tito at Bleiburg…and the subsequent fate of the smaller body of Croats who remained in Austria following the Bleiburg tragedy…numerous smaller bodies of Croatian soldiers and civilians had succeeded either in arranging a formal surrender to British forces, or in infiltrating undetected into their zone of occupation. Since it was clearly unnecessary to guard people who were desperate to remain in British custody, the fugitives were either directed to large camps improvised for their reception, or simply told to stay put where they found themselves. By 15 May 5 Corps reported to 8 Army that they held some 25,000 Croats…During the third week of May arrangements were made for all Croats in Corps custody to be transported into the hands of Tito… "

In other words Tolstoy has made a distinction between what happened to some Croats 'already held' behind the British lines, and those who never crossed behind British lines. Unfortunately many Croatian writers in the 21st century still have not understood this distinction, or perhaps they do not believe that it is as important as I do.

In "The Minister and the Massacres" more unsourced information appears, for example that the Croats returned from Bleiburg had to cross the Drava River. Although this route cannot be confirmed or denied with the documents I have, at least Tolstoy acknowledges that most of the Croats were not killed inside Austria, but afterwards in Yugoslavia. Scott's Report online, refers to a quick route out of Bleiburg after the surrender, yet the freshly transcribed War Diaries within the same website of the 38th Irish Brigade, do make mention of a crossing of the Drava River.

> Tolstoy: "In 1945, the overwhelming majority of Croatian people returned to Yugoslavia from Austria were not killed at Bleiburg itself, but following their recrossing of the Drava."

The various accounts are conflicting and leave me confused. If vast numbers of Croats arrived at Bleiburg, and they were "herded" back within 24 hours, then it is unlikely that this could have happened by crossing the "Drava". The Drava River is not on the closest route to the Yugoslav frontier from Bleibug.

During the British trial against Tolstoy, Michael Barnard referred to it in an article in Melbourne's Age newspaper on 28 November 1989 entitled, "Betrayed: a war's legion of the lost". Barnard writes about the British High Court months-long trial which had resulted from Tolstoy's accusations in pamphlets against Lord Aldington. Lord Aldington, also known as Brigadier Toby Low, had been Chief of Staff of the British V Corps in post-war Austria. In this article Barnard writes about the repatriations of 70,000 Cossacks and anti-Tito Yugoslavs, including Serbs and others, and the justification for those actions in the British military and political command.

There is no mention of Bleiburg in that article because the repatriations Toby Low described occurred later in May.

An official British Report, which included Bleiburg, was prepared for the British Trial against Tolstoy, in response to accusations in his book, because Tolstoy's book had included Bleiburg. Lord Anthony Cowgill in his Report described the Croats attempting to escape to Bleiburg in the context of the Yugoslav aggression. My review of "The Repatriations from Austria in 1945: The Report of An Enquiry, 1990--Chp. 5, Bleiburg: The End of the Croat Incursion--15 May" can be found in the next chapter. However, an important part of the Cowgill Report, in response to Tolstoy's allegations, is below.

> Cowgill: "The most serious problem remaining for 5 Corps was thus that posed by the approach of the main body of Croat troops (reported as being 200,000 in number), accompanied by huge numbers of Croat civilians, who were attempting to escape into Austria via Dravograd, towards the small town of Bleiburg just inside the Austrian frontier...This column stretched many miles back into Yugoslavia, and no reliable figures exist as to how many people, troops and civilian refugees, were actually involved...But Tito's forces were anxious to stop them escaping into Austria, and on 13 May Tito instructed [KP 88] his First Army:
>
> Tito: "A group of Ustashis and some Chetniks, a total of over 50,000 men, is reported by Third Army in the...area towards Dravograd. ... You must move your forces most urgently from the Celje area...in order to concentrate for an attack aimed at the annihilation of this column".
>
> (Cowgill continues): ...on 14 May, as the head of this (Croatian) column began to cross the frontier between Dravograd and Bleiburg, Tito's forces were massing in considerable strength on both sides of the frontier around them."

In reference to Cowgill's Report, it is hard to imagine that any rifle fire could have been heard from the Bleiburg castle from Poljana as he suggests, but perhaps it is possible. A mass grave of Croats is located at Poljana today, of those murdered following their surrender to Yugoslavs on the 15th May, according to both Wikipedia and a Slovenian Commission on Yugoslav post-war massacres. I do believe rifle fire could be heard at the castle from Bleiburg field or Libuce, where grave sites are now located to remember an estimated small number of Croatian victims shot there.

Subsequent to the verdict ruled against Tolstoy, a Reuters bulletin published in July 1990 entitled, "General has Tolstoy down for the count", reported that the former British general had won his legal battle against Count Nikolai Tolstoy.

"The Minister and the Massacres" (1986) – reports and criticisms

Several articles have been written about Tolstoy and Macmillan in many countries that Tolstoy visited to talk about his book. Therein one of the critics, Christopher Booker, in "A Looking Glass Tragedy: The Controversy over the Repatriations from Austria in 1945" writes that Tolstoy distorts his facts concerning Bleiburg – that no massacre happened at the Bleiburg field. Most of the articles about Tolstoy's book, though interesting, are very repetitive and offer nothing new by way of facts. Below I have reviewed a couple of them, but some criticisms can also be viewed on Wikipedia (as at December 2015) under "The Minister and the Massacres".

"Nikolaj Tolstoj u Toronto" (Nikola Tolstoy in Toronto), Marin Sopta, page 12 in Hrvatski Tjednik, Melbourne, 28 July 1986

This article in Croatian is about Tolstoy's visit to Toronto. It describes how Tolstoy's book "The Minister and the Massacres" has been criticized in the media. For example Dr Robert Knight found 36 big mistakes in Tolstoy's book. Canada's the "Globe and Mail" reported on Tolstoy's book on 23rd May 1986, and in the Toronto Star on 22 June 1986, in "Harold MacMillan povezan s ratnim pokoljem" (Harold MacMillan associated with wartime massacre). It's not clear whether the Toronto Star or this Croatian newspaper referred to the return of 200,000 Croatian soldiers.

"Harold Macmillan linked to wartime slaughter", Olivia Ward, Toronto Star, reprinted on page 13 in Hrvatski Tjednik, Melbourne 29 July 1986

Underneath a large photograph of Tolstoy the caption reads:

> "Historian is campaigning for a parliamentary inquiry into the deaths of some 70,000 Cossacks and Yugoslavs … ".

The first sentence of this sensationalist article by Olivia Ward says that "Britain has blood on its hands". The article suggests that Macmillan acted "in violation of the Yalta agreement". Tolstoy refers to the alleged political policy of silence of the BBC and censorship of the British press. Tolstoy refers to the shooting of Yugoslavs in a Slovenia pit. Tolstoy suggests that Macmillan knew that a certain death awaited those turned over. Most of this article, like Tolstoy's book, deals with the fate of the Cossacks, but there is one reference to Croats.

> Toronto Star: "A retreating Croat army of 200,000 men who fought with the Germans approached Austria to surrender to the Allies, but were turned back. Instead they were pressured to give themselves up to Tito's Army".

In this article it is alleged that Tolstoy believes Soviet pressure was the motive for the repatriations. The reporter also refers to Robert Knight's criticism of Tolstoy's book.

> Knight: "Tolstoy's understanding of the historical context is deeply flawed. ... he pooh-poohs the central theme of Macmillan's guilt or conspiracy ... the handing back of the Cossacks and Yugoslavs was part of a complex and bloody extended war. ..."

This article also alleges, that according to Knight, Alexander had

> "sanctioned the turning back of 200,000 Croat soldiers to Tito. Although Fifth Corps appeared to be acting out of order in handing over the others".

In this case the "others" refers to events far west of Bleiburg, and whilst there were 200,000 Croats 'near' to Bleiburg, nowhere near 200,000 actually crossed into Austria. Thus, once again, the numbers (of Croats) given in association with British policies is highly exaggerated. It is quite possible that Knight's words, which are taken from a "Times Literary Supplement" are used out of context.

Olivia Ward also wrote another article, "Survivor recalls praying for a quick death" about a Slovenian survivor of the Kocevje Massacre. After leaving Viktring the Slovenian was told by the British that they were going to Italy. It is sad that a Croatian survivor from Kocevje was not interviewed also.

"UK Official History: Trieste and Austrian Crises – UK Official History", Gen. Sir William Jackson & Group Capt. T P Gleve, HMSO, in "The Mediterranean and Middle East Volume 6: Victory in the Mediterranean Part III: November 1944 to May 1945" online Military History Network, London, 1988

The official UK history by this military historian published online is both informative and interesting. First this paper describes in detail the crises created by Tito's Yugoslav Army in Trieste, Venezia Giulia, and Carinthia Austria. Secondly the numbers of prisoners-of-war are given, and Bleiburg is also briefly mentioned on pages 11 and 12.

Since my focus is on the number of people involved and on Bleiburg I will mention these issues first. The numbers below in reference to Croats on the move in the east, or in reference to Croats already in camps in the west, generally agree with the numbers given by most sources I have reviewed so far.

The Yugoslavs: According to Alexander by 6th May the Fourth Yugoslav Army already had about 60,000 troops just in Venezia Giula. In Austria by 15th May there were about 16,000 troops in south-east Carinthia of the First, Second, and Third Yugoslav Armies, with another 25,000 troops just south of the border. In the meantime the Fourth Yugoslav Army was moving towards Villach.

The Germans: First we learn that about one-third of the German Army Group E was still south of the Austrian border on 8th May 1945. General Lohr joined the approximately 150,000 officers and men to try and surrender to the Yugoslavs, which was carried out at Topolsica in Slovenia, south-east of Mezica. The German Army Group E was one of the last to surrender in the Third Reich.

The Croats: V Corps had signalled on 14th May that hundreds of thousands of Croats and Germans and civilians were moving north towards the Austrian border. There were 300,000 Germans and 200,000 Croats to total 500,000. (The number of 600,000 initially reported was changed to 500,000--so this would account for some confusion in reading the documents.) The soldiers were accompanied by 500,000 civilians including women and children.

Others: Also already surrendered POWs inside Austria included 100,000 Germans, 46,000 Cossacks, 15,000 Hungarians, 25,000 Croats, 24,000 Slovenes. These groups totalled 220,000 but according to this paper by Jackson there was confusion regarding the numbers.

When it comes to the issue of British repatriations the numbers sent back by train, to Yugoslavia instead of to Italy, are discussed briefly on page 348. The British involved included members of the "36th Brigade" and "1st Guards Brigade", both who had found the unpleasant task "most unsavoury".

> "The evacuation by rail to Yugoslavia of all Yugoslav nationals who were already in Austria began early on 19th May and continued into June."

Bleiburg is only briefly mentioned in this paper. Brigadier Scott of the "38th Brigade" was operating under "46th Division headquarters" under orders of General Keightley. According to this paper, on 14th May 1945 the movement of "a whole Croat nation" and Germans towards the Austrian border, actually contributed to the order to repatriate those who were already inside Austria. In this context, the paper explains what happened at Bleiburg on page 348.

> "(the)...threatened influx at Bleibug, which had sparked off the train of orders, was quickly resolved by the mediation of an experienced British brigade commander, who persuaded the Croats to surrender voluntarily to their Yugoslav pursuers in return for guarantees of humane treatment and orderly trials of any accused war crimes."

Although this paper barely mentions Bleiburg it does provide information about the "politico-military" crises caused by Tito's scheming and lack of cooperation with his 'Allies'. This paper's focus is on Venezia Giulia and not on south-east Carinthia. It is interesting to note that the term "Venezia Giulia" also includes Gorizia, Trieste, Istria (Pula), Carnaro (Fiume/Rijeka), and Zadar! It was the intention of the Allies to administer the Venezia Giulia, except for Zadar, and this conflict of interests brought direct confrontation between the British and the Yugoslavs. The Yugoslav Army occupied the whole area by the beginning of May, and "clandestinely" even earlier in 1945.

It was also the Yugoslav "objective to occupy all ground up to the River Drava" in Austria. But "To close the Austrian frontier would be incompatible with Alexander's current orders that British troops were not to shoot except in self-defense."

A British policy of non-confrontation was adopted due to the fact that at the time the "British were still operationally and logistically over-stretched". Many exchanges between the western Allies took place at both a political and diplomatic level about what approach they would take towards the "already established" Yugoslav occupation. By 19th May the Yugoslavs informed the British that Yugoslavs were to withdraw.

"An emissary carrying the same message in fact visited 5th Corps Headquarters that evening".

Ultimately, military action was being discussed behind the scenes between the American and British in the event that the Yugoslav Army did not withdraw from Austria.

"British intelligence officer with 1st Guards Bde, 6th Armoured Div south Austria May-June 1945: organisation of transportation for repatriated Croatians from Austria to Yugoslavia", Nigel Nicholson Interview, produced by Michael Palaich, in online Archives of the British Imperial War Museum, London, 1988

In February 2015 my husband and I listened to this audio interview, and other full recorded audio interviews on the Imperial War Museum website.

Some sources are just as important for what they do 'not' say regarding the Bleiburg issue. A lengthy interview with Nigel Nicholson, OBE, recorded before the trial of Nikolai Tolstoy, but during the time that the Cowgill Report was being finalised, is referred to on the website of the British Imperial War Museum. This is the same Nicholson who has often been quoted by both Tolstoy, and Michael Palaich whose Youtube film will be discussed later in my book.

Nicholson describes, in detail in Tape 1, his geographical area of responsibility as being "12 miles wide and 15 miles deep", south of Klagenfurt between the lake and the Yugoslav frontier. Of course this area is nowhere near Bleiburg. Because his area is some distance from either Trieste, or Klagenfurt, according to Nicholson, the situation he has to deal with was not chaotic.

Nicholson describes how various groups were streaming over the Yugoslav frontier from different directions between 8th May and 15 May 1945. Nicholson also goes on to say that Viktring Camp and other camps in the area contained the following groups:

> "15,000 Hungarians, some Bulgarians, Greeks, and Poles, 40,000 Cossacks who were fighting Tito during the War, Croats and some Germans, Serb Chetnik Royalists who fought on same side as Germans, Slovenes who had also feared the Partisans"

Nicholson's numbers are summarized below and correspond more or less to Alexander's telegram of the 17th May mentioned in my opening chapters, along with Tolstoy's mention of 12,000 Royalist Chetniks and White Russians. Alexander's numbers, according to Nicholson, are repeated below.

- 100,000 Germans
- 46,000 Cossacks
- 15,000 Hungarians
- 25,000 Croats
- 24,000 Slovenes

Nicholson described a conflict between the two occupying forces in his area. According to Nicholson, Tito "our Ex-ally" was occupying parts of Istria and Carinthia including Klagenfurt, to proclaim a "Greater Yugoslavia". The British, under Alexander's orders, were to liberate and restore the area to its pre-war boundaries, but that the upcoming Peace Conference would be the time to finalise these boundaries. I quote Nicholson in reference to the situation in the week after the German surrender.

> "It could have led to a very ugly situation but it didn't."

The situation did not turn "ugly" because, Nicholson emphasises, the British policy was not to interfere, even when the Yugoslavs were helping themselves to the German arms dumps, although Yugoslav attempts to do so were sabotaged as much as possible by the British.

In this audio interview Nicholson goes on to say that Tito was to withdraw his army on 17th May or 18th May from Klagenfurt. At the same time on about 17th May the return of all anti-Tito groups to Yugoslavia was to begin. The Cossacks were also to be returned to the Russian occupied zone of Austria. According to Yalta each of the groups would be returned to the other, in reference to the British and the Soviets.

In Nicholson's area for example at Viktring Camp there had been "30,000" disarmed Croats, Serbs, or Slovenes etc. The Croats were the first to leave. It was five to ten miles from Viktring to the stations Maria Elend and Rosenbach, where there were forested areas on either side of the train tracks.

In Tape 2 there is no question of how heavily the order to send back the Croats had weighed on Nicholson's mind, even to the time of this interview. The deception by V Corps that Croats were to go to Italy from these stations is described in detail by Nicholson with considerable remorse. Nicholson's orders were "disgraceful" because they knew that the trains would instead go through the eight-mile long tunnel to Yugoslavia instead of to Italy, the destination they had been told. These repatriations occurred between the 19th May and 1st June according to Nicholson. The rest of Nicholson's interview deals with his emotional account of the hand-overs at the above-mentioned railway stations.

While listening to Nicholson it should be clarified that there is no eight-mile-long train tunnel near Bleiburg, and that Viktring Camp is ninety miles from Bleiburg. At Bleiburg the Croats did not get behind British lines, because their surrender had not been accepted, and three alternatives were given instead. At Bleiburg there was 'no' British deception, but there was a Yugoslav deception! The Yugoslav Commissar, in front of witnesses including an interpreter, promised to honour international law regarding Prisoners-of-War but broke his word once out of sight! In conclusion, what happened at Bleiburg had nothing to do with Nicholson's testimony, British deception, or his remorse. In other words, if one carefully listens to Nicholson's whole testimony it is as important to note what he has 'not' said, as it is to note what he has said.

Why Michael Palaich edits Nicholson's interview, and leads his Youtube audience to believe that Nicholson is speaking about Bleiburg, is best known to him. Nicholson mentions the repatriation of the Cossacks, though in the case of the latter without detail because he says he was not there. Nicholson does not discuss Bleiburg either. Indeed, he makes no reference at all to it in any way in the tape.

It is interesting that Nicholson's interpretation of Yalta was that it never mentioned Yugoslavia, and that he makes a judgemental guess that the matter had been dealt with at a higher level. Nicholson strongly disagrees that there was a conspiracy, as incorrectly alleged by Tolstoy in his book. According to this interview, Macmillan's testimony regarding the decisions he made were mentioned several times in the official biography of Macmillan by Sir Alistair Allan Horne published in 1988.

"Djilas: a moral man in an amoral age", Edward Kynaston, page 14 Weekend Australian Magazine, Canberra, 4—5 January 1986

This is a book review about Milovan Djilas's book "Rise and Fall". Djilas, a well-known Yugoslav dissident, is described as a WWII Partisan, the vice-president of post-war Yugoslavia, and president of the National Assembly until 1954. Sadly this review does not mention anything about Tito's massacres of his opposition, and I don't know if Djilas does so in this book as I have not read it. I mention this article because I have quoted Djilas a couple of times in my book regarding Bleiburg. This review does at least print a sombre picture of the Yugoslav state in 1986 which was a "microcosm of the Soviet macrocosm". Yugoslav socialism ended up as national socialism, with forced labour camps, compulsory 'volunteer' labour brigades, internal secret police, informers, dogmatic ideology, rigid bureaucratic structures, communist slogans and the replacement of freedom by unquestioning obedience"! There are many refugees from Yugoslavia in Australia and around the world who could attest to this lack of freedom and volunteer labour.

"Harold Macmillan as the villain", Edward Kynaston, page 14 of The Weekend Australian Magazine, Canberra, 26-27 July 1986 (reprinted in Hrvatski Tjednik, Melbourne, 19 August 1986)

This is a book review in an Australian mainstream newspaper of Tolstoy's "The Minister and the Massacres". The article written by the same journalist who reviewed Djilas's book, begins by describing the repatriation of the Cossacks. Kynaston is defensive of Macmillan in reference to Tolstoy's unjust accusations. Unfortunately Kynaston then reveals his bias by casting judgement on the "savagery" of all nationalist groups in Yugoslavia. Written mostly about the extradition of the Cossacks to the Soviets, the review then mentions the surrender of "some thousands of Slovenes and Serbs" in a camp near Klagenfurt. No less than 'eight' times, on this half-page article, the journalist repeats how Fifth Corps repatriated Slovenes and Serbs on 24th May 1945 who ended up in mass graves!

> Kynaston: "...some thousands of Slovenes and Serbs...Fifth Corps began the forcible repatriation of the Slovenes and Serbs. Over 20,000 were returned and were massacred by the Titoist forces...(and)...thrown into a huge pit in the forest of Kocevski. ... Force was used to repatriate Slovenes and Serbs when it had been expressly forbidden by Allied Forces Headquarters...repatriation of the Serbs and Slovenes...The forced repatriation of the Serbs and Slovenes...the Slovenes and Serbs...By June 4 most of the Serbs and Slovenes had been returned to be massacres."

This book reviewer criticises Tolstoy's book for its poorly organised presentation and its needless repetitiveness, but then he praises its detailed research. The journalist says that Tolstoy's attempt to link together

> "the Cossack, and Slovene and Serb repatriation is an unnecessarily confusing factor."

1980s

NAZIONI UNITE
Ufficio dell'Alto Commissariato per i Rifugiati
in Italia
Via Caroncini, 19
ROMA

Data : 26.3.64

Rif :

La Commissione Paritetica

Governo Italiano / Alto Commissariato delle Nazioni Unite per i Rifugiati nella sua seduta a Trieste il giorno 26.3.64

ha riconosciuto

MARINOVIC Ante di Stanko

RIFUGIATO POLITICO IN ITALIA

ai sensi della Legge 24 luglio 1954, N. 722 (G.U. N. 196 del 27 agosto 1954) che ratifica e dà esecuzione alla Convenzione relativa allo Statuto dei Rifugiati, firmata a Ginevra il 28 luglio 1951.

Il Delegato delle Nazioni Unite
Alto Commissariato per i Rifugiati

Political Refugee document of Ante Marinovic, 1964 – United Nations High Commission for Refugees, Trieste

But Tolstoy does mention the repatriation and massacre of Croats at the Kocevski pit in his book. Yet for some unknown reason Kynaston, in his review, has totally ignored the presence of 25,000 Croats around Klagenfurt, who were repatriated and massacred 'before' the Slovenes or Serbs. To say that Kynaston is selective is an understatement!

> "...(On)May 14 there were still large numbers of Tito partisans in the Klagenfurt area, a quarter of a million German prisoners, and the Cossacks and the Slovenes and Serbs."

Kynaston ignores the surrender negotiation at Bleiburg. Indeed, Bleiburg is not mentioned by Kynaston at all even though Tolstoy does in his book. Finally we have Kynaston's motive for excluding the fact that Croats were also massacred. Kynaston tries to link the massacre of Serbs and Slovenes to the "incursion" of "200,000 armed Croats" from Yugoslavia, as if those several hundred thousand Croats were approaching the Klagenfurt area. He does not say otherwise. In the following misrepresentation of historical events as covered in Tolstoy's book, Kynaston's ulterior motive is further exposed.

> Kynaston: "On this day, of all days, Fifth Corps was informed that 200,000 armed Croats were approaching from Yugoslavia accompanied by half a million civilians... The Fifth Corps succeeded in turning them back into Yugoslavia."

> Kynaston continues: "...Confusion reigned following the crisis of the possible Croat incursion. Allied headquarters ordered all surrendered Yugoslavs to be retained on May 17. On May 23 Fifth Corps asked permission to return all Yugoslavs...On May 24 repatriation of the Yugoslavs, by force, began. By June 4 most of the Serbs and Slovenes had been returned to be massacred."

For reasons best known to himself Kynaston has omitted the start of the British repatriations, of Croats, around 19th May, a date more or less agreed on by various sources. Perhaps Tolstoy's "rhetoric" in his "voluminous" book has confused Kynaston. After all, Tolstoy's book will not really help Kynaston to understand everything about the negotiations at the Bleiburg castle. But Tolstoy does mention Bleiburg!

I agree with this journalist on one point at least. Tolstoy has been criticized for his prejudice, blind spots and illusions in his effort to look for a "sinister conspiracy". Nevertheless, according to Kynaston, Tolstoy has "performed a necessary service to history" by bringing attention to "hitherto concealed atrocities". Kynaston, who has totally ignored the Yugoslav atrocities against the Croats in Tolstoy's book, then finishes with the following sentence about atrocities! How ironical!

"One hopes there are no more to be revealed."

"Letter to the Weekend Australian", Shirley Stedul, republished in Hrvatski Tjednik, Melbourne, 19 August 1986.

This letter to "The Weekend Australian", never published by them, is a response to the Kynaston book review of 26-27 July 1986. Shirley Stedul, of Scottish descent, is the wife of Nikola Stedul who was hit by several bullets in a well publicised Yugoslav assassination attempt outside their home in Kirkcaldy Scotland in 1988. Stedul survived and the assassin was caught. A Scottish television series "Crime Story", called "Hitman" was screened in 1994 about the assassination plot.

Shirley and Nilola Stedul wrote the novel, "Krizar: The Soul of Freedom" (Crusaders) about the events leading up to 'Bleiburg' and afterwards. On page 52 it is alleged that the number of "approximately 500,000" have been gathered at the Bleiburg field". This explains her suggestion that "hundreds of thousands of Croatians" were repatriated, in her Letter to the Editor.

In an emotional style Stedul criticises the journalist's selectivity, and then criticizes Kynaston's reference to a Croatian "incursion". She points out the interesting contradiction that if it were actually an "incursion" why would the approaching Croats need to be accommodated and fed, as Kynaston remarks.

Then Stedul refers to how Kynaston completely ignores the role of Macmillan in the repatriation of an alleged "hundreds of thousands of Croatians". But, it's important to note here, that most sources agree there was 'never' any repatriation of "hundreds of thousands of Croatians" from Austria. Nowhere near that many Croats ever crossed into Austria in the first place because they had not escaped capture by the occupying Yugoslav Army. In other words, the "Death Marches" began inside Slovenia, and at the time the British were barely established eastern Carinthia. The "Death Marches" happened, but they did not begin in Bleiburg, in other words!

"Twelve Responses to Tragedy", or "The Yalta Memorial", Wikipedia online (last modified on 3 February 2016), 1986

Reference to this Yalta Memorial is in the 1980s chapter because it refers to the period between 1982 and 1986, although it would have been put on the internet much later. This Yalta Memorial can be found in the 'Yalta Memorial Garden' in west

London next to the Victoria and Albert Museum. The site is accessible at all times. It commemorates those people who were displaced due to the Yalta Conference after WWII.

According to Wikipedia, in May 1980 the Yalta victims memorial was approved by P.M. Margaret Thatcher over protests from the USSR and the British Foreign Office. Then in 1986 a second Yalta Memorial replaced the original vandalised 1982 memorial – a fact recorded in its inscription. The 1986 Yalta Memorial was dedicated by the Bishop of Fulham. In addition another inscription on the curved stone plinth reads:

> Inscription: "This memorial was placed here by members of all parties in both houses of parliament and by many other sympathisers in memory of the countless innocent men women and children from the Soviet Union and other East European states who were imprisoned and died at the hands of Communist governments after being repatriated at the conclusion of the Second World War. May they rest in peace."

In relation to this issue, an American author refers to the immediate British response to news of the fate of those repatriated to the Soviets or Yugoslavia under the Yalta Agreement (pages 314--318). Franklin Lindsay in 'Beacons in the Night: With the OSS and Tito's Partisans in Wartime Yugoslavia' (1993), is reviewed later in this book.

Lindsay refers to the mixed groups who crossed into Austria at several points by 7th May 1945 and then refers to their repatriation (here Lindsay does 'not' refer to Bleiburg). Separately Lindsay does refer to "200,000" others who did not reach the Austrian border.

> Lindsay: "Altogether some 70,000 Cossacks, Ukrainians, and Yugoslavs were forcibly repatriated. At the same time the British and Americans pressed Tito to withdraw behind the prewar Yugoslav border. When Stalin did not back them (the Yugoslavs), the Yugoslavs complied and withdrew."

According to Lindsay Tito's Yugoslavs were surprised by the policy of the newly elected British Labor Party's Foreign Secretary. Ernst Bevin gave a speech opposing Soviet expansion into Eastern Europe and stopped the forced repatriations.

> Bevin: "Bevin also took the lead in ending the forced repatriation of prisoners and displaced persons to Russia and Yugoslavia."

The British halted the repatriations but the Yugoslavs continued to commit genocide. Regrettably neither Yalta Memorial referred to victims of the 'Yugoslav' government, a deliberate omission no doubt which reflected the Cold War foreign policy of the day.

The British government has remembered the innocent victims they repatriated, who were later imprisoned or died at the hands of the Soviet Union or other East European Communist states. The 70,000 victims of Yalta, mentioned by Lindsay, included up to 26,000 Croats according to official documents.

In stark contrast to the British memorial in London, there is no monument to Croatian victims of genocide in the Croatian capital city. The only monument to "victims of Bleiburg and the Way of the Cross" is situated away from the general public view in the Mirogoj Cemetery. Unfortunately, on the Mirogoj monument there is no inscription which explains what 'Bleiburg' means. 'Bleiburg' represents the biggest massacre of Croatian people in their long history. In 2014 a British reporter for the UK Daily Mail, Nigel Jones, listed Tito's Yugoslavia as the 13th most murderous regime in the world, where over half a million were massacred by Tito's regime. Statistics and other evidence has proven that those massacred were mostly Croatian. This number was also confirmed by Tito's right-hand man Rankovic. Even the infamous Yugoslav dissident Djilas acknowledged that under Tito the Croats had to die so that Yugoslavia could live. The monument at Mirogoj mean little to the general public if they come upon it because it does not reflect the huge scale of the massacres which was unprecedented in Croatian history, or the perpetrators.

"Hiding Bleiburg Won't Lessen the Guilt", Jean Marinovic, Hrvatski Vjesnik, Melbourne, 29 May 1987

This is the first article I have written which mentions Bleiburg, although two poems of mine about Bleiburg were published before this time, also reviewed in this chapter. This article has appeared in the "Students' Page" of Melbourne's Hrvatski Vjesnik which publishes in the English language. No photograph accompanied this article. In my article I hardly mention Bleiburg, and instead I ramble on about several issues happening over a forty year period. Basically all I refer to in this article is the "trickery" of the British officers. While this may be true of those officers who deceived the 25,000 Croats that their train-cars were going to Italy, it is not true of the situation at Bleiburg far away! I still had not joined-the-dots on that one!

I was absolutely wrong when I suggested that if Croatian generals had understood British history better they would not have retreated to them. Today my thinking has changed – I believe that the opposite is true. Today I believe that the Croats need to understand their own history better, including how Yugoslavia was created. No

Yugoslavia--no Bleiburg! I knew none of this at this time. I had not yet studied about the former Yugoslavia at university, and at this time I had not yet sighted some of the other books written before 1987, and since read and reviewed here. To be a little fair on myself, access to material about Bleiburg, in Australia, was limited to libraries or whatever the Croatian community was distributing. There was no internet and I trusted what I was reading at the time.

The Australian government knows just how many tens of thousands of Croatian refugees from Yugoslavia settled in Australia at the time, without official recognition of their identity! So another issue which was worth mentioning in my article I believe was the mass Croatian emigration which began because of and after the "Death Marches" and Tito's mass killings.

My article also discusses the inaccuracy, and "lies and omissions" of the 1986 Encyclopaedia Britannica about Yugoslavia, but unfortunately in an un-professional way.

In retrospect I recognize that many of my opinions were based on misinformation about the Bleiburg. Yes I had read the book "Operation Slaughterhouse" but the books published since then by Omrcanin or Tolstoy were the most fresh in my memory. Tolstoy's visits around the world contributed to an enduring false impression about Bleiburg on the collective memory of Croatian communities.

I am angry about the false accusations written against the British. But I sincerely believe that I am not alone as others have also been duped. We cannot change the past however. I continued my writing and being published about Bleiburg and making errors now and then along the way. In hindsight I have unfortunately been part of the problem, part of the propaganda machine, and so now I am writing this book to present all the facts I can find about Bleiburg and to seek closure.

"We Will Not be Fooled Anymore", Jean Marinovic, Hrvatski Tjednik, Melbourne, 24 November 1987

In this article I only discuss Carinthia, but I am including it here because I would not want to be accused of censoring my own mistakes! In writing this article I have been influenced by the propaganda trail. The Tjednik published a photograph with this article with the caption "Tito in discussions with Field Marshall Alexander, after he had obtained recognition from the Allies". I actually allege, just because the Allies sent supplies to Tito during the war, that the British gave clandestine assistance to Tito in a "trap set for Croats and others in Austria, 1945" is unbelievable.

I have come to the wrong conclusion because many important points have been missing in most of the books I read, or the facts have been presented in an unorganised, inconsistent and unchronological order! The "trap" I refer to in this article is about those Croats and others in camps around Klagenfurt, not Bleiburg, but I did not comprehend that point at the time.

> Marinovic: "(The British)...re-assured Croats in train-cars that their destination was Italy when they knew it to be Slovenia (Yugoslavia). The British still have a bad conscience about this today."

I discuss the decline of the British empire and other events that happened over a forty year period. I mention Orwell's dislike of "imperialism" and I discuss the western supplies and munitions to Yugoslavia during WWII. In this context I also mention in this article that my father worked in the war office to defeat Nazism from 1941 to 1946, and that he was awarded the M.B.E. by Field Marshall Alexander, who had become the Governor General of Canada after the war.

After studying the history and politics of the former Yugoslavia, and Nazi and Fascist ideology at university, and after private research, it is clear that the Allies were working together to defeat Nazism and Fascism. I am proud of my father's contribution and his MBE in that fight against those totalitarian regimes.

"CROATIA 1941—1945: BEFORE AND AFTER", IVO OMRCANIN, SAMIZDAT, WASHINGTON DC, 1988

In this lengthy book the author once again tries to arrange facts and figures to back up a conspiracy theory. Omrcanin delves into many centuries of history in Croatia in his arguments and adds many documents at the end, as he does in most of his books. Like with most of Omrcanin's books unfortunately there is no index.

Bleiburg is mentioned on page 84 under the sub-heading of "IV History of the Genocide of Croatians" and once again there is more misinformation than information.

> "There were about 300,000 army personnel and about 250,000 civilians. On May 15, 1945, all of them were extradited from Bleiburg, Austria, by the British to the Yugoslav Bolsheviks of Tito. All of them were slaughtered."

Perhaps this typical incorrect version of 15th May 1945 'in a nutshell' has been further propagated to back up his conspiracy theory in this book. By this time however Tolstoy had somewhat 'stolen the thunder' from Omrcanin and added more confusion on the issue.

"Prijegor Bleiburga: iz Knjige "Bleiburg Uzroci i posljedice" (Dedication Bleiburg, from book Bleiburg Causes and Consequences), Mladen Schwartz, Hrvatski Tjednik, page 18, Melbourne, 30 August 1988

Schwartz's article gives an overview of information included in an anthology edited by Vinko Nikolic on the 40th anniversary of the Bleiburg tragedy and lists a few of the books in it. A photograph with this article allegedly depicts the Bleiburg field, "Hrvatska Vojska Na Bleiburgu Nakon Predaje" (Croatian Army at Bleiburg after surrender) but because the background is faded it is difficult to verify the location without a source.

Schwartz briefly mentions the events at Bleiburg and instead discusses the English (the "perfidni Albion") who, he alleges, created the first Yugoslavia, and who helped Tito and Drazi (Mihailovic). He mentions Nikica Martinovic who was assassinated by the Yugoslav state security police (UDBA) in 1975, because he had looked after the Bleiburg memorial.

The Yugoslav dissident Milovan Djilas gives numbers of various groups massacred regarding Bleiburg and elsewhere.

> Djilas: "20-30 tisuca ustasa i domobrana i slovenskih domobranaca i srpskih cetnika . . . i Basta, premda priznaje, da je hrvatskih vojnih snaga na Bleiburgu bilo preko 130 tisuca"

> (Djilas: "20-30 thousand Ustasha and Croatian Home Guards and Slovenian Home Guards and Serbian Chetnicks . . . and Basta already admitted that the Croatian military strength at Bleiburg was more than 130 thousand.")

"Partisan Warfare in the Bilingual Region of Carinthia", Thomas M. Barker, in "Journal of the Society for Slovene Studies", online, 1989

This article is important for its description of the military situation in Carinthia at the end of WW II, and about the Partisan procrastination at the end of the war.

Information about the situation on the ground is important if we are to get at the truth. For example leading up to the end of WWII the Yugoslav

> "... policy was to extract maximum logistical support in return for minimum cooperation with Wilkinson's goals."

Tito openly had declared his annexation policies from September 1944. Barker also describes the increasing numbers of Partisans who were east of Eisenkappel and active in the Meza Valley. Barker states that the policy of the Slovene Partisans was relatively "inactive and unsuccessful" after 1944, due to their policy of building-up their strength, until the collapse of the German army in Slovenia. Barker quotes a despatch by P.M.N. Moore of the Royal Engineers:

> "Britain is regarded with intense dislike and suspicion by the partisan authorities, who fear we may oppose their territorial claims ..."

A memorandum from another SOE man, Sir W. Deakin on 28th April 1945, concerned the "propagandistic revival" of Slovenian claims to the region in the context of their 1919-1920 referendum defeat.

Meanwhile a "vast traffic jam of Axis soldiery" was being pursued by the Bulgarians under the command of the Austrian/German General Lohr. This "Axis soldiery" was mingled with "200,000" Ustashi and other troops under Ante Pavelic, including 40,000 from the German Army Group Southeast, amalgamated with the German Army Group E. Of course we know from my Chapter 4 that the Pavelic group was on an earlier separate retreat.

In this Journal for Slovenian Studies, Barker estimates that at the time the Yugoslavs had 40,000 men. We later learn, in 2010 from an outdoor Exhibit in Poljana, that the Yugoslav Army numbers in Carinthia were later reinforced in eastern Carinthia.

Barker estimates that Keightley's Fifth Corps had 55,000 men, spearheaded by the Sixth Armoured Division. However because it took several days for the British Fifth Corps to move into eastern Carinthia, the number of British there on 15th May was more like 25,000 as per the 1997 book by C. Booker, "Through a Looking Glass Tragedy". Booker's book and the Exhibit are reviewed in later chapters.

According to Barker, the British advancing Sixth Armoured Division made it to Klagenfurt on 8th May 1945 three hours before the Partisans. However Booker goes on to say that the Partisans, together with an 'Austrian' provincial Government already there, were seeking to establish their own administration.

One Day in May – Bleiburg 1945

On 11th May Tito was requesting, unsuccessfully, the big powers to allow him to share in the post-war occupation of Austria. Moscow did not support Tito's occupation of Carinthia and so on 12th May Alexander asked Tito to withdraw from Carinthia.

By 13th May instead of withdrawing however the Yugoslavs simply re-shuffled and continued fighting the Ustashi, according to Barker. Barker continues that, by 14th May in Belgrade, Tito was still asserting his right to pursue the Ustashi and Domobrans who had not capitulated. On the same day, 13th May, MacMillan flew into Klagenfurt for his brief visit.

> Barker: "...confirmed that Keightley's soldiers were installed there but could not stop that Yugoslavs'...'minor reign of terror'... (and) 'high-handed actions'."

Barker then states that there were "500,000" enemy troops and civilian refugees already in Carinthia, and by 15th May MacMillan signalled that the Yugoslavs outnumbered the British in Volkermarkt.

> Barker: "...(Yugoslavs) were installed in Volkermarkt, the HQ of the Fourteenth Shock Division which counted some 6000 men alongside the 100-man, British-equipped motorized detachment of the YNLA's Fourth Army".

In the following two days around the Meza valley and Slovenian Styria over 2000 Yugoslav troops had entered Lavamund, as well as another two divisions of the Yugoslav Fourth Army being readied. Alexander was concerned in this context with the weakness of the British Fifth Corps which were dispersed over a wide area. These conditions around Lavamund have also been described in detail on the website of the 38th Irish Brigade.

Barker's article however is more about the Slovenians and the Yugoslav attack at Ferlach than with Bleiburg. The actual events at Bleiburg are referred to in one puzzling sentence.

> "Sixty people had been abducted from Pliberk/Bleiburg".

Barker's version of why the Yugoslavs left the region after the 19th May was that Tito had lacked support from the USSR, and I believe this is a more credible reason than the reason suggested by some Croats that an alleged "trade-off" of Croats was made for territory, or that there was some conspiracy going on!

"UK historian ordered to pay $3M damages", The Weekend Australian, AFP, page 19, Canberra, December 2-3 1989

Count Nikolai Tolstoy and Mr Nigel Watts were ordered to pay $3 million in damages for writing that Lord Aldington (Toby Low) was responsible for the massacre of thousands of World War II prisoners. The two would appeal immediately. A pamphlet published in 1987 accused Lord Aldington of playing a

> "key role in the forcible repatriation of 70,000 Cossack and Yugoslav war prisoners after the armistice, sending them back to what was certain death."

It was alleged that the British "knew" that the soldiers and civilians they would be tortured or killed once repatriated, but Lord Aldington maintained that he did not know that "the prisoners would be summarily executed." There were about 50 witnesses for the defence, including some British war veterans and some who had escaped from trains.

It is unfortunate that when this news does reach a mainstream newspaper that Tito's victims are not identified.

CHAPTER 7

1990s

"Slavs find mass grave",
The Australian, page 9, Canberra, July 2 1990

This is a small entry in The Australian newspaper on page 9, with no author other than that its source is Zagreb's daily newspaper, "Vjesnik".

It opens with the news of a discovery of a mass grave of "anti-communist Ustasha fighters" who were "executed by Yugoslav partisans in 1945". The grave, discovered by Vjesnik journalists, was reported to be in the Zumberek mountains. Wounded enemy soldiers were killed or "finished off" before being thrown in.

It is rare that any mainstream newspaper acknowledges the identity of the victims, unless of course, readers don't know that "Ustasha" were Croatian. The so-called "Slav" reporters published a book later in 1990, in Zagreb, about this grave, "Jazovka". Unfortunately this article does not indicate that these were 'post-war' graves or how many there were.

"Jazovka",
Zelimir Zanko, Nikola Solic, Vjesnik, Zagreb, 1990

This book is all in the Croatian language so it is difficult to translate everything. The book documents the discovery of the 40 meter deep karst 'sink hole' (known as Jazovka) mass grave in Croatia some 40 miles west of Zagreb. More than one pit has been located. These pits open into caves at the bottom and thousands of naked bodies were covered in lime and dirt. A single bullet hole in the skulls reveals that they did not die in battle. Their wrists were tied together with rusty handcuffs. The location is sometimes referred to as "Sosice" after the name of the village.

The Croatian journalists who exposed 'Jazovka' travelled to Australia with a book they had published, and brought a couple of the makeshift barb-wire handcuffs as evidence. The Croatian journalists gave speeches to the Croatian community. As I held these rusted wires in my hand a sudden chill ran down my back.

At the end of "Jazovka" there are a couple of pages of newspaper reports about the grave discovery.

One newspaper from the London "Independent on Sunday" reported on the mass grave in the Jazovka sink hole which mentions that it happened after the war. In another article from the Italian "Il Giorno" on 2nd July 1990, the number of the "Ustasha" victims in the mass grave was given as 40,000!

The Los Angeles Times ran a rather biased article on 4 November 1990, written by Carol J. Williams, the bureau chief in Budapest. Although multi-party elections may have been held successfully in Croatia for the first time Yugoslavia was still intact at that time.

> Los Angeles Times headline: "Yugoslav Killing Fields: A grisly Secret Comes Out: Atrocity: Communists executed thousands after the war. Those who revealed it hope the message is heard."

In this article it has been acknowledged that these mass killings occurred after "the war was over" for days as truckloads of victims were brought to the site and either shot in the head, or hit in the head with a sledgehammer, after their hands were tied with wire. Jazovka is described as a "hilltop cavern" in Croatia and the identity of the victims is given as "Nazi collaborators" or "Ustashas" or "fanatical SS-like Croatian nationalists". The villagers had kept quiet for "45 years" under the former Yugoslavia due to fear of the Communist regime. Although the journalist refers to the "ghosts of Sosice" I would say also that the "ghosts of Bleiburg" have risen to haunt Yugoslavia.

> "... ghosts of Sosice have risen to haunt Yugoslavia."

But then early into the article the journalist Williams changes her tone when, instead of blaming the Communist perpetrators of the atrocity, she blames the victims! She follows typical Yugoslav propaganda with the often-heard claim that the Croatian nationalists allegedly killed hundreds of thousands of Serbs, Jews and Gypsies during WWII.

> Williams: "... disclosure ... has confronted those who lived through the last war with a shocking reminder of the human costs of indulging nationalist zeal. ... the victorious Communists settled the score ... slain in retaliation."

The number mentioned by Williams is "40,000". Williams 'fears' this discovery of mass graves will reopen old wounds, instead of raising the issue of justice! It is my contention that what many journalists and authors actually 'fear' is that Yugoslavia might collapse. At least the number of the victims is mentioned in this article, unlike in The Australian.

And within Croatia itself at a government level, Williams reports that Mario Nobilo, the aide to the Croatian president Franjo Tudjman, remarked that Croats should "forget the past and turn to the future". This was the official policy of the government at the time, no "revanchism" (no revenge) and they "declined to order" a further search or "exhumation of the bones". It is likely however that the 'buffer state' bankrupt Yugoslav regime would have collapsed soon after the dismantling of the Berlin Wall in late 1989 and 'glasnost' and 'perestroika'.

It is my strong belief that twenty years after the collapse of Yugoslavia the "past" needs to be investigated and justice delivered. Williams does not say that such crimes need to be investigated however even though she writes that villagers were eye-witness to days of massacres. Dirt and lime was thrown on top to hide the smell.

> Williams: "... daily arrivals of more than 1,000 people for four to six weeks after the war ended."

"Otvoreni dossier Bleiburg" (Open Dossier Bleiburg), Marko Grcic, Editor, START magazine, Zagreb, 1990

This is a paperback book in the Croatian language written by several authors and edited by M. Grcic. The chapters include an interview with N. Tolstoy, Lord Aldington, and an article about Anthony Cowgill. As with the two volumes by Vinko Nikolic, it is beyond the scope of my time to translate and review 224 pages in the Croatian language. It appears at a glance to follow the general theme and topics which I have reviewed so far in other books.

This book is the only one to accredit several photographs which have been used in various Croatian books and newspapers. The photographs have been taken from the following: "Fotografije kao svjedocanstva Snimci: Koruski pokrajinski muzej revolucije u Slovenj-Gradecu i Miroslav Lilik; presnimci: Alojz Borsic". (Photographs as a testimony records, from the Koruska Provincial Museum of the Revolution in Slovene Gradec and Miroslav Lilik; pictures copied by Alojz Borsic.)

> "Miroslav Lilik, pratilac britanskog majora D.C. Owena, snimio je veci dio fotografija o situaciji na jugoslavensko-austrijskoj granici potkraj i neposredno

poslije rata. On smatra da su fotografije (u ovoj knjizi) snimljene 13 svibnja 1945. U nekim se slovenskim izdanjima navodi datum 15 svibnja. Vecina fotografija ovdje reproduciranih potjece iz Korusko pokrajinskog muzeja revolucije u Sloven Gradecu."

(Miroslav Lilik, escort of British Major D.C. Owen, took many of the photographs of the situation on the Yugoslav-Austrian border immediately after the end of the war. He considers that the photographs (in this book) were taken on 13 May 1945. Some Slovenian sources say the date is 15 May. Most of the photographs reproduced here come from the Koruska Provincial Museum of the Revolution in Sloven Gradec.)

My Note: D.C. Owen was with the interpreter Robert Plan as part of the OSS at the end of the war, as mentioned in Lindsay's, "Beacons in the Night".

The photographs from the book "Operation Slaughterhouse" have been reprinted, by A. Borsic, though not accredited to the book of their origin. Some of the photographs (from British Imperial War Museum) have also been taken from Tolstoy's book, though not directly accredited. The photographs in this book include several shots of the signpost area at the Volkermarkt-Dravograd junction in Slovenia from various angles; a picture at Sentvid Slovenia after capitulation; a large scene at the P.O.W. camp at Dobja Vas in Koruska (Carinthia); the congested road at "Mreznici" on 13 May 1945 (perhaps should say Mezica because Mreznici is located in Croatia).

In this book I will discuss a couple of the photographs from "Otvoreni dossier Bleiburg" which have appeared in various other books or articles, with their various conflicting captions. (see review of Vukusic's 'Bleiburg Memento' book in 2000s chapter) As it says, the photographs are a sort of testimony record. I believe it is fairly safe to say that these photographs refer to places and people as they were 'before' Bleiburg. By the photographer's own admission they were probably taken 'before' the 15th May 1945.

"BLEIBURG: THE END OF THE CROAT INCURSION—15 MAY" IN "THE REPATRIATIONS FROM AUSTRIA IN 1945: THE REPORT OF AN ENQUIRY – THE DOCUMENTARY EVIDENCE", ANTHONY COWGILL, SINCLAIR-STEVENSON LTD, PAGES 41—48, LONDON, 1990

This Enquiry devotes a chapter to the events at Bleiburg. Cowgill's report is very revealing about the conditions at the time. There is also a map of the Croatian advance to the Bleiburg field on page 45, and a map of the British and Yugoslavs in post-war Carinthia on page 123. On some points the eye-witness reports in

"Operation Slaughterhouse" compare with the findings of the Lord Cowgill Enquiry which begin by stating that

> "the Partisans were already occupying the Bleiburg area in considerable strength".

Lord Cowgill described the "approaching" group as

> "600,000 Germans and Croats" and this huge mass of "fugitives" stretched back for miles into Yugoslavia.

According to Cowgill, most of the Croats as well as the Germans retreating with this group were cut off by Yugoslav Partisans by 13th May before reaching Austria.

> Cowgill: "The vast majority" of Croats never reached Austria, as by 14th May Tito's forces were "massing in considerable strength on both sides of the frontier around them".

This fact in Cowgill's Enquiry is important in determining the number of people who actually came to Bleiburg.

Cowgill continues: The main body of Croats numbered 200,000, and were accompanied by "huge numbers of Croat civilians" who had been attempting to escape via Dravograd. In Cowgill's Enquiry we also have it 'from the horse's mouth' so to speak that on 13th May Tito instructed his First Army as follows (KP 88).

> "a group of Ustashis and some Chetniks, a total of over 50,000 men, is reported by Third Army in the …area towards Dravograd. It includes Pavelic, Macek, the Croatian Government and a huge number of criminals. They are attempting to cross at Dravograd and give themselves up to the British…You must move your forces most urgently from the Celje area…in order to concentrate for an attack aimed at the annihilation of this column."

Although Cowgill does not emphasize it, the key word here is "annihilation" which means complete destruction or obliteration. This document represents Tito's unmitigated intention to commit genocide. Of course the British did not know of this instruction at the time as it was between the Yugoslavs. It is also interesting to note that not even Tito seemed to know that the Croatian government members had already escaped from their clutches days earlier, so that they were not with the long columns he intended to "annihilate".

On 15th May at 0830 hours, Cowgill describes the very decisive 5 Corps signal (KP 112) to the British Eighth Army signal.

"200,000 CROATS wishing to enter AUSTRIA via BLEIBURG. YUGOSLAVS determined to oppose CROATS and will not allow their surrender to BRIT troops. 46 DIV have reinforced this area with one Battalion Infantry and one squadron tanks and are preparing to support YUGOSLAVS in event CROAT advance. Parley still in progress and possibility CROATS will withdraw into YUGOSLAVIA when faced by BRITISH troops."

More relevant information is then raised by Lord Cowgill. His Enquiry describes a separate meeting on the morning of 15th May at Klagenfurt. Lord Aldington, known during WWII as Brigadier Toby Low, had been Chief of Staff of the British V Corps in post-war Austria. This meeting of 15th May was between the British Brigadier Toby Low (Lord Aldington) and the Yugoslav Lt. Col. Hocevar, Commissar of the Fourth Yugoslav Army, together with the senior Yugoslav commander in Austria, Major Dubajic.

The British minutes of this meeting with the Fourth Yugoslav Army have survived (KP 115). The recorded minutes of this meeting reflected the changed British policy, changed no doubt after Macmillan's visit to Klagenfurt on 13th May 1945. In the Cowgill Report the four points considered on 15th May in Klagenfurt were as follows.

1. The Yugoslav claim to share control of Carinthia is rejected by Low.

2. Low rejects Hocevar's request for Yugoslav joint-responsibility for camps which included already-surrendered 'Yugoslav' nationals or so-called "Yugoslav Quislings", but Low agreed that 5 Corps would "as soon as possible, send into YUGOSLAVIA all the CROATS in our area..."

3. The German Army Group E and General Loehr were to be the responsibility of the Yugoslavs.

4. "Low raised the question of the situation around Bleiburg." The Yugoslav policy was that "Croats should be bottled up in the pass leading to Austria and later disarmed." Low stated that any Croats escaping into Austria would be guarded, disarmed and put into a camp and later returned to Yugoslavia. Hocevar expressed his gratitude to the British.

Evidently there did not seem to be any knowledge during the British-Yugoslav meeting that Croats had already reached Bleiburg that day, judging by the content of the fourth point. Both the British and Yugoslav policies are clear.

Cowgill's Report does not give many details regarding the Bleiburg castle surrender meeting except to say that they were assisted in the investigation for this Enquiry by the castle's owner Dr Thurn-Valsassina and Robert Plan of the OSS. Cowgill simply refers to a "remarkable episode" at Bleiburg when Brig. Scott, commander of the 38th (Irish) Infantry Brigade held "tripartite discussions" in the Bleiburg Castle. The British reference to the Bleiburg episode is given as KP 128 and the other source is the journal of the Royal Irish Fusiliers. Cowgill (not Scott) also refers to KPs 89 and 105 regarding Tito's assurances that war criminals would be tried by military courts.

> "(After)...assurances that surrendered Croats would be humanely treated and that only 'war criminals' among them would be tried and punished...Brig Scott managed to persuade the Croat generals ...to surrender to Tito's forces."

Cowgill concludes by saying that neither Tito's troops or the Soviets honoured their assurances.

> "All we can say is that assurances were given, and that for a short time they were accepted as having been given in good faith; but they were not honoured."

Cowgill then discusses the "confusion" about what happened after the 'surrender' to the Yugoslavs, under the sub-heading of "The Bleiburg Massacre". He questions the validity of Tolstoy's incorrect allegations in his book "The Minister and the Massacres" on pages 103 to 109 about the fate of the Croats at Bleiburg.

> Tolstoy alleges: "...no sooner had the 20-30,000 Croats assembled at Bleiburg laid down their arms (they also included many civilians) than Tito's partisans opened fire from the surrounding woods causing an immense massacre...on 15 and 16 May..."

Cowgill refers to the terms "Bleiburg Massacre" and "Bleiburg Tragedy" as having been used by historians sympathetic to the Croats such as in the Croatian-authored book "Operation Slaughterhouse: Eyewitness Accounts of Post-War Massacres in Yugoslavia". Tolstoy had quoted "Operation Slaughterhouse" as "as one of his sources" but Cowgill points out that Tolstoy could not have read anything about a massacre on the Bleiburg field in "Operation Slaughterhouse"!

> Cowgill: "...this book...does not actually make any mention of a massacre at Bleiburg in the immediate aftermath of the Croat surrender on 15 May 1945. It states that the Croats were marched back into Yugoslavia, and it was only there that the mass-killings by Tito's supporters began".

Brig Scott's account also refers to the evacuation of Croats within a 24 hour period.

> Scott: "…as far as I could see, during the next twenty four hours, all the arrangements in connection with the surrender and evacuation were carried out by the Yugoslavs speedily and efficiently."

The Cowgill Enquiry was written after an investigation at Bleiburg with the help of Dr Arip and Thurn Valsassina, owner of the castle, and with Robert Plan, OSS, who Cowgill says was leading the Croatian columns to Bleiburg and who was present during all the tripartite negotiations.

> "… (R. Plan) led the leading column of the Croats to Bleiburg"

This would explain how Robert Plan was available at the negotiations, and it would also suggest that the Allies did not prevent, or could not prevent, the entry of the Croatian columns into Austria around Bleiburg.

The conclusion by Cowgill is that "30 to 50" Croats are buried locally. What actually happened after the Croats were "force-marched" out of Austria was that many were "machine gunned" near Poljana and are buried in a mass grave there.

British troops had thus only witnessed the initial treatment by Tito's partisans of the Croats surrendered around Bleiburg, including many civilians who were marched north-east through Austria by mounted Yugoslav troops towards the Yugoslav frontier near Lavamund. They had been taken across country in the pouring rain instead of by road. But it was only a month later that the statement of the Durham Light Infantry (D.M.C. Worrall and Maj. J.G. Denny) came to light. Another British statement of 45 Recce Regiment (Maj. J. Laugham) referred to a dense mass of barefoot Croats being urged by Partisans who were "discharging arms in all directions."

In any case the Croatian columns had been separated before some of them made it to Bleiburg.

> "… (the) partisans had already managed to cut the main column in two on 14 May and the rear of the main column was surrendering piecemeal to the partisans before the Bleiburg surrender took place…many of these were marched towards Maribor… subsequently the mass-slaughter of many thousands of Croats took place."

What is important to remember according to the Cowgill Enquiry is that

> "None of this was known to the British at the time".

More surrenders to Yugoslavs occurred over the following days, when considerable numbers of Croats in the 5 Corps area had managed to cross into Austria along the frontier but were met by Yugoslavs and not the British. I stress the point that this had nothing to do with the negotiations at Bleiburg. On 17th May (KP 143a) the Brig Mitchell agreed with the Yugoslav 14th Division that

> "all CROAT soldiers SOUTH of the RIVER DRAVA, within 26 Armd Bde area are the prisoners of Marshal Tito's forces."

Also on 18 May (KP 176) the 1st Guards Bde reported that the Croats should be left on the South bank of the DRAU. At this time "1 Welch Regt" witnessed the wounding of some 30 to 40 Croats. A 5 Corps summary of 17th May gives some numbers for surrendered personnel. (My note: Sittersdorf is 9 km north of Eisenkappel and 15 km west of Bleiburg.)

> "(KP 142)...10,000 Croats from 12th Croat Division at Sittersdorf. The handing over of some 12,000 Croats to Tito's forces in the days after 19 May will be referred to in later sections of the (Cowgill) report."

"The Mills of God", Chapter 23 in "Front of the Line: Adventures with the Irish Brigade", Colin Gunner, Greystone Books, Antrim, Northern Ireland, 1991

This book is mostly about WWII, but towards the end a couple of chapters are devoted to the post-war situation. Although 1991 is claimed as the first publication of this book both the Foreward and the Preface refer to the 1970s suggesting that it was available earlier in a different format. My interest in this book, regarding the topic of Bleiburg, is due to Colin Gunner's mention of the "Ustachi". In addition, Gunner's words have been misrepresented by Nikolai Tolstoy in his book, and in an online interview by 'Hrvatski Svijet' of Michael Palaich, reviewed in a separate chapter in this book.

For example, I soon discovered in chapter 23 that Gunner was never in Bleiburg as implied by Tolstoy in "The Minister and the Massacre (1986). Gunner's use of the term "Mills of God" from an English poet suggests retribution. It is unclear to me however whether Gunner believes that the Partisans took retribution against the Ustachi or is he just referring to God's retribution against either or both forces?

My endeavour to make sense of the use of Colin Gunner's testimony, by Tolstoy, could be compared to an attempt to put together a jigsaw puzzle without the picture on the lid of the box. I'm not sure what the whole picture is. It seems Gunner's testimony is a piece of the puzzle which does not quite fit neatly in where others want it to. A word-for-word quotation straight from Colin Gunner's book is used without any accreditation to Gunner, in Tolstoy's "The Minister and the Massacres", a book otherwise full of footnotes. In my mind there has to be a reason why Tolstoy did this.

Even Gunner's own account is a bit ambiguous, as most of the time he seems to refer to Hogan's testimony about the Ustachi when he says, "he stood by" or "I was told" or that the Germans turned their eyes to "Hogan". In parts it's as if Gunner is just repeating what Hogan told him. Only in a separate paragraph, about a German, does Gunner begin his sentence with "Hogan and I". At the time Gunner's Brigade ("the Faughs" or "The Royal Irish Rusiliers") was in the area around Lavamund, but some were partly under new orders to re-locate according to War Diaries. The situation on the ground was changing daily. Orders had been further changed on the 16th of May subsequent to earlier changes on the 14th or 15th.

In an adjoining paragraph, also used by Tolstoy, Gunner refers next to an incident about a "Bulgar". In this case Tolstoy 'removed' key words from Gunner's testimony in his use of this quotation, which would suggest that this incident was un-related to any eye-witness account about watching the Ustachi. Instead, it seems it was just another re-telling of a different story in hindsight about Bulgarians. Gunner writes

> "I had told Hogan of that little girl's body. Before we parted he said: 'I've heard about those cameras. Where's mine, you miserable sod'."

As a result of Gunner's testimony, and Tolstoy's use of it, in 1989 Michael Palaich interviewed Colin Gunner (available on Youtube). I have reviewed it in a different chapter in my book. Underneath a photograph taken from Gunner's book (though not accredited) either Palaich, or 'Hrvatski Svijet' in their interview has inserted a caption which refers to an alleged watching of the Ustasha for

> "three days and nights."

The words "three days and nights" are not in Gunner's book.

It is quite possible that, according to other sources, the incident referred to about witnessing the Ustachi, occurred at or near Lavamund. At Lavamund there was a crossing of Croats over the Drava River to Yugoslav/Bulgarian-occupied territory. This was a separate tragic extradition, when about 800 Croats from a camp in Wolfsberg were returned via Lavamund, according to the British War Diaries and is not related to Bleiburg.

It seems safe enough to acknowledge Gunner's testimony as honest about witnessing the Ustachi being driven across the Drava bridge. What is unclear is whether the event Gunner witnessed involved the Ustachi who were brought from Wolfsberg. Or, alternatively, were Croats force-marched by the Yugoslavs to Lavamund from Bleiburg and this is what Gunner witnessed? The distance between Bleiburg and Lavamund is long no matter whether through Austria, or through Slovenia. Since Scott referred to a speedy exit from Bleiburg it would seem likely that so many thousands were led either straight east towards the Slovenian border, or south-east.

On this issue, in his book "A Looking-Glass Tragedy", Booker refers to the repatriation routes of Croats by the Yugoslavs on page 193. Booker also refers to a subsequent massacre of Croats at Poljana, and thus it is conceivable that they were marched via the Slovenian route towards Lavamund.

> Booker: "The truth of what happened after the Croat surrender at Bleiburg is shocking enough in itself ... After the Croats had been disarmed, they were force-marched back into Yugoslavia – some to the south-east and south towards Celje, others to the north-east, via Lavamund, towards Maribor."

The Cowgill Enquiry does not refer to Gunner's testimony in reference to Lavamund, but to 'other' eye-witness testimony, as in my review of Cowgill.

The questions about Colin Gunner, and to him, on Hrvatski Svijet's website interview of Palaich are rather loaded, so to speak, where the question already implies the answer. For example,

> H.S. Question to Palaich: "... directly involved in extraditions of Croatians to their deaths and a key witness to the British involvement in the Bleiburg Tragedy. Tell us about your interview with him (Gunner)."

Palaich's reply mostly is a paraphrasing of Gunner's account taken out of context!

> Palaich's Answer to H.S.: "Captain Colin Gunner continued forcing Croats across the bridge in Lavamund, Austria even after watching them being killed and thrown over the bridge. He admits watching these murders for three days and three nights, because the procession of Croats passing over the bridge lasted that long. The murders he saw included women and children. He (Gunner) states: "... Tito slaughtered. Tito didn't have time for people in his way. The bastard slaughtered.""

In actual fact Gunner did not imply that the British were "forcing" Croats because the two British officers were "watching" Yugoslavs drive the Croats over the bridge! Palaich then contradicts himself in answering the next question, when he states that Gunner sat in a military vehicle at the foot of the bridge at Lavamund, as the Croats were being forced across and murdered by the Partisans.

The caption below Gunner's photograph incorrectly suggests that in this interview Gunner had said the following.

> "The Croats were killed by beating them into the head and were thrown off the bridge, a hundred times. Children were killed. There were babies in arms of mothers. Three full days and nights they passed over the bridge, 300,000 of them. We are ashamed that we couldn't tell the commanders to go to hell".

The fact that so much conflicting and unsourced material exists is the reason my focus is on one day, 15th May 1945. It is difficult enough to ascertain the nature of events on just that one day! Suffice it to say I am convinced that Gunner was not at the Bleiburg field, as suggested by Tolstoy, because Bleiburg is not near the Drava River.

"CROATIAN TRAGEDY: CROATIAN GENOCIDE--LEST WE FORGET", MIRA GLADOVIC, KLOKAN, PAGES 17—19, SYDNEY, MAY 1991

Written on the 46th anniversary of the Bleiburg tragedy, Mira Gladovic wants to remind people of the terrible tragedy of Bleiburg. The article has been translated into English by Sime Dusevic. The author correctly states that pro-Yugoslavs fear the issue of Bleiburg, because it is a reminder that Yugoslavia's foundations lie on skeletons.

The numbers killed, and the plan to retreat from Zagreb to cross the Austrian border, are discussed in this Klokan article. The author, Gladovic, correctly describes an initial meeting in the field with the British on the 14th May but that by the 15th May the situation had changed from the previous day.

The author discusses a 1.00pm meeting at the Bleiburg castle with a British General and Croatian generals amidst continuing attacks by the Yugoslav Partisans present at Bleiburg. However a brief paraphrasing of the meeting, although not inaccurate, leaves too much out. Included in this interpretation was the fact that the British general did believe that the Partisans would abide by international laws. But what is not included in this version, unfortunately, are the options given to the Croats by the British commander.

The Serbian and Slovenian Yugoslav negotiators joined the British and the Croats at the meeting, but then Gladovic incorrectly alleges that the "British General was losing patience". Original testimony, already analysed in my opening chapters, indicates that it was actually the Serbian spokesman Basta who was losing his patience!

It is true to say that the British did promise support to the Yugoslavs regarding the surrender decision at the castle, but the author fails to state that it had been the decision of the Croatian spokesman to surrender to the Yugoslavs, and that the real pressure came from the Yugoslavs! There is no mention that the Yugoslavs outnumbered the British there at the time.

After describing the tragic "Death Marches" perpetrated by the Yugoslavs, and after ignoring key testimony of the negotiations at the castle, the author refers to the general introduction of "Operation Slaughterhouse" and Willoughby's Foreward, both which misrepresent some the facts inside the book that they introduce!

"Croatia: Myth and Reality", Michael McAdams, Croatian Information Service, Sacramento, 1992

In this small book in the chapter entitled "Myth: There was no retribution against the Croatians after World War II", we come to the sub-heading, "Bleiburg" on page 55. McAdams correctly asserts that

> "To Croatians, the single word "Bleiburg" summarises the pain endured by an entire nation."

McAdams cites the following sources, "Operation Slaughterhouse"; "In Tito's Death Marches and Extermination Camps" (Hecimovic); "Operation Keelhaul" (Epstein); 'Bleiburg' (Nikolic); and "The Minister and the Massacres" (Tolstoy); and briefly describes the Croatian 'retreat' which ended up in Bleiburg which included some "200,000" Croatian civilians, and some "200,000" Croatian soldiers, sailors, and airmen. He mentioned the Croatian Emissary's journey to Italy, who had the intention of meeting with Field Marshal Alexander, but who ended up in a P.O.W. camp.

Under the sub-heading of "Deception and Betrayal", McAdams writes,

> "One of the first groups to arrive at British headquarters was a contingent of 130 members of the Croatian government headed by President Nikola Mandic. All were told that they would be transferred to Italy as soon as possibly by British Military Police. All were then loaded into a train and returned to the Partisans for execution. It was the intent of the British to turn over all Croatians, as well as Serbs and Slovenes, to the Communists from whom they had fled."

This group of Croatian leaders mentioned above, were amongst those who had left Zagreb before the main Croatian retreating columns by a different route and never came to Bleiburg.

In my book I have discussed how these Croatian government members were not anywhere near to the hundreds of thousands of Croats who found themselves stopped and re-routed by Bulgarians, and attacked by Yugoslavs at Poljana, before some thousands made it across the Meza River to Bleiburg. Nevertheless I have no doubt that McAdams was sincere in what he wrote at the time in 1992.

Under the sub-heading "Denial and Discovery" I concur with some of what McAdams writes, as follows, but I disagree with him in his estimation that western governments sought to cover-up or ignore the crimes. According to Omrcanin's book "Dramatis" on page 98, reviewed in my chapter 5, the British Public Record Office was opened for research on 1st January 1972.

> "The total number of people liquidated may never be known, but figures of 100 to 180 thousand have been voiced by some, up to one-quarter of a million by others ... the Yugoslav government denied that the Bleiburg-Maribor massacres or any subsequent liquidation of anti-Communists occurred. As late as 1976 special teams were active in Slovenia and southern Austria covering up evidence. ... The American and British governments, implicated in the forced repatriation that led to the slaughter also sought to cover-up or at least ignore the crimes."

Camp X secret spy training camp site WWII memorial at Whitby on Lake Ontario in 2003

"Beacons in the Night: With the OSS and Tito's Partisans in Wartime Yugoslavia", Franklin Lindsay, Stanford University Press, Stanford, 1993

In Franklin Lindsay's book, "Beacons in the Night: with the OSS and Tito's Partisans in Wartime Yugoslavia", we learn that agents of the OSS (Office of Strategic Services) were in the Slovenian mountains in the last year of WWII. This book is very relevant to the topic of Bleiburg because Lindsay documents the well-armed and supplied Yugoslav Partisans' intention to annex southern Austria! In addition readers learn that the interpreter at the Bleiburg castle negotiations, Robert Plan, was with this OSS group. Finally, the Partisans' sabotage and stockpiling of Allied munitions and supplies is of particular interest to me as I have stated in my Preface.

For example, Lindsay describes in his OSS reports how the Partisans were stockpiling the munitions dropped for their own post-war purposes.

> "The Partisans were gathering up the weapons and, we became convinced, were putting their attacks on hold as they buried in mountain bunkers a large part of the drops. Our reports of this change in their strategy seemed to have no effect in slowing down the rain of arms from the sky."

According to Lindsay in order to achieve their goals to annex Carinthia the Partisans had begun obstructing Allied efforts to create a separate 'Austrian' resistance. By the summer of 1944, and with a growing awareness of Partisan intransigence, Lindsay described how the Allied and Partisan objectives were increasingly diverging as the Partisans wished to prevent any independent resistance in southern Austria. The Slovenian Partisans wanted to use their manpower to strengthen brigades in Stajerska in order to move "in force" into Austria at the end of the war. The Moscow Declaration of 1943 had expressed support for Austrian independence. Lindsay writes that by April 1945, the Yugoslav Partisans had displayed

> ". . . non-cooperation, bad faith, (and) obstructionism ...(Tito)... had not even hinted to Alexander in Belgrade that he intended to use Allied arms and supplies to get to Trieste ahead of the British Eighth Army".

Lindsay documents this theme throughout his book. For example at Trieste where there were

> "... continuing battles with the Yugoslavs. They were past masters at agitation and propaganda and the Allied command was completely unprepared for the political warfare unleashed against them. ... We had concluded they were conserving their forces, and our supplies, for a final move into prewar Austria and Italy. Now the evidence was clear".

In summary, Lindsay's book provides information which explains the well-stocked Partisan presence in Carinthia and throughout the areas of the Croatian retreat towards Dravograd. This information is crucial to understanding how and why the Croatian retreating columns were either re-routed to Maribor or ended up at Bleiburg.

"The Holocaust that no one cares about", Anne Applebaum, on page 14 'Opinion-Analysis', republished from "The Spectator", in The Age, Melbourne, 10th March 1994

In this article, inset next to a picture of Stalin is the caption "Stalin: responsible for the murder of up to 20 million people".

> Applebaum: "Popular culture is full of images of the Holocaust, but there are no memorials to the victims of Stalin ..."

In this article Applebaum informs those who don't know that Stalin was trying to cover up the murder of up to 20 million Russians, Ukrainians, Poles, Balts and others – not including those who died in the second World War. She notes that Stalin killed twice as many people as did Hitler.

> Applebaum: "… almost no one in the West feels these crimes to have been evil in the same visceral way that they felt Hitler's crimes to have been evil. The lack of interest is academic as well as popular. Until five or six years ago, the historian Robert Conquest was often considered a paranoid alarmist for claiming Stalin had murdered millions."

I had the privilege of attending an address by the tireless anti-Soviet campaigner and author Robert Conquest at La Trobe University in Melbourne. I also attended Tolstoy's address at the same university. At the time I was studying a stream of Communist political systems and so was aware of the scheduled visits of those authors on campus.

Applebaum refers to Tolstoy's account of how the British Government used "force to send thousands of Russians and Yugoslavs home after the war." I disagree that the British used "force" in connection with sending thousands of 'Yugoslavs' home. For example, British historians acknowledge that the British used 'deception' to return 25,000 Croats by train to Yugoslavia; and that there were 'surrender negotiations' between the British, Croats and Yugoslavs at Bleiburg.

According to Applebaum evidence is now available, using the example of "Katyn", and in addition, skeletons in the Ukraine (the Kulaks) have been dug up. There were no "war crime trials" regarding the Soviets and George Urban, a former director of 'Radio Free Europe', thinks this is why the West does not believe the crimes were "so terrible".

Applebaum correctly points out, that such crimes were undertaken to consolidate power and that is why I have mentioned her article in my book about Tito's "revolution".

> "in the name of the revolution and of the proletariat, and were clearly part of the regime's consolidation of power."

"Balkan Warfare",
Jonathan E. Lewis, in "Reviews and Commentary", pages 245—248 of "Intelligence and Counterintelligence", Volume 7, Number 2, 1994

Lewis highly recommends Franklin Lindsay's "Beacons in the Night: With the OSS And Tito's Partisans In Wartime Yugoslavia" in this book review because of its attention to detail. This book review is worth mentioning here because of the importance of Lindsay's book in describing the Partisan's lack of cooperation with the Allies against the Nazis. Lindsay's book, also reviewed in my book, chronicles how the Partisans changed their attitude towards the western Allies, and how this increasing Partisan "distance" contributed to the "first skirmish" of the Cold War, known as the "Trieste Crisis of 1945". The effectiveness of the Partisan's communication network described by Lindsay was replaced by Partisans who were intentionally uncooperative, according to Lewis. Lewis highlights that the Allies munitions air drops continued in spite of the OSS intelligence regarding Tito's lack of cooperation, and for this Lewis places blame on Fitzroy Maclean. Lewis also blames the way in which OSS intelligence was interpreted, or not, during the war. Maclean was the British general in charge of Allied intelligence activities in Yugoslavia. According to Lewis it was the Chetniks who were the main opponents of the Partisans "for control of a postwar Yugoslavia".

Lewis concludes with a positive judgment on Lindsay's valuable history book which offers insight into the future.

> "The best histories inform about the past to help better understand the present, and offer useful insight into the future."

"Thoughts on a Commemoration: Our Debt to the Victims of Bleiburg", Dr Radovan Latkovic, on pages 16—18, Klokan, Sydney, winter 1995

The size of the retreat of the Croatian population in May 1945 is correctly described by this author as a

> "flood of some general national exodus of biblical proportions".

However the execution of the new order by General Scott, of the Allied High Command to the British Eighth Army in Austria, is interpreted incorrectly in this article. It appears in this article that the Croatian army was disarmed by the British before handing over to the 'Partisans'. In this way the author can set the scene to question whether or not the 'handover' was part of the price paid for the Partisan withdrawal from Carinthia. I believe the situation was more complicated.

In fact the discussions at Klagenfurt with the Yugoslav commander Hocevar about the Yugoslav withdrawal occurred on the same day as the negotiations at the castle. And we know from other testimony that the British had already decided not to accept any more surrenders based on the Yalta Treaty, and that the Russians did not support Tito's occupation of Carinthia.

Dr Latkovic of Buenos Aires lays the blame for the slaughter of Croats after WWII on the Serbian rule which followed the creation of Yugoslavia, and correctly mentions the tragic involvement of some Croatian politicians in that process.

A decision regarding the massacres after Bleiburg is attributed to Josip Broz Tito in Belgrade, Latkovic asserts, mentioning Milovan Djilas in his argument. Latkovic writes that the commemoration is held at Bleiburg field because it is the scene of a "symbolic" grave.

> "...three hundred thousand" (Croats died)..."the symbolic grave of thousands of Croatian martyrs, a battlefield..."

"Fifty Godina Bleiburga: Zbornik radova o Bleiburgu i kriznim putovima s treceg medunarodnog znanstvenog simpozija u Bleiburgu 14. i 15. svibnja 1995" (Fifty Years at Bleiburg: Proceedings of Bleiburg & Way of the Cross at Third International Symposium at Bleiburg 14–15 May 1995), Nakladnik Croatiaprojekt, (publisher Croatiaproject), Zagreb, 1995

This book cites many authors who give their version of events regarding Bleiburg. Of interest are the quotations on page 96 which refer to the Yugoslav admission of guilt in the massacre of Croats. There are also a couple of summaries, in English. I will chose a couple of passages at random, especially concerning numbers. It is impossible for me to translate 300 pages from Croatian to English.

Milovan Djilas koji bez stida, drsko i hladno daje izjave u Svetu br. 207 od 1990 i u svojoj knjizi "Wartime" (str. 446 i 447) ovako:

(Milovan Djilas unashamedly, brazenly and coldly gave statements in 'Svetu' number 207 of 1990, and in his book "Wartime" on page 446 and 447 told it like this:)

Djilas: "...cetnici, ustase, domobrani i slovenski domobrani...svi su poubijani osim zena i mladezi ispod 18 godina... bili su ubijani odvojeno i svaka skupina tamo, gdje su bili preuzeti kao zarobljenici... tako je najjednostavniji izlaz bio, da ih se pobije i rijesi problem".

(The Chetniks, Ustasha, Croatian and Slovenian Home Guards...all were killed except for young people under 18 years of age...they were killed separately in groups where they were taken as captives...the simplest way out was to kill them and solve the problem.)

Kosta Nadj, komandant 3. armije, daje u tjedniku Reporter od 13.1.1985. na str. 26. izjavu, da je oko 150,000 neprijatelja palo u njevove ruke, pa drsko ne stideci se izjavljuje:

(Kosta Nadj, Commander of Third Army, gave a newspaper reporter on 13 January 1985, on page 26, information that about 150,000 enemies fell into his hand, and unashamedly and brazenly stated that:)

Nadj: "naravno, da smo ih na kraju likvidirali." (Of course, we finally liquidated them.)

Kosta Nadj also wrote that from 9th to 15th May "zarobljeno oko 60,000 pripadnika 'Pavelicevih jedinica'" ("captured about 60,000 of Pavelic's units".) in "Spektar" in Zagreb 1980 on page 215.

A sub-heading by **Dr. Ante Lausic** is "Procjene broja zarobljenih Hrvata kod Bleiburgu". (Estimates of the number of Croatian prisoners at Bleiburg.) Lausic gives the estimated numbers at Bleiburg according to various authors. He acknowledges that most of the massacres occurred after Bleiburg.

Milan Basta wrote in his book "Rat posle rata": "bilo oko 100,000 Pavelicevih vojnika, ne racunajuci cetnike ni one koje smo ranije zarobili, kao ni civilne izbjeglice". (In his book "War after the War" Milan Basta wrote: there were about 100,000 of Pavelic's soldiers, excluding previously captured Chetniks, and civilian refugees.)

Nicholas Bethell in "The Last Secret" wrote on page 85 that general Scott had written that on "dana 14. svibnja primio vijesti da se dvije skupine hrvatske vojske, koje u svemu broje oko 200,000 ljudi, kreću prema britanskim linijama kod Bleiburga...Oni su pratili oko 500,000 civila i htjeli su prijeci u britansko podrucje da bi se predali i stavili pod britansku zastitu." (Scott had written that: on May 14 received news that two groups of Croatian army, which in all amount to some 200,000 people, moving towards the British lines near Bleiburg...they were followed by some 500,000 civilians and they wanted to cross into British territory to surrender and be put under British protection.)

Josip Djakic wrote in "Od Bleiburg do nasih dana" …"15. svibnja 1945…izrucena (200,000 hrv. Vojske i 100,000 zena, djece, staraca, invalida, itd.) To je ucinjeno od Engleza" (Josip Djakic wrote in "From Bleiburg to the present day": From Bleiburg to the present day"… 15 May 1945… extradited (200,000 Croatian Army and 100,000 women, children, the aged and invalids, etc.) This was done by the English.)

I must comment about Djakic's interpretation. Nowhere near that number of Croats were extradited by the English from Villach, etc.; and it was not the English who sent back the Croats from Bleiburg.

Dr Ante Lausic wrote that on 15 May Vladimir Sklopan wrote "u zbjegu kod Bleiburga naslo oko 200,000 ljudi (Sklopan ne pravi razliku izmedju vojnika i civila)." (Vladimir Sklopan estimated that on 15 May: In refuge at Bleiburg were about 200,000 people (Sklopan does not distinguish between soldiers and civilians)."

Lausic finishes with a brief summary in English of his contribution. He writes that "historiography" still hasn't cleared up the whole truth. He refers to the alleged "indisputable fact" that "Englishmen handed over "Croatian applicants of policical asyl to Yugoslav partisans in Bleiburg". What he says needs more research is the "Death Marches", the "number of captured Croats at Bleiburg", and the "total victims" on the 'Ways of the Cross'. For his "indisputable" facts he has used Tolstoy and Bethell as the source.

Tolstoy was, as we know, less than accurate in his description of the events at Bleiburg and on page 102 mentions the generals at the castle but not the three alternatives given by Scott to the Croats. Bethell does mention the castle negotiations in more detail and briefly summarizes Scott's three alternatives to the Croatian generals on page 86 of "The Last Secret". Lausic cites "Operation Slaughterhouse" in his "Literatura" but does not use the testimony in it about the full negotiations at the castle.

Kazimir Katalinic also has a summary in English and a photograph of a different monument at Bleiburg in front of the pine trees but the quality is poor, and the words unreadable. Most of the summary is about the census before the war. One sentence at the end gives Katalinic's estimate regarding victims as "around 154,000 Croat victims…(soldiers and civilians) "at and after Bleiburg".

One author, **Zvonimir Kulundzic**, repeats the testimony of Daniel Crljen under the sub-heading "Pukovnik Danijel Crljen o Kapitulaciji i predaji 700,000 hrvatskih vojnika i civila u Bleiburgu". (Col. Daniel Crljen about the surrender and capitulation of 700,000 Croatian soldiers and civilians at Bleiburg.) I have no way of knowing whether or not Crljen mentioned the figure of "700,000 Croatian soldiers and civilians at Bleiburg" in another source. In any case it is an exaggeration of the numbers who were 'at' Bleiburg.

Dr Marko Veselica has a rather surprising summary in English written in an historical and fatalistic style. To his credit Veselica criticizes Pavelic's failure to change to the side of the Allies much earlier.

Veselica puts the tragedy of Bleiburg into the context of a geo-strategic struggle to take over Croatian land. He makes the point that the division within Croatian society between the left and right is the result of the influence of "World imperialistic factors". Veselica does a great dishonour to the Croatian victims when he indirectly blames the alleged Serbian Ally, the British. It seems to me that Veselica had been reading Engels whose hatred of Croats is well-known. Engels is the source of the racist hatred of Croats over the past century and a half!

It was not the British, but Friedrich Engels who wanted to wipe 'Slavs' including Croats from the face of the earth! And it must be said that it was the Bishop Strossmayer who was accused by the "British" London Times for trying to sacrifice Croats for the sake of some pan-Slavic dream to unite the east and west churches in the 19th century. The following quotation from Veselica's summary in English is so illogical it is laughable.

> Veselica: "...British Intelligence Service and its military camarilla, had as its objective the definite destruction of the Croats as people and the genuine subject of history, and wipe them away from the European and the World political scene, to disappear completely."

Veselica's rationale for placing ridiculous accusations against the British become clear when he argues that the Bleiburg tragedy should not cause ideological divisions in Croatia.

> Veselica: "(Bleiburg)… should not become the source of new disputes, ideological and other divisions and conflicts inside the Croatian people's corpus."

In other words, Veselica has minimized the domestic guilt and blames the tragedy on "foreign imperialist strategies". What a pity Veselica has forgotten that it was Amnesty International, founded in England, which made him a "Prisoner of Conscience" in 1983! In addition, the United Kingdom was one of the first to recognize the independence of the Croatian Republic in 1992, yet anti-British arguments persist into 1995, and beyond.

In "Tragicne posljedice Bleiburga" (The Tragic Consequences of Bleiburg) **Pero Bosnjak** refers to the Bleiburg Tragedy as the biggest catastrophe for Croatian people in history. A whole generation was lost, and if there had been no Bleiburg tragedy there would be nine million Croats in Croatia. However, he does not say much about what happened at Bleiburg because he is writing about the consequences of the tragedy.

He refers to the withdrawal to Bleiburg of 200,000 Croatian soldiers and 300,000 civilians, which is an understatement of British sources of an approaching 200,000 Croatian soldiers and half a million Croatian civilians. Bosnjak poses questions about what would have happened if there never was a Bleiburg. For example, he asks what would have happened if the English had not extradited the Croatian army to the Partisans. He alleges that the Croatian army gave their weapons to the English, who betrayed them, by handing them over to the Partisans. Until that point in time the author suggests that the Croatian army had been undefeated. On another issue Bosjnak also mentions, like other sources, that the Chetniks joined the Partisans near the end of the war.

In this version of the Bleiburg Tragedy it could appear to a reader who was not acquainted with the issue that the English, rather than the British, simply handed over all 500,000 Croats to the Partisans after disarming them. There is no mention of how many Croats were at the Bleiburg field and no mention of negotiations and surrender options.

Another summary about Bleiburg, in the English language, is by **Petar Vucic**. Vucic writes that Bleiburg was not an accidental episode in Croatian history. He points out that 'Bleiburg' represents for Serbs and Serbia a conquest of Croatian lands. But then he alleges, without any supporting facts that "for Great Britain it was a way of ensuring a sphere of influence in the Balkans"!

But then typically this Croatian author goes back to the year 1102 and the centuries of East-West geopolitical struggle. According to Vucic, Great Britain wanted to limit the spreading of German influence in the Balkans and so Bleiburg can be explained in that context!

In summary, first he blames 'Bleiburg' on the geopolitical interests of the victors, primarily Britain. Secondly he blames the geopolitical interests of Greater Serbia;

and last but not least he blames the political interests of the Partisans to get rid of its political rivals in Croatia.

The last entry in this book "50 Godina Bleiburg" is by **Zvonimir Zoric**, and he also finishes with a summary in English. He gives testimony under the heading "Confirmation of Bleiburg Tragedy Based on Excavations", and it was written at "Dravograd Bridge, Wednesday 16th May, 1945 — at dawn".

Being the 16th May it is about what happened 'after' the Croats left Bleiburg. Zoric repeats the often-told brief version of what happened at Bleiburg.

> "All of these people were handed over to Partisans the evening before after the ultimatum and the massacre that had taken place on Bleiburg field approximately 20 kilometers away. They were handed over by the English army after having been disarmed."

He then moves forward in time to a football field at Maribor where the Croats were divided up according to their uniforms or as civilians. Vucic was among these people who were then loaded into trains at Maribor Slovenia. On 17th May 1945 people came to understand that the train was headed towards Croatia. He saved himself by jumping out but found out later that twenty thousand were massacred in that Maceljska forest. In 1995 he reports that excavations are underway in the region.

I have taken the time to review the English summaries because each of them, in a nutshell, reveals a misunderstanding about what happened on 15th May 1945.

"BLEIBURG: THE MASSACRE THAT NEVER WAS" IN PART II OF BOOK, "A LOOKING-GLASS TRAGEDY: THE CONTROVERSY OVER THE REPATRIATIONS FROM AUSTRIA IN 1945", CHRISTOPHER BOOKER, GERALD DUCKWORTH & CO LTD, LONDON, 1997

This thick book is a response to the investigation and subsequent Tolstoy libel trial 'verdict' in London. Booker is concerned mostly with the Cossacks like Tolstoy's book, "The Minister and the Massacres", but nevertheless it is an indispensable book for researchers on the topic of Bleiburg. On the front cover of this book, and inside, is the photograph of the 15th Cossack Cavalry Corps in a field near Griffen after their surrender to the British 6th Armoured Division on 11 May 1945 (source: Sgt W.G.Johnson, British Imperial War Museum, NA 24020). In the photograph the Cossacks are pictured throwing 7.92 mm Mauser carbine rifles when surrendering.

I also discuss a similar photograph of the same scene in another chapter where it is incorrectly alleged that it is a photograph of the Bleiburg field.

In this lengthy book there is some important and interesting information for those who wish to read it further. I am only concerned about whether or not we can learn more about the Bleiburg Tragedy, especially given the controversial and misleading title of the chapter, "The Massacre That Never Was"!

Because no public investigation would be forthcoming, Anthony Cowgill organised a thorough investigation into Tolstoy's allegations about the post-war repatriations in 1945. Cowgill's Report has been reviewed earlier in this chapter. Actually it was Christopher Booker, author of an earlier article about Tolstoy's book, who had inspired Cowgill to investigate further.

In my book I focus on the events around the 15th May so I will try to confine my comments to that time-frame. Booker's version of the Croatian journey towards Bleiburg is somewhat inconsistent with other accounts. Booker seems to suggest that "some" columns of Croats got through the Bulgarian front and crossed into Austria via Lavamund. Here he seems to be taking Tolstoy's version at face value that some Croats moved passed the Bulgarians, a point which I have already argued against. Otherwise Booker could be referring to Pavelic's group which crossed the border many days earlier, but it is unlikely because this statement is about Bleiburg per se.

> Booker: "Some were heading for Lavamund, but the largest number were advancing, via Dravograd, towards the small town of Bleiburg... This column stretched some 30 miles (48 km) back into Yugoslavia"

But just to add confusion, in this above-mentioned group Booker incorrectly assumes that it includes "Pavelic, Macek, the Croatian government and a huge number of criminals". Booker then links the message of Tito of the 13th May to this government group, by adding

> "... You must move your forces from the Celje area ... in order to concentrate for an attack aimed at the annihilation of this column".

We know however that Pavelic's elite government group was already in north Austria before 13th May, and that the Croatian 'government' group did not travel via Celje. Tito's 13th May order obviously referred to the main Croatian exodus columns still moving beyond Celje. Yet about the evasion of capture by the Croatian Ustasha leader Pavelic, Booker acknowledges that most of the Croatian Cabinet met with a different fate.

There is more than one way of looking at what Booker has to say though. Booker has referred to the main columns being cut off from those at the front before entering Bleiburg, some via Lavamund. It is possible that those entering via Lavamumd consisted of the group of Croats which had split from the Pavelic group a few days earlier.

In fact, as described earlier, the Croatian vanguard which arrived in the area from the 13th May on were in fact cut off by the Bulgarians. They were re-routed towards Poljana and along the Meza River, some finally possibly crossing into Austria via Mezica, or via Poljana, after a well-known battle at Poljana. Indeed, Brigadier Scott himself had referred to the Bulgarian refusal to allow Croats to pass. At this point a Croatian memorandum of 13th May 1945 is written to the western Allies at Klagenfurt, which I review under a 1998 article by Zeljko Kruselj.

Booker gives his estimate of the number of Croats actually at the Bleiburg field as between 20,000 and 30,000 soldiers and civilians. This number differs from most but not all sources. Tolstoy, in his "Minister and the Massacres" chronology, refers to the number of 20,000 Croats. It would appear as if Booker has accepted many things Tolstoy has said at face value except for the part about a massacre on Bleiburg field. At least Booker does acknowledge more than Tolstoy regarding the negotiations.

Booker does present most of Scott's testimony regarding the negotiations including the Yugoslav threats and impatience. In his book Booker lists Scott's three alternatives. Those alternatives can be seen in Part I of my book, but the following quotation from Booker also sums up Scott's Report on page 192.

> Booker: "After five minutes they (Croats) sensibly decided on the first course. The Yugoslavs were brought back into the room, and I told the interpreter to explain...an agreement was then made in my presence and signed by the two armies...the terms of surrender were fair enough--the Croatian Army was to be treated as prisoners of war with the exception of political criminals, who would be tried by Allied courts, while the civil population was to be fed and returned to Croatia by the shortest route. With five minutes to spare the Croatian Army signified their surrender, and the handing in of arms commenced forthwith."

Regarding the massacres at the Bleiburg field Booker concurs with the "Operation Slaughterhouse" original eye-witness accounts that 'no' mass slaughter actually happened at Bleiburg--contrary to Tolstoy's account which came under scrutiny at the Trial.

In his book, Christopher Booker also discusses a lot about the cross-examination of Tolstoy during the trial by QC Mr Charles Gray. About events at the Bleiburg field, it was revealed that Tolstoy had grossly exaggerated the accounts about what actually happened there, in his book. And on his visit to Bleiburg with Nigel Nicholson in 1988 Tolstoy already admitted that only a

> "score or so were shot on our side of the frontier…"

On page 369-370 Booker describes in detail Tolstoy's shocking admission 'under oath' at the trial. Booker describes how Tolstoy, under oath, explained how he had erred.

> "… (Tolstoy) erred on the generous side".

> Tolstoy continued: "Yes I think it might be fair to say, in the light of what I have said, that I have shifted my view very considerably since then, as a result of very intensive work and meeting a great many more people who were involved…I was putting forward perhaps too extreme a view of the most charitable view that could be adopted."

Personally I have never seen a finer example of Orwell's 'doublespeak'.

It is difficult to understand why a well-known and respected author like Tolstoy would exaggerate or distort facts! We know that to accomplish his version of the events at Bleiburg Tolstoy had used Colin Gunner's words out of context. In conclusion, Tolstoy's admissions, that there was 'not' a large mass killing on the Bleiburg field, now concur with accounts written by Croatian eye-witnesses in the book "Operation Slaughterhouse".

At the Tolstoy libel trial the topic came up that Brigadier Scott had been given assurances by the Yugoslavs that treatment of those surrendered Croats would be according to law. And at the trial the QC Gray asked Tolstoy if he thought the British should have seen through those assurances, and Tolstoy admitted that what he had first written was unlikely! In addition, Robert Plan, the American-Croatian interpreter present at the negotiation, was also of the strong opinion that the British officers at Bleiburg were convinced that Croats would receive fair treatment.

I guess everyone is entitled to a mistake—I have certainly made a few in the past on the topic of Bleiburg, particularly when I also took Tolstoy at face-value. In my book I have endeavoured to acknowledge every source in the Bibliography.

Booker makes the point, after the surrendered Croats at Bleiburg had been marched "north-east across the countryside towards the Yugoslav frontier near Lavamund", that the British were not aware of the machine-gunning of unarmed Croats across the border at that time. From Booker we learn, later after the fact, that British soldiers there at the time had witnessed the Yugoslav shocking treatment of Croats.

> "The route taken by the convoy was across country, through fields of corn, over walls, banks and ditches, through fast flowing streams. There was no apparent reason why the road should not have been used, as it was free at the time. ... No attempt at organised march was made whatsoever, but by the time the Croats, both soldiers and civilians, had passed the road junction . . . leading to Bleiburg, they had been stripped of everything they possessed. ... Over the next few days considerable numbers of Croats in smaller groups did manage to cross over into Austria at various points along the frontier. ..." (Lt. Col. D.M.C. Worral MC; Maj. J.G. Denny, Durham Light Infantry; Major J. Langham, 46th Recce Reg.)

Booker also writes that many Croats did manage to penetrate the British lines elsewhere. In his book it is clarified, at last, that Montenegrin Chetniks who were allegedly with Croats going towards Bleiburg had in fact come by a different route and were taken to Viktring camp. There were no Montenegrin Chetniks represented at Bleiburg, as sometimes claimed by several sources, but they probably had been amongst the retreating columns, columns which became split before crossing the border. The 13th May Memorandum is co-signed by one Montenegrin as well as by Herencic and Crljen but that is the only documented mention I have come across of Montenegrins.

Booker's book is important, especially regarding revelations of Tolstoy's misrepresentation of events at Bleiburg. Regarding Tolstoy's book it is impossible to overstate just how much of an enduring impact it has had on the psyche or 'collective memory' of Croatian communities around the world. During the long Cold War Croatian victims believed that at last there was someone who had exposed the Bleiburg tragedy! It was not a bad thing that Tolstoy had brought the issue of repatriations to the public's attention again. But in the case of Bleiburg I believe Tolstoy may have done more harm than good, in the long term, because of his inaccurate and misleading portrayal of events there.

In retrospect the Croatian gullibility, and mine, regarding Tolstoy's initial claims is another tragedy!

In his book, Booker also discusses some of Tolstoy's comments regarding other repatriations, however he does not challenge the events surrounding the British handover of Croats at Rosenbach and Maria Elend from the 18th to 23rd May 1945.

Booker also gives details regarding meetings with Yugoslav commanders and the repatriations, and Tito's decision on 19th May to withdraw the Yugoslav Armies from Carinthia. Booker agrees with other sources on the topic of the cautious British policy. British policy regarding its dealings with the Yugoslavs had been formed since the Yugoslav attempt to takeover Venezia Giulia, and this had a direct bearing on later British policies in Carinthia! Like many other sources Booker explains the chaos at the time. He mentioned that five days after the end of the war the British were outnumbered by Yugoslavs and still had only 25,000 men in an area "100 miles long and 50 miles wide". (160 km by 80 km) In this book on page 207 we learn again about the British attitude and potential plan towards Tito's intransigence in the area.

> Booker: "The operation, code named 'Beehive', would involve all 5 Corps' three divisions...The intention of Beehive was 'to secure complete military control of the Corps area', and this was to be achieved by 'capturing or destroying all Tito troops in the Corps area'-- now estimated at up to 30,000 men, or a strength rather greater than that of 5 Corps itself."

Although we learn about the surrender of Croats to Yugoslavs, and their subsequent treatment during the evacuation, Booker's text does need some criticism. The title of the chapter about Bleiburg is misleading and unjust, as is one map which incorrectly indicates that Bleiburg is north of the Drava River! The map-scale is in miles rather than the kilometres in use at the time.

Also misleading, regarding the Bleiburg time frame, is Booker's chart entitled, "Chain of Command and Military Styles" about the British Army in May 1945. In immediate post-WWII Austria I believe that Brigadier Scott's Brigade should be listed as the "38th (Irish) Brigade" and not the "1st Irish Brigade".

Mention needs to be made regarding Booker's 'Chronology/Index'. The only reference to the Croats approaching Bleiburg is on 14th May, as a "Croat emergency". The 15th May is not mentioned.

When comparing Booker's chronology with Tolstoy's the two are different. Tolstoy mentions "the approach of 200,000 Croats" on 14th May and on 15th May that "20,000 Croats" are turned back by Fifth Corps.

The fact that there was not an actual huge 'massacre' at the Bleiburg field is the rationale used by Booker for the title of his chapter "Bleiburg: The Massacre That Never Was". At first glance, the title can be misconstrued by readers that there was no massacre at all! The choice of title is perhaps due to Tolstoy's admission that he had virtually "erred" about events at Bleiburg. At the end of the chapter Booker does refer to subsequent massacres across the border, after being force-marched away from Bleiburg as "shocking" on page 193. (See also my review of Colin Gunner's book where I mention Booker.) A subsequent massacre just across the border is a point also acknowledged by Cowgill in his 1990 Report.

In conclusion I must criticize Booker's choice of title for this chapter because I believe the whole situation was a tragedy by every definition! It was a tragedy from everyone's perspective except the Yugoslav's who have interpreted the whole situation in the terms of "freedom" at their Poljana Exhibit in 2010. This Exhibit is reviewed in another chapter of my book.

Booker also opines, I believe incorrectly, that that the 'tragedy' which Croats are referring to is the defeat of the Croatian state by Tito's Yugoslavs in a civil war! Well of course no people want to become stateless victims, but this statement diverts attention from the ongoing investigation of mass graves being unearthed until this day! At least Booker acknowledges the following reference to massacres on page 196.

> Booker: "When Croat historians have subsequently spoken of the 'Bleiburg Tragedy' this is what they really mean. The massacres which were to follow, in many parts of northern Yugoslavia in the weeks and months ahead, were among the consequences of that victory and that tragedy. But at Bleiburg itself on 15 May, despite Tolstoy's six pages of 'eyewitness evidence', no massacre of the type he described had taken place."

In conclusion, when Croats speak of the 'Bleiburg Tragedy' they are, as he said above, referring to the hundreds of thousands of victims of post-war massacres by Tito's Bolsheviks. For Croats this Bleiburg tragedy includes the terms "death marches" and "the Way of the Cross". These massacres were acknowledged around the world. For example, in "Strategies of Containment", Gaddis writes that the former American President Truman remarked "Tito killed more than 400,000 of his opponents in Yugoslavia before he could finally establish himself as a dictator". Also, in "Hoodwinking Churchill", Batty writes that to establish his power, "Tito allowed more than 400,000 of his own people to perish".

"Tko je Tko u NDH: Hrvatska 1941–1945",
Z. Dizdar, M. Grcic, S. Ravlic, Darko Stuparic,
Editors, Minerva, Zagreb, 1997

This book in the Croatian language, organized alphabetically by name, has nearly 500 pages. I believe it would be an important book for researchers as it includes names and photographs of key individuals at Bleiburg, on the Croatian retreat, and in the Independent State of Croatia (NDH). The biography, photograph, and war-time roles of the Croatian generals such as Crljen, Herencic, or Stancer, at Bleiburg are included. There is a chronology of events at the end of this book and for May 1945 the following dates mentioned are relevant to 'Bleiburg'. Once again an incorrect sweeping statement suggests that there were mass executions at the Bleiburg field, carried out by the Yugoslavs. There is no mention of the British at Bleiburg in this chronology however.

> "...6 svibnja oruzane snage NDH, zajedno s njemackim jedinicama, povlace se prema Sustriji s ciljem predaje zapadnim Saviznicima, Poglavnik i Vlada napustau Zagreb; (6 May Croatian armed forces together with German forces retreated to Sustriji with the aim of surrendering to the western allies, the Leader and government left Zagreb.)

> ...7 svibnja kapitulirao Njemacki Reich; (7 May capitulation of German Reich.)

> ...8 svibnja u Zagreb ulaze jedinice Jugoslavenske armije; (8 May arrival of Yugoslav Army in Zagreb.)

> ...15 svibnja na polju kraj gradica Bleiburga (Pliberka) partizanske jedinice izvrsile masovna pogubljena opkoljenih pripadnika oruzanih snaga NDH i civila." (15 May on field near town of Bleiburg (Pliberka) the Partisan units carried out mass executions of members of the Croatian armed forces and civilians.)

In the glossary at the end of the book Bleiburg is listed. The "Death Marches" are mentioned as well as various camps of death inside Yugoslavia. This time it is alleged that Bleiburg is the place where the mass killings began rather than where they were executed en masse.

> "...partizanske jedinice otpocele pogubljenja zarobljenih vojnika i civila, dok su masovna ubojstva obavljena u okolici novoosnovanih logora u Sloveniji...Na Bleiburskom polju, a potom jos vise na tzv. marsevima smrti (krizni put) stradali su deseci tisuca ljudi...Bleiburag se u sirem smislu rabi kao sinonim za stradanje hrvatskog naroda (vojna i civila) nakon sloma NDH".

(...Partisan units began executing captured soldiers and civilians, while mass murders were carried out around newly established camps in Slovenia...On Bleiburg field and then even more on "Death Marches" (Way of the Cross) were killed tens of thousands of people... the term Bleiburg is broadly used as synonymous with the suffering of the Croatian people (soldiers and civilians) after the breakdown of the Croatian state (NDH).

Ironically after the surrender amongst the successful escapees to the West were Crljen and Herencic. General Ivan Herencic was the general who had originally intervened to prevent Croatia from joining the Allies in 1944. The book "Tko je tko u NDH" published in Zagreb, is informative on the topic.

"Testimony of an Officer Who Led 900 Croats to their Death", Zeljko Krusel, Croatia Weekly, Page 13, Zagreb, No. 8, March 5, 1998

This notarized testimony reprinted in Croatia Weekly is an interview, with a British officer Bernard O'Sullivan, in Vecernji list, Zagreb. This officer's testimony has been preceded by an introduction about the Bleiburg Tragedy. In the introduction it is alleged that Yugoslav Partisans had, at Bleiburg, executed tens of thousands of captured Croats in May 1945.

Immediately the first question asks what happened on 24th May 1945, as if to suggest to readers that O'Sullivan was stationed at or near to Bleiburg. Or perhaps readers are to 'assume' that reference to Bleiburg is merely symbolic, but I believe that I was not the only one to initially think O'Sullivan may have been referring to Bleiburg. I did not have a decent map of Carinthia at the time.

The British officer categorically denies that he had any idea of what would happen as a result of his orders. He was to hand over three Croatian generals and about 900 Croatian soldiers to Welsh Guards near Rosenbach, southeast of Villach. He acknowledged that both Stalin and Tito had entered Austria.

In the next question O'Sullivan is asked to describe how he had to fetch the Croatian prisoners from Spittal in about forty trucks. O'Sullivan had not tried to conceal the destination from the prisoners and he was aware of their objections. On arrival at Rosenbach the Welsh Guards drove the Croatian soldiers towards Tito's Partisans.

Finally O'Sullivan was questioned about his knowledge of what happened later to the Croats. Actually O'Sullivan had no knowledge about the killings until reading about the incident in an issue of Life magazine a year later. He then began to consider the incident as a war crime

> "in which I unconsciously took part, through a series of unfortunate circumstance ..."

Until reading this Life magazine article O'Sullivan had thought his role in the repatriation of Croats had been an isolated incident. O'Sullivan then became influenced by the arguments in Tolstoy's "Minister and the Massacres", and like many others who read Tolstoy's book, he became convinced that the "clearing of the decks" was part of a deal to get Tito to withdraw from Austria.

I believe that this article about O'Sullivan's testimony leads to some misunderstanding about the Bleiburg Tragedy. Actually the incident described is not about Bleiburg at all. The incident happened 'after' Bleiburg to prisoners who had surrendered 'before' the 15th May 1945, and who found themselves at Villach far to the west. These 900 Croats were not part of the main Croatian columns which moved towards Dravograd, and may have been part of those who left earlier with Pavelic to arrive in Carinthia before Croats arrived at Bleiburg. O'Sullivan is honest when he says he did not know what the fate of the Croats would be, but then he is influenced, like many others, by Tolstoy's arguments that there was a British-Yugoslav deal.

I argue in my book that the situation was very complex, because of the Yalta Conference, and because many various national groups were sent back, not just the Croats! Finally, it is not well understood in this interview with O'Sullivan that although the British did repatriate Croats the number they repatriated was about 26,000. It was a tragic situation. However there is neither logic nor evidence which points to a conspiracy or a cover-up. This officer's testimony that he did not know what would happen matches the contemporaneous testimony of other British officers. It also matches the testimony given by Robert Plan, the interpreter at the Bleiburg castle. The British repatriations were stopped within a few weeks, but the Yugoslav massacres did not stop.

Mural dedicated to WWII secret spy training Camp X Memorial Park Oshawa near Whitby Canada 2003

"Apel saveznickoj vojsci da sprijeci krvoprolice" (Appeal to Allied Army to Prevent Bloodshed), Zeljko Kruselj, reporter in Vecernji list, republished on page 14, in Nova Hrvatska (New Croatia), Sydney, 21-27 July 1998

This full-page article, in the Croatian language, is about Robert Plan, the American-Croatian translator at the Bleiburg castle, who was on a trip to Slovenia. Robert Plan, also known as Bob Perry, had come to Slovenia on the occasion of the translation, into the Slovenian language, of Lindsay's book "Vatre u noci" (Beacons in the Night: With the OSS and Tito's Partisans in Wartime Yugoslavia).

Published on this page is also an incomplete image of an appeal written on 13th May 1945 in Slovenia. Unfortunately the document's contents are incomplete and practically unreadable. This document, in Croatian, is addressed to

> "Glavaru Angloamericke vojske za Starjerskum Korusku i Gorejsko", Celovac. (Leader of the Anglo-American armies for Styria, Carinthia and Goriska, Klagenfurt).

The document is signed by the Croatian representatives at the Bleiburg castle, Ivo Herencic, Prof. Daniel Crljen; and one Montenegrin Dr Dusan Krivokapic.

Robert Plan, after being informed by Basta that a huge column of Croats was coming towards Dravograd, put up a white flag and went to the Croatian Ustasha and Domobrani camp. This incident is also referred to in Booker's "A Looking-Glass Tragedy: The controversy over the repatriations from Austria in 1945".

> Booker: "... in May 1990 Tony Cowgill visited Austria to carry out an on-the-spot investigation into what had happened. This was assisted by Dr Ariprand Thurn-Valsassina, the owner of Bleiburg castle (one of Tolstoy's 'Patrons') and Mr Robert Plan, of the American OSS, who in 1945 had led the leading column of the Croats to Bleiburg. Both men had been present when Brigadier Scott received the Croat generals.

The article also refers to Robert Plan's conviction that the British at Bleiburg were convinced that the Yugoslavs would treat the Croatian refugees fairly.

> Kruselj: "...Plan uporno ponavlja, da su saveznicki casnici bili uvjereni da su od partizanskih ... predstavnika Milana Baste I Ivana Kovacica Efenka dobili cvrste garancije o tretiranju hrvatskih vojnika kao ratnim zaroblenika nad kojima nece biti dopustena kolektivna odmazda..."

> (... Plan strongly emphasized that the Allied officers were convinced by Partisan representatives Commisar Milan Basta and Ivana Kovacka Efenka, who gave firm guarantees on treatment of the Croatian soldiers that they will not be subjected to collective revenge)

"Britain and the Bleiburg Tragedy", Suzanne Brooks-Pincevic, Leon Publications Ltd., Auckland, 1998

This is a folio-size book of a series of paintings by the author, an excellent artist from New Zealand. On the first page Brooks-Pincevic quotes Nikolai Tolstoy who was interviewed in the BBC *True Stories* documentary "Betrayal" about fighting for the truth. She then acknowledges the sources for her work as Tolstoy ("The Minister and the Massacres"), Prcela & Guldescu ("Operation Slaughterhouse"), McAdams ("Croatia—Myth and Reality"), Bethell ("The Last Secret"), Beljo ("Yu-Genocide"), Rees for the BBC ("Betrayal"), and two Croatian Heritage Foundation Symposiums. I have reviewed most of the above sources myself and discovered that they all do not agree with each other about the events or numbers involved at Bleiburg.

I am reviewing Brooks-Pincevic's book seventeen years after its publication and launch, and since then some of my views about what happened at Bleiburg have changed considerably. Although I had been writing about Bleiburg myself since then

I realize that I had been both deceived and confused by some of the sources above. Self-criticism of my own work appears throughout the chapters of my book. Tolstoy in particular admitted, under oath, he had "erred" regarding the events at Bleiburg.

Part 2 of her book is dedicated to "The Bleiburg Set" (set of paintings). The first part of the book entitled "The Liberation of Croatia series" is about the siege against Croatia between 1991 and 1995. After an introduction to World War II the author Brooks-Pincevic explains how and why she was contacted to paint about Bleiburg in New Zealand after an Exhibit.

Some of the verses of her poem "The Bleiburg Tragedy" at first glance seem similar in a style to my first and second poems about Bleiburg written in 1984 and 1985 (see chapter on 1980s). However the numbers of victims given in Brooks-Pincevic's poem at 'Bleiburg' are higher. The Brooks-Pincevic poem mentions "300,000" at Bleiburg field, and another "200,000" approaching. The number "500,000" is repeated three times in reference to the British who "deceived foreign people at the border". Although there is a clear mention of British deceit in my poem, the attribution of overall guilt to the British is generally much stronger in Suzanne's poem "The Bleiburg Tragedy". This attribution of guilt to the British is strong because she merges all repatriations and all of the various ethnic groups together.

For her Foreword Brooks-Pincevic repeats the 1968 Foreword in "Operation Slaughterhouse" by the American Major General Charles A. Willoughby. I have already criticized some of Willoughby's generalisations in my book. Following the Foreword is a map which illustrates the "Death March" routes throughout post-war Communist Yugoslavia. On this map Dravograd is incorrectly located south-west of Bleiburg. Dravograd is east of Bleiburg at the Drava River, hence its name, and south of the Austrian/Slovenian border.

Brooks-Pincevic's first painting in Part 2 is entitled "The Betrayal of Croatia—Bleiburg 1945". We know the artist is referring to a British betrayal because Alexander, Macmillan and Churchill are depicted as surreal 'larger than life' figures tearing up the Geneva Convention. The painting is accompanied by an explanation. The "Tavern" is depicted (I assume she means "Hrust") where there were meetings between the Partisans and the British, although it is not mentioned that this was the Partisan Headquarters, as far as I have been able to find out. The "Thurn-val-sassin" castle on the hill overlooking Bleiburg is described as a "Chateau". I would describe it as a medieval fortress.

The artist claims that Bleiburg is "near the Carinthian town of Klagenfurt", the British military base, but I would suggest that 55 kilometers is not very near. It is alleged that the British "held military control in the region" and no mention is given of the Yugoslav occupation there until the last part of her essay. For her source about the Yugoslav threat she refers to the biased BBC documentary "Betrayal" and the view of Sir Charles Villiers (SOE) who alleged that the Yugoslav threat was "exaggerated". But this documentary is about locations nowhere near Bleiburg and Croats are not mentioned, which is why I did not review it in my book.

Bleiburg is introduced by a discussion of the many groups who were "fleeing the Partisans". The British extradition of those particular Croats who were told they were being "transferred to Italy" is then mentioned. Next, "From 14th to 15th May", readers learn of the approach of Croats farther east.

> "...a second—much larger group of more than 400,000, arrived en masse along the borders of Austria—mostly centering on Bleiburg...it included some 200,000 soldiers, over half of whom were Ustase and the remainder Domobrani...the Army was joined on the roads to Austria by over 200,000 civilians..."

> "...and here Herencic was forcibly persuaded by the British to surrender to the Partisans...When Herencic came out of his meeting with Brigadier Scott it was sundown...soldiers were persuaded to hand over their arms to the British..."

> "...Thus, this huge second group of refugees...were forced to turn back, across the river Drava, into Slovenia, and the waiting Partisans...Basta gave the order for which Tito's Yugoslav Partisans were waiting. They appeared from the camouflaging shadow of the trees—faceless and soulless..."

No doubt this is why the author paints the Partisans without faces, to match her text, or vice-versa. We know however from Scott's Report that when he arrived at Bleiburg all he could see were "Yugoslavs", and we also know that the negotiations finished in the late afternoon. Sundown in May occurs several hours later.

I am not being hypercritical out of any personal judgment because, like me, this author had too many conflicting versions to choose from in her research. I am simply trying to excavate the truth from several sources and join-the-dots in the right order. Anyone who has tried to join dots in children's books will know what I mean.

Brooks-Pincevic suggests that "over 90,000" Croats were in the camps tens of kilometers west of Bleiburg which included the first groups surrendered earlier, plus many who had escaped from Bleiburg. Most sources agree that only about 25,000 to 26,000 of these Croats were repatriated. We know that many Croatian government members lived out their lives overseas, in another article I have also reviewed. Brooks-Pincevic suggests that on Bleiburg field on 15th May perhaps "a thousand" or "as many as three thousand" died.

The author acknowledges that the ordinary British soldiers eventually made it known to their officers that the Yugoslav treatment of refugees was horrific. She does not add that the handovers stopped however. The author tries to understand why the British extradited the Croats and others but gives too much attention to the Geneva Convention, and no attention to Yalta, or the Yugoslav occupation of the area. Many critics acknowledge that the Geneva Convention articles applied to conditions 'during a war' and V.E. Day had already been celebrated a week before 15th May 1945.

This author correctly acknowledges that the testimony of Nigel Nicholson of the Grenadier Guards, as per the BBC documentary film "Betrayal", deals only with those who were deceived they were being sent to Italy.

Brooks-Pincevic then includes an extract from Tolstoy's "The Minister and the Massacres". First she discusses the BBC documentary film "Betrayal", which was on New Zealand television in 1992. This documentary refers to the unveiling of a memorial opposite the "Victoria and Albert Museum" in London which commemorates the "sufferings of innocent people in the repatriations—sufferings still felt to this day." This documentary, which uses Tolstoy as a Research Consultant, focuses on Orthodox victims and on the Cossacks.

Pincevic compares the betrayal of the repatriated victims to a betrayal by the "west" in the form of an arms embargo, which affected the self-defence of Croats who were under siege by Serbs between 1991—1995. In the extract Tolstoy gives the numbers of Croats.

> "...well over 100,000 (at the Bleiburg field)...".

This 100,000 had allegedly crossed the frontier at Dravograd, a crossing which we have learned was thwarted by the Bulgarians.

Tolstoy's version of the negotiations at the castle is less than thorough in comparison with "Operation Slaughterhouse" which Brooks-Pincevic has not chosen to quote, no doubt because it is very lengthy. She does repeat the testimony by Tolstoy about an alleged slaughter at the Bleiburg field—a slaughter Tolstoy himself denied at the libel trial under oath a decade before the publication of Brooks-Pincevic's book.

Brooks-Pincevic's second painting (8a) in the book is entitled, "Operation Slaughterhouse—Zagreb 1945", and it also has a descriptive essay next to it in her book. A second "Operation Slaughterhouse" painting (8b) depicts the Zagreb Cathedral and the statue of King Tomislav.

In her text the author refers to the recognition of Tito's Yugoslavia by the British and Americans. She incorrectly alleges that Tito acquired Yugoslavia "by default". The "Russian threat" and the "British betrayal",

> "put into his (Tito's) hands, unarmed, those he feared most as a threat to his ambitions and thus it was a simple matter to liquidate his opposition."

In fact other sources have described how most Croats on retreat had already been turned back by Yugoslavs before crossing the Austrian border. And, in response to the above suggestion that Yugoslavia was acquired "by default" history tells us that as far back as Yalta the Tito-Subasic government was accepted as the successor to the first Yugoslavia.

Later in her text we read her conclusion.

> Brooks-Pincevic: "Tito's Yugoslavia was achieved by murder and intimidation. Not only did Tito kill his own people, but worse still he turned his people against his people, and the world against his people".

Truer words were never written! We know that it was after the Stalin-Tito split that criticism of Tito was hushed in the media for many years. Such was the nature of the Cold War. By this time many thousands had actually survived in the British refugee camps.

Also, it has been established that the British extradited up to 26,000 Croats back to Yugoslavia but that this did not happen at Bleiburg or near Bleiburg. In conclusion therefore at Bleiburg the British did not accept any more refugees, and more importantly it has been acknowledged by many reputable sources that most of the retreating mass of Croats never escaped the clutches of the Yugoslavs, or the Bulgarians to a much lesser extent, in eastern Slovenia.

In this chapter of Brooks-Pincevic's book the victims of the "Death Marches" are described and depicted in the paintings. Croatian soldiers are depicted marching from the Maksimir Park in Zagreb in columns to their death. In the background is the Mirogoj Cemetery in Zagreb, and to the side the gate to the Maksimir Park is depicted. In the foreground Tito is pictured watching naked victims being killed in deep ravines, by the Yugoslavs. The ravines are found throughout Slovenia and

Croatia. The biggest massacres at Maribor were of some "60-70,000" and a pit at "Kocevski Rog" holds "20-30,000" victims. These unmarked mass graves hold mostly Croats, but also Slovenian Home Guards and some Serbian Chetniks, as well as civilians.

In Part 2, the BBC "Betrayal" documentary is once again referred to, this time in relation to an interview with the Serbian Major General in Tito's Partisans, "Simo Dubajic". It is acknowledged here that it was Dubajic who "had helped to negotiate the repatriations with Brigadier Toby Low, of British 5th Corps". In another book review I have itemized the meeting between Low and Dubajic (and Hocevar) on 15th May at Klagenfurt. The refugees and repatriations referred to at that meeting were not from Bleiburg however. Here Brooks-Pincevic quotes "Betrayal" that it was Dubajic, after 25th May, who was ordered by Tito to "finish the job" at the Kocevski pit, which was later dynamited.

Blame is attributed to those giving the orders, whether British or Yugoslav. Blame is not attributed to the soldiers by this author/painter, and this is why the Partisans have not been given faces in her paintings. But this approach, which falls into the category of the 'equal guilt' of 'all leaders' is a view adopted by the International Criminal Court established during the 1990s regarding the former Yugoslavia. She refers to Dubajic's self-described 'conditioning' yet Dubajic was not a regular soldier to be excused but a Major General! Then the Irish testimony, as per Tolstoy's book, is given in relation to 'Bleiburg' but in my book we have learned that Colin Gunner's words "orders are orders" (from a Palaich filmed interview) do not actually refer to Bleiburg per se.

In criticism I disagree that the British officers and the Yugoslav officers share equal responsibility. It was the Yugoslavs who planned and carried out the genocide, and the British officers had no foreknowledge this was going to happen. In addition, we learn from many versions reviewed in my book about the "Death Marches" that the Yugoslav soldiers were taking their "revenge" against Croats—"revenge" would not be admissible in a court as an excuse, but the constant mention of "revenge" as an excuse for the mass killings does suggest that guilt does not only lie with the 'leaders'.

Finally, eye-witness testimony (written in 1952) is revealed about the return of the defeated Croatian soldiers and civilians to Zagreb. Their miserable state is emotionally described. Some resistance and shooting occurred from some who had never left but was ineffective. From the Maksimir Park they were killed and buried in mass graves behind the Mirogoj Cemetary and elsewhere. Massacres all over the former Yugoslavia are briefly described. For example at Lasko there were at least "3,000", and at Hrastnik "7,000". At Kosice, near Celje (Slovenia) 100 war prisoners were murdered.

The power of the visual arts is strong. The original paintings brought to show in Australia from New Zealand are 'huge' and would only find a suitable wall space in a large gallery. Prints were available for sale but too expensive for most at the launch. The book itself is the lasting legacy of this author/painter. It was distributed around the world to Croatian communities who were asked to donate them to the Australian Returned Services League or to a library. I did not participate in this campaign due to the depictions of Alexander, Macmillan and Churchill looking down on Bleiburg field. I do not regret that decision as I believe that Tito and Stalin, or perhaps the three leaders at Yalta, could dominate the skyline above Bleiburg. I do not agree that the outrageous concept of "equal guilt" applies to Bleiburg, e.g. the alleged equal guilt of the British and Tito!

"The Bleiburg Massacres" in "An International Symposium Southeastern Europe 1918-1995", Ante Beljo, Croatian Heritage Foundation & Croatian Information Centre, online www.hic.hr, 1998

This interview with Nikolai Tolstoy has been written 'after' his defeat in the British libel trial where Tolstoy admitted under oath that he had "erred on the generous side" in his book about Bleiburg! This interview does not mention that however.

Tolstoy acknowledges at the outset that most of the Croatian people returned were not killed at Bleiburg but then mentions the alleged British decision to hand the Croats over "to be slaughtered". Tolstoy writes that Croats were killed "following their recrossing of the Drava" after their "involuntary repatriation".

In my previous chapters I have already presented first-hand testimony about the events at Bleiburg. Bleiburg has little to do with any "involuntary" repatriation of Croats which had occurred far to the west of Bleiburg. The Allies' decision to repatriate people after WWII originated from Stalin, Roosevelt & Churchill at Yalta. In addition, the British could not have predicted a mass slaughter on a genocide-scale that would follow. When reports of massacres filtered through weeks later the British repatriation policy changed. Tito's policy did not change however!!

In summary, there does not appear to be any great mystery as Tolstoy suggests about the repatriations which have already been historically acknowledged by the British.

The only mystery for me is why those who remember the Croatian victims continue to complicate and confuse the Bleiburg issue by generalisation or omission!

In conclusion, after a misleading introduction, Tolstoy seems to contradict himself although 'mysteriously' the date given is incorrect. Is this a typing error? Although I have mentioned this in another chapter the point cannot be emphasized enough and so is worth repeating. For example, Tolstoy gives the date 12th May instead of 15th May 1945.

> Tolstoy: "...an important matter needs to be emphasised. That is the distinction which should be drawn between the tragedy of the Croats driven back to Tito at Bleiburg on 12 May 1945, and the subsequent fate of the smaller body of Croats who remained in Austria following the Bleiburg tragedy."

In reference to the actual Bleiburg castle surrender negotiations, in this article by Tolstoy, Crljen is referred to as Herencic's interpreter. The suggestion that Scott would prevent the Croatian exodus is not given in the context of the three options given to the Croatian commanders. At least Tolstoy mentions that Basta promised the Croats would be treated humanely.

Tolstoy then refers to the arguments on "both sides" at the castle as "passionate" at this symposium. Surely if the British were actually guilty of planning a slaughter with their Yugoslav allies, Tolstoy would have said "all sides"! There is no doubt that the Croatian representatives presented a passionate plea to surrender to the British, but it is misleading to describe the Yugoslav Commissar Basta's arguments as "passionate"! Basta's belligerent behaviour was designed to bully everyone present when he threatened to start killing the Croats in 15 minutes! In addition, in the context of Bleiburg, no mention is made by Tolstoy that the Yugoslavs outnumbered the British in the Bleiburg area according to many sources. This Yugoslav capability would definitely have contributed to Basta's behaviour.

But Tolstoy is also inconsistent. In contrast to his description of Basta's behaviour at Bleiburg as "passionate", Tolstoy then describes the Yugoslav "atrocious" and "inflammatory" behaviour around Carinthia.

> "(The Yugoslavs)...openly declared their intention of annexing Southern Carinthia, where their troops were behaving with increasing truculence."

Throughout the essay Tolstoy continues to suggest a British "conspiracy". Tolstoy has already lost a court battle and acknowledged that he "erred" regarding Bleiburg, so it is disappointing to read the following unsupported anti-British propaganda.

> "...in memory of all those Croatian victims who died at the hands of the British and their Communist allies during the dark days of 1945 ..."

My disappointment turns into angry disbelief and frustration when the surrender at Bleiburg, which has been misrepresented early in this essay, is then described differently in later pages! All of a sudden, in a separate part of the essay which weaves the Bleiburg issue in and out between other repatriations, we are told by Tolstoy that Herencic, after all, did "agree to surrender to Basta" and that the British forces at the time were insufficient.

> "(insufficient) ... to obstruct the passage of the Croatian exodus for long".

Why therefore does he not say that the British forces were insufficient to obstruct the Yugoslavs at the time!!

In addition, any reference Nigel Nicholson's comment, in connection with Bleiburg, is beyond my understanding because Nicholson was at Ferlach, nowhere near Bleiburg. Of course Tolstoy is not the only person to make this incorrect inference but he is one of the sources of it.

"BRITAIN AND THE BLEIBURG TRAGEDY: AN ARTIST'S IMPRESSION: SUZANNE BROOKS-PINCEVIC", "NEW GENERATION", EDITOR, IN HRVATSKI VJESNIK, MELBOURNE, 21 AUGUST 1998

This is an article which promotes the launch of the author's new book in conjunction with the Australian Croatian Association in Melbourne on 30th August 1998. A similar presentation will be held at the Croatian Punchbowl club in Sydney in September.

In "Britain and the Bleibug Tragedy" the author discusses a century of genocide against Croatian people and the unjust stigma applied to the Croatian name, according to this article.

Concerning Part 2 of the book, the part about Bleiburg, the author/painter admitted in an interview that she didn't know much about Bleiburg until a year earlier.

> "Until a year ago, I knew only a little (about the subject) but during this past year I have read numerous books on Croatia's past—especially Bleiburg...I have talked to...John Prcela (author of Operation Slaughterhouse) in America and Count Nikolai Tolstoy in England (an author of a very controversial 1986 book about the British betrayal at Bleiburg)."

Suzanne's motive for writing and painting on this topic, apart from being married to a Croat, is "to give readers in the West a better understanding of Croatia and its violent rebirth" and to reveal the truth, giving a quotation from Tolstoy which was also in her book.

"Podignimo do Zvijezda Prah Heroja",
Poem, Ante Marinović, Poličnik, 1998

> Od Bleiburskog polja pa na dalje pale su tri generacije
> Od jedne male u srednjoj Europi tad nesretne stare nacije
> Petnaestoga Svibnja otjerani u smrt Hrvat star ne jak i mlad
> U Jugoslavenskim šumama i jamama od njih prah i kosti leže sad
>
> Baš ondje pod tuđim vedrim nebom crveni genecidni krvožedan vrag
> Započeo nastavio i ostavio po jugi svoj strašan krvavi trag
> Gdje je majki zarobljen mučen i pogubljen otac muž kći i sin drag
> Oni koji su od smrti pobjegli nisu smjeli doma natrag na svoj prag
>
> Vidim brate da želiš i hoćes opisati to strašno bolno tuđe polje
> I od Bleiburga poći naprijed na istok u pravcu Balkana dalje
> Pripremio sam zate brate bure tinte i breme penkala i olovki
> Za opisat stotine tisuća masovni grobnica Huda Jama i Jazovki
>
> Bleibursko polje je najveća nesreća i grobnica u povijesti Hrvata
> Tito i Ranković naredi i pobi djeda baku oca majku sestre i brata
> Do zvijezda prah heroja živili za Hrvatsku slobodu i samo Bogu rob
> Da vjetar nosi u milu domovinu da zagrle Starčevića oca domovine grob
>
> Slavimo i našeg velikog Tuđmana oca države i njegovu junačku Oluju
> Ljubimo i čuvajmo lijepi Božji dar Hrvatsku jedinu grudu svoju

This poem by Marinović is about the suffering of a small European nation, which lost three generations, following the Croatian surrender at Bleiburg field to Yugoslavs after 15th May 1945. The bones of soldiers and civilian Croats, young and old, lie in mass unmarked graves throughout Communist Yugoslavia. Croatian people have not forgotten this tragedy, this genocide, perpetrated by Yugoslavs after the end of the second World War. The author writes that it would take a barrel of ink and a stack of pens and pencils to describe the hundreds of thousands of Croats who vanished in gorges, trenches, ravines and pits. Bleiburg, for this author, is the biggest massacre in Croatian history. The Bleiburg Tragedy happened when Tito and Ranković ordered the killing of innocent grandfathers, grandmothers, fathers, mothers, sisters and brothers. The poet says to lift to the stars the ashes of heroes who only lived for

Croatian freedom and be slaves only to God. Let the wind take their ashes to their beautiful homeland to embrace the grave of Ante Starcević, father of the Croatian nation. Croatian people honour the father of their country, Tudjman, and Operation Storm, and cherish their homeland Croatia God's gift.

Jean and Ante Marinovic at Bleiburg Monument 2014

"BRITAIN AND THE BLEIBURG TRAGEDY SELLS OUT AT NEW ZEALAND PREVIEW WITHIN MINUTES", DAVORIN OZICH, NEW GENERATION, IN HRVATSKI VJESNIK, MELBOURNE, 21 AUGUST 1998

This is a small piece which is inset into the page about Brooks-Pincevic in the "New Generation" of 21 August 1998. The writer Davorin Ozich in Auckland New Zealand referred to the private showing of Brook-Pincevic's paintings and book on 9th August 1998. Ozich writes that "It is recorded in a way that can be understood by everyone".

"THE BLACK BOOK OF COMMUNISM: CRIMES, TERROR, REPRESSION", MARK KRAMER, CONSULTING EDITOR, ONLINE BOOK, HARVARD UNIVERSITY PRESS, CAMBRIDGE, 1999

I will discuss the entries in this book under the headings that they appear. Part I of this book is about the Soviet Union.

"The Comintern in Action", chapter 16 in Part II, "World Revolution, Civil War, and Terror" S. Courtois & J. Panne Editors

Courtois and Panne have mentioned Bleiburg on pages 323 to 326. Yugoslavia's collapse, the "resistance", WWII and Tito's coming to power are briefly described. The Croatian retreat is described, but no "Death Marches" regarding Croats is included! The number of Croats actually "on retreat" is reduced, a number which totally disagrees with established British-recorded numbers! The acknowledged order of events is drastically and inexcusably changed in this book which purports to be about the crimes of Communists. The death marches of Chetniks and Slovenians are described even though we know that these groups were in camps situated nowhere near to Bleiburg! The massacre at Kocevje is mentioned in relation to Slovenes even though it has been acknowledged that Croats were massacred there first because Croats were the first to be extradited from Villach.

> "As the German surrender approached, Pavelic and his army, his aides, and their families—in all, tens of thousands of people—set off for the Austrian frontier. Slovenian White Guards and Chetniks from Montenegro joined them in Bleiburg, where they all surrendered to British troops, who handed them over to Tito. Soldiers and policemen of all types found themselves forced to walk to their deaths, hundreds of miles across the country. The Slovenian prisoners were taken back to Slovenia near Kocevje, where as many as 30,000 were killed. In defeat, the Chetniks were unable to avoid the vengeance of the partisans..."

Surely an extensive study of Communist crimes and terror can do better than this! Yes, well in Part III the above version is expanded.

"Central and Southeastern Europe" chapter 20 in Part III "The Other Europe: Victim of Communism" Karel Bartosek, Editor

On pages 397 to 398 Bartosek refers to the Communist bloodthirsty "monopoly on power" in Yugoslavia under Josip Broz "Tito". The wartime and post-war bloodbath in Yugoslavia is discussed where 1 million people died but the ethnicity of the victims is not identified.

> "...and the genocide and purges ensured that at the moment of liberation, Tito and the Communist Party had hardly any political rivals left. They swiftly set about eliminating them all the same."

In conclusion it is a travesty of justice and a tragedy that Croatian victims have not been identified in this book written several years after the collapse of Yugoslavia.

"Cetverored: Prica o Bleiburgu", Jakov Sedlar, film for Croatian television and VHS, Zagreb, 1999

This film in the Croatian language tells the story about Bleiburg, as written by Ivan Aralica. The retreat of Croatian civilians and soldiers from Zagreb in early May 1945 is illustrated by a dramatisation of the events. My interest in this film is to only to see how the surrender at Bleiburg is interpreted, and whether or not the numbers there are mentioned.

Considerable dramatic license has been employed by Sedlar in the re-enactment of the surrender negotiations at the Bleiburg castle. When the British general is talking in English, sub-titles in Croatian are used. In my opinion Sedlar's film does not accurately represent the negotiations at the Bleiburg castle and instead it distorts the truth. Sedlar's dramatic license has no limits. For example, the film-maker attributes the words of Winston Churchill to Brigadier Scott, in a fictitious conversation between Scott and his adjudant.

In the first scene at the castle Scott is telling the Croats that the British army cannot accept their surrender in reference to Yalta. Scott allegedly says to the Croats that "Tito is our Ally—-you were fighting against him—therefore you are Tito's prisoners." But Scott never actually said any of this to the Croats at the time. Scott wrote something similar in his Report a few weeks later in reference to orders from a higher authority.

Next the scene is set with the Yugoslav Commissar Basta and the Croats together, in another case of the use, or misuse, of dramatic license. We know however that such a meeting between the Yugoslavs and the Croats did not happen, from original testimonies and Reports. What actually happened was that the first meeting was between Scott and Basta; the second meeting was between Scott and the Croats; and the third meeting was with all armies present.

In this re-enactment of events in the second scene Basta allegedly speaks to the Croats about the terms of surrender even though Sedlar has not yet mentioned them in their correct context.

> Basta: "You may not like it and we may not like it—but we must do it—can we please stick to the terms of the surrender."

Then the Croatian General Herencic allegedly says that they would have surrendered to the Partisans in "our own country" and that they (Croats) went on this journey to surrender to the western Allies because Communists don't recognize international conventions of war.

In the next scene the written words from Scott's later Report are allegedly spoken to Herencic about there being no need to leave Croatia. As Herencic is speaking the camera turns to the Yugoslav Commissar sitting by himself.

Scott continues and he allegedly tells Herencic that he is deceived because

> "Tito personally promised to General Alexander that all prisoners would be humanely treated".

Herencic made the case that this surrender was about ordinary people asking for political protection from western countries. Scott retorted that as a soldier he did "not wish to discuss politics please". In another misuse of dramatic license, in reality, parts of this conversation between Scott and the Croats did not take place in front of the Yugoslav Commissar.

The next scene shows an arrogant Basta laughing and smirking to himself as he is alleged to have immediately demanded that the Croats "must surrender". Basta made it clear that the Croats had one hour, or else they would be attacked from air and land after 15 minutes. It did not matter that civilians were there according to this version.

It is important to note at this point that in Sedlar's version no interpreter appears or is mentioned. It's important because immediately following Basta's brazen threats Scott is alleged to have immediately answered back to him, in yet another distortion of the events.

> Scott: "This is a humane and reasonable offer and in accordance with agreement with all our Allies."

In actual fact this statement by Scott was given to the Croats when Basta was not present, and it was in relation to the three options given to the Croatian representatives at the negotiations. Scott did not say this in the presence of Basta, and on the contrary Scott actually protested to Basta about the time-frame! This is another clear case of dramatic license being used to distort the chronological order of events and change the nature of what happened at the castle. It distorts the eye-witness testimony of those present as presented in the book "Operation Slaughterhouse" two decades earlier.

The scene then shows all three military groups together as Herencic asks for a few minutes to consult, to which Scott agrees. We know from eye-witness testimony that it did not happen like that. The Croatian leaders consulted with each other in a separate room from Basta. In the next scene the three Croatian representatives talk amongst themselves, though still in the same room with the others, for less than one minute in the Croatian language. In this scene by Sedlar the Croats then complain to the British general that more time was needed to inform their units.

The Yugoslav Commissar Basta then interrupts and nastily threatens that one hour is enough.

> Basta: "not one minute longer."

At this time the British Brigadier Scott said the Croats should be given two hours. In reality Scott asked for a "longer" time. Basta reaffirmed that the time limit is one hour. Herencic, using Scott's suggestion, asked Basta why he does not take Scott's advice, and Basta is shown smiling throughout the negotiation.

Sedlar's final scene shows two British, three Croats, and one Partisan. In actual fact there were two or more British, three Croats, two Partisans, and an interpreter. This next scene is the worst when it comes to dramatic license. Scott allegedly leans forward with a very stern look to speak.

> Scott: "Gentlemen we must finish this—-you are surrounded by British tanks".

Speaking then to Basta, Scott asks him to initiate the surrender "under your own terms" and that his tanks and aircraft are at his disposal in one hour. In actual fact, this logistical position by Scott was delivered privately to the Croatian generals as part of one of three options, and not in the presence of Basta.

Drums play loudly in the background as Herencic allegedly tells Scott that history will not forgive him.

> Herencic: "(if) ... you let 300,000 Croats to be massacred by Partisans and Greater Serbs".

This comment would suggest that there were 300,000 Croats at the Bleiburg field. In an alleged response to this Basta is alleged to have answered Herencic.

> Basta: "Fascist propaganda."

This fictitious dramatisation of the castle negotiations finishes showing the British general with a somewhat devious expression on his face!

Many Croats would not understand why it is important to correctly represent 'how' the negotiations played out because they believe the film generally portrays the truth. So why is it important to make a distinction between what was said, where, and to whom, and when?

For one thing, Sedlar's version does not really highlight Basta's acknowledgement to Scott that the Yugoslavs would treat the Croats fairly according to international law. In addition, we know from many sources that the British aims and the Yugoslav aims were different. At that time the war-weary British were under orders to pacify the occupying Yugoslavs to avoid another war, and also not to accept the surrender of any more refugees. In contrast, the goal of the Yugoslavs was to carry out a violent revolution and liquidate the Croats. This was the 15th May 1945. There had been no other repatriations up to this time!

"Yalta and the Bleiburg Tragedy", Michael McAdams, online Dalmatia.net, 1999

This is a condensed version in English from a chapter in a book "Od Bleiburga do Nasih Dana" (Edited by Jozo Marovic, Skolska Kniga, 1995) presented at an "International Symposium for Investigation of the Bleiburg Tragedy" in Zagreb in May 1994.

The author Michael McAdams alleges that the Bleiburg-Maribor massacres were part of Operation Keelhaul although today this does not appear to be accepted as fact. International treaties and laws are discussed in this presentation, and I strongly disagree with the following strange statement by McAdams.

> McAdams: "Bleiburg is a model for all the forced repatriations in post-war Europe".

This argument cannot be sustained when all the facts were revealed. Once again, like in several other sources, the retreat of several other nationalities is incorrectly mentioned in the context of Bleiburg.

This presentation refers to the post-WWII departure of the "Croatian officials" and that the Archbishop Metropolitan Aloysius Stepinac was given charge of the government in their absence, until the arrival of the Partisans. McAdams mentions that by 1st May a "peace emissary", Minister Vrancic was sent to Italy, and that it was on 1st May that 200,000 civilians and as many Croatian armed forces began their exodus from Zagreb, to arrive at the Austrian border by 7th May 1945. These dates are incorrect because they do not apply to the bulk of the retreating soldiers and civilians from Zagreb. Next the text jumps to the arrival at Bleiburg by 14th or 15th May.

Then at this point the group of government ministers is mentioned. Typically, the description of the Croatian retreating columns, some of whom made it through to Bleiburg, is integrated with the situation experienced by various other groups (including some Croats) who, in fact, were to be sent back to Yugoslavia from a different region at a later date.

So far in this so-called investigation it would appear that the Pavelic group, government ministers, all Croatian columns, and those interned elsewhere were all part of the same event at Bleiburg. In addition, even though Bleiburg is supposed to be a "model" the surrender negotiations are not even mentioned!

This integral Bleiburg model is justified by McAdams like many authors before him.

> McAdams: "... the tragedy of Bleiburg was not a single event, but hundreds of events over a long period of time ..."

I believe it's because of this type of generalisation, which ignores eye-witness testimony, that the truth about Bleiburg is disappearing into a black hole. Of course I include myself amongst those who have been misled and as a result have written articles about Bleiburg which give either incorrect information or little analysis.

"Outcast Without Guilt or My Way of the Cross: Four Months of a Young Home Guard Alias Hrvatski Domobran", Zvonko Springer, online www.cosy.sbg.ac.at/~zzspri/, 1999

Zvonko Springer has published a free book online of his post-war experiences during and after May 1945. This book is an autobiographical version of his withdrawal from Zagreb with other soldiers and civilians, their capture by Yugoslavs, and the "Death Marches" or "Way of the Cross".

I mention this book because equally it's important to note what it does not say, in helping us to establish the numbers who actually crossed the Austrian border into Bleiburg. None of his chapters mention Bleiburg. Chapters 12 to 15, deal with

> "Withdrawal of Croatians"; "Night of Surrender"; "Surrender and Imprisonment"; and "Begin of My Way of Cross".

The withdrawal route of Croats from Zagreb is described in detail from Krapina, Rogaska Slatina, Celje, along the Paka River to Velenje, Dolic, Straze, Turiska Vas, Smartno, to Slovenj Gradec on 14th May 1945. He describes a St. Ana church and a hill Otiski Vrh which is about five miles from the Drava River. He mentions a junction of roads "Hanzic and Kotije".

On the night of 14th May his group of Home Guards surrendered to the Yugoslavs and joined others who were herded back to Yugoslavia. Not everyone took the same exact routes and this author alleges that the Ustasha were in command of the retreat of the Home Guards most of the way. A photograph appears in Springer's book from an "undisclosed" location. The location in this photograph appears to be the same as in the signpost photograph discussed in a later chapter with other photographs.

"Maribor Building Monument to Post-WWII Victims", Vlado Zagorac, "Croatia Weekly", Zagreb, No. 71, June 10 1999

In 1999 another mass grave made headlines, and this time in Slovenia. Yugoslavia as a multinational state was gone and Slovenia and Croatia were independent since 1992. Slovenia was already in the European Union. The article's opening statement describes the "Death Marches" and post-WWII massacres.

> Zagorac: "... thousands of Croats, prisoners of war, who were forced to walk from Bleiburg, an Austrian place where many soldiers and civilians surrendered to the Allies after World War II to their homeland (an ordeal referred to by the Croats as the "Way of the Cross") and then slaughtered in massacres on the outskirts of Maribor."

It was along the "Slivnica – Pesnica highway" that the mass graves were discovered during the highway's construction work. The anti-tank trench was 70 meters long. According to the Mayor of Maribor the monument will be dedicated to 'post-war' victims.

> "all war victims after May 9, 1945."

Here the government "protected area" is referred to. Although this article refers to victims from "Croatia and Montenegro", later DNA tests and other investigations confirmed that the remains were of Croatian people on "Death Marches".

"Preserve Maribor World War II Genocide Evidence", Jean W. Marinovic, Hrvatski Vjesnik, 23 July 1999

Although my original heading referred to "**post-World War II**" **genocide**, the heading and text was published as "world war II" genocide. I refer in this article to the discovery of 1179 skeletons during construction of the Slovenian 'Slivnica – Pesnica' section of highway (Maribor's eastern bypass highway). In any case I make a typical and confusing mistake when I write that the 'Bleiburg Genocide' described tens of thousands of Croatian POW bodies and others who had been told by British forces in post WW II Austria that they were being transported by rail to Italy. I cite "Operation Slaughterhouse" and "The Minister and the Massacres".

My article however is more about the alleged decision of the Maribor City Council to have these remains 'cremated' and I argue that there is no historical precedent for this. I must have read this information somewhere at the time, but it seems to contradict the article (read later) I have reviewed about the creation of a Maribor Monument to the victims. In my article I suggest that Croats should follow the example of others I discussed such as a Katyn memorial or the Cambodian data base of victims of Pol Pot.

> "... in Croatia ... a data base, a memorial 'wall', and an 'Interpretive Centre' ... (should be created for post-war Croatian victims)".

I finish by concluding that "every Croatian family has its own Bleiburg victim". My original 1999 internet "web-site Croatia Zadar" was also published with this article, www.tenex.com.au/users/antem/index.html

A Slovenian government 'Commission on Concealed Mass Graves in Slovenia' was created in 2005 and gave its report in 2009. I will mention this in more detail in a subsequent chapter.

CHAPTER 8

2000s

"Ethnicity and Identity in the Cold War: The Carinthian Border Dispute, 1945-1949", Robert Knight, 'The International History Review', University of Toronto Press, (pages 253—504) Downsview, 2000

Robert Knight's analysis in the "International History Review" of the Carinthian border dispute is helpful in understanding Tito's motives at the end of the war, and their immediate effect on his former Western Allies.

> Knight: "Southern Carinthia became an epicentre of East-West conflict within hours of the end of the Second World War … After British and Yugoslav troops confronted each other in the Carinthian capital of Klagenfurt on 8 May … the stand-off lasted for two weeks until Marshall Tito, under Western and Soviet pressure, ordered a withdrawal…"

"Do Not Bury Bleiburg", Suzanne Brooks-Pincevic, Nova Hrvatska (page 11), Sydney 25—31 January 2000; and in 'New Generation', Hrvatski Vjesnik (page 2), Melbourne, 28 January 2000 Melbourne, (January 2000)

This article, published in both the Melbourne and Sydney Croatian-Australian newspapers, is placed in the context of today's political turmoil in Croatia. The author discusses the importance and relevance of remembering the Bleiburg Tragedy. The BBC and CNN are attacked for their anti-Croatian slander and pro-Serbian reporting. In the 'Nova Hrvatska' version of this article, Brooks-Pincevic resorts to coarse provocative language to make her point. She switches back and forth between 19th century history, the history of WWII, and the 1990s Serbian war of aggression. In spite of the title "Do Not Bury Bleiburg" the author barely mentions Bleiburg! Nevertheless Brooks-Pincevic asks readers to purchase her book, "Britain and the Bleiburg Tragedy" and to circulate it. The New Generation article, in Hrvatski Vjesnik has published a condensed version without some of the 'unsophisticated' language!

"Bleiburg in today's 'anti-fascist' political culture", Jean Lunt Marinovic, page 17 Spremnost Hrvatski Tjednik, Sydney 25 July 2000

As the title suggests this article is a tirade about an alleged anti-fascist culture. I argue that if a book is to be published in the western mainstream society it must not cross any politically correct boundaries. I suggest that Communist ideology has actually gained currency in the west since the fall of the Berlin Wall. Because there have been many ideological about-faces in European history I surmise that it is difficult to find lasting support regarding responsibility for the Bleiburg genocide. Time will tell.

Within this framework I compare and contrast the book by the late Jerry Blaskovich M.D., "Anatomy of Deceit: An American Physician's First-hand Encounter with the Realities of the War in Croatia", with books such as A. McAdam's "Croatia: Myth and Reality". A debate in the Australian-Croatian media between Blaskovich and Brooks-Pincevic is the focus of my article. In this article I describe Brooks-Pincevic's book as a "graphic reminder" about Bleiburg, and I commended Blaskovich's candid eye-witness account of the 1990s Serbian siege on Croatia. However I criticized Blaskovich on his opinion about Bleiburg.

In an article in Spremnost Hrvatski Tjednik on 23rd May 2000 Blaskovich writes that Bleiburg was of little significance in Croatian culture!

> Blaskovich: "Bleiburg has little relevance in any discussion of the events of 1990-91 ... Bleiburg wasn't by any stretch of the imagination a holocaust ... few Croats living in Croatia had heard of Bleiburg ... (Bleiburg) wasn't in anyone's thoughts in the 1971 movement ...

"Pokraj tvornice Impol 1948. spaljena trupla 4000 Hrvata" (Next to the factory 'Impol' 1948 were burned 4000 Croatian corpses), Suzana Barilar, Kristina Turcin, page 8 Hrvatski Vjesnik, Melbourne 2001

The title tells the story of yet another mass grave in Slovenia. A photograph shows the entrance to the mass grave in 'Slovenia Bistrica' where remains of 4000 Croatian

Ustasha, Domobrani and civilians were interred. It is alleged in this article that these 4000 came from Bleiburg to this location which is 20 kilometers from Maribor.

A sub-heading "Grobnica Paveliceve vlade" (Graves of Pavelic's government) states that in Slovenia there are graves of up to 190,000 Croats. 1000 mass graves are discussed in this full-page article in the Croatian language.

"Englezi, Bleiburg i Stjepan Mesic!", Marjan Bosnjak page 12, Hrvatski Vjesnik, Melbourne, 18 May 2001

Above the author's title his concluding statement is also part of a header.

> Bosnjak: "Tesko je vjerovati da, unatoc nepobitnim povijesnim cinjenicama, vodeci ljudi u sadasnjoj vlasti jos odlaze na partizanske proslave i jos pohvalno govore o "drugovima" i o "narodno—osloboditeljskoj borbi" ("It is hard to believe that, despite the undeniable historical facts, leading people in the present government still attend partisan celebrations and deliver commendable speeches about "comrades" and the "Peoples Liberation War".)

After the author's title is another sub-heading, also part of the author's conclusion which, like the title itself, suggests that the "English" are responsible for Bleiburg and for the betrayal of western values and customary norms of war.

> Bosnjak: "Petnaestoga svibnja 1945, u reziji engleske politike, dogodio se dan prevare i dan izdaje gotovo svih proklamiranih zapadnih vrijednosti i uobicajenih ratnih normi." (Bosnjak: On 15th May 1945, as directed by English politics, came the day of deception and betrayal of all proclaimed western values and customary norms of war.)

Of course the war was already over one week before the 15th May 1945.

In this full page article in the Croatian language, according to Marjan Bosnjak, on 14th May 1945 the English were aware of the approaching Croatian soldiers numbering about 200,000 plus 500,000 Croatian civilians, in a column which stretched back for 50 kilometers. Bosnjak describes the commanding officers present at Bleiburg as an English general who had come from Klagenfurt, Brigadier Scott, and General Herencic, Servatzy and Colonel Crljen. Like many others he does not mention the interpreter who was present at all negotiations.

It is interesting that some authors refer to an English rather than a British army. For example, many officers were of Scottish ancestry. In addition, it was the Yalta agreement which determined the outcome of already surrendered POWs in Austria before the 15th May and not English politics.

Bosnjak's version of the actual meeting at Bleiburg Castle is very brief however and he gives an impression which differs from what actually happened. For example he did not mention the guarantee of the Yugoslavs that the surrendered Croats would be treated according to international law. Instead it appears in this article as if the "ultimatum" came from both the English and the Partisans when, in fact, from the beginning it was the Partisans who were expressing impatience and an unreasonable time frame. He has not mentioned the strong Yugoslav occupying armies who were already in Austria at the time but instead suggests that the Partizans arrived at Bleiburg a few hours before.

According to this author at a 1pm meeting the Croats were informed that Scott had the explicit command of Marshal Alexander and Winston Churchill that Croats must surrender to Tito's Partisans. The English would support the order with the strength they had in the Bleiburg area. Then at 3pm the Croats and English would meet with the Partisan Colonels Milan Basta and Ivan Kovacic and that, at this meeting, the Partisans and English commanders delivered an ultimatum that the surrender must occur in 15 minutes after returning to the field.

Bosnjak does not acknowledge that the ultimatum was coming solely from the Yugoslav side and that the British officer actually objected to the time frame.

The author writes that the Croats were taken away from Bleiburg by both the Partisans and the English and in this way they were deceived about their destination and thought they were going to the west instead of to Maribor.

> Bosnjak: "... partizanskih i engleskih vojnika odvedena preko austrijskog teritorija (kako bi mislili da idu una zapad), ali natrag prema Mariboru." (...Partisans and the English took them through Austrian territory [thought was going to the west], but back to Maribor")

It is likely, according to sources reviewed here, that the routes taken 'away' from Bleiburg were to the south-east or the north-east. Is it possible that Croatian officers and soldiers did not know they were going through Austria along the same direction from which they came? One British eye-witness reported that the Croats were taken across the fields and not by roads.

The article continues that a massive liquidation apparently started at Bleiburg, in contradiction to facts since revealed that the "Death Marches" began 'before'

Bleiburg. At least Bosnjak quotes Milovan Djilas which at last attributes blame to the Yugoslavs! The author deduces that between 200 and 300 thousand Croats died – 100 thousand soldiers, 100 thousand civilians, and the rest who escaped overseas.

> Djilas: "Hrvati morali umrijeti kako bi Jugoslavija mogla zivjeti" (Croats must die that Yugoslavia can live.)

This article describes the mass grave locations and lays blame on Yugoslav "bratstvo i jedinstvo" (brotherhood and unity) and on English policy, as suggested in the text and also in the heading.

Because the author does not mention the Yalta convention, or that the Yugoslav Commissar guaranteed that the Croats would receive fair treatment as POWs, or the crisis in Carinthia caused by the large belligerent Yugoslav Army, the alleged "day of deception and betrayal" can be tied to "English politics".

The author Marjan Bosnjak, who lived in Melbourne for many years, translated the book "Bleiburg memento", 2005, and is the son of Pero Bosnjak whose comment on Bleiburg appeared in "50 Godina Bleiburga", 1995. He also became a leading member of the "Only Croatia" Movement founded in 2007 which lobbied against Croatian membership of the EU or NATO.

"Jedino Hrvatska" (Only Croatia) signs in Zadar 2007 an anti--EU, anti--NATO Movement for Croatia. Croatia joined NATO in 2009 and EU in 2013

"Bleiburg i BBC" (Britain and the BBC), Marina Skrobica, page 7 Spremnost Hrvatski Tjednik, Sydney, 22 May 2001

This article, in Croatian, is about a BBC program "Reflections on the Holocaust" screened on 27 January 2001 on BBC2. In this article Skrobica suggests that an objective BBC editor would have mentioned Bleiburg. The author incorrectly claims that this BBC program does not mention Bleiburg because the British in Bleiburg sent 150,000 Croatian refugees in cattle wagons like in Auschwitz.

Of course this did not happen at Bleiburg, not by any stretch of the imagination! Also, the British did not send back to Yugoslavia in train cars the number of 150,000 Croatian refugees. The number of 25,000 Croats has been given by British officers, who also repatriated Slovenes and Serbs south of Klagenfurt.

"Bleiburg i Krizni put kao opomena" (Bleiburg and The Way of the Cross as a Warning), M. Barisic, page 12 'Vjesnik', Zagreb, 15—21 May 2001

This article discusses the situation at the Bleiburg field where tens of thousands of Croatian soldiers and civilians were trapped. Some numbers of Croatian victims are mentioned. According to this article, Djilas said that between 20,000 and 30,000 Croats were liquidated. Tudjman puts the figure at between 35,000 to 40,000 and Tolstoy mentions 60,000 who died on "Death Marches". There is no information in this article about the surrender at Bleiburg, and a photograph without caption appears of a camp. I notice that Vukusic in his book "Bleiburg Memento: fotomonografija" (2005) has identified this camp as being located at Maksimir.

"Kako je 1945 Izrucena Hrvatska Drzavna Vlada" (How The Croatian State government was extradited in 1945), Josip Davorin, (in Argentina in 'Godisnjak' 1954), published in 3 parts in Spremnost Hrvatski Tjednik, Sydney, page 7 -- 15 May 2001; page 12 -- 22 May 2001; page 5 of 29 May 2001

This three-part article is about the extradition of the Croatian government from the British zone to Yugoslavia in 1945 after the war. It is important to mention in my book because it shows the distinction between this Croatian "government" extradition and what happened at Bleiburg field. Next to the article a photograph shows the Maria Elend train station in Austria. The map shows Klagenfurt (Celovec), and Villach (Beljak) in Austria, and Jesenice inside Slovenia. Bleiburg, farther to the East, is not on this map.

"52 Obiljetnica Bleiburga, Austria" (52ⁿᴰ Anniversary of Bleiburg), Dr Ante Simonic, page 7 Spremnost Hrvatski Tjednik, Sydney, 29 May 2001

The representative of the Croatian government for education, science and culture, Dr Simonic, gave an address on Bleiburg during his stay in Sydney Australia. Commenting on the importance of remembering the Bleiburg tragedy, he said that it was the largest symbol of Croatian national suffering since the sixteenth century. The sixteenth century battle of Krbava Field was a defensive battle against the Ottomans; and the eleventh century battle of Gvozd Mountain was against the Hungarians. On this same page another article on Bleiburg appears, under the heading, "Fra Nikola Mate Roscic" and it is mentioned below.

"GOVOR FRA NIKOLA MATE ROSCIC" (A TALK BY FATHER NIKOLA MATE ROSCIC), FR N. M. ROSCIC, PAGES 7—8 SPREMNOST HRVATSKI TJEDNIK, SYDNEY, 29 MAY 2001

In his talk in Croatian at Bleiburg field Fr Roscic describes Bleiburg as "Our Katyn Forest". Personally I no longer accept this comparison with Katyn, because Bleiburg happened at the end of the war, and Katyn happened during the war. The Katyn tragedy is similar only because it involves a mass grave, and it remained hidden from public scrutiny for a time. The "Death Marches" and mass graves of Croats 'after WWII' are on a far bigger scale both numerically and geographically than Katyn.

After a general description of events and the "Death Marches" or "Way of the Cross" in a religious context, he says in reference to the castle at Bleiburg, and the Bleiburg field, that for Croats hell began there. In his talk Fr Roscic quotes Nigel Nicholson, and Lord Cowgill. Nicholson was referring to his post-war zone of Austria, which we now clearly know was nowhere near Bleiburg. Fr Roscic then misinterprets Cowgill's remarks about the British General Scott.

> Fr Roscic: "Brigadni britanski general, Patrick Scott je priopcio i savjetovao da se s kolonom iz Hrvatske "trebalo postupati kao s ilegalnim bandama". Tako su, nazalost, i postupili najodgovorniji engleski politicari i vojni zapovjednici, kako se jasno moze utvrditi iz brojne pouzdane dokumentacije o Bleiburgu koju nije mogao presutjeti i zanemariti ni takozvani "Cowgillov izvjestaj". Oni su odgovorni!" (Fr Roscic: The Brigadier General Patrick Scott announced and advised that the Columns from Croatia 'should be treated as illegal bands'. Thus unfortunately the most responsible English politicians and military commanders, as can be clearly ascertained from numerous reliable documentation about Bleiburg which even the so-called Cowgill Report could not keep silent and ignore. They are responsible!)

To complete this annual coverage about Bleiburg, on the same page as this article, yet another article appears, "Medju nama: ... Bleiburg, Bleiburg ..." and below is a brief review.

"MEDJU NAMA:...BLEIBURG, BLEIBURG..." (AMONGST US: ...BLEIBURG, BLEIBURG ...), DAMIR BOROVCAK, PAGE 8 SPREMNOST HRVATSKI TJEDNIK, SYDNEY, 29 MAY 2001

Beside a photograph of Count Nikolai Tolstoy this author discusses the Bleiburg tragedy in general, relying heavily on Tolstoy's book, in the context of Operation

Keelhaul and Toby Low. Operation Keelhaul of course deals with the British repatriations to the Soviet Union as does the majority of Tolstoy's book.

Because Borovcak relies so heavily on Tolstoy, it is important for me to add a criticism I have not focussed on until now, about his book "The Minister and the Massacres". One cannot help but notice a moral injustice because throughout Tolstoy's book the Orthodox victims have "souls", and the Croatian victims have "bodies"!

"Lessons from Bleiburg", Jean Lunt Marinovic, Melbourne; page 10 Nova Hrvatska, Sydney, 22—28 May 2001; page 15 Spremnost Hrvatski Tjednik, Sydney, 29 May 2001

The editor of Nova Hrvatska has put an impressionist painting which represents Bleiburg along with my article. The editor in Spremnost used a photograph of the original monument at the Bleiburg field, and at the bottom the 'signpost' photograph appears. In this article I delve into Croatian history in a typical narrative which includes a "history of duplicity" across the centuries. I also tie the censorship of Bleiburg in the world media to the ongoing 1990s Yugoslav aggression against Croatia, and the policies of UNPROFOR. In this article I mention that, at the time of the collapse of Yugoslavia, I was at university studying the nature of Yugoslav politics!

The talk around the campus in 1990—1991 by the pro-Yugoslav 'left' groups was that Tito was a "Stalinist". The professors had been teaching that all along, that is that Tito had a Bolshevik phase between 1945 and 1948 before Stalin's split with him. The extreme 'leftists' were holding lunch-time meetings on campus to suggest that the 1990s 'Balkan civil war' was the fault of so-called nationalist imperialist leaders such as Milosevic and "Tudman [sic]".

When it comes to details about Bleiburg itself, in this article, I make the same mistakes as many others whom I have already criticized. I discuss the Geneva Convention and how "hundreds of thousands of disarmed Croats after WWII lost their lives". Seeming to suggest that "hundreds of thousands" made it to Bleiburg, I then surmise that an official Allied acknowledgement of the Bleiburg massacres should be forthcoming. On the point about the Geneva Convention and the Allies I am incorrect, because I had not done enough research. It is the pro-Yugoslavs in Croatia, since the collapse of Yugoslavia, who should be acknowledging the Bleiburg massacres officially and clearly rather than justifying it! It is the Yugoslavs who disregarded the Geneva Convention in their pursuit and treatment of their enemy who was trying to escape being slaughtered after the war.

I am critical of Cowgill's Report on the repatriations from Austria in 1945. In this article it would appear that I prefer Tolstoy's version about massacres in the Bleiburg field rather than Cowgill's. On this point I am wrong but I did not know it at the time. I also make my own judgment that Cowgill does not say where the border is except "the frontier between Dravograd and Bleiburg ". I now believe that the original borders were accepted by the British. I have since reviewed more books on the topic to discover the truth.

I make another error when I criticize Cowgill's Report that there was a confrontation between Tito and the British, and suggest instead that the Allies helped and encouraged the Partisans to penetrate Austria. Since reading the entire book by Lindsay "Beacons in the Night" it is obvious that the Allies had one intention, namely to defeat the Nazi's in Austria, while the Partisans' intention was to sabotage the Allies and occupy part of Austria after the war.

My article concludes with a comment that a chronic source of instability across the centuries in the Balkans has been the competition by "rival imperialists". But then I suggest that regional stability also depends upon the ability of Croatian people to reconcile their own historical issues, instead of looking outside their borders for approval. This point has been paraphrased by the Editor as a sub-title in Nova Hrvatska. Unfortunately I cannot blame anyone but myself for that because I do not tie-in the issue of Bleiburg in my conclusion.

"Dr Jere Jareb Komentira Izjavu Ljubljanske Drzavne Tuziteljice Grobistu Kraj Radovljice: Ministri NDH Nisu Pokopani u Sloveniji" (Dr Jere Jareb Commentary on Statement of the Ljubljana State Prosecutor about the graves near Radovljice: Ministers of NDH [Independent State of Croatia] are not buried in Slovenia), Zeljko Kruselj, page 8 Hrvatski Vjesnik, Melbourne, 2 November 2001

Some articles are important for what they do not say as well as what they do say. In this article Zeljko Kruselj reports that a Slovenian Zdenka Cerar was investigating the mass grave near Radovljice Slovenia, south of Jesenice. It was thought that some of those Croatian government ministers who left Zagreb at the beginning of May might be buried there. However Dr Jere Jareb, a Croatian historian, claimed that the mass grave did 'not' hold the government ministers but rather those who served under them, or members of the military of Independent State of Croatia (NDH).

Kruselj discusses the fate of the various Croatian government leaders including some who were killed during the war. According to this source only five state ministers were repatriated on 18th May 1945, by train via Jesenice to Radovljice, and the rest escaped to the West. It would be safe to conclude that these Croatian government ministers were never at any time close to Bleiburg.

"The Former Yugoslavia", in "Stupid White Men ... and Other Sorry Excuses for the State of the Nation!", Michael Moore, Penguin Books, Camberwell, (page 188—190), 2002

This might seem like an odd book to review, in a book about the Bleiburg Tragedy, but Moore's scandalous claim about Tito makes it relevant. Perhaps Moore has been duped by Yugoslav propaganda, or perhaps he is pro-Yugoslav, or perhaps he just thinks the former Yugoslavia is good material for a joke.

Initially Moore describes the former Yugoslavia as a "godforsaken" place which has been the source of the world's "collective misery" for a century. He asserts that millions died in the twentieth century due to Yugoslavian misbehaviour, but his solution to end Yugoslav violence is to raise Tito from the dead in a billions-of-dollars "Lazarus Project"!

> Moore: "for nearly forty years the people of Yugoslavia stopped killing each other. They became a civilized country . . . Then Tito died and all hell broke loose. Croats started killing Serbs. Serbs killed Muslims in Bosnia. Serbs killed Albanians in Kosovo..."

Moore is wrong on two main points. Many people knew by that time that Tito had massacred over half a million unarmed people after WWII, and that Yugoslavia had more Amnesty International political prisoners per capita than the Soviet Union. The peace, for Croats, under Tito was the peace of the grave.

In addition the world media reported that the recent war in the former Yugoslavia began when Serbs inside Croatia began bombing Croats. That is how it began and that is why UNPROFOR was first created. For example, in Australia a respected academic and renowned author, Robert Manne, wrote "We Must Rescue Croatia" on 13th December 1991 (Herald Sun newspaper, Melbourne). Manne described the one-sided Yugoslav aggression against Croatia and Croatian civilians by the Yugoslav

Army, Air Force, and Navy, and that in the most savage aggression since WWII over 10,000 Croats have been killed by bombs, and 100,000 homes and 200 Catholic churches have been destroyed.

"The Balkans Conspiracy",
Vladimir Orsag, Ginninderra Press, Charnwood ACT, 2002

This is a 327-page novel by Vladimir Orsag in the English language. The novel is set against the backdrop of Tito's brutal regime and an alleged conspiracy between the eastern and western intelligence "fraternities". Orsag's one-page Epilogue refers to General Willoughby's Foreward in "Operation Slaughterhouse", and the BBC documentary "Betrayal". He refers to an English journalist's (George Urban) interview, in Encounter (December 1979) with Milovan Djilas. Djilas was the vice-President of Yugoslavia until 1954. Orsag quotes Djilas who generalizes about the fate of "these people".

> "The British did the completely wrong thing in putting these people across the border, as we did the completely wrong thing in shooting them all!"

Orsag writes that this media revelation resulted eventually in the inscription "Yalta Victims Memorial" on a memorial plaque which he criticizes for its failure to identify the perpetrators or victims. Orsag questions whether this Yalta memorial is just "another example of the global conspiracy against humanity". Yet again the facts about the Bleiburg tragedy are interwoven with conspiracy theory allegations.

"Kako Je u Posljednjih 60 Godina Nestalo 2.5 milijuna Hrvata"
(How in the past 60 years 2.5 million Croats have disappeared),
Don Anto Bakovic, Editor, pages 12—13
Narod, Zagreb, 15 February 2003

This well-known author in Croatia who deals with demographic issues writes in the Croatian language. Under this heading, ten issues have been raised which have contributed to a falling population in Croatia. The second issue raised is entitled, "Tragedija Bleiburg" (Bleiburg Tragedy).

Bakovic describes the Bleiburg tragedy as the biggest slaughter of Croats in Croatian history. He typically claims that the Croatian columns surrendered to the English, and that the English disarmed them and submitted them to the Partisans. Bakovic puts all the deaths of all Croats after WWII into the symbolic context of Bleiburg.

"Promocije – Cuvari Bleiburske Uspomene" (Promotion – Guards of the Bleiburg Memory), Ivana Rora, page 51 Matica Casopis Hrvatske matice iseljenika, no. 5, May 2003

This article, in Croatian, appears in the "Croatian Heritage Foundation" journal. It is a promotion for a new book entitled, "Cuvari Bleiburske Uspomene" by Josip Jurevic, Bruno Eish, and Bozo Vukusic. No details about the surrender at Bleiburg are in this promotional article.

"Commemoration of 'Bleiburg': Croatia's Reason To Be...", Suzanne Brooks-Pincevic, page 4 New Generation in Hrvatski Vjesnik, Melbourne, 13 June 2003

This article is a prime example of anti-western, anti-British, and anti-English hatred, and unfortunately it is in English. Much of the information has come from the book by Ivo Omrcanin, "Enigma Tito" which I have reviewed in my book. The British are incorrectly blamed for their "interference" in creating the first Yugoslavia. Typically, in addition, the British are blamed for their creation of Communist Yugoslavia. Such claims need to be criticized. However, I do not blame anyone for believing the arguments of Ivo Omrcanin and some others who look for fault outside their own borders. I was also influenced by the same propaganda for many years.

Yes, it is partly true that the British did help to facilitate the Tito-Subasic union but in the fight against Nazism who else did they have to turn to? First I would suggest that no second Yugoslavia could have been created without the Croats who were in both Tito's and Subasic's government. Secondly, the Allies had no one else to turn to in the region, because unfortunately Croatia was the only nation in Europe which remained loyal to the Fascists and Nazis until the final hour on VE day! Any attempt to 'change sides' came too late when the war was over! The Croats even thwarted an earlier Croatian pro-western plot during the war.

As for the claim that the British created the First Yugoslavia, the truth is finally coming out that the pan-Slavic diehards in Croatia were responsible for that idea also. (see my Appendix) Two thirds of the way through this article by Brooks-Pincevic, after setting an anti-western scene, the topic of Bleiburg is mentioned. But is there any information? No, just more anti-British diatribe. Nothing is mentioned of the crisis that Tito created in Carinthia against the British. After all, the Cold War had a lot to do with the support of Yugoslavia, as a buffer against the Soviet Union, but now it is time to move on and focus on the Yugoslav-Bolshevik crimes against humanity.

Thankfully we now live in an atmosphere of free speech and a lot of new information is coming to the fore about Bleiburg.

"Bleiburg Massacres: Untold Holocaust – the Shame of the British Army and Yugoslav communists", Lijepa Nasa Domovina website, online, Zagreb, 2004

This article begins with a typical inflammatory headline and includes a Michael Palaich video which is allegedly about Bleiburg, reviewed elsewhere in my book. Another YouTube film (referred to in this article) has been terminated due to copyright infringements.

"Bleibursko Polje Crvene i Bijele Boje" (Bleiburg Field of Red and White colours) Poem, Ante Marinović, Melbourne, 2004

> Bleibursko polje tvoje ime tumačiću svakom
> Uzduž i širom svijeta skim se ja god sretnem
> Crveno i bijelo polje gdjegod dođem ti si sa mnom
> I kad spavam o strašnoj tvojoj tragediji sanjam
>
> Bleibursko polje na tvom tlu bio sam pet puta
> Pola milijuna Hrvata do Bugarske ti si proguta
> Cetrdeset pete za nas Hrvate tragedija najveća
> U našoj trideset slavnih burni i mračni stoljeća
>
> Bleibursko polje ti si bio lava u grlu vulkana
> Od petnajstog svibnja četrdeset i pet godina
> Devedeset prve vrisnu tvoja u Hrvatskoj lava
> Iz Hrvatskih grudi junačkih srca i duha zdrava
>
> Htjeli su je spriječiti sto i više zli država
> Tvoja brza jaka usijana lava krči Hrvatska prava
> Devedeset pete kao feniks se diže Hrvatska država
> Uskrsnula je Hrvata sloga 'Oluja' i pomoć Kristova
>
> Bleibursko polje vrijeme svoje bere i mrve crvi
> Te dvi boje tvoje od Hrvatskih kosti i krvi
> Vječno će nam oprezna jasna i živa opomena biti
> Da se vampir juga više nikad nesmije ponoviti
>
> Nakon devet burnih stoljeća slobodna je Hrvatska moja
> Hrvatska je ja i ime moje Hrvatska me sa svijetom spaja

This poem by Marinović is about the tragedy at the Bleiburg field, the worst tragedy in 30 centuries of Croatian history. Even his sleep is disturbed by the haunting Bleiburg Tragedy. In this poem the colours of white and red represent Croatian bones and blood. The author visits Bleiburg and remembers how after WWII half a million Croats were driven in "Death Marches" as far as Bulgaria. The memory of the Bleiburg tragedy, for Croatian people, is always in their hearts and minds. The Bleiburg tragedy is compared to a dormant volcano by the author. And, the poem goes on, when Croatia was under siege in 1991, that dormant volcano erupted in Croatia spilling its hot lava into the hearts and minds of the nation. The legacy of the Bleiburg tragedy, of that volcano and its hot lava, was the indomitable Croatian 'Storm' which wiped-out Yugoslavia from the world maps and Croatia, like a phoenix, which rose from the ashes. For this author the freedom of Croatia, after nine turbulent centuries, is everything. Now at last his identity and his name belongs with the rest of the world.

"Forced Repatriation, Operation KeelHaul and Bleiburg Tragedy", Axis History Forum, online, 2005

This Forum discussion on the topic of repatriation is candid and interesting because it illustrates a widespread confusion on the topic. All perspectives are responded to in a professional manner, including the British viewpoint, and there is no necessity to repeat the various perspectives here except for one new point.

One point is relevant to some of the various claims made in relation to repatriations. The Hague Convention of 1907 which covered Prisoners-of-War is mentioned and quoted here.

> Forum comment: "After the conclusion of peace, the repatriation of prisoners of war shall be carried out as quickly as possible. ... The fact the British were sending them back to a nation of which the ruling power considered them to be traitors, is not addressed by any international law."

This is an important point and the Geneva Convention of 1929 also included an 'article' about repatriation. According to the 1929 Convention regarding Prisoners-of-War Section II is quoted here.

> "Release and Repatriation upon Cessation of Hostilities, Article 75"

states that after an armistice belligerents shall come to an agreement regarding repatriation:

> "...repatriation of prisoners shall be effected with the least possible delay after the conclusion of peace..."

"BLEIBURG: JUGOSLAVENSKI PORATNI ZLOCINI NAD HRVATIMA" (YUGOSLAV POST-WAR CRIMES AGAINST CROATS), JOSIP JURCEVIC, DIS, ZAGREB, 2005

This book of 438 pages is entirely in Croatian and contains many original documents, photographs, and details about the war and post-war events. A review of such a thick book about Bleiburg is outside the scope of my book because of its length and because it is not in the English language. Jurcevic has published another book in English which I will review entitled, "The Black Book of Communism in Croatia: The Crimes of Yugoslav Communists in Croatia in 1945" (2006). Suffice it to say that both books reflect his opinions at the time.

"HISTORY OF WORLD WAR II: REMEMBER BLEIBURG THE MASSACRE THE WORLD CHOSE TO FORGET", FR ZVONIMIR GAVRANAVIC, ANNALS AUSTRALIA, ONLINE, SEAN O LACHTNAIN HOME PAGE, (JLOUGHNAN.TRIPOD.COM/BLEIBURGH,HTM), APRIL/MAY 2005

Fr Gavranavic, also the author of a book about Cardinal Stepinac, wrote an article in English about 15th May 1945, and it has been published on line and in an Australian Catholic magazine. In this six-page interpretation the Bleiburg tragedy represents acts of brutality which are barely known to the English speaking world. Fr Gavranavic gives the numbers of Croatian soldiers as from 120,000 to 140,000, and also many tens of thousands of Croatian civilians who were all allegedly at the Bleiburg field.

> "...encamped on a large field just outside Bleiburg"

According to Fr Gavranavic's incorrect version it was the British who requested that the Croats lay down their arms and who then herded the unarmed Croatian masses across the border to waiting Tito's Partisans and the beginning of the liquidation.

Fr Gavranavic also describes the British repatriations elsewhere, which were between 30 to 40 kilometers away, in places such as Villach, Lawamauend, Krumpendorf, Griffen, all which were near to the Slovenian border. Fr Gavranavic correctly states that it was these Croats who were disarmed by the British and crammed into railway cars and deceived about their destination.

It is helpful that this article at least acknowledges that there was more than one repatriation location, but the events at Bleiburg per se are grossly misrepresented. The various extraditions are compared rather than contrasted for their differences.

It is disappointing that this Australian Catholic magazine has seen fit to publish this article which alleges that the brutality used against the Croats on subsequent "Death Marches" is tied with wartime events, as if to justify Bolshevik crimes against humanity because of 'Serbian' revenge!

I believe that post-WWII massacres need to be considered in a post-war context and not tied-in to excuses about war-time revenge. International law has come a long way at the time this article was written. For example at the International War Crimes Tribunal at the Hague the Croatian defense team, for "Operation Storm" was not allowed to use 'revenge' as an excuse to justify alleged 'criminal enterprise' activity. No way! No connection was allowed to be made between prior Serbian aggression against Croats and fresh allegations against Croats, much less permit 'revenge' as part of any defense or justification! Nevertheless the Yugoslav post-WWII crimes against Croats are still continually being justified and excused due to 'revenge' -- revenge for something that allegedly happened during WWII and not after the war!

Harold Macmillan's trip to Klagenfurt on 13th May 1945 is mentioned in reference to his diary "Tides of Fortune 1945-1955", but Fr Gavranavic then adds in brackets that Klagenfurt is near to Bleiburg! This is misleading because Klagenfurt is much closer to the places mentioned earlier such as Villach, than Bleiburg, and it was within a different British military jurisdiction. Nigel Nicholson clarifies his zone of operation in the interview reviewed in an earlier chapter. Then, to further confuse the issue, after mentioning that Slovenes, Montenegrians, Serbs and Cossacks were repatriated, Gavranavic straight-away jumps to the scene at Bleiburg field.

The author then gives examples of the tragic fate of all groups who were put onto train box cars and returned to Yugoslavia including Croats, Slovenians, and Montenegrians at Kocevje forest. There in Slovenia some 30,000 to 40,000 Croatian, Slovene, German, and some Serbian prisoners were slaughtered between 27th May and 5th June. Other mass graves at Jazovka are described and Gavranavic estimates that up to 200,000 Croats were killed during the two months after the war.

Fr Gavranavic has painted a tragic picture in this article and poses the question of how we should respond to the tragedy sixty years later. Although entitled "Remember Bleiburg" unfortunately most of what he has described in his article was about the extraditions elsewhere, including massacres of peoples around the world.

Fr Gavranavic believes that the "way to go" is to take the model of the "South African Truth and Reconciliation Commission" which was headed by Bishop Tutu. I strongly disagree with any comparison between the genocide of Croats after WWII and the later situation in 'Apartheid' South Africa!

> "(Tutu)... sought not to punish the perpetrators of crime in the former regime, but just seek acknowledgement of the crime by the perpetrators, and once it is acknowledged all parties can then go forward building a new South Africa."

In some kind of 'equal guilt' scenario Fr Gavranavic then suggests that first the British government should come clean, as if they have not done so prior to this time!

> "... British government must come completely clean with the role played by British civil and military authorities in Southern Austria at the time".

Next according to Gavranavic the Serbian authorities must acknowledge the brutality of the Royalist Yugoslavia, and of those Serbs or Croats in Tito's Partisan movement! Finally the brutality of the WWII Ustasha regime should be acknowledged. Fr Gavranavic finishes by 'imagining' the following unprecedented and extremely unlikely scenario.

> Gavranavic: "On the 15th of May many Croatians as well as Slovenes, Austrians, possibly some Serbs and Montenegrins will be gathering in the field at Bleiburg, Austria, to commemorate this surrender...(and)...It will be commemorated and prayers offered, not for the purpose of vengeance and hate, but for reconciliating and forgiveness".

I have reviewed many books and articles about Bleiburg over the decades for my book and have come to some conclusions. According to my analyses of the Bleiburg commemorations this is not the way things have happened because Bleiburg was an exclusively Croatian post-war event. Before any reconciliation or forgiveness happens as per the South African model, the truth needs to be exposed and those who did the mass killing condemned and punished. This article does not go far in that direction. Fr Gavranavic quotes an eye-witness account about the "Death Marches" at Maribor from the book "Operation Slaughterhouse" but does not refer to the testimony about the Bleiburg field from the same book.

"Bleiburg Memento fotomonografija" (Bleiburg Photo-Monograph Memento), Boze Vukusic, Croatian Calvary Association, Zagreb, 2005

Vukusic's book contains a large collection of un-sourced photographs which allegedly portray the whole of the Bleiburg tragedy, from the retreat to the "Death Marches" and gulags inside Communist Yugoslavia. The introductory explanation, a few pages long, is in the Croatian, German, and English languages. Thus, in this book published on the sixtieth anniversary of 'Bleiburg 1945' we have a version of the events in a nutshell. The Editor is Bruna Esih, and the English language section has been translated by Marjan Bosnjak, and the German by Monika Lovric.

Each chapter is introduced by various artists, who have been accredited in the book. Of note, the 'Bleiburg' artwork by Suzanne Brooks-Pincevic has not been used in this book. Artists include Anton Cetin, Kristijan Krekovic, Ivan Lackovic, Ivan Rabuzin and Kuzma Kovacic.

The bibliography refers to "Private Collections" and Croatian archives; and the maps, by Ivica Rendulic, show the retreat routes from NDH towards Austria, the "Death March" routes, post-war Yugoslav concentration camp locations, and post-war mass grave sites. The first retreat routes map does not show the Slovenian/Austrian border, so it's as if the entire Carinthian area claimed by the Yugoslavs is a fait accompli. The other maps do indicate the border.

Colour photographs taken recently are of Memorial monuments are shown at Unter-Loiback (1976), Eisenkappel (1983), Klagenfurt (1977), Mirogoj (1994), Tezno (1999), Celje (2004), and Kocevski rog. A small photograph of the original monument is shown (2004). The new monument is not in any photograph, and indeed it was allegedly Vukusic who changed the wording of the new monument, as discussed elsewhere in my book. An uncompleted restoration of the Bleiburg memorial site is captured in a photograph.

The photographs, the purpose of this book, are mentioned in the brief Afterword "Editor's Message" but no original sources are given! This is highly irregular for a book of photographs. Professional publications require photographs to be accredited in order to comply with copyright law. The photographs are divided into several chapters in Vukusic's book, namely, "The Retreat", "Bleiburg Field", "Death Marches", "Mass Graves", and "In Remembrance". According to the editor these photographs have already been published in other publications but some have been published in Vukusic's book for the first time though it's up to the reader to guess which ones they are. Most of the photographs are over sixty years old. One Mr Miroslav Ambrus-Kis restored the photographs "to extract the best out of them". Then in this Afterward the editor gives vague sources for the photographs.

> Bruna Esih: "I wish to express my greatest gratitude to the members of the Bleiburg Honorary Guard and to other Croats in the Diaspora —- from whose collections some of these photographs came from..."

For the purposes of my book I will discuss the introductory text, and the photographs in the "Bleiburg Field" section. The opening sentence sets the scene with a vague allegation about the Allied countries' intention to abolish all Axis states after the end of WWII. This book is in the English and German language and readers new to the topic could be forgiven for believing that the "Axis" created the Croatian state. This point may be debatable but it is worth pointing out.

> Vukusic: "...Allied countries which had beforehand decided to abolish all States established by, or with the consent of, the Axis Powers and to re-establish those which had ceased to exist for the same reasons."

In fact Yugoslavia was not actually re-established because its government-in-exile had 'not' ceased to exist and it had agreed to join Tito to form a new government (1944) at the war's end. Vukusic by innuendo leads readers to believe that the second Yugoslavia was created by the Allied powers. Indeed, as we have already learned in my book, some Croatian authors would have us believe that the victorious Allies created both the first and second Yugoslavia.

At the war's end Vukusic suggests that the NDH government "sent recklessly" its soldiers and civilians on retreat on a route towards Celje. It is alleged that the retreating Croatian soldiers and civilians had to "fend for themselves" because the routes from Celje to Maribor or Dravograd were "completely blocked" by abandoned German war machinery.

An unsuccessful negotiation with the Partisans on 13th May 1945 prompted General Herencic and Colonel Crljen to send a "Memorandum" to the Head of Anglo-American forces, citing international conventions, asking for protection during surrender.

> "(surrender of)...200,000 Croatian soldiers and about half a million Croatian civilians".

Vukusic has not mentioned the Bulgarians; and adds that the Memorandum had no effect due to an earlier agreement.

> "...an earlier in-principle agreement with the Allies on handing-over surrendering soldiers to local allied forces."

Although several columns reached Austria, many others were already captured within Yugoslavia by the Yugoslav Army. Those at the Bleiburg field were

> "...quickly surrounded by Partisan units."

The negotiations at the castle on 15th May 1945 are summed up in a couple of sentences which do not mention Basta or the options given to the Croats, one of which was chosen. Vukusic misrepresents what Scott said to the Croats and is able to do this by omitting Basta from the analysis.

> Vukusic: "(Scott)...told the emissaries of the retreating Croatian soldiers and civilians, General Ivan Herencic and Colonel Danijel Crljen, that the Croatian Army must surrender its weapons to the Yugoslav Partisans. All other explanations and negotiations were futile. The surrender of the prisoners-of-war to the Yugoslav army followed."

Vukusic writes that according to Yugoslav reports some 341,000 enemy soldiers were captured and about 100,000 were killed. There is no mention by the Yugoslavs of the civilians, and Vukusic does not indicate that the Yugoslavs referred to Croats in particular.

The rest of Vukusic's book is not relevant to the focus of my book, although it is important regarding the "Death Marches" and the Commission to investigate some 700 post-war mass grave sites. A further 90 post-war mass grave sites were found in Bosnia and Herzegovina, and a further 200 (of Croats) post-war mass grave sites in Slovenia.

Vukusic estimates the total number of victims of "post-war vengeance" of mostly innocent civilians.

> Vukusic: "several tens-of-thousands to more than one hundred thousand".

Vukusic does distinguish between the events at Bleiburg and the hand-over by the British to the Yugoslav Partisans from camps around Klagenfurt. Many of those 40,000 Croatian refugees in those camps around Klagenfurt had survived however and they "quietly established" the "Bleiburg Honorary Guard". The purpose of this Honorary Guard was "to keep alive the memory of the victims of the Bleiburg Tragedy". Here we see that the Bleiburg Tragedy is a symbolic term for all surrenders and all repatriations.

The rest of Vukusic's book is about the improvement of the Bleiburg memorial site, and he also mentions the assassination of Nikica Martinovic, who was regularly maintaining the site. He mentions that both the Catholic church in Croatia, and the "Meshihat of the Islamic Community" in Croatia, participate in annual commemorations.

He finishes by explaining that he does not enter into any detailed interpretation of events but instead offers documentary photographs which "speak volumes without saying a word".

It is the photographs used by Vukusic, in particular the ones under the "Bleiburg Field", which caught my attention. A picture of Volkermarkt, or the Bleiburg castle, are interesting but do not "speak volumes".

One photograph on page 8 falsely describes the location as Bleiburg, of the disarmament and surrender of the Croatian army in May 1945 – this picture is almost identical to another which actually "speaks volumes" about surrendering Cossacks near Griffen and is from the British Imperial War Museum (see Booker's "A Looking-Glass Tragedy").

The background of the photograph on page 9 appears to be a bad job of 'restoration'.

The photograph on page 10 is alleged to be of a deserted Bleiburg field after the hand-over of Croatian POWs to the Partisans. Given that the other photographs do not represent Bleiburg, and the similarity to the same scene in this shot, it's unlikely that it is Bleiburg.

If the Bleiburg Honorary Guard had these shots why did they not use them when the book "Operation Slaughterhouse" was re-published in the 1990s?

Also, photographs are used to depict Croats "near" Bleiburg. The familiar 'signpost' photograph is a case in point. An almost identical location and scene in a photograph also appears in an online book by Zvonko Springer, but 'without' the signpost where he describes the location as "undisclosed".

I cannot place this 'crossroads signpost' anywhere on a map, especially if the extra third directional sign is added onto the same post which depicts "Griffen 19 km" and underneath "Bleiburg 3 km".

Many of the photographs which appear in Vukusic's book, including the 'signpost' photograph, are actually sourced in the book 'Otvoreni dossier Bleiburg" and accredited to one Miroslav Lilik and held in the "Korusko pokrajinskog muzeja revolucije" (Carinthian Regional Museum of Revolution) in Sloven Gradec. (see in my 1990s chapter)

Vukusic's photograph with the caption "Maksimir Prisoner-of-War camp in Zagreb May 1945" has also been described in the 'Otvoreni dossier Bleiburg' book as being at "Zarobljenicki logor u Dobroj Vasi u Koruskoj snimlje s visine" (Prison camp in Dobja Vas in Carinthia recorded from a height). The 'Dobja Vas' settlement is next to the Meza River and the wooded background would suggest that the location is really taken in Carinthia and not in Zagreb. This photograph has been taken probably between the 13th and 15th May 1945 according to the source.

My critics may well say "so what"? There is proof that the Bleiburg Tragedy happened. Most have acknowledged, in their own way, that negotiations took place, that a surrender to Yugoslavs occurred, and that there were likely some tens of thousands at the Bleiburg field. A picture which reinforces the fact is a good idea because it "speaks volumes". But a photograph without an 'identifiable' background or a source does not "speak" about anything. It is clear that some of the photographs in Vukusic's book do not depict what he says they do and this in no way attracts justice and closure.

In my book I am attempting to excavate and sift the facts about Bleiburg from the mountain of propaganda. What might seem irrelevant to most readers, especially those of a Croatian background, will matter a great deal to others. It is surely not in the best interest of the victims to portray their case fraudulently. Tolstoy found this out the hard way. It appears already that a YouTube interview regarding BLeiburg has also been removed for copyright infringement. So the question is raised in my mind about the target audience of Vukusic. I imagine it has been written for a Croatian audience, including the 'diaspora' of the first and second generations, who speak Croatian, German or English. The author Vukusic wants to inform the Croats abroad about Bleiburg and that is not a bad thing. The misrepresentation of a photograph is not a good idea however. People might think, well if one of the pictures is not real, perhaps many others are not real either. And by extension, perhaps the whole Bleiburg Tragedy narrative is also propaganda.

Finally, Vukusic has claimed that in 1995 the Croatian Parlament proclaimed 15th May as a Public Holiday or a Day of Remembrance. In actual fact this annual Day of Remembrance for Bleiburg in Croatia occurs on the Sunday closest to 15th May, so it is not a Public Holiday in the same sense that Anzac Day is in Australia.

Collage illustrates parts of photographs from 1945 which appear with different captions in various books or articles

"Slovenija: U jami Konfin pronadjeni posmrtni ostaci 26 Hrvata surovo ubijenih po svrsetku Drugoga svjetskoga rata: 60 Slovenaca, 26 Hrvata, i 2 Srba" (Slovenia: In sinkhole Konfin was found the remains of 26 Croats brutally murdered at the end of the Second world war), Hina, re-published in Hrvatski Vjesnik, Melborne, 29 September 2006

Fortunately this article has also been published and translated online, and of course one must always be careful when using Google Translate to make sure it agrees with the original. Online the title is "In the pit Konfin in Kocevski Rog and the remains of 26 Croats". This article is about the discovery of another mass grave in Slovenia, one of 500 mass graves from "after the war". Konfin is one of ten which have been investigated so far. The Slovenian government historian is Joze Dezman. Evidence confirms that they were killed on the night of 24 June 1945 after being taken from a Ljubljana hospital. According to this article, moderate estimates are that in the first two months after the end of WWII, up to 80,000 people were killed. Other post-war mass graves to be investigated include the camp Stental near Celje, and in the Pohorje near Maribor.

"Bleiburg Massacre",
Wikipedia, online, as 'printed' 21 January 2006

This Wikipedia entry which constantly changes, by its very nature, is brief in comparison to what is on Wikipedia about Bleiburg in 2015. My 2006 "Bleiburg Massacre" print captures the Wikipedia interpretation in time.

But in 2015, the same 2015 entry entitled "Bleiburg Massacre" is automatically redirected to another Wikipedia page then entitled the "Bleiburg Repatriations". The theme has not changed much however between this version and a lengthy 2015 version.

After the Bleiburg Massacre is defined, the massacre is immediately attributed to Yugoslav Partisan reprisals, with or without the knowledge of Tito. The numbers are still "undefined", according to this source, who were

> "...executed without trial as an act of vengeance for the crimes committed by the Ustase regime..."

It is alleged that British archives on the topic of "Operation Keelhaul" has received little attention because Communist Yugoslavia was not criticized in the post war period. It is misleading however to attribute the West's later position on Yugoslavia to the immediate post-WWII period, because that change in foreign policy happened after the Stalin-Tito split in 1948.

> "(Yugoslavia was)...the West's protégé and the buffer zone to the Soviets in the post-war period."

Two schools of thought about the number of victims are described, namely, demographic, or according to the number of mass graves discovered since. The latest version sites a third school, namely eye-witness accounts.

The later version has expanded and added the retreat routes of the Croats; it has referred to some British historians on the topic; and it discusses the commemorations. Unfortunately the surrender negotiations are not even mentioned.

However, what is mentioned in this 2006 Wikipedia article, ostensibly about the "Bleiburg Massacre" of Croats, comes under the heading of "Criticism of the massacre claims". It is grossly misleading to portray Tolstoy's mention of Bleiburg out of context. This reference to Bleiburg in Tolstoy's book was actually about a handover of Slovenian civilian refugees from Viktring to Tito's partisans on 31st May 1945.

> "(Slovenians)...taken to Rosenbach and Bleiburg the following day, to be handed over to Tito's partisans."

The Wikipedia source is on page 202 in Tolstoy's book. But on this page Tolstoy refers to Bleiburg only as a part of a journey (of Slovenian "Domobranci") which ended at the Kocevje mass grave at the end of May, and it has nothing to do with what happened two weeks earlier to Croats at the Bleiburg field. A secondary train route had been ordered by Toby Low which passed via Bleiburg to Dravograd Yugoslavia at the end of May 1945.

"Why are we Croatians so afraid of the Bleiburg truth?" Ivan Pavletic, online Croatian World Network, (Croatia.org), May 2006

Ivan Pavletic has been motivated to write this article because his family members were post-WWII victims. This article is amongst the few which claim that the Ustasha escaped execution during the post-war massacres of Croats. The author adds, in a bold statement, that the Ustashas at Bleiburg had a "plan B" as an exit strategy and moved into Zones A, B, and C, into Istria and Italy.

He asks why, so many years after the end of Communist Yugoslavia, the topic of Bleiburg is seemingly ignored. He argues that it is in the interests of both the Right-Wing pro-Ustashas and the Left-Wing pro-Communists to minimize the number of Croatian victims, and to distract Croatian people from the truth and blame "that we had done this to our selves".

The numbers 300,000 and 500,000 Croatian victims of the "Way of the Cross" are mentioned; and that 180,000 Croatian victims now being already excavated in Slovenia were "mostly Domobrani" (Croatian Home Guards).

> Pavletic: "(The Bleiburg Way of the Cross) ... was never the punishment death marches for the war criminal Nazis, Ustashas and Chetniks, as propagandized by the Communists to justify it".

Pavletic raises another important point when he says that the crimes were typical of a Stalin-type mass murder and so are not "reprisals". In this context the content of this article certainly contradicts the Wikipedia sources above which justify the massacres because of "reprisals".

By stating that the Croatian columns of civilians and military stretched a long way back it is evident that all of them never could have reached Bleiburg.

> Pavletic: "(columns) ... as far as 60 km from Bleiburg into Slovenia..."

Pavletic discusses the Yugoslav attacks against these retreating Croats on the move, but a large part of this article attempts to answer the question as to why the "truth about Bleiburg" remains largely unknown. He asks the question whether or not Croats are still divided, as if still stuck in 1102 when "we lost our original independence." He alleges that the real victims of Bleiburg were

> "...caught between the two very selfish political rivalries".

He concludes that the truth of this genocide is being covered up and minimized. However, once again similar to many authors, the negotiations at the Bleiburg castle are being distorted by Pavletic, although perhaps not intentionally. According to Pavletic, Milan Basta, the Yugoslav Commissar, had already made deals on 14th May with the British, alleging that Field Marshall Alexander

> "...had already arranged the mass repatriations..."

Pavletic alleges that Alexander made a deal, in exchange for absolute British control of Carinthia "long before" negotiations with Croats were made. A British-Yugoslav meeting regarding the repatriation of (already surrendered) Croats and a Yugoslav evacuation did occur on 15th May 1945 at Klagenfurt, not on 14th May. This meeting did not include Milan Basta who was in Bleiburg at the time. See my review on Anthony Cowgill, "Bleiburg: The End of the Croat Incursion—15 May" in "The Repatriations from Austria in 1945: The Report of an Enquiry – The Documentary Evidence" (1990).

This author alleges there were personal deals between Brigadier Scott and Basta before the arrival of the Croatian generals at the Bleiburg castle about the Croatian "unconditional surrender". I would agree that there were discussions but I would not describe them as "deals" because the Yugoslav occupation in Carinthia was not discussed at the time.

Unfortunately Pavletic eliminates the testimony of Crljen and the meeting between Scott and the Croats, and the option chosen by the Croats at the castle. Pavletic jumps to the meeting of all three commanders and says that Scott and Basta bluntly told Croats to surrender

> "...hundreds of thousands in a period of one hour".

We have already learned that the British—Yugoslav—Croatian discussions did not play out in this order, and that there were not that many at the Bleiburg field. Also not mentioned by Pavletic, and of critical relevance to the outcome of the meeting, is the belligerent Yugoslav behaviour and demands, and actual crisis the Yugoslavs had created throughout Carinthia, which gave them the upper hand to deliver ultimatums at the Bleiburg castle.

It is true that Brigadier Scott offered to back-up the Yugoslavs with military support, but this was said 'after' the Croatian acceptance of the option to surrender to the Yugoslavs, and after Basta had assured the British that they would respect international law.

"BLEIBURG ANTHOLOGY",
JEAN LUNT MARINOVIC, ONLINE CROATIAN VIEWPOINT WEBSITE, MELBOURNE, 2006; CROATIAN WORLD NETWORK WEBSITE, NEW YORK, 18 MAY 2006

This anthology was originally on my own website, and it remains on The Croatian World Network website at the time of writing this book. Unfortunately, I disagree with some of the entries I have published about Bleiburg. I have mixed up the British repatriation from Klagenfurt with the retreating Croats who did not reach Bleiburg.

In this article I also discuss the 50-50 Stalin-Churchill Yalta issue, Italian irredentism, and the history of pan-Slavism. I give a little history about clerical pan-Slavism in Croatia to argue that Yugoslavia was not a "British invention".

The only time I briefly mention Bleiburg is when I refer to the Croats being without their leader who had vanished with the help of the Vatican to South America. I conclude that genocide was never intended by the British and their help for Tito, during the war, was for the purpose of defeating the Axis. Many sources today have concluded that there was no "conspiracy".

"THE BLACK BOOK OF COMMUNISM IN CROATIA: THE CRIMES OF YUGOSLAV COMMUNISTS IN CROATIA IN 1945",
JOSIP JURCEVIC, CROATIAN HERALD—MELBOURNE, IN ZAGREB, 2006

This book, translated into English, represents another Croatian version of the events surrounding the Bleiburg tragedy. The publisher is the Croatian Herald in Melbourne. The co-publishers include "Bleiburg Honorary Guard" in Klagenfurt; "Institutum Historicum Croaticum" in Vienna; and "Dokumentacijsko informacijsko srediste" in

Zagreb. The chief editor is Tomislav Vujeva. The executive editor is Boze Vukusic, and consulting editors are Zdravko Dizdar and Dubravko Jelcic. The translation was done by Tomislav Bosnjak, and language editing by Katarina Basic-Brozovic. Ivica Rendulic is responsible for the chartography and Borut Bencina for the design.

For the photographs there is no source, although the author does list Marko Grcic in the literature so he must have been aware of some of the sources. (I have reviewed the book edited by Grcic in my book under the 1990s.) Some old photographs are re-published by Jurcevic which include the 'signpost' photograph and the photograph with is allegedly of "Maksimir". (refer to book reviewed, by Vukusic in 2000s)

Because the book is not too long, this version of the story of Bleiburg is available 'in a nutshell', or so one would expect. In this book very little space has been devoted to the actual negotiations at Bleiburg. Jurcevic only briefly mentions the European Parliament's condemnation of Communist Crimes, or the insufficient treatment of Tito's post-war crimes against Croats in the "Black Book of Communism" (1999). To suggest that an opportunity has been missed is an understatement.

Although the book describes the crimes of the Communists in Croatia, once again there is an underlying anti-British bias.

The book's Preface is by Janko Vranyczany Dobrinovic, a Bleiburg survivor. He refers to an alleged 200,000 soldiers and 500,000 civilians, and that the head of these columns were,

> Dobrinovic: "...held up by British troops in Bleiburg Carinthia ... disarmed and handed over to the Yugoslavian communist Partisans, who had joined the Allies ... Immediate mass liquidations and death marches of prisoners right across Yugoslavia ..."

Dobrinovic's Preface concludes by setting the scene of the failed "Lorkovic-Vokic Coup d'etat" and their presumed execution by the Croatian regime. He also refers to the Yugoslav head of the Secret Service, one Alexandar Rankovic, who reported on page 6 that 686,000 prisoners were liquidated between 1945 and 1951. But according to this Preface there should be no "sweeping guilt" placed on the Partisans. (Refer also to review of 9 March 2016.)

In the Introduction Jurcevic begins his explanation of why the Bleiburg tragedy occurred. Although he inaccurately argues (pages 18—19) that the Croats (at Bleiburg) were "handed over" by the British Army, he correctly points out on page 18 that only a small proportion of the Croats reached Bleiburg.

> Jurcevic: "an ill-prepared and chaotic retreat towards the Austrian border …the exodus was joined, on their own initiative, by a huge number of civilians, driven by fear…Most of these Home convoys of military personnel and civilians were captured, by the Yugoslav Army already stationed on the territory of Slovenia, while a smaller proportion of the fleeing convoys, had succeeded in breaking through to Austrian territory…where the British Army was stationed…were subsequently handed over (or, extradited) to the Communist Yugoslavia by the British. …it is recognized that only a smaller proportion of the Croatian convoys actually reached the vicinity of Bleiburg, in Austria, and that there were no mass killing of Croats in Austria itself."

Historical errors make this one more book which I cannot pass on to the English-speaking public. The author incorrectly alleges on page 23 that a solution at 'Versailles' led to the establishment of Yugoslavia. Jurcevic should have said that the creation of the first Yugoslav state, known as the Kingdom of Serbs Croats and Slovenes was 'recognized' at Versailles.

> Jurcevic: "the establishment of the first Yugoslav State was one of the least successful solutions of the Treaty of Versialles (where) a series of peoples were pushed into the same state framework…who were very different…(and that)…the entry of Croatia into the Kingdom of Serbs, Croats and Slovenes…was never ratified by the Croatian Parliament…"

It would appear that a common allegation by many authors is that the first Yugoslavia was created as a result of "Versailles" and perhaps this is included in the context of Bleiburg, without evidence, to establish an alleged continuity of British actions against Croatia. I can only guess why.

In the Appendix of "One Day in May Bleiburg 1945" is an article about how the "State of Slovenes Croats and Serbs" existed first in Zagreb, before it was joined by Serbia and became a kingdom. In my Appendix also is another article which describes in detail the 1928 Serbian assassination of five Croatian parliamentarians, sitting in the front bench, in a Belgrade session of parliament. I only mention this because Jurcevic's description of the 1928 assassinations, which made world headlines, is limited to one sentence. This can be contrasted to the attention given to Versailles in the same section.

Getting back to 'Bleiburg' and the Yugoslav revolutionary occupation of Carinthia, is Jurcevic's discussion of Yugoslav propaganda in WWII (page 38). This systematic creation of printed propaganda matches the detailed description of Partisan requests for printing material in Lindsay's "Beacons in the Night".

> Jurcevic: "With the end of the war approaching, propaganda was becoming all inclusive, more uniform and more systematic ... Areas intended for military conquest were targeted for social and detailed propaganda activity. Plans were drawn for the takeover of print shops and radio stations, with texts of proclamations, slogans and banners planned and thought out in advance (including)... several thousand periodicals...prose, poetry, various brochures."

Jurcevic pays a lot of attention to the demographic losses during WWII, and those liquidated after the war. He describes the scene leading up to the Bleiburg tragedy. Importantly, he refers to Tito's edict of 2nd April 1945 on page 43.

> Jurcevic: "It is then that the Yugoslav Army was given its end of war objectives (1) to encircle, force to capitulate or destroy the principal forces of the Occupier and its collaborators...to free all parts of Yugoslavia including those which were taken away unjustly after the end of WWI, primarily Trieste, the Slovenian Littoral and Carinthia."

Another interesting judgment in Jurcevic's book is his referral to an alleged British position at the time, and their fight in the Po Valley.

> Jurcevic: "...the British Foreign Office examined the possibility of how useful it would have been if the Ustasha and Homeguard forces kept Tito around Zagreb and Ljubljana to allow the Allies to occupy, unhindered, the Julian Region and Carinthia."

Finally, in Jurcevic's description of the Croatian position, he points out the Croatian leadership's loyalty to the German Army under General Lohr, and the retreat from Zagreb. Jurcevic explains how the plan to retreat towards Istria and North Italy was abandoned, and mentions a Croatian memorandum of 3-4 May 1945 to the Western Allies, and the retreat of the Croatian government. True to Tito's edict, the Yugoslavs were already in Carinthia including the Slovenian Partisans, and the Fourth Yugoslav Army with its six Divisions. Other areas occupied were also occupied by various other Yugoslav armies and are described in detail in this book.

On page 47 he discusses the routes taken by the Croats from Zagreb as

> "Zagreb – Novi Dvori – Rogatec – Celje; Samobor – Zidani Most – Celje; Varazdin – Ivanec – Krapina – Rogatec – Celje, and then from Celje in two broad directions – towards Maribor and Dravograd (which) were blocked .. "

Of relevance to the Bleiburg tragedy, he correctly describes how Maribor had been occupied by the Yugoslavs and cut off to the Croats by 11th May 1945. This blockade had forced the retreating Croats towards Dravograd, where they were then blocked by the Bulgarian Communists, and the 51st Yugoslav Division which had arrived on 12th May 1945.

On page 49 Jurcevic states that the Croats sent belated representatives to the head of the Anglo-American Mission for Styria, Carinthia and Alpine Slovenia in Klagenfurt. On page 50 Jurcevic, apart from his introduction that the British handed over the Croats at Bleiburg, finally for the first time writes about what happened Bleiburg.

> Jurcevic: "...14th of May, and that same day, several tens of thousands of Croatian military personnel and civilians crossed the Austrian border and arrived on the agricultural fields near Bleiburg, where they were met by Units from the 38th Brigade of the Fifth Army Corps of the Eight Allied Army, namely, these were the British Units commanded by General Patrick Scott."

Jurcevic also mentions on page 50 that the British were aware of 200,000 military personnel and half a million civilians in dispersed convoys which were not all at Bleiburg, but were

> "... on the move towards Austrian territory".

Unfortunately, in the same paragraph, he confuses his readers into thinking that other groups were also headed towards Bleiburg.

> "...Most of these were Croats, and only a small proportion (a few tens of thousands) were Slovenians and Chetniks who were also escaping ahead of the communist repression."

In the next sentence comes the heading, "British Extradition of Croats from Austria".

Jurcevic incorrectly insinuates that the British extraditions which occurred elsewhere in Austria, similarly occurred at Bleiburg.

> Jurcevic: "...and on the 15th May 1945, the British began handing over Croatian military personnel and civilians from the Bleiburg Field and other areas of Carinthia which were under their control, to the Yugoslav Partisans."

At this point Jurcevic briefly mentions the negotiators at the Thurn-Valsassina castle about which he says that Croatian authors place too much weight on the judgment of the British General Scott after short negotiations to "extradite the Croats and others" (page 50). This then is Jurcevic's whole description of the castle negotiations.

> "...witness accounts...always placed decisive weight on the short negotiations ... thereby, creating the impression that the decision to extradite the Croats and others, was left to the authority and judgment of the British Army (at that time, Generals P. Scott or H. Alexander) who could have – or it is most often thought – decided otherwise, that is not to hand over the Croatian prisoners of war to the Yugoslav Partisans."

Jurcevic then mentions Tolstoy's book about the role of Macmillan and how Tolstoy alludes to alleged British 'interests' in the region as if those interests were somehow unwarranted. In actual fact Macmillan's visit resulted in a decision not to accept any more refugees, because of a decision from higher up that the Yalta Agreement terms would be carried out.

I would pose the following questions. Did the defeat of the Nazis and Fascists in Northern Italy not reflect the interests of all the western Allies? Was not the war-time Allied support for the Partisans given directly for the purpose of defeating Nazism? Is it not true that all the western Allies had an interest in preventing the Soviets from advancing into western Europe? Or perhaps the situation would have been better if the British had given the area to Tito!

Jurcevic eventually refers on page 53 (of an 80 page book) to the border dispute with Tito and the strong post-war Yugoslav occupation.

> "British military experts assessed on the 12th May that if Tito refused the demand to withdraw from Austria, a very difficult situation would arise for Alexander, as he only had one division in Austria at the time."

Up to this point in the book there has been no actual reference to other camps such as Viktring, and no detail regarding the negotiations at the castle, even though in his "Literature" Jurcevic lists both Bethell's and Cowgill's books. Instead he suggests that there had been a deal between the British and the Yugoslavs.

> Jurcevic: "(a)... direct or tacit deal between the highest levels of the British Kingdom and the new Yugoslav Communist authorities".

Newspaper reports of the day suggest otherwise as intense discussions between Tito and the big powers about the Yugoslav withdrawal from not only Trieste and Gorizia but also from the Austrian province of Carinthia made headlines. For example, in the Advertiser, from Adelaide Australia, on 21st May 1945, the heading reads "Growing Crisis over Trieste, Tito's Reply to Note 'not Acceptable', Urgent Talks in Progress".

> "The crisis over Marshal Tito's claim to certain territory in the Austrian province of Carinthia ... has reached an acute stage, and urgent talks are in progress between Britain, America, Russia, Yugoslavia and Italy in an effort to resolve the problem!

In reference to Article 2 of the Geneva Convention Jurcevic makes the ridiculous suggestion, on page 55, that there was a "state of war" between Croatia and Britain! Using Stjepan Hefer as his source Jurcevic makes the following assertion about the surrender at Bleiburg by calling it a "capture".

> "...the Croatian Army and civilian population had in fact become Prisoners of War of the Armed Forces of Great Britain, and therefore, from the moment of capture, a legal relationship was established between Great Britain and the captured citizens of Croatia".

Like a few other authors in my book, Jurcevic distorts some facts, and omits others, to build a case for a "tacit deal" between the British and the Yugoslavs. In this way less blame is placed on the Yugoslavs. In this context Djilas's propaganda in Orsag's "The Balkan Conspiracy" comes to mind again.

> Djilas: "The British did the completely wrong thing in putting these people across the border, as we did the completely wrong thing in shooting them all!"

Other portions of Jurcevic's short book discuss the Communist massacres which happened after Croats and others were back inside the Yugoslav frontier. He constantly argues that revenge against the Croats was the reason behind the massacres. One would wonder therefore why other groups such as the Serbs or Slovenes were massacred!

He has a short chapter on the "Consequences of the Bleiburg Tragedy". On page 71 the legacy of negative effects are discussed such as liquidation and torture and Tribunals and persecutions, in the context of Croatia being "pushed into the new Yugoslavia" in 1945.

The final chapter also deserves some criticism and it provides another reason why I find myself unable to offer this book to any of my peers.

Mate Mestrovic, in "The Bleiburg Tragedy of the Croatian Nation", begins with a general statement about the Croatian surrender to the British and delivery to Tito from Austria. Of course there were surrenders to the British, and extraditions, but why is all this put under the heading of Bleiburg? Are such over-generalizations acceptable because Bleiburg is a symbolic term? If all this confusion is due to a single symbolic "Resolution" made by American Croats, then it should be acknowledged as such, rather than be presented as fact. For readers of a British background, Mate Mestrovic PhD, American professor and Croatian-American activist, is the son of the late Ivan Mestrovic, famous Croatian artist and sculptor who was also a member of the Yugoslav Committee in 1915.

Mate Mestrovic partly attributes blame for the Croatian retreat and the Bleiburg Tragedy to the belief of Pavelic and of the Yugoslavs that war between the Soviet Union and the Western Allies was imminent.

Perhaps Mate Mestrovic could have acknowledged that the only party who believed that war was imminent was the British regarding Yugoslav threats. It was British policy to avoid another war and thus it was not imminent. Typically the alleged British contravention of the Geneva Convention is referred to but not the Yugoslav or Russian violation of it!

It is important to keep reinforcing the fact that at Bleiburg the British did not extradite the Croats. The British officer was following orders not to accept any more refugees. The occupying Yugoslavs turned-back the Croats from Bleiburg after negotiations and Croatian acceptance of the Yugoslav terms of surrender.

It is also incorrect to say that the Independent State of Croatia was a "satellite" state created by Hitler and Mussolini.

> Mate Mestrovic: "...(Croatia) was established by Hitler's Germany and Mussolini's Italy as a satellite state"

Such historical mythology compares with the equally poor version of history that Yugoslavia was somehow established at Versailles. Actually the Croatian people in unison and peacefully accepted the declaration of Croatian independence after the collapse of Royalist Yugoslavia, and before the arrival in Zagreb of Pavelic. The Croatian state was subsequently occupied by Hitler and Mussolini who were originally the Allies of Royalist Yugoslavia.

In addition some blame for the events at Bleiburg and casualties afterwards is also attributed to Pavelic by Mestrovic.

> Mate Mestrovic: "...had Pavelic's government not decided on a large scale, and organized withdrawal into Austria, and (instead) had allowed the soldiers to throw away their uniforms, scatter, surrender individually, or hide until conditions settled down somewhat. Then their fate might have depended on chance..."

Mate Mestrovic concludes his reference to Bleiburg by confusing Bleiburg with different surrender locations. By innuendo Mestrovic suggests there was a British/Yugoslav deal, and he also suggests that the Pavelic regime shares responsibility for the Bleiburg tragedy.

> Mate Mestrovic: "The responsibility for the Bleiburg tragedy of the Croatian nation is shared by the Pavelic regime, Tito's Communist leadership and the British who handed tens of thousands of disarmed Croatian soldiers and civilians to their terrible fate in return for the withdrawal of the Yugoslav forces from southern Austria."

Road junction sign: Volkermarkt 18 km; Bleiburg 3 km on way to Bleiburg from Klagenfurt, 2014

"BRITAIN AND THE BLEIBURG TRAGEDY: RADIO INTERVIEW WITH SUZANNE BROOKS-PINCEVIC", SPREMNOST HRVATSKI TJEDNIK, PAGES 13—14, SYDNEY, 6 FEB, 2007

This interview is mainly about the translation into the Croatian language of the book "Britain and the Bleiburg Tragedy", and the organisation of donations provided. In an interview with Blago Peric, on the Sydney Croatian Community Radio, the three publishers for the Croatian version are acknowledged as "Domobran Officers 242 Klub of Zagreb"; the "Croatian Intercommittee Council of NSW"; and the "Croatian Victimology Society of Zagreb".

There is little information about the Bleiburg tragedy in this article, and nothing about the surrender. The article finishes with a criticism of the European Union. She correctly makes the observation that other countries are not afraid of incorrect propaganda and commemorate in a positive way events like Gallipoli or Bastille Day.

One of the enduring myths is mentioned by Brooks Pincevic, that "Croatian forces never invaded any country" during WWII, a myth hard to defend when the Croatian unit at the battle at Stalingrad is considered. A Croatian stamp was printed, "Hrvatska Legija Stalingrad".

Research also reveals that during WWII Croats also trained in a southern French town under German command. On that occasion, the Croats took part in an anti-Nazi mutiny at Villefranche-de-Rouergue. Today there is a street named after them, "Avenue of the Croats", as well as a grave and memorial. Those Croats who escaped execution afterwards were known for inspiring the French resistance in Aveyron.

To her credit Brooks Pincevic exposes and criticizes the newly changed Bleiburg memorial which was installed under the auspices of the Croatian government. She also criticizes the books by Bozo Vukusic and Josip Jurcevic on the Bleiburg tragedy. According to her, after the sixtieth commemoration was finished,

> Brooks Pincevic: "Vukusic sneaked back to remove the wording from the Bleiburg monument – he took out any reference to Croatia or the Croatian army."

The original monument has been restored and my 2014 photograph of it is in my book. If I believed the Australian-Croatian newspapers up until the time of the 2015 commemoration at Bleiburg, I would have believed that incorrect monument was still there! Vukusic's book "Bleiburg Memento fotomonografija" does not have a photograph of the infamous new monument.

"Kako su nas Ubijali" (How They Killed Us), Hrvoje Hrvatin, page 3 Spremnost Hrvatski Tjednik, Sydney, 15 May 2007

This is a sincere account of how Croats were treated and slaughtered in Yugoslavia from July 1945 onwards. It is accompanied by a large often-used and un-sourced photograph of the Croatian retreat under the signpost which says "Volkermarkt and Unterdrauburg".

"Tajni Britanski Dokumenti Potvrduju: Bleiburg: Hrvati su bili zrtvovani" (Secret British Documents acknowledge: Bleiburg: Croats were sacrificed), Davor Ivankovic, online Vecernji.hr 19 May 2007; Spremnost Hrvatski Tjednik, Sydney, 29 May 2007

Because of my British background one of my motivations for writing this book has been to provide factual information to an English-speaking audience. English translations on the internet can sometimes be very misleading because the Google translation may be misleading. In this review I am looking for Ivankovic's perspective on the surrender at Bleiburg. I am wondering if the title of the article is misleading in the context of Bleiburg.

For example the documents mentioned are hardly secret as they have been available for decades. Nevertheless as I struggle through the article I have discovered that, as the gap widens between 1945 and the present, some new information does emerge.

The article is typical in its general discussion of all post-WWII locations. For example, in the same paragraph, Scott's awareness of 200,000 military forces and 500,000 civilians approaching is followed by mention of 30,000 to 40,000 Serbs, 8,000 Montenegrins, 30,000 Slovenians, 100,000 Germans and 40,000 Cossacks. Ivankovic at least then correctly informs readers that the

> "...greatest human torrent was stopped before the Austrian town of Bleiburg".

Ivankovic discusses Macmillan's plane trip to Carinthia, and the aggressive behaviour of Tito's forces which had penetrated the location to Klaenfurt, with the intention of occupying Carinthia, as in Trieste. The deception, by the British, used against the Croats in the "camps" to repatriate them is mentioned. The problem is that readers could believe that all the numbers mentioned above involved British deception when that was not the case.

I have been looking for a clarification of various surrenders of Croats, in order to compare and contrast all surrenders, and numbers, in reference to Bleiburg. Unfortunately I have only encountered more confusion in Ivankovic's article. I understand that Croatian readers may be more interested in any information about the victims and the mass graves, however I believe that only with a better articulated narrative will any pressure be turned towards those guilty Yugoslavs.

To my disbelief, the Australian-Croatian media print version omits the crucial online ending of "Vecernji.hr"! For example, online text describes how some victims miraculously survived the Partisan executions by spending days in the mass graves or pits amongst the dead, before exiting. And it is this part of the removed online article that refers to Alexander's telegram about ending the repatriation of "Yugoslavs" on the 17th May 1945, thus changing the order of the 14th May. This telegram is discussed on page 128 of Tolstoy's book.

It is towards the end of the article that the Croatian Commission for War and Postwar Victims is mentioned. This Commission had collected documentation about the victims but it was abolished in 2000! Its closure, according to Ivankovic, has allowed the debate over numbers of victims to poison the political culture in Croatia.

"Bleiburska Tragedija i krizni put Hrvatskoga Naroda Godine 1945" (The Bleiburg Tragedy and the Way of the Cross of the Croatian people in 1945), Andjelko Mijatovic, Hrvatski Svjetski Kongres (HSK), online, Zagreb, 2007

This lengthy essay by A. Mijatovic was published in the Croatian language online by Dr S. Coric of the Croatian World Congress. Mijatovic describes in detail the many various routes of Croatian government members, the Pavelic group, and various long columns of Croatian soldiers and civilians. Because of its length and because it essentially repeats the information I have already reviewed from different sources it is unnecessary to repeat it all again here. In addition it is extremely difficult for me to review a lot of material in the Croatian language due to time constrictions. I want this book published as soon as possible and lengthy translations would add several months to my schedule.

I focus on one day, 15th May 1945 and also try to ferret out those who don't say anything about the castle negotiations. The poorly sketched maps used by Mijatovic are taken from the same source as the pro-Yugoslav Permanent Exhibit in Poljana, which was later mounted in 2010. He uses photographs which have been used in various other Croatian books or newspapers.

Mijatovic describes the scene. The arrival at the Loibach field (also known as Bleiburg field) just before Bleiburg on 15th May was headed by 30 Croatian armed vehicles, and included wounded and civilians. Also present were brigades of the 51st Division of the Third Yugoslav Army. This source alleges that there were also Montenegran soldiers and civilians amongst the Croats who had been collected up in the Meza Valley by the Yugoslav Army in the chaos. Montenegrins were not represented at the castle surrender negotiations and elsewhere in my book I confirm that they were re-routed in another direction.

On page 24 Mijatovic mentions an American-Croatian man who I believe to be Robert Plan and what he says would explain how Plan came to be at Bleiburg, as described elsewhere in my book.

> "... pred Dravogradom dosao je i jedan pripadnik americke armije, podrijetlom Hrvat. S njim su ... razgovarali general Vladimir Metikos i pukovnik Danijel Crljen..."
> (... before Dravograd came one member of the American Army, of Croatian descent. With him ... spoke general Vladikir Metikos and Colonel Danijel Crljen...)

He believes that probably this American Croat could have delivered a Croatian memorandum about surrender to the "glavaru angloameriacke misije za Stajerskum Korusku i Gorenjsku" u Klagenfurt. (Head of Anglo-American Mission for Carinthia Styria and Gorenja) in Klagenfurt.

Mijatovic believes that many Croats had not made it to Bleiburg and over 100,000 were re-routed to Maribor. He writes that at Bleiburg there were about 150,000 people of whom up to 140,000 were Croats.

The author mentions that there were British Spitfire planes at eleven o'clock on the morning of 15th May flying above the Loibach field. The negotiations are described under the heading, "Pregovori o predaji HOS-a" (Negotiations on the surrender of Croatian Army). In the middle of a difficult international situation after the war talks were to be held between the Yugoslav Partisans, who were already deep in Carinthia, the British 38th Irish Infantry Brigade and the Croatian Ustasha. Before describing the negotiations Mijatovic mentions the brief meeting of the 14th May 1945 between the British and some Croatian generals at Hrust near Bleiburg. Hrust, located next to the Bleiburg field, has been described in other sources as the local Partisan headquarters.

At twelve noon on 15th May, at the Thurn-Valsassina Castle above the town of Bleiburg, members of each side attended the surrender negotiations in the presence of the British brigade commander Scott. The Croats represented included, according to Mijatovic, the Generals Herencic, Servatzy and Colonel Crljen. The Yugoslav Army was represented by the political Commissar of the 51st Division, Colonel Basta, and Commander Kovacic, a Partisan of the 14th Slovenian Division. According to Mijatovic the talks were very agonizing. Nowhere can I find mention by Mijatovic of the presence at the castle of the American-Croatian interpreter Robert Plan whose presence was crucial to the talks! In addition eye-witnesses do not place Servatzy in the room where negotiations took place.

Anyways, according to Mijatovic, Scott first spoke and told the Croatian delegation they could not surrender to the British, and that they should surrender to the Yugoslavs. Basta also gave the condition that after they returned to their columns they must raise a white flag in one hour. Basta declared that the women and children would be returned to their homes, the army would become prisoners, and officers would be put on trial if they were guilty of war crimes. Herencic sought a 24-hour delay and higher British advice, but in this version, Brigadier Scott suggested two hours and offered military help to the Yugoslavs. Basta arrogantly and immediately refused British help and said the hand-over should begin immediately upon the Croatian officers' return to their columns. Herencic protested that there was not enough time to organize the surrender of so many people, but Scott then allegedly threatened at that time that, if the surrender was not accomplished, after one hour we will "start bombing". This point by Mijatovic needs to be criticized because eye-witness sources attribute these threatening words to Basta, not to Scott!

> Mijatovic: "...Scott zaprijetio: 'Ako se to ne izvrsi, mi cemo vas poslije jednog sata poceti bombardirati'..." (Scott threatened: If this is not executed, we will after one hour start bombing)

Some Croats might wonder what difference it would make who said these words and when but an international court would disagree. It does make a difference who said what, and when it was said, and whether or not there was an interpreter, and whether or not there had been separate meetings before a combined meeting! None of this is clear in this version of events. It is probably better that this is not in the English language. At least this way, by reviewing the material, I can qualify some of the statements made.

In conclusion it is unethical to make it appear that the British were the main aggressor at the Bleiburg negotiations, because it was Basta who was doing all the threatening, emboldened by the presence of thousands of Yugoslav forces at this time.

Another attempt to negotiate with the British is briefly mentioned in this essay which occurred in the field. The Croatian Domobran (Home Guards) General Stancer tried to negotiate with the Yugoslavs in the field but to no avail, as the castle talks had already been completed. It is also alleged, by this author, that a leader of the Montenegrins in the field also failed at this time to negotiate. I have not seen this written anywhere else.

"THE HAGUE COURT AND THE BLEIBURG GENOCIDE", JEAN LUNT MARINOVIC, CROATIAN VIEWPOINT WEBSITE, MELBOURNE, 2007; PAGE 10 NOVA HRVATSKA, SYDNEY, 20—26 NOVEMBER 2007

I connect the Bleiburg genocide to the Hague Court in my first sentence.

> "The concept of 'equal guilt' applied at the ad hoc Tribunal for the former Yugoslavia is unsustainable unless the post WWII genocide of Croatian people is kept hidden from the world. When international law has to serve an agenda of 'equal guilt' the victim is justice."

I allege that the discrepancies in the ICTY indictments and pattern of arrests suggest that an "equal guilt paradigm does exist". After a brief introduction, this article is a word-for-word repeat of my article "Lessons from Bleiburg", 2001. In that article I hardly discussed Bleiburg. It is time that people who write about Bleiburg, like myself as a prime example, should explain what happened there instead of writing about anything and everything but ...!

For this article in Nova Hrvatska I have supplied one of my photographs of the UN Peacekeeping monument in Ottawa which illustrates that 'reconciliation' is the mission of the UN Peacekeepers.

Peacekeeping is defined generally as active maintenance of a truce especially by an international military force. There is no mention of 'reconciliation' in this definition. In 1956 Lester Pearson, a famous Canadian, created the United Nations Peacekeeping concept and its purpose was to ensure peace and monitor events. The UN Peacekeeping forces are recognizable by their "Blue Helmets". It is only more recently that a 'reconciliation' ideology has been heard of a lot.

I mention 'Peacekeeping' because the website of the 38th Irish Brigade has a link to Scott's eye-witness Report (which includes Bleiburg), as well as the Brigade's month-by-month diary. On the website Part 6 of Commanding Officer Scott's Report is entitled "Peacekeeping Duties" although no such concept or force existed in 1945. Scott however entitled his original Report "Balkan Troubles". Testimony from many sides illustrates that post-war 'reconciliation' was not the purpose of the 38th Brigade at Bleiburg. Their order was to avoid the outbreak of another war (with Tito); and (by 14 May) not to accept any more refugees because the refugees already held behind British lines were to be repatriated.

"Reconciliation" monument in Ottawa Canada, 2003 – Inscription: "We need action not only to end the fighting but to make the peace... My own government would be glad to recommend Canadian participation in such a United Nations force, a truly international peace and police force."

"THE BIGGEST KNOWN POST-WWII EXECUTION SITE IN EUROPE: TEZNO FOREST, SLOVENIA, HOLDS REMAINS OF MORE THAN 15,000 POST-WWII VICTIMS", BRIAN GALLAGHER, CROATIAN WORLD NETWORK WEBSITE, NEW YORK, 17 AUGUST 2007

Brian Gallagher has published several links with texts to various world websites regarding the post-war massacre near Maribor at Tezno Forest in Slovenia. I will go through them in the order they appear. At the time Slovenia was in the EU but Croatia was not until 2013.

"WORSE THAN SREBRENICA?" THE VANCOUVER PROVINCE, WWW.CANADA.COM, CANADA, AUGUST 10 2007

Officials are exhuming a post-war mass grave in Tezno Forest in northeastern Slovenia thought to hold the remains of more than 15,000 victims of the former communist regime. The identity of the victims is not given. The article quotes "Slovenian

Commission on Concealed Mass Graves". The Tezno grave was found during a 1999 highway construction. I have already reviewed this in 1990s, but this article gives an update on the number of victims. At the time Slovenia was in the European Union but Croatia was not until 2013.

"Post-War Execution Site 'Core' of Croatian Army Buried Near Maribor?"
Ivona Baric, www.javno.com , Croatia, 9 August 2007

A Slovenian historian Mitja Ference asserts that the number of victims is important to find out if

> "the core of the Croatian army lies there"

This anti-tank trench near the new Maribor cemetery 'Dobrava' may hold

> "those Croats who were singled out among those departing from Bleiburg . . . members of the Croatian Home Guard (Domobrani) who were taken back to Yugoslavia after surrendering in the Bleiburg field."

The victims were sometimes described as "class enemies" according to Joze Dezman, the President of Slovenia's commission for hidden mass grave sites. The probe of the trench in several places has been funded by Prime Minister Janez Jansa. There is a brief discussion of opposition to this initiative from both the left and the right. Although some governments have an agreement with Slovenia on the burial of the victims, namely Italy and Germany, "such an agreement with Croatia does not exist". Slovenian historians say

> "that there is not much enthusiasm in Croatia for resolving the issue"

Bozo Vukusic, president of the Honorary Bleiburg Guard, thinks it best for Croatian remains to be exhumed and placed in a mausoleum in Slovenia. I believe there are many ordinary Croatian people who would not agree with him.

"Execution Site Probe" is another link by the same source, and journalist, as above and it reports on the 'Press Release' of the Honorary Bleiburg Guard to the Croatian government to sign an agreement with Slovenia.

"Slovene mass graves reopen historic wounds: A WWII historian has unearthed 570 hidden sites, Few want to deal with the finding, and revisionists want to blame the communists", Christine Spolar, The Chicago Tribune, online, February 24 2008

This journalist sarcastically alleges that Slovenia "can't rest its bones". It appears in this account that more than 570 hidden grave sites from World War II have already been unearthed. Slovenia currently holds the European Union presidency so this is being brought up to allegedly have a "fair accounting of the past". In an even more inappropriate remark Spolar remarks that

> "History has long known that Slovenia was a field of vengeance... killing --- a level that few imagined."

It turns out that Ference's "greatest – or worst discovery" is about the anti-tank trench originally found in 1999 during a highway construction. At that time 1179 skeletons were found. Military gear indicates that as many as 15,000 dead German or Croatian solders lie there. According to this article Slovenia had one million people at the end of WWII and now it has two million. Joze Dezman acknowledged that on a local level people knew of the graves throughout the time Slovenia was in the former Yugoslavia. The retreat of

> "Thousands of Slovenes, Serbs, Cossacks, Romanians and others ... joined German troops and collaborators including thousands of Croats"

Spolar writes that the British in Austria "turned back most" following Allied Command orders, or they were "handed over" to Tito's fighters." Slovenia's right-wing government argues that there was a clear post-war "communist agenda". But then the journalist makes a judgment call instead of reporting on what was happening. This journalist has used the words of an ageing partisan to call those who wish to find justice for the victims "revisionists".

> Spolar: "The revisionists want communism blamed for the mass graves ... Before we had the partisan mythology – and ... now we're seeing the construction of another mythology".

Apparently a political cartoonist Franco Juri, a former member of parliament said that "The truth is somewhere in between". Really, how so?

"Commemoration of the 63rd Anniversary of the Bleiburg Tragedy", Informativna Katolicka Agencija (Catholic Press Agency), www.ika.hr, Zagreb, 18 May 2008

From this time forward many articles about Bleiburg describe commemorations there, and rarely introduce factual information about what happened. This online article of the Catholic Press Agency, available in English and in Croatian, discusses the commemoration at Bleiburg field on 17th May 2008. This was one of the few commemorations, organized by the "Bleiburg Honor Guard" which was sponsored by, and attended by, members of the current Croatian Parliament.

In 2008 the commemoration began at the local cemetery "Unter-Loibach" and then a procession moved to the Bleiburg field. There were about 10,000 present from Croatia and Bosnia & Hercegovina, and the Mass was held by Bishop Slobodan Stambuk, on behalf of the Bishops' Conferences from there. Several members of the church were also there. The Bishop refers to Unter-Loibach as the "first station of the Croatian cross" and the "valley of tears".

In my humble opinion reference to Bleiburg as a symbol, in place of specific details about the event, is becoming an obstacle to proving that genocide was planned and executed against Croats.

> Bishop Stambuk: "(Bleiburg is) ... a symbol of everything that followed and lasted for a full 45 years."

During the Mass the Bishop referred to the commemoration the year before which was attended by the Archbishop of Zagreb, Cardinal Bozanic. He urged people to acknowledge the location of mass graves. He also contrasts Jasenovac and Bleiburg.

> Bishop Stambuk: "it was not permitted even to mention the victims of Bleiburg which was deemed to be a crime in itself!"

According to Bishop Stambuk there are 1,300 mass graves throughout Croatia.

"Red Stars, Black Shirts: Symbols, Commemorations, and Contested Histories of World War Two in Croatia", Vjeran Pavlakovic, National Council for Eurasian and East European Research, University of Washington, online www.ucis.pitt.edu/nceeer/2008_822-16h_Pavlakovic.pdf, 2008

This lengthy work discusses the so-called "red-black" division in Croatian society by comparing and contrasting Jasenovac and Bleiburg, which were allegedly "nationalized to fit into competing narratives of World War Two". According to this work, it is generalized that the Bleiburg commemoration memorializes

> "the thousands of Croatian and Bosnian Muslim soldiers, i.e., Ustase and Domobrani (Home Guards, regular NDH army), and civilians who were handed over to the Partisans and liquidated in the final days of the war".

The author then directly refers to numbers of victims without mentioning what happened at Bleiburg. I would add that the "Bosnian Muslim soldiers" were included in the Croatian Ustasha forces and not a separate entity. This is why the Islamic 'star and crescent' symbol is engraved on the Bleiburg monument as well as a cross.

The focus here is on the commemorations and the controversies about them. By eliminating dates and facts about the exclusively Croatian surrender at Bleiburg on page 14 and throughout, Pavlakovic could lead readers to believe that both Jasenovac and the Bleiburg tragedy happened during the war.

Pavlakovic acknowledges that the number of victims in reference to Bleiburg had been suppressed in Yugoslavia. Only émigré Croats had been at the Bleiburg commemorations for decades. On pages 16—17 the author makes a general statement about what happened at Bleiburg.

> Pavlakovic: "Bleiburg as a site of memory is important because it is the place where the retreating armed forces of the NDH and accompanying masses of civilians attempted to surrender to the British, and were turned over to the Partisans on May 15, 1945, nearly a week after the Third Reich had capitulated."

The author then adds that only a limited number of killings took place at Bleiburg and that no mass war or crimes happened there. Pavlakovic alleges that the mass deaths were part of military casualties who had died during the closing battles of WWII at the hands of the Allied-supported Partisans. This allegation is incorrect. Mass killings occurred 'after' those "closing battles", and at this point the Partisans were acting on the orders of Tito who had stopped cooperating with the Allies at that time.

> Pavlakovic: "(Croats) ... suffered during the closing battles against the Allies and the Partisans, who were part of the Allies".

Then mention is made, in addition to NDH units, of thousands of Germans, Montenegrin and Serbian Cetniks, Slovenian White Guards and Cossacks in the context of leading up to the surrender at Bleiburg! Next the author claims that the numbers are subject to considerable exaggeration from between 45,000 to 600,000. Pavlakovic is throwing all groups into the same basket and in this way false propaganda can be supported. In addition such an allegation can only be uttered if facts about the exclusively Croatian surrender are censored. The following statement is a shocking example!

> Pavlakovic: "the victims of Bleiburg were nationalized and became exclusively Croats in the dominant narrative of the commemoration."

After a detailed analysis of the Jasenovac memorial and commemoration, it is acknowledged that individuals who went to Bleiburg and its aftermath did so at a "great risk to their lives". The first commemoration was held in 1952. In 1965 the Bleiburg Honorary Platoon purchased land at Bleiburg and in 1987 a monument was erected.

The rest of the 39 pages discuss the history of controversy regarding commemorations held since, and the Croatian government's funding of construction at the Bleiburg field. The author hopes that the influence of the European Union will encourage a more positive dialogue regarding "World War Two".

The death marches to mass grave locations did not happen 'during' World War Two, but after it! This is certainly not clear in this investigation and it will not contribute to truth and justice.

"The Systematic Oppression of Croats in the First and Second Yugoslavia through Economic Abuse and Hegemony", Dr Juraj Petricevic, page 7 "History" in "CroExpress" Sydney, 19 February 2009

Although the text does not say anything about Bleiburg a large photograph of the Bleiburg Monument at the Bleiburg field accompanies the article. The monument shown has the controversial new inscription which has removed any reference to Croats.

> Inscription: "U Spomen na neduzne zrtve Bleiburske Tragedije Mai 1945" (In memory of the innocent victims of the Bleiburg Tragedy in May 1945).

Of course the wording on this new monument contradicts the suggestion in the review, "Red Stars, Black Shirts: Symbols, Commemorations, and Contested Histories of World War Two in Croatia" that the Bleiburg tragedy was later "nationalised" to make it exclusively Croatian! I mean, which is it? How can people be nationalizing a single ethnic group if they are removing reference to them! Also, the month of May is written as "mai" and not in the Croatian "svibanj".

"Gassed to death: 300 victims of Yugoslavia's communist regime found in mass grave", Graham Gurrin, online, Daily Mail UK website, 11 March 2009

Another Slovenian post-war mass grave 90 kilometers east of Ljubljana made the headlines. This mass grave is in the Barbara-Rov" (Barbara Trench), known also as "Huda Jama" near Lasko. Is a 15-meter long (and 2.5 meter wide) underground tunnel situated 400 meters from the cave entrance. It is part of an investigation into 500 suspected mass graves in Slovenia. A picture accompanies the online article of hundreds of bones of "pro-Nazi soldiers" which had been covered in lime. Piles of military shoes were found at the mass grave according to Joze Balazic of the Institute for Forensic Medicine in Ljubljana.

Some Online comments after the article, which I printed in 2009, refer to the fact that the British handed over about 20,000 of these victims to the Yugoslavs.

Collage illustrates bones discovered at Huda Jama & locations of some post-war mass graves of Croatian victims

"Barbara Pit: two pits are hiding thousands of victims – witnesses and after 54 years in fear", Danas, online, Zagreb, 8 March 2009

The abandoned mine known as "Barbara Pit" is in the Slovenian village "Huda Jama" near to "Lasko". The historian Dr Mitja Ferenc leads the committee for concealed post-war mass graves. So far they have discovered the remains of between 200 and 400 victims. It is likely that the graves contain the remains of Slovenian Home Guards or the Croatian Ustasha. It is believed that in the old coal mine "Trbovlje-Hrastnik" there may be at least 1000 remains of liquidated prisoners from the Teharje camp near to Celje. Details of the ongoing investigations, and the fear of the people living around there, are discussed in this article.

"Bleiburg Memorial",
Axis History online Forum, online (printed 2012), April 2009

The topic is introduced of the new memorial at Bleiburg in 2005 to honour the victims at the sixthieth commemoration. Present on this occasion were the authors Bozo Vukusic, Josip Jurcevic (and Bruno Esih) who had written a "new" Bleiburg history.

After an emotional argument on this forum one person with an English surname reminds members that inflammatory "rhetoric" does not qualify as informed research. Some books, and a documentary link are mentioned, on the issue of Bleiburg, all of which have been reviewed in my book herewith. An interesting fact emerges that West German compensation after WWII was tied to the alleged number of victims in Yugoslavia during the war, after which the numbers became inflated.

CHAPTER 9

2010s

"And What is the Price of Freedom: End of World War II in Carinthia"
Carinthian Regional Museum,
Author: M. Linasi, Design: E. Koraca, Review: M. Osojnik, Translation: E. Kozar, maps: T. Ferenca, Photographs: from museum, Poljana, 10 May 2010

Situated just outside the town of Poljana is a museum exhibit which presents a pro-Yugoslav interpretation of the so-called final battle of WWII. Poljana is on the bank of the Meza River in Slovenia. The permanent outdoor Exhibit Boards are located across the highway from another sculpture in the so-called Memorial Region of 'Freedom and Peace'. This Exhibit is located close to the Austrian/Slovenian border crossing at Holmec on the main highway. Also near to the Exhibit is a mass grave of the Croatian soldiers and civilians who were 'liquidated' after the Bleiburg surrender to Yugoslavs of 15th May 1945.

In cooperation with the Prevalje Municipality, the expressed aim of the permanent Exhibit Boards is to give visitors concise and clear information about the events which took place there. The text is in both the Slovenian and English languages. I was keen to scrutinize the narrative, and the photographs, to find out more about the surrender to Yugoslavs at Bleiburg, the purpose of my book.

ONE DAY IN MAY – BLEIBURG 1945

Carinthian Regional Museum "Freedom and Peace" Exhibit at Poljana 2014

Exposed to the harsh mountain climate, this open-air permanent exhibit is displayed on six Exhibit Boards, each of which I captured separately in a photograph. After reading the boards it is clear that the exhibit narrative boasts about the bold Yugoslav occupation of Carinthia. Unfortunately only a single sentence on the sixth Exhibit Board mentions the surrender to Yugoslavs at the Bleiburg castle. Nevertheless it is helpful to analyse the Partisan's movements to understand what happened at Bleiburg, and what did not happen there!

Exhibit Board 1: This Exhibit is divided into six sections, the first being an introductory overview of the wider region. Exhibit Board 1 depicts events on the European and Yugoslav battlefields, from the Srem Front breakthrough in mid-April 1945, until the end of the war. The number of retreating enemies is given, and this number is misleading because it includes groups which did not enter Austria from anywhere near to Poljana. The goal of the retreating groups to escape into Austria is described, as well as the goal of the Partisans to prevent them escaping to Austria. The Exhibit describes how most routes were blocked across a wide front by the four Yugoslav Armies and the Slovenian Partisans, even though only the Third Yugoslav Army is relevant to Poljana. The numbers are listed below.

Interestingly, a huge map is described as "the sketch of the 'Slovenian' territory with the withdrawal directions". In fact this area is not all Slovenian territory nor was it ever all included in Yugoslavia. The map includes the wider Koroska (Carinthia) area including Ljubljana, Celovec (Klagenfurt), Celje, Maribor, Dravograd, and Pliberk (Bleiburg).

Thus, at the outset it is obvious that this exhibit narrative includes all Yugoslav Armies, and all surrenders of various ethnic groups all over Southern Austria as well as Trieste. For example, not all of the advancing groups described in the exhibit, were near Poljana but this is not clarified, except to say that the Yugoslavs "liberated Trieste" and seized "all the Karavenken Mountains passages".

> "...quick advances of the four Yugoslav armies, the German Army Group E... It counted about 400,000 men along with 200,000 members of the NDH troops (Independent State of Croatia)...15,000 Montenegrin chetniks ...500,000 civilian refugees. . .18,000 members of the Slovenian Homeguard and chetniks together with about 6,000 civilian refugees..."

All possible withdrawal routes were "cut off by the Partisan forces" and the Third Yugoslav Army, regarding the Bleiburg issue, from Celje towards Dravograd or the Meza Valley to Holmec Pass to Libuce field near Bleiburg.

The other five exhibit boards are dedicated to individual larger "battlefields" in Carinthia such as in Austrian Carinthia, Dolič, Dravograd and Libuče near Pliberk (Bleiburg)--where the last larger group went, consisting of the NDH State's soldiers (members of Croatian Ustaša and Domobranski pokret movements).

Exhibit Board 2: The second Exhibit Board does not discuss the Bleiburg surrender. Of relevance to the wider issue, the second board describes the Partisan occupation of Southern Carinthia between "May the 3rd and 8th 1945" which was "feverishly" competing with the "British Ally Army". The Fourth Yugoslav Army and the Third Yugoslav Army are described as "huge claws". The right claw, relevant for the Bleiburg issue, included the Prekmurje Brigade, a Red Army unit, and units of Bulgarian troops. Areas inbetween the right and left claws were taken by Slovenian and Carinthian Partisan units which are all identified.

On the second Exhibit Board fierce fighting is mentioned near Borovlje (Ferlach), between Partisans and German and Homeguard units, for passage across the Drava River. Ferlach is nowhere near Poljana or Bleiburg!

Exhibit Board 3: The third Exhibit Board refers to the Cossack Calvary Corps and other withdrawing "defeated formations" including

> "NDH forces and Montenegrin chetniks"

north of Celje. Continuing fights between the Yugoslavs and "Ustasha units" are described.

The third Exhibit Board gives us some important information in relation to the issue of retreating groups towards Bleiburg. Here we learn of a split in the retreating Croatian columns, and the route towards Eisenkappel (Zelezna Kapla) is described. This Eisenkappel group which split from the retreating columns never reached Bleiburg.

> "A part of the withdrawing armed column and civilians moved slowly further towards Mislinja, Slovenj Gradec and Dravograd ... while a part of the column before Dolic withdrew back into the Saleska valley and on May the 14th broke through the upper Savinja valley over Zelezna Kapla and further to the northern side of the Drava river."

Exhibit Board 4: The fourth Exhibit Board describes the situation on the 13th of May at Dravograd. Apart from the other NDH column who had entered Austria towards Eisenkappel, other NDH soldiers and civilians were trying to pass through Dravograd. But the Yugoslavs had "seized" the Dravograd region, and were occupying the area along with the Bulgarians and a Red Army unit. Here the retreating columns are referred to as "attackers".

> "...the NDH forces tried to break through across the Drava river" (and to) "unsuccessful negotiations" on May 13th, and how "the pressure upon both Dravograd bridges ceased" (as the) "attackers (were) directed along the Meza valley".

Exhibit Board 5: The fifth Exhibit Board refers to the situation on 14th May around Poljana. The attempted escape of the German General Lohr to the British occupying zone is described, towards Holmec, but this area was already "seized" by the Yugoslav brigades. The Yugoslav brigades are described on this board as the 1st and 2nd Battalion of the Tomsic Brigade, the 1st Battalion of the Slander Brigade and the 2nd Battalion of the 7th Vojvodina Brigade which were awaiting them on the hills around Poljana.

> "...NDH forces and Montenegrin chetniks directed towards the Meza valley in order to break through to the Britains over Holmec ...(but that the Yugoslavs) awaited them on the hills around Poljana. Fierce fights that commenced at 9 o'clock on May the 14th lasted till night. The main body of the column outflanked both Tomsic Brigade battalions and worked their way through both railway tunnels ... (and that the)... attackers suffered heavy losses."

Also described is the 3rd and 4th Battalion of the Tomsic Brigade which "led the captives column over Jezersko pass to Kranj and these locations are farther to the south-west of Poljana.

Loibach west of Bleiburg field with Petzen Mountain in background

Exhibit Board 6: The sixth Exhibit Board describes the arrival and entrapment of the NDH columns, and allegedly also the "Montenegrin Chetniks" at the Bleiburg field. This entrapment happened during the evening of the 14th May to the morning of 15th May 1945. The Bleiburg field is referred to here as the Libuce field. At the Bleiburg field, the exhibit boasts of the Yugoslav blockade of the Third Battalion (Tomsic Brigade), the Third Battalion (Zidansek Brigade) and other battalions. Even the Drava River well north of Bleiburg at Lippitzbach had been seized by the Third Battalion (Slander Brigade).

Of direct importance to the exclusive Croatian surrender at Bleiburg was the presence of units of the 51st Vojvodina Division of the Third Yugoslav Army. However the negotiations which involved the 51st Vojvodina Division are referred to but not described at all, and instead only the British are referred to.

> "Meanwhile the British received the command not to accept any more fugitives from the Yugoslav territory and they had to extradite to the Yugoslav Army also all those who had meanwhile already fled to their occupying zone...After negotiations the surrender occurred in the afternoon of May the 15th, accompanied by a short conflict..."

This brief Yugoslav version of the surrender and negotiations does not contradict most of the Croatian versions where the negotiations are usually skipped over or sometimes even distorted. However when it comes to the numbers and identity of those present at the Libuce field, the Yugoslav version does contradict the testimony that the Montenegrin Chetniks were actually cut-off earlier and were not at Bleiburg. See reference to this below in this review of the Exhibit. The numbers are conservative.

> "...12 NDH generals, the Montenegrin chetniks command, about 30,000 NDH soldiers and Montenegrin Chetniks as well as about 20,000 civilians..."

The fate of those who had made it to Bleiburg, along with others who had not made it, after attacks at Poljana etc. is then described. Afterwards the columns had been taken "in rapid pace" to Maribor which they reached on 18th May 1945. A claim is made that many prisoners had died on the way and that the Croatian Homeguard and civilians were released, in contrast to the Ustashas who had been killed.

> "...met their tragic end at places of mass killing at the antitank defence trench at Teznot, in Dogoze, on the Pohorje slopes and elsewhere."

The discovery of the remains of the Homeguards in mass graves around Maribor tells of a different story however. See the article reviewed in 2007 "Post-War Execution Site 'Core' of Croatian Army Buried Near Maribor."

I would add a comment that a good map which shows the "Pohorje" slopes south-west of Maribor is in Lindsay's "Beacons in the Night".

An analysis of the whole exhibit at Poljana reveals a broader agenda than is suggested by the Museum's mission, on its website, which is to clarify exactly what happened "here". The question is asked "What is the Price of Freedom" but it is not clear whose freedom is at stake here. Does this exhibit wish to portray the "battlefields" at various locations, or the return of soldiers and civilians "in rapid pace" as attempts to create "freedom"?

In this exhibit the variously described fleeing armed forces and civilians are deemed to have been engaging in battles along their route to escape the marauding Yugoslav armies. But it is not always clear just who initiated those battles at the "battlefields", though the Yugoslav goal to stop the columns from escaping is given. It is also unclear why locations had to be "seized" by Yugoslavs -- seized from who? Or was the real intention to simply occupy and block all escape routes and liquidate everyone, as per Tito's order of 13 May 1945, which is not mentioned in this exhibit for obvious reasons. The "tragic end" of the Ustashas at mass graves is greatly minimized even though by 2010 several hundred post-war mass graves have been exposed.

One could deduce that the Yugoslav belligerent and traitorous behaviour throughout Austrian Carinthia (so described as part of Slovenia in this exhibit) towards the Western Allies is not mentioned, because this would refute the idea that peace or freedom was the Yugoslav goal or policy at the time. If it was the Yugoslav intention to block Croats, or Slovenians or Montenegrins from leaving Tito's Yugoslavia, then why was it in their interest to block the retreating Germans and others? The answer could be that all these expendable retreating columns were simply 'in the way' of Yugoslavia's mad rush to consolidate their occupation of southern Austria.

Another point needs to be stressed that the surrender at Bleiburg was an exclusively Croatian surrender, and no representatives of any "Montenegrin chetniks" were represented. Certainly no Chetniks have ever expressed interest in creating any monument, like the Croats have, anywhere near there.

We have read elsewhere that the "Montenegrin chetniks" surrendered at a different location. According to page 135 of the book "Operation Slaughterhouse", full of documents and eye-witness testimony, no Montenegrin chetniks every reached the Bleiburg field! The "Commander-in-Chief Marshall of Yugoslavia, J.B. Tito, M.P. at Belgrade, May 15, 1945" described how the Chetniks never made it to Austria.

> "...troops of our Third Army cut off the retreat of the remaining German and Ustasha-Chetnik bandits, and after surrounding them in the area around Gradec-Gustanj--Dravograd in Slovenia, destroyed them and forced them to surrender after a bitter three-day battle...along with the Ustashas, a great number of Chetniks have been captured..."

In contrast to the repeated mention of Montenegrin Chetniks it is seldom mentioned, in any English language source, that the Croats at Bleiburg included members of both the Catholic and Moslem faith, which is why both symbols are on the Croatian monument to this day. (See photograph on back cover.)

The Chetniks, for the most part, had joined the Partisans after an announcement to them by the Serbian king-in-exile near the end of the war. In addition, Tolstoy describes the surrender in early May of another group of Serbian Chetnik Royalists close to Italy. The groups described on the first Exhibit Board surrendered at other points on the map, after various retreats northwards, for example from Ljubljana.

The single sentence in the Exhibit which refers to the new British orders to extradite others who had already surrendered, taken by itself, is not incorrect if it refers to the several groups at places nowhere close to Bleiburg. However the Exhibit is vague about the surrender to the aggressive Yugoslavs at Bleiburg, and the sixth Exhibit Board minimizes the numbers who were represented there. In this way the numbers of Croats in retreat to Maribor, and the numbers in mass graves, can also be minimized. Basically, the Exhibit focuses on events which lead up to the surrender at Bleiburg, and other "battlefields".

Finally, the Yugoslav version of events about Bleiburg differs from Western accounts of Yugoslav betrayal because its ideological position is so different. Much is left to the imagination about the Bleiburg surrender, and the belligerent conduct of the Yugoslavs there. Little is mentioned about the number of British forces who were at the time still on their way from Trieste.

In conclusion, regarding this exhibit, the Yugoslav perspective about the events in question is ideological, selective, and incorrect, and it glorifies the Yugoslav intransigence and occupation of Carinthia. I have yet to see any serious Croatian challenge to the Yugoslav version, although there may be one. In Croatia the anti-fascist political leadership still has an influential following, which keeps the Croatian nation out of touch with the current European anti-Communist political culture.

"Regret is Not Enough in Slovenian Tragedy", Charles Crawford, online Radio Free Europe/ Radio Liberty, 30 October 2010

This article written by a former British Diplomat in Yugoslavia, refers to the "thick fog of oblivion, confusion, and dishonesty generated over many decades by Europe's communist regimes."

The article is about an "ecumenical Mass of Reparation" held in an English village in Buckinghamshire on 29th October 2010 by the Catholic bishop of Northampton, the Anglican bishop of Buckingham and the Archbishop Metropolitan from Ljubljana. The article criticises the fact that no one from the British government attended the Mass, although an official message was sent. Remembered were the 12,000 Slovenians who were forcibly repatriated by the British Army to Yugoslavia where they were murdered. This event was the result of the efforts of the "British Slovene Society". The "Commission on Concealed Mass Graves in Slovenia" speaks of 600 mass graves from the era. It is unfortunate that Croats are not mentioned as those post-war graves contain mostly Croatian victims!

Although Croats and Bleiburg are not the subject of this article it is still important, because it mentions Tolstoy's book, and a comment by a British spokesman. The Minister for Europe, David Lidington, expressed regret, but that the decisions in that era

> "…did not have the benefit of hindsight (because the)… indiscriminate slaughter (was only understood later in August as a) ghastly mistake".

Crawford suggests that "regret" is not enough.

"Britains ancient shame in Slovenia", The Economist, online, London, 30 October 2010

The Economist article refers to the ecumenical Mass and quotations from the article by Charles Crawford, and I only mention it because of its omission of any reference to Croats in the context of the mass graves.

"The Croats and the Serbs: A history of an aversion, Jakov Sedlar, a film (currently available on YouTube, 2016), Panorama 360, Zagreb, 2011

In this film Sedlar interprets the history of the Croats and Serbs from the first millennia to the present time. About 45 minutes into the film Bleiburg is mentioned, after a segment on the Second World War in Croatia. According to Sedlar the Poglavnik (leader) left Zagreb in May 1945 and troops and civilians followed.

> Sedlar: "The Croats who retreated across Slovenia and north of the Drava into the British zone of Austria did not escape the tragedy. According to British documents there were about 450,000 of them. The British Field Marshall Alexander handed them over to Tito's communists."

Then the film mentions that Croats were killed by the Communists at Dravograd, Maribor, Ljubljana, and Kocevje, etc. in this post-WWII genocide. The numbers of Croats massacred has not been established – between 80,000 and 350,000 massacred, and no one has been held accountable for these crimes. Sedlar states that Bleiburg is symbolic of all crimes, because from Bleiburg the largest number of Croats were led to their death, and also Slovenes and Serbian Chetniks.

This film's portrayal about Bleiburg is vague, and at times inaccurate, because it seemingly combines the repatriation of Croats, Slovenes and Serbs, which happened far away from Bleiburg, with events at Bleiburg. You cannot justify ambiguity or errors by stating that Bleiburg is a symbolic term. No one, least of all myself, is trying to deny that genocide against Croats happened. But it did not happen the way Sedlar portrays it. And as for accountability for the crimes, I agree that no one has been held accountable. However, after reading several books and countless articles on the topic it would seem that not only the Croats, but the British in particular have been subjected to a trial by media!

Field Marshall Alexander did not hand over 450,000 Croats to the Yugoslavs because in fact 26,000 were repatriated by the British from Rosenbach. Only a few tens of thousands of Croats made it to the Bleiburg field because the rest had been blocked and re-routed inside Slovenia by the Bulgarians and Yugoslavs. At Bleiburg there were negotiations after which the Croats surrendered to the Yugoslavs. Even the number of 450,000 is incorrect, because according to British documents there were about 200,000 Croatian soldiers and half a million Croatian civilians approaching the border!

"An Exclusive interview with Michael Palaich, Producer of the Documentary Bleiburg Tragedy: Great Britain Shares Responsibility for Post-World War II Mass Executions of Croatians by Tito's Communist Forces", Hrvatski Svijet -- Croatian Information Portal), online, HRsvijet.net, Zagreb, 2011

This interview with Michael Palaich is about the May 1945 alleged extradition to Tito, and his Partisans, of Croatian civilians and the military who had allegedly been disarmed by the British (at Bleiburg). This grossly misleading description of the Bleiburg situation is however not different to the many statements written in earlier years by various authors. "Hrvatski Svijet" explains that this calamity is known as the "Bleiburg Tragedy" or the "Krizni Put" (Way of the Cross), and that the

> Hrvatski Svijet: "extradition began near the town of Bleiburg in Austria ... and that the British authorities knew well what would happen to those who were forcibly handed over to the communists."

According to "Hrvatski Svijet" Palaich's documentaries are an indispensable historical source. In this "Hrvatski Svijet" interview Palaich resorts to the use of speculative accusations to condemn the British by comparing the British "co-conspirators" with the war crimes prosecuted at Nuremburg as he writes

> Palaich: "...testimony of British Army co-conspirators involved in Bleiburg and the repatriation of Croats...corroborated by the British co-conspirators to the war crimes."

In this "Hrvatski Svijet" interview, we read that Palaich's interviews have been deposited at the British Imperial War Museum under the subject of "forced repatriations". When or if readers listen to this original interview at the British Imperial War Museum they will notice that "Bleiburg" is not mentioned by British officers, such as Nigel Nicholson, who identifies his area of control to be far away from Bleiburg.

Continuing with the co-conspiracy allegations, also found in the title of the "Hrvatski Svijet" interview, the following provocative and judgmental heading appears as the introduction to the testimony of British officers.

> Hrvatski Svijet: "The interviewed British officers and their role in the murder of Croatians--horrific accounts."

Palaich's first mentioned interview, quite out of context, is with one Gerald Draper who was not associated with any post-war repatriation. In fact Gerald Draper was a Prosecutor at Nuremburg and who stated in this interview that Tito could have been put on trial for crimes against humanity.

In answering "Hrvatski Svijet's" loaded question about the "British responsibility in the Bleiburg Tragedy", Palaich then spoke of Nigel Nicholson's interview about his role in deceiving Croats who were put onto trains that they were going to Italy! Once again I must repeat that those who actually consult Nicholson's entire interview will realize that his zone of responsibility was tens of kilometres away from Bleiburg!

Another interview is with Captain Colin Gunner, of the First Royal Irish Fusiliers of the British Eighth Army, who according to "Hrvatski Svijet" was allegedly a

> Hrvatski Svijet: "key witness to the British involvement in the Bleiburg Tragedy".

Palaich, like Tolstoy years earlier, has incorrectly asserted that Colin Gunner was at Bleiburg. We have since learned otherwise from Colin Gunner's book "Front of the Line" published in 1991. This Palaich interview has taken place years after the release of Gunner's book. Before we watch Palaich's Gunner interview, from 1989, Palaich introduces it by mentioning Gunner had to watch Croats being forced across a bridge at Lavamund, as if this has a direct connection to Bleiburg.

Information now on the internet, discussed in my earlier chapters, suggests that this scene refers to a different group of 800 Croats brought to Lavamund from Wolfsberg. Whilst this does not make the Yugoslav's actions any more palatable, putting events into the correct context would widen the scope of Tito's intention to commit genocide because the "Death Marches" began from locations over a much wider area than from Bleiburg!

A misleading and untruthful caption appears directly under Gunner's photograph (taken from Gunner's book) in the "Hrvatski Svijet"--Palaich interview, with words allegedly attributed to Gunner, which are 'not' in the Palaich-Gunner interview at all!

> Hrvatski Svijet: "The Croats were killed by beating them into the head and were thrown off the bridge, a hundred times. Children were killed. There were babies in arms of mothers. Three full days and nights they passed over the bridge, 300,000 of them. We are ashamed that we couldn't tell the commanders to go to hell".

The above fiction has been distorted and amended from Gunner's interview and Gunner's book, "Front of the Line", 1991, and also from Tolstoy's book from 1986, both which do refer to a slaughter of Ustachi who were being driven along a road to death by Tito's troops. The actual Gunner text is as follows.

> Gunner: "The column seemed endless as they were driven over the Drau bridge to the Yugoslav side; men, women, children and babies in arms, all were starving but kept moving by Tito's men mounted on ponies and carrying the infamous steel-tipped Cossack whip . . . some died on the bridge with Father Dan present . . . "

In the Palaich interview, Gunner does talk about the repatriation of the Cossacks, but only after prompted by Palaich does Gunner add, "Yes, Croats too". It appears obvious that some of the words attributed to Gunner in relation to Croats are a fabrication: For example, "Three full days and nights they passed over the bridge, 300,000 of them..." For a start, we know by now that no where near the number of 300,000 Croats actually crossed the border into Austria in the first place!

Also, it is possible that the Yugoslavs were driving the 'Ustachi' across the bridge, suggesting this event had something to do with some Croats (not "300,000") allegedly driven on foot there by Yugoslavs from Bleiburg, rather than from Wolfsberg. Separate groups of Croats at Wolfsberg are also referred to in "Operation Slaughterhouse". We know that Gunner's First Royal Irish Fusiliers regiment was in the Lavamund area but not near Bleiburg.

Nigel Nicholson's interview with Palaich is also carefully edited to make it appear as if it is Bleiburg being discussed although Nicholson is actually talking about British extraditions tens of kilometres away. Nicholson's full interview is discussed in a previous chapter.

The photographs used for this interview of Michael Palaich by "Hrvatski Svijet" are the same as used by many others and are discussed throughout this book because of the variety of incorrect or misleading captions attributed to them.

Incorrect or misleading information, and the numbers present, on the field appear as headings in the "Hrvatski Svijet" interview.

> Hrvatski Svijet: "British are legally accountable for the Bleiburg crimes." ... or ... "There were 200,000 disarmed Croatian soldiers and 500,000 civilians on the fields of Bleiburg."

"Why Croats Commemorate the Bleiburg Genocide at Bleiburg: The Bleiburg Genocide – Croatian Tragedy!" Jean Lunt Marinovic, online Croatian World Network Discussion Forum, www.Crotia.org, New York, 23 April 2012; also: page 10 Nova Hrvatska (New Croatia), Sydney, 1 May to 7 May 2012

This article was published in the Croatian-Australian media and online just before the annual commemoration ceremony at Bleiburg in 2012.

Pictured at the top of the newspaper edition is a photograph of the new monument at Bleiburg which has been the topic of criticism. All of the historical information in this article is also in my book.

I introduce the topic by arguing that the Bleiburg tragedy is symbolic of a long-term Yugoslav intent to destroy and occupy the Croatian nation, and that those who did not perish in post-war Yugoslavia, or later escape from there, ended up being bombed between 1991 and 1995.

Tito's apologists in Croatia have suggested that commemorations should be held at various massacre sites instead of at Bleiburg because "not only Croats" were killed by Partisans after WWII. In addition I add that the new monument mentioned above had replaced reference to "Croatian victims" with "innocent victims". I criticize this whole approach because Bleiburg was an exclusively Croatian surrender to Yugoslavs at Bleiburg. I discuss the double standard towards the Srebrenica genocide in comparison with Bleiburg.

I also argue that the "legacy of genocide for Croatian people has been profound". I criticize the current "reconciliation overtures", the "equal guilt" platform and the pro-Tito politically correct culture in today's independent Croatian state.

> **Marinovic: "(Since Bleiburg) ... More than a quarter of their population, an estimated million Croats either escaped, emigrated or perished since WWII, a catastrophe for a small nation. But Croatian people have lost much more than territory and population since the beginning of Tito's dictatorship, they have also lost their human rights. People have a right to grieve but in place of closure they are stigmatized ... Croatian survivors of 'Bleiburg' are still victims of genocide as expressed in ongoing depopulation, stigma, and a dishonourable reconciliation process."**

I conclude that Yugoslavia is wholly responsible for the systematic genocide of Croatian people resulting in Croatian demographic decline and ongoing stigma against them. By way of self-criticism there are little details about what actually happened at Bleiburg in my article, and it is more of an overview of the historical period.

Author at Bleiburg Memorial 2014

"The Croatian Surrender at Bleiburg", Jean Lunt Marinovic, online Croatian World Network Discussion Forum, www.Croatia.org, New York, 13 May 2013

In this lengthy article I analyse the exclusive Croatian surrender to Yugoslavs at Bleiburg on 15th May 1945. In a way this article is a synopsis of the events covered in this book "One Day in May – Bleiburg 1945". Importantly I clarify that the Croatian surrender to Yugoslavs at Bleiburg and their return to Yugoslavia was distinct from other 'British' repatriations of various groups from another location. I finish with some conclusions about the need to place blame for genocide where it is due onto the Yugoslavs.

> Marinovic: "... it's not rocket science to understand why the neo-communist Yugoslav Partisan advocates in the Croatian parliament today would like to shift blame for their sinister past to the dustbin of history. Therefore it is totally in the Partisan's interest if blame is placed onto the British. What is less logical however is why most Croats continue to focus on an alleged British 'conspiracy' at Bleiburg when the facts tell otherwise."

I finish by suggesting that a new narrative about the Bleiburg genocide needs to "avoid past ambiguous generalizations".

> "It is important to be historically correct, not 'politically correct' if Croatian people wish to have any international or academic support on this tragedy."

"Iron Curtain: The Crushing of Eastern Europe 1944–56", Anne Appelbaum, The Penguin Group, London, 2013

In this lengthy book Applebaum does not mention Bleiburg, but criticism of Tito is included. I briefly review this book because it discusses the nature of the post-war Yugoslav Communist regime. In addition, on page 21 the author discusses Roosevelt's main concern at Yalta.

> "the shape of the new United Nations ... he needed Soviet cooperation to construct this new international system."

She states that the Soviet Union had transformed "an entire region, from the Baltic to the Adriatic". There is a lengthy introduction which is introduced by Churchill's well-known 'Iron Curtain' speech which starts out "From Stettin in the Baltic to Trieste in the Adriatic, an iron curtain has descended across the Continent." On page 10 she alleges that Yugoslavia lost 1.5 million people during the war.

On page 296 Appelbaum mentions what may be "Goli Otok".

> "Tito's Yugoslavia built labour camps too, including one on an Adriatic Island, where water was scarce and the main torment was thirst."

On page 270 Appelbaum describes Tito as unpopular both at home and unpopular with Stalin. Here we see that it was Stalin who broke off with Tito and not the other way around – perhaps an arguable point.

> Appelbaum: "the little Stalin of Yugoslavia … Although he had plenty of enemies, and although he disposed of them qite brutally … the rest of the bloc agreed to expel Yugoslavia from the Cominform."

"Predsjednica će ići na Bleiburg, ali neće držati govor" (The President will go to Croatia, but will not make a speech), HRT Croatian Radio and Television, online, vijesti.hrt.hr, 28 April 2015

In an interview with Croatian Radio and Television (HRT) the President of Croatia, Kolinda Grabar-Kitarovic, confirmed her attendance at the 70th anniversary commemorations at Bleiburg but that she would not make a speech there, and there would be no media. In taking a neutral position on the issue of the genocide of Croats, even though there are hundreds of known post-war mass graves sites containing the remains of Croatian victims, the politically-correct Croatian president condemned 'all' totalitarian regimes.

"Hrvatska Drustva, Udruge, Kao i sve Hrvatske Organizacije Prireduju Komemorativnu Akademiju u cast 70 Godina Blajburske Tragedije Kriznog Puta" (All members of Croatian Society, Associations, and all Croatian Organisations prepare for a Commemoration Academy in honour of 70 Years of Bleiburg Tragedy and the Way of the Cross) – Advertisement Hrvatski Vjesnik, Melbourne; Boka Cropress, Sydney, 29 April 2015

This advertisement mentions various locations in Sydney to commemorate the 70th anniversary of the Bleiburg tragedy and "Way of the Cross" (Death Marches). A photograph of the well-known 'signpost' showing "Griffen and Bleiburg" is shown.

"Komemoracija Za Svibanjske Zrtve: 70 Obljetnica Bleburske Tragedije" (Commemoration for the Victims in May) – Advertisement
Boka Cropress, Sydney, 13 May 2015

In Croatian, this is a large advertisement to attend a mass and presentation in Sydney about the 70th anniversary of the Bleiburg Tragedy on 17th May 2015. A well-known sketch of a grieving mother at Catholic and Moslem graves is shown.

"I ove godine hodocasce od Zagreba do Bleiburga"
(This year's pilgrimage from Zagreb to Bleiburg),
Hrvatski Vjesnik, Melbourne, 13 May 2015

This short article pictures a group on pilgrimage to Bleiburg on foot which will arrive on the evening of the 15th May 2015. The pilgrimage follows a route where post-war mass graves are located. The article also mentions that amongst those going to Bleiburg this year are the Archbishop Josip Bozanic and the new Croatian President Kolinda Grabar Kitarovic. Unfortunately no information about the actual events in Bleiburg is mentioned in the article.

"Bleiburg i Krizni put bili su masakr nad nevinim civilima"
(At Bleiburg and on the Way of the Cross there was a massacre of innocent civilians),
Hrvatski Vjesnik, Melbourne, 13 May 2015

This short article mentions Tolstoy's accusations against the British, the trial against Tolstoy, and a reference to an alleged new book being written about Bleiburg by Tolstoy.

Instead of referring to what happened at Bleiburg the article refers to a later British repatriation and deception at a separate distant location. Tolstoy's picture from an apparent Youtube video appears with this article. A quick internet search reveals a Youtube video about an event which featured Tolstoy which I will review separately. This article incorrectly refers to the alleged British handover to Tito's Partisans of hundreds of thousands of surrendered Croats.

This article must be criticised because in fact the hundreds of thousands of Croats in question never reached Austria. The "Death Marches" began inside Yugoslavia before many were able to cross the Austrian border.

"Croatian leader pays tribute to killed pro-Nazi collaborators" news.yahoo, online, 14 May 2015

There was little objectivity and a lot of unwarranted criticism on the internet about the Croatian President's visit to Bleiburg, even though her visit was separate from the commemoration proceedings! In this typical critique the Croatian President's visit to Bleiburg is incorrectly described as a tribute to Croatia's pro-Nazi collaborators and civilians who were killed by Communist Partisans in Austria and Slovenia after the war. The short article then goes on to report that the President also said,

> Grabar-Kitarovic: "The end of World War II and the victory against Nazism to which Croatian people gave a big contribution marked one of the most tragic chapters of Croatia's history".

Typically the Croatian President is also reported as having referred to the Ustasha's persecution and killing of hundreds of thousands during WWII.

In this article the order of events at Bleiburg is generalised and an inaccurate description of who arrived at Bleiburg is given. Thus much confusion still clouds the Bleiburg issue even on this anniversary date. Regarding the attempt to escape, by the Ustasha and Croatian civilians, and allegedly Slovenians also, the article refers to the British refusal of their surrender, and subsequent execution of the Ustasha 'authorities' by the Communist Partisans. Of course those familiar with the issue know that there were no Slovenians refugees near Bleiburg, but that Slovenians did surrender to the British at a separate location and time. Such is the nature of vague inaccurate propaganda!

The annual Croatian commemoration is deemed "controversial" in this article and estimates of those killed is between a few dozen to tens of thousands.

It is also worth making a comment that I do not know of any commemorations, which are symbolic of massacres, of anyone anywhere in the world that are deemed to be "controversial". The families of victims, and their communities, have a right to mourn and express their grief without being slandered and ridiculed. The Japanese are not condemned for commemorating the victims of the Hiroshima, just because the Japanese army had attacked members of the Allied forces during WWII. Not even the Slovenians who, like the Croats, had been on both sides during WWII are regularly singled out and condemned for commemorating the deaths of Slovenian post-war victims!

"Bleiburg 70 Years on: Our wounds will never heal, nor will we ever forget!"
Hrvatski Vjesnik, "New Generation", Melbourne, Volume 19, No. 825, 20 May 2015

This full front-page 'English supplement' in the "New Generation" pages shows a picture of the crowd and inset is a picture of the original monument. Reviewed below are a couple of articles in this edition.

"Kolinda in Bleiburg on Thursday": The President of Croatia Kolinda Grabar-Kitarovic visited the Bleiburg field "by herself", as well as visiting Macelj and Tezno, on the Thursday before the main commemorations. A Press Release was also published on a few web pages. The President's Press Release gives the following carefully worded politically-correct statement. I note she feels she has an "obligation" to say something rather than a wish or opportunity to speak out. I also note that for Croatia's president this is not an opportunity to speak out for justice but for a spirit of harmonious living. I cannot find any similar placatory examples about Genocide around the world in recent history, since the definition of the word!

> Grabar-Kitarovic: "in paying my respects to the victims of the Way of the Cross in Bleiburg, Tesno and Macelj, I have the obligation to morally condemn the regime that persecuted and killed people. A crime is a crime and it cannot be justified by any ideology ... how important it is to promote the spirit of democracy and harmonious living as a guarantee of peace and a better future."

"Two Commemorations": Mladen Leko contrasts the pious commemoration at Bleiburg, the best attended in history, with the poorly attended commemoration of self-proclaimed anti-Fascists in Jasenovac weeks earlier. Leko explains that for 45 years Bleiburg was a taboo topic in Croatia and that since independence the subject has only furtively surfaced and been subjected to stigmatizing remarks. He contrasts the humble monument at Bleiburg with the "enormous, bland and grotesque 'Sun Flower' at Jasenovac". He also contrasts the open common knowledge about events at Bleiburg amongst Croatian people, with the "many contradictory accounts" about Jasenovac. Leko alleges that the same people are responsible for banning investigation into both locations. Many large photographs of the 2015 commemoration appear on this page.

"Croatian Community sponsors buses for 70th Bleiburg Commemoration": Paul Saric wrote this article about Fifteen Croatian Australian associations, organized by AHD Geelong, who provided $20,000.AUD to sponsor twelve buses of people to attend the 2015 commemoration at Bleiburg. Details of the organization of the

Commemoration also appear in this article, accompanied with the following typical general statement about what allegedly happened at Bleiburg.

> Saric: "... tens of thousands of NDH soldiers were killed at Bleiburg, in May 1945. Their intention was to surrender to the allies, but the British Government turned them over to the Yugoslav Army. Some were killed in the field and many more died in the following months..."

2015: "Obiljezavanje 70. Godisnjice Bleiburske Tragedije: Hrvatska zajednica sponzorirala autobuse za odlazak u Bleiburg" (Commemoration 70 years Bleiburg Tragedy: Croatian community sponsored buses to go to Bleiburg), Paul Saric, Hrvatski Vjesnik, Melbourne, 20 May 2015

This article is similar to the same author's article in the English language. The pictures are different however, showing a line of buses as far as the eye can see coming to the Bleiburg field, and a view of the open-air chapel and crowds at the Bleiburg field surrounded, it would appear, by security guards.

"Htjeli su zrtvama zatrti svaki spomen i trag groba -- Vise od Sesdeset tisuca ljudi u Bleiburgu" (They wanted to destroy every victims monument and marked grave -- More than Sixty thousand people at Bleiburg), Hrvatski Vjesnik, Mebourne, Volume 32, No. 1548, 20 May 2015

This headline appears on the front page with a photograph of the 2015 crowd at the Bleiburg field, and the information in this short article is similar to that reviewed in the English "New Generation" immediately above. Part of the address of the Croatian Cardinal Bozanic is quoted. Also (not the words of Bozanic) this brief article states that

> H.V.: "...mnostvu hrvatskih vojnika i civila koje je britanska vojska predala Titovim partizanima"...(multitudes of Croatian soldiers and civilians who the English handed over to Tito's partisans)

"Pocast Vise od Sezdeset Tisuca Ljudi Na Komemoracij Nevinim Zrtvama na Bleiburskom Polju: Deseci tisuca ljudi dosli su odati pocast nevinim zrtvama" (Homage by more than 60,000 people at the Commemoration of the innocent victims at Bleiburg Field: Tens of thousands of people came to commemorate to the innocent victims), Hrvatski Vjesnik, Melbourne, 20 May 2015

It is interesting that the heading of this article, on top of a photograph of the crowds at Bleiburg field, pictures the controversial monument which has been removed from Bleiburg. The words "Neduzne Zrtve" on the controversial since-removed monument, mean "Innocent victims" just as the words in this headline in 2015 "Nevinim Zrtvama" also mean "innocent victims".

Yet the words on the monument currently pictured on the pages of "The New Generation" of the same newspaper read "Croatian Army Killed" instead of the words on the since-removed monument, the "tragedy of the innocent". The monument was controversial because it had removed any reference to the Croatian Army victims. On our visit in 2014 the monument pictured, by the Hrvatski Vjesnik, in 2015 had been replaced with the original monument.

"Svibanj '45. pamtimo po strasnim pokoljima pocinjenima pod znakom zvijezde petkorake" (May 45, we remember the terrible massacres which began under the sign of the five-pointed star.), Hrvatski Vjesnik, Melbourne, 20 May 2015

This article in Croatian is similar to an article in the English pages of the same paper. The information is the same.

Under a sub-heading "Milanovic u petak u Teznom", a visit to the Tezno mass grave near Maribor by the Croatian Premier Zoran Milanovic, the President of the Croatian government, Josip Leko, and the Minister of Defence, Ante Kotromanovic is mentioned. The article describes the 15,000 to 20,000 Croatian soldiers and civilians buried in the mass grave at Tezno. Two other articles appear on this two-page coverage of this year's Bleiburg commemorations.

"Vratio sam se sa 36 kilograma, ni majka me nije prepoznala" (I returned, weighing 36 kilograms, and my own mother did not recognize me.), Hrvatski Vjesnik, Melbourne, 20 May 2015

This is a story about Vladimir Fucek who survived the "Death Marches". He describes his journey northward from Zagreb after the war from 7 May 1945 to 14 May 1945, when he and his father arrived near the Austrian border, to arrive eventually at Bleiburg and Unterloibach (Loibach). He then describes the situation at Lavamund where the Partisans ordered the columns to go back towards Celje. He writes that "Ni u najcrnjim mislima nismo mogli predvidjeti strahote koje sun as cekale" (Not in his darkest thoughts could he foresee the horrors that awaited them.)

"70th Commemoration of Bleiburg: More than 60,000 gather from all over the world to remember victims of Bleiburg", Marko Barisic, Hrvatski Vjesnik, Melbourne, 20 May 2015

This year's commemoration was organized by the "Honorary Bleiburg Leader", under the auspices of the Croatian President Kolinda Grabar-Kitarovic, and Bosnia-Herzegovina parliamentary representative Dragan Covic.

Barisic introduces this article with a brief description of the tragedy that happened seventy years earlier at Bleiburg. Barisic generally states that the British Army had handed countless numbers of soldiers, civilians, and children to Tito's Partisans, who were then killed along the 'Way of the Cross' filling hundreds of mass graves from Bleiburg to Macedonia.

This is the same typical narrative that we have heard so often over the past seventy years. It is difficult to know whether this introduction is representative of what was actually said at Bleiburg on the day, or was it added into the article by the author. I probably will never know.

The article describes the tens of thousands of peoples' journey to Bleiburg in 2015 who had come from all around the world. The mass at the Bleiburg field was held by Croatia's Cardinal Josip Bozanic and some of what he said is written in this article. Cardinal Bozanic referred to the crimes against humanity committed under the five-pointed star, and that the 'Way of the Cross' (also known as the Death Marches) had begun at Bleiburg. The Zagreb Archbishop blamed the current Croatian government for re-igniting ideological divides, in particular a "new antifascist ideology" not seen in modern countries which feeds off "the invention of a fascist Croatia".

But then the Cardinal calls on those at Bleiburg on the occasion of the 70th anniversary to not let anti-Fascism and anti-Communism create divides. Bozanic expressed his sorrow that more truth had not been exposed. Commenting on this remark, I ask myself the question of how much more truth about several hundred mass graves of Croatian post-WWII victims the Archbishop needs! I note here too that too much is made of "ideology" and not enough on "post-war guilt".

Also in attendance on behalf of the Moslem victims at Bleiburg was the President of the Islamic Community in Croatia, the Mufti Aziz Hasanovic.

"SJECANJE NA MNOSTVO KOJE JE ZADNJI PUT VIDJENO NA BLEIBURSKOM POLJU" (IN MEMORY OF THE MULTITUDES WHO WERE LAST SEEN AT BLEIBURG FIELD.), MARKO BARISIC, HRVATSKI VJESNIK, MELBOURNE, 20 MAY 2015

This article is situated along side three photographs. The caption of the first picture showing the signpost "Griffen" and "Bleiburg" reads "Bleibursko polje u svibnju 1945" (Bleiburg field in May 1945).

The caption of the second photo, probably the same location from a different angle, reads "Jedna od kolona na Kriznom putu" (One of the columns on the Way of the Cross).

The caption on the third photograph reads "Ulaz u Hudu jamu" (Entry to Hudu Cave), showing a blocked entrance to a non-operational mine which is south of Celje.

The article contains information similar to the English version in the pages of the same newspaper, but it is far more comprehensive. Herein the author mentions the organiser of the massacres in different locations.

> Barisic: "OZNA Trece jugoslavenske armije, egzekutori iz 15. majevacke brigade, a naredbodavac vrh jugoslavenske komunisticke vlasti" (OZNA (UDBA Yugoslav Secret Police) Yugoslav Third Army, executor of 15th Majevac Brigade giving orders from the top Yugoslav authorities).

Several of the post-war mass graves are mentioned such as Tezno, Huda Mine near Lasko, and Koceve (a mass grave which followed repatriations elsewhere far away from Bleiburg).

"SVEHRVATSKO ZAJEDNISTVO NA BLEIBURSKOM POLJU—1945—BLEIBURG—2015" (ALL CROATS TOGETHER AT THE BLEIBURG FIELD—1945—BLEIBURG–2015), IVO BUTKOVIC, HRVATSKI VJESNIK, MELBOURNE, 20 MAY 2015

This article in Croatian includes a picture of the author Ivo Butkovic, a former editor of the Hrvatski Vjesnik, and a picture of the 2015 crowds at Bleiburg field. The comment is made that the Austrian police were in disbelief at the multitudes coming in by bus to Bleiburg.

After giving similar information about the event as reviewed in other articles from the same newspaper, another generalisation of events is given once again.

> Butkovic: "Da, na Bleiburskom polju na kojem su zapadni saveznici, predvodjeni Englezima, izrucili hrvatsku vojsku, civile, zene i djecu jugokomunistickom molohu koji ih je zlocinacki mrcvario i ubijao od tog mjesta..." (Yes, at Bleiburg field from where the western Allies led by the British, extradited the Croatian Army, civilians, women and children to the Yugo-Communist monster who tormented and killed from that point...)

"ODLASKOM NA BLEIBURG JE POSLANA PORUKA VLADAJUCIMA" (DEPARTURE TO BLEIBURG, IS A MESSAGE SENT TO THE GOVERNMENT LEADERS), BOKA CROPRESS, SYDNEY, VOLUME 3, NO. 135, 20 MAY 2015

The heading on the front page, accompanies a photograph which pictures throngs of Croatian pilgrims walking on a paved road in a forested area on the way to the Bleiburg field. Also referred to on the front page in this edition is "Sjecanja na Bleiburg i Zrin--mjesta hrvatske zrtve koju nikad ne smijemo zaboraviti" (In memory at Bleiburg and Zrin--place of the Croatian victims we must never forget).

"ISELJENICI OSIGURALI 12 BESPLATNIH AUTOBUSA ZA BLEIBURG" (IMMIGRANTS GUARANTEED 12 FREE BUSES TO BLEIBURG), TOM SARE, BOKA CROPRESS, SYDNEY, 20 MAY 2015

The article relates to the 70th anniversary of the suffering of Croatian soldiers and civilians which began in Bleiburg field to be held on 16th May 2015. The commemoration was organized by the 'Honorary Bleiburg Platoon' under authority of Croatia's President Grabar-Kitarovic, beginning with a prayer led by Zagreb's Archbishop Bozanic. In the article Tom Sare alleges that "tens of thousands" were killed at Bleiburg in May 1945. But then the article goes on to say they were not actually killed at Bleiburg. Those unacquainted with the events, hearing of this for the first time, will be misinformed and confused by many contradictory statements.

> Sare: "...the British Government turned them over to the Yugoslav Army. Some were killed in the field and many more died in the following months on marches back to the then Yugoslavia known as the "Way of the Cross" marches."

According to this article, and similar others, the Croatian president paid respects to victims of the communist regime at Bleiburg, Tezno, and Macelj, "without media attention". I would add that unfortunately the Croatian President's visit, on a different day, was also without the Croatian people!

This 'lone-wolf' President's visit has allowed the ideological gap to widen between the leadership and the people. And I believe this is the core of the problem -- What is needed is a unity between the leader and the people on the justice of an issue, not a unity between two opposing ideologies and injustice! Those sentiments are felt by others too, but too seldom expressed.

"BLEIBURG—ISTINA KOJA NAS SVE OSLOBADJA" (BLEIBURG—THE TRUTH THAT FREES US ALL), BOKA CROPRESS, SYDNEY, 20 MAY 2015

The Editor comments on the 70th Anniversary Commemoration and the reaction in the Croatian media. He concludes by saying,

> Editor: "Nema mira i pomirenja bez pravde i istine...Bez iskrene osude zlocina ..." (There is no peace and reconciliation without justice and truth ... Without sincere condemnation of the crimes.)

"DVOSTRUKI ODNOS TITOISTA PREMA JASENOVCU I BLEIBURGU POKAZUJE NJIHOVO ANTIHRVATSTVO" (THE DOUBLE RELATIONSHIP OF TITOISTS TO JASENOVAC AND BLEIBURG SHOWS THEIR ANTI-CROATIAN ATTITUDE), MARKO FRANOVIC, ANTE MILINOVIC, BOKA CROPRESS, SYDNEY, 20 MAY 2015

A large photograph of Cardinal Bozanic and the Croatian clergy in front of the Croatian crowd comes with the caption, "Dostojanstvena komemoracija na Bleiburgu pokazala je sto hrvatski narod doista misli o zlocinima komunizma" (A dignified commemoration at Bleiburg illustrates what the Croatian people really think about the Communist crimes).

The article opens by saying that for 25 years in Croatia every spring brings an escalation of the issue of the dispute between the historical truth of WWII Croatia, and the attitude of Titoists to the new Croatian state. Once again yet another article side-steps the issue of what happened at Bleiburg and instead deals with the current controversy about it.

This is a full-page article in Croatian. The authors discuss the revisionist anti-Fascist pro-Communist Croatian leadership's interference and lies, concerning the remembrance of the Bleiburg tragedy, and Jasenovac, and the number of Croatian victims. Several post-war mass grave sites are mentioned including those around Maribor, Koceve, Barbara trench and the Huda mine.

A sub-heading is "Informativna blokada istine o zlocinima titoizma" (Information blockade regarding the truth of Tito's crimes).

For example, one Croatian historian, Slavko Goldstein maintains that Tito did not know about Bleiburg and that Rankovic was the operative.

An inappropriate comparison of the dispute between 'anti-fascists' and 'fascists' in Croatia to an "old schizophrenic dispute" is tactless, uninformative, and not politcally correct.

"Povjesnicar u Emisiji 'Bujica': Broj Ljudi Na Komemoraciji je Velika Politicka Poruka" (Historian on the Show 'Bujica': The number of people on the Commemoration is a strong political message), Boka Cropress, Sydney, 20 May 2015

This article refers to a Croatian television show and a discussion about the 70th Bleiburg commemoration. It also criticizes the suggestion by the Social Democratic Party (SDP) political party, P. Grbina. I agree that the assertion is ridiculous that tens of thousands of people attending the 70th commemoration were there to show their 'regrets' for the NDH!

> P. Grbin: "...da je komemoracija u Bleiburgu bila zaljenje za NDH, a ne za zrtvama" (that the commemoration at Bleiburg was about mourning for the WWII Independent State of Croatia, and not because of the victims).

"Na Bleiburgu--Bozanic: Ponovno se namecu podjele, Hrvaska je dobila novi totalitarizam" (At Bleiburg--Bozanic: Divisions re-imposed, Croatia has a new Totalitarianism), Direktno.hr, online, Zagreb, 20 May 2015

This article is mostly about the Homily given by the Croatian Archbishop Cardinal Bozanic who attended the Bleiburg field 70th anniversary commemoration in 2015.

He referred to the words of Pope John Paul II, who in Croatia in 1998 referred to the evils of Fascism, Nazism and Communism. In this context the Cardinal expressed his regret over the ideological divisions in today's Croatia. Taking a neutral position at Bleiburg Cardinal Bozanic spoke of an alleged absence of the complete truth about all war-time and post-war victims in relation to all nationalities, religions and political sides. It is unfortunate that the occasion of the Bleiburg commemoration is used for a political platform of 'equal guilt' and in this context for an inappropriate agenda of reconciliation.

> Cardinal Bozanic: "... bez obzira kojem naroda ili vjeroispovijesti pripadali, bez na kojoj su strani ili bez strani pale, te da im se zagarantira principjelan pijetet." (... which ever nation or religion they belong to, which ever side they fall on, and that they are guaranted the principle of piety)

Once again it seems that the only reconciliation the people need is one between the people and their leaders who do not take sides against injustice.

Unfortunately in this article the only explanation of events at Bleiburg in 1945 came at the end, alleging that the tens of thousands of Croatian soldiers and civilians wished to surrender to the Allied side but were allegedly extradited by the British at Bleiburg.

> Direktno: "...htjeli predati saveznickim snagama, ali ih je britanska vojska izrucila jugoslavenskoj. Neki su ubijeni na Bleiburskom polju, a mnogi su stradali iducih mjeseci u marsevima danas poznatima kao 'krizni putovi'." (... wanted to surrender to Allied forces, but the British Army extradited them to the Yugoslav (Army). Some were killed at Bleiburg field, and many were killed in the following months, on marches known as "Way of the Cross")

"Vodio sina na Bleiburg, da vidi gdje je bio i njegov djed" (He took his son to Bleiburg, to see where his grandfather had been), Tomislav Karamarko, online, index.hr, Zagreb, 16 May 2015

Tomislav Karamarko, the President of the Croatian Democratic Union Party (HDZ) went to Bleiburg with his son this year according to an online article. Amongst the 50,000-plus crowd were thousands of young people.

"Miro Kovac: Milanovic radi na podjelama, on je zabranio pokroviteljstvo Bleiburga" (Miro Kovac: Milanovic is working on divisions, he forbade the patronage of Bleiburg), Direktno.hr, online, Zagreb, 20 May 2015

This article is about an interview with Miro Kovac on a Croatian radio show, "Polygraph" on HTV4. In criticism of the Croatian Prime Minister Milanovic, of the SDP (Social Democrat Party) Miro Kovac highlights the fact that there is no consciousness about responsibility for the "Bleiburg" atrocities.

> Kovac: "...u Hrvatskoj nema svijesti da postoji odgovornost za zlocine u Bleiburgu i na Kriznim putevima..." (... in Croatia there is no awareness of the accountability for crimes at Bleiburg and Death Marches (Way of the Cross...)

"Croatia: Bleiburg Massacres of Victims still Hostages of Communist Ideology", Ina Vukic, Boka Cropress, Sydney, 20 May 2015

Ina Vukic, a weekly contributor to Boka Cropress comments on the discrepancies in the media regarding the numbers who attended the Bleiburg commemoration on 16th May 2015. The Croatian media mention 30,000 in attendance, but Austrian sources say up to 50,000 were at the field.

This full-page article discusses those present at the commemoration and what they have said there, and so I will not repeat the same facts again here, except to refer to Vukic's comment about the numbers of victims.

> Vukic: "records of numbers that perished have not surfaced as yet ..."

Surprisingly the numbers on retreat appear to be reduced here. The number of "60,000" retreating civilians is mentioned together with about "100,000" soldiers. It is not clear whether Vukic said this or somebody else. Most sources, including

British sources, agree that there were about 500,000 civilians on retreat towards the Austrian border, and most say 200,000 soldiers. The retreat of such large numbers is the reason why the retreat has been referred to as an 'exodus' or "the migration of an entire nation".

The fact that many Croatian Home Guards did not join the Ustasha forces, or in fact joined the Partisans is discussed by Vukic. Also the fact that many escaped death is revealed in this coverage of events by Vukic.

> Vukic: "Most Ustashi leaders had fled to South America after WWII, (and) were not among the masses ... at Bleiburg".

Bleiburg is described as being "symbolic" of all massacres after the war under the Tito. It is correct to say that, because the issue has remained open, it has become a political jumping-board, and in the place of justice there remains an ideological dispute in Croatian political culture.

The only comment I would make is concerning Vukic's sweeping statement regarding the turning over to the Yugoslav Army by the British Army after their refusal to accept the Croatian surrender. This generalisation that Croatia's Communists are still hiding their crimes by "rubbing shoulders with the Allies" requires some mental gymnastics! This could be taken as a subtle criticism of Croatia's membership of the EU and of NATO and a suggestion that those western alliances are hiding the crimes of the Communists. Of course if that is what Vukic meant to say then, for example, what of the EU's condemnation of all totalitarian crimes against humanity?

"Bleiburg--Istina i Samo Istina Ce Osloboditi Hrvatsku" (Bleiburg--The Truth and only the Truth will free Croatia), Dinko Dedic, Boka Cropress, Sydney, 20 May 2015

Dinko Dedic discusses how the truth about Bleiburg is manipulated in Croatia today. A large photograph of the multitudes, from the back, takes up half a page. On a separate page of photographs the number 61,235 pilgims is given. Dedic gives the example that even the foreign media reported that 50,000—65,000 actually attended the Bleiburg 70th Anniversary commemoration, in contrast to the Croatian television's estimate that 20,000 attended.

Dedic describes how the truth is slowly leaking out, in spite of Yugoslavia's attempt to bury the facts deep, but then alleges that even Great Britain is still hiding the facts also!

Dedic: "Istina curi na vidjelo svakog dana ...(Jugoslavija) pokrila liscem da se nikad ne pronadju i makar Velika Britanija, koja se ocito stidi svoje uloge u tom genocide, jos uvijek odbija deklasificirati dokumente iz tog vremena, istina izbija na povrsinu svakog dana i sa svih strana ... kao sto Turska ne moze zataskati armenske zrtve ..." (The truth is leaking light on the past each day ... Yugoslavia covers the (the past) with leaves to never find the truth and even Great Britain, which is obviously ashamed of its role in a genocide, still refuses to declassify documents from that time, truth comes to the surface every day from all sides ... just as Turkey cannot cover up the Armenian victims.)

It's true that every side has its own truth, but unfortunately the whole truth has not been accurately portrayed in this article. British documents concerning Bleiburg have already been opened, and compared and contrasted with available Yugoslav documents. British officer interviews, diaries, journals, declassified documents, a successful trial against Tolstoy, reports, films and books, etc. -- all of these sources have provided sufficient detail to sufficiently understand the events at Bleiburg; and at repatriation locations elsewhere along the Austrian/Yugoslav frontier.

Many British officers and others have expressed regret regarding how some of the repatriations were carried out, however the British are not "ocito stidi" (not obviously ashamed) of their alleged role in genocide because Yugoslavia is fully responsible for the planned genocide!

"Obljetnica 70. godina Bleiburske tragedije "Kriznog puta" u Hrvatskom centru u North Fremantleu" (Commemoration 70 years of Bleiburg tragedy and "the Way of the Cross" in the Croatian centre in North Fremantle) Stjepan Asic, Hrvatski Vjesnik, Melbourne, 20 May 2015

An academic event, dedicated to the Bleiburg victims, was held by Croatian clubs in North Fremantle.

"Croatia: Stjepan Mesic And The Scourge of Communist Past", Ina Vukic, Boka Cropress, Sydney, 27 May 2015

As the title suggests this article focuses on the remarks of the former Croatian President Stjepan Mesic – on his immoral and unethical accusations against those Croats who gather at the Bleiburg memorial to mourn, and on his stubborn refusal to acknowledge Tito's crimes against humanity. Mesic calls those who mourn at Bleiburg field "nazifascists", and accuses anyone who calls Tito a criminal and murderer of being "liars". Mesic contrasts the killing of innocent people at Jasenovac with those who "deserved death" at Bleiburg, or after the war, who had "lived an orgy for four years". Mesic certainly does not mince his words!

The only problem I have with this article as with many others, including my own, is the way in which the events at Bleiburg in 1945 are speciously integrated with other later surrenders and repatriations. Right through my book I maintain that this is not the ideal way to portray the genocide against Croatian people. For example,

> Vukic: "... when they surrendered at the Bleiburg field the members of the Croatian armed forces fleeing Croatia became British prisoners of war and the tens of thousands of civilians fleeing became asylum seekers ... But the British handed them all to Tito and his communist murderers..."

Comment is needed to correct the above quotation. In fact at Bleiburg the Croats never became British Prisoners of War, and the 'entire' Croatian exodus never managed to escape across the border. At Bleiburg surrender options were accepted by the Croatian commanders who then surrendered to the Partisans. These events have been detailed and supported by first-hand testimony in the first part of my book. The principles of the Geneva Convention apply to surrender during a battle in wartime but at Bleiburg the war was over. On this occasion also, Yalta superseded other international laws and after WWII the terms of the Yalta agreement were adhered to. At Bleiburg in particular it was the bullying and deliberate deceit of the Yugoslav Commissar Milan Basta which should be focused on.

Article 75 of the 1929 Geneva Convention refers to prisoners "at the end of hostilities" as analysed in Wikipedia. Article 76 stipulates how victims or prisoners of war should be treated or buried! It is Yugoslavia who has contravened the Geneva Convention.

> Article 75: "The release of prisoners should form part of the armistice. If this is not possible then repatriation of prisoners shall be effected with the least possible delay after the conclusion of peace. This particular provision was to cause problems after World War II because as the surrender of the Axis powers was unconditional there was no armistice, and in the case of Germany a full peace treaty was not signed..."

> Article 76: "Article 76 covers prisoners of war dying in captivity: they should be honourably buried and their graves marked and maintained properly..."

"Sunshine Odrzana Komemoracija uz 70. Obljetnicu Strasne Bleiburske Tragedije" (Sunshine holds Commemoration for 70ᵗʰ Anniversary of the horrible Bleiburg Tragedy), Petar Gelo, Hrvatski Vjesnik, Melbourne, 27 May 2015

This article is accompanied by a picture of Croatian community members holding candles, who attended the Bleiburg commemoration at the Croatian Sunshine Croatian Catholic Centre in Melbourne, on 17th May 2015. With the article also is a sign below the stage which states:

> "70. Obljetnica Bleiburga i Kriznih Puteva: Najveci Poslijeratni Zlocin Jugokomunista Waltera Tite nad Hrvatskim Narod". ("70th Anniversary of Bleiburg and the Way of the Cross: Biggest post-war crimes of the Yugo-communist Walter Tito on the Croatian people."

The article refers to the alleged arrival at Bleiburg of "200,000" Croatian military and more than "500,000" Croatian civilians of all ages. The speaker, Petar Gelo, is a leading member of the Melbourne-Croatian community, a 3ZZZ radio announcer, and the President for the Croatian Democratic Union (HDZ) in Australia and New Zealand. The article quotes a sentence or two from Gelo's address on the occasion that 'Bleiburg' was a crime which was not prevented but could have been, and that the crime is today concealed and that the European Union does not put those war criminals on trial.

My main criticism is that not many facts about the events at Bleiburg are in this article. I have already commented in my book that the crime at Bleiburg is not concealed any more.

"Bleiburg 2015, Sydney--Svecana Komemorativna Akademija Odrzana u Hrvatskom Drustvu Sydney" (Blessed Commemoration Academy held by Croatian Community in Sydney), Tomislav Beram, Boka Cropress, Sydney, 27 May 2015

This lengthy article is accompanied by photographs of the occasion taken by Milena Sopic. The commemoration was organized by the Croatian Coordinating Committee in Sydney for 17th May 2015. The emotional speeches, and prayers, are published.

"Komemorativna akademija Bleiburske tragedije u hrvatskom klubu "Bosna" un Sydneyu" (Commemoration Academy for Bleiburg Tragedy held in Croatian Club "Bosnia" in Sydney), Ivica Glamatovic, Boka Cropress, Sydney, 27 May 2015

This article describes events of the Sydney commemoration about the Bleiburg Tragedy and has no historical content.

"Sramota Hrvatska! Sramota!" (Shame Croatia, Shame!), Dinko Dedic, Boka Cropress, Sydney, 27 May 2015

This article should perhaps have been entitled 'Sramota Jugoslavia, Sramota' or 'Sramota Tito, Sramota' because as it is the ambiguous heading could be inadvertently misconstrued as anti-Croatian propaganda.

As well as picturing post-war columns on "Death Marches" another photograph of Mesic appears with a caption.

> "Kaze Mesic da ce se boriti protiv revizionizma. Kako ce se boriti, s kim i s cim?" (Mesic says that we will struggle against revisionism. How will we struggle, with whom and with what?)

Another picture of Tito also has a caption in Dedic's article.

> Caption: "Marsal Tito cije se velike rijeci "Majku vam Bozju!" moraju ukopati u svijest svakog antifasiste." (Marshall Tito's great words were "Mother of God" we must dig antifascism into everyone's consciousness."

"Genocide Memorial: Sculpture Destined for Preston Reserve", Julia Irwin, Preston Leader, Preston Victoria, page 5, September 15, 2015-11-29

This Victoria Australia newspaper has a short article and big photograph by Josie Hayden.

> Caption: "Members of Darebin Ethnic Communities Council Sofia Kotanadis, Nalliah Surlyakumaran and Katarina Brozovic in Ray Bramham Gardens".

This is Australia's first memorial for victims of genocide. Brozovic describes this memorial as a place for those of all religions.

Brozovic: "(a) ... place where those who had family members or friends brutally killed in places such as the Republic of Congo, Srebrenica, Germany and Greece could remember their dead when there was no gravesite."

The Memorial marker will be unveiled on December 6 to coincide with an important date in history.

"(the) ... date of the adoption of the United Nations 1948 Convention on the Prevention and Punishment of the Crime of Genocide on December 9, 1948."

"Genocide memorial on hold after complaints received", Harrison Tippet, Preston Leader, Preston Victoria, page 5, December 15, 2015

The installation of the victims of genocide memorial, "Victims of Genocide and Genocidal Acts", has been held back due to a few community opposition groups. At the time of publication of my book no further news has been published in the Preston Leader newspaper. This opposition to a memorial in a Melbourne location suggests that controversy over the issues of genocide and responsibility exist in other places across time.

"Purging Croatia of Darkness of Tito and Communism", Ina Vukic, Za Dom Press, Sydney, 11 November 2015

From time to time mention is made of Bleiburg in various articles in the Australian-Croatian press. The newspaper "Boka Cropress" changed its name to "Za Dom Press" in late 2015. There is a photograph of a large crowd and a large panel of speakers with the backdrop reading,

"Hrvatsko Nacionalno Eticko Sudiste ... Eticke osude J.B. Tita, totalitarizma i Zorana Milanovica" (Croatian National Ethical Tribunal ... Ethical conviction of J.B. Tito, totalitarianism and Zoran Milanovic)

Thousands of people filled a hall in Zagreb on 31st October 2015 for an Ethical Tribunal and conviction against Tito. This Tribunal has drawn large crowds since 1990.

"posthumous judgment against Josip Broz Tito, the President, the Marshall, the Judge , the Jury and the Executioner, the Dictator of the former communist Yugoslavia delivered by the Croatian National Ethical Tribunal for his crimes against the Croatian people ... (for genocide)."

One speaker, the Slovenian M.P. Franc Breznik referred to the event as being the "Croatian Nurenberg". Other speakers included Dr Marko Veselica, Nikola Stedul, Anto Kovacevic, Ante Glibota (of European Academy of Sciences and Arts and Literature), Roman Ljeljak, Dr Zvonimir Separovic. The Tribunal President was Zvonomir Separovic, and members included Nikola Debelic, Zdravko Tomac, Josip Jurcevic, Zdravko Vladanovic, Zvonimir Hodak, John Kozlic, Bozidar Alic, Ante Beljo, Nevenka Nekic and Tomislav Josic.

Zoran Milanovic was also convicted and condemned for being "Tito's and his ideology's follower". Over the past year convictions have also been delivered against Ivo Josipovic, Stjepan Mesic, Vesna Pusic, Milorad Pupovac, Budimir Loncar, and Vesna Terselic.

> Zdravko Tomac: "(Milanovic) ... a man who even after the discovery of 1700 mass graves and Huda pits he has the audacity to repeat that Tito was the best thing that Croats ever had."

"MILE KEKIN OGNJISTARIMA POSLAO 'MOCNU' PORUKU" (MILE KEKIN SENT HOME A POWERFUL MESSAGE), ZVONIMIR HODAK, ON PAGE 27 OF WEEKLY COMMENTARY, HRVATSKI VJESNIK, 9 MARCH 2016

My main interest in this lengthy article is the mention of the official number of atrocities committed by the Yugoslavs after WWII. Hodak refers to Alexandar Rankovic's admission in his report to the Federal Assembly of Yugoslavia in 1952 about the liquidation of 586,000 "enemies of the people"! (Note: the number 686,000 is given in Jurcevic's 'Black Book of Communism in Croatia' (2006) reviewd in my Chapter 8). The author comments that the whole lost generation of Croatian people of that era have not been able to catch up.

"THE TRAGEDY OF BLEIBURG AND VIKTRING 1945", FLORIAN T. RULITZ, NORTH ILLINOIS UNIVERSITY PRESS, USA, 2016

This is an important book based on Rulitz's dissertation, and translated from German by Andreas Niedermayer. The Foreword is by Paul E. Gottfried and Postface by Tomislav Sunic. My interest in 'The Tragedy of Bleiburg and Viktring 1945' is his interpretation of negotiations at the Bleiburg castle but unfortunately only a couple of pages refer directly to the castle negotiations.

According to Rulitz's version the British 38th Army arrived at Bleiburg on 12th May 1945 and their headquarters was at the castle. The British were aware of the approach of 700,000 Croats near the Austrian/Slovenian border due to air surveillance, according to Rulitz. Rulitz describes the various routes to Austria in detail and mentions the presence of the Bulgarians at Dravograd since the 9th May 1945. He says that the Croats rejected an unconditional surrender at Dravograd and he alleges that the Bulgarians blocked the bridge under "Soviet orders". According to his book only a few Croats managed to escape across the Drava River to eventually reach Wolfsberg. After battles along the way to Poljana, between the Croats and the Yugoslavs, the Croats eventually moved towards Bleiburg via Loibach (Libuce).

On pages 38--39 Rulitz describes separate talks at the castle between Scott and the opposing Croatian and Yugoslav representatives. For his sources Rulitz uses Beljo, Bethell, 38th Brigade war diaries, Aralica, Tolstoy and others. His very brief portrayal of the negotiations is correct as far as it goes but I believe more attention to detail is warranted to avoid misunderstanding. But of course the main focus in Rulitz's book is on the Slovenians, on all Yugoslav murders in Austria, and on British repatriations in the context of Viktring.

I have a couple of criticisms of his book. I believe it is incorrect to suggest on page 38 that Dr Dusan Krivokapic, the Montenegrin Chetnik representative, was at the Bleiburg negotiations together with Herencic "to persuade Scott to protect the refugees". In my book I have mentioned an appeal document signed by Herencic, Crljen and also Krivokapic on 13th May 1945 two days before Herencic attended the castle negotiations. I also disagree with Rulitz's suggestion that part of the Bleiburg field stretched into Slovenian territory at the border. The railroad cuts through a narrowing space before Holmec. In addition Yugoslav sources indicate that the Croats were surrounded at the "Libuce" field area. In addition it is a stretch of the imagination to suggest that the "edge" of the Bleiburg field reaches as far as Poljana. Rulitz writes that there is a mass grave of Croats at Poljana which lie underneath the Victory Memorial

> "in Poljana at the southeastern edge of the fields at Bleiburg ..."

Rulitz referred to Scott's car telephone not working on 15th May, so Scott could not refer the matter higher up, and had to deal with the situation by himself at Bleiburg. We know from other sources that Scott had received orders the previous day not to accept more refugees behind the British lines. It's clear that the Bleiburg tragedy is unique and different when compared to the repatriations around Viktring. Any "horse trading" alleged by Rulitz happened around Viktring many miles west of

Bleiburg by road. Rulitz accuses the British of using the presence of refugees around Viktring as leverage for inducing Partisan withdrawal from Carinthia, on pages 168-9. For these reasons I do not agree that the situation at Bleiburg was part of any alleged "horse trading", a point I have argued throughout my book.

There is information about the removal of bodies from the Bleiburg field by Yugoslavs in lorries after some killings there, according to the local farm residents, who vary in their estimates about the number killed at the field. It is likely that about 1000 were killed at the field, however Rulitz includes a lot of territory in Bleiburg field that is not actually in the Bleiburg (Libuce) field.

This author Rulitz is very clear about the responsibility of the Serbian Partisans on pages 40-41, who were the ones shooting and killing at the Bleiburg field. More than once Rulitz stresses the point that Slovenian or Carinthian Partisans had no part in the killings, and that the mass of killings happened in Slovenia and not in Austria. Partisans were gone from Bleiburg by the 17th May. According to one Partisan deserter Kersche,

> "Serb Partisans left a trail of blood running through all of northern Slovenia".

The separate retreat of the Croatian government ahead of the main Croatian exodus is confirmed by Rulitz on pages 53-54. At Grafenstein and Krumpendorf POW camps the NDH leadership was together with Pavelic's bodyguard and up to 50 priests and theologians. Between 50 and 80 cars took them away, and some authors say that many of these, though not all, made it to safety abroad.

The tragedies are discussed in the context of the post-WWII killing and mayhem created by Tito's Yugoslav Partisans in Austrian Carinthia. He argues that the murders, which were not "random", must be seen in the context of the "NS" brutality during WWII. Thus Rulitz suggests the murders can be explained somewhere between "revolution and revenge justice". Although he mentions Croats, Slovenes, or Serbs, and Montenegrins or Chetniks etc. Rulitz often simply refers to "slavs". He also cites Yugoslav intolerance of Croatian secession as a motivating factor for the post-war murders, and that murders and assassinations continued for years by UDBA.

Rulitz's book cover depicts the iconic 'signpost' photograph, which he alleges is taken at Bleiburg field, "north of the railroad embankment opposite the country inn Hrust". This is one of a few suggested locations for the signpost and unfortunately I cannot find a source for the photographs in Rulitz's book, although it is always possible that I have missed it. On page 11 or 58 of my book is my photograph of the Hrust tavern on the other side of the railroad tracks from the Bleiburg field.

The translation of Rulitz's book is important because new information is available for English-language readers interested in the topic, myself included. I suspect that some information which is new to English-speaking readers may not be new for Croatian researchers because so much information still remains hidden in thousands of pages about Bleiburg in the Croatian language.

CHAPTER 10

CONCLUSIONS

SEARCHING FOR THE TRUTH

In "One Day in May – Bleiburg 1945" I have tried to discover how and why the unique Croatian surrender to Yugoslavs at Bleiburg occurred. It has been difficult to fit together pieces of information about the 15th May 1945 from so many sources. After searching through a mountain of musty old newspapers and several books on the topic I became confused because many authors do not correctly or consistently reflect the order of events or numbers involved. Most sources agree about some basic facts, but from that point on the many confusing theories contradict each other. Indeed, the large number of different opinions I found shocked me. For example, most sources reviewed in this book concur that tens of thousands of Croatian soldiers and civilians arrived at the Bleiburg field by 15th May 1945, but only a few of those sources describe the surrender negotiations which took place at the Bleiburg castle. So I have had to analyse the material to determine some fundamental truths. To give another example, it is obvious to me that Tito's post-war genocidal intentions were expressed and demonstrated against Croatian soldiers and civilians at Bleiburg and even before Bleiburg, but this fact is not always evident in the case of some literature!

Thus, my original mission narrowed and evolved, to describe the "Bleiburg Tragedy" in its correct historical context, by separating fact from fiction, and the victims from the perpetrators. Every Croatian family has been touched by the Bleiburg Tragedy and they want and deserve justice and closure.

AN OVERVIEW

The situation in post-war Carinthia: The Yugoslav Army officers were ordered by Tito to occupy Austrian southern Carinthia and claim it as part of a Communist greater Yugoslavia; and liquidate their biggest opposition, the Croats. For example the Yugoslavs occupied Trieste and Klagenfurt and other locations, and they outnumbered the British forces at the time in southern Carinthia.

British Army officers on the ground were ordered to avoid a war, and not to confront the occupying Yugoslav Army, except in self-defense; and not to accept more refugees behind British lines. The terms of the Yalta Agreement between the big powers were to be carried out to repatriate already held prisoners-of-war back to Yugoslavia or the Soviet Union.

The Croatian government leadership, which had taken a different route, ordered the colossal Croatian columns to follow a single retreat route from Zagreb through southeast Slovenia; to escape the Bolshevik Yugoslavs; and to surrender to the British. The Yugoslavs were attacking the hundreds of thousands of Croats along their retreat and turned a majority of them back. The situation on the ground was changing daily and more Yugoslav troops were constantly arriving and ultimately outnumbered the British at that time.

The Attempted Croatian Retreat: It was through eastern Slovenia that the largest post-war Croatian columns of up to 200,000 soldiers and 500,000 civilians were moving northward with hopes of escaping Tito's Yugoslav Armies. These Croatian columns were separate from and no where near to the other major retreating ethnic groups. In addition, the number of retreating Croatian people vastly outnumbered other groups some of which were also trying to escape the Yugoslav attempts to liquidate them. Most of the Croats were blocked before reaching the Austrian border and were re-routed by the Bulgarians and Yugoslavs towards Maribor, but a few tens of thousands reached Bleiburg, a newly created post-war British Army outpost.

The Croatian Surrender to Yugoslavs: The British commanding officer at Bleiburg was given the strict new British order not to allow any more refugees to cross the British lines. Therefore in this context the British officer gave three options to the Croatian representatives at Bleiburg in a separate meeting with them. A Croatian-American interpreter was an important part of the process and he was present throughout the negotiations. But even the separate talks between the British and the Croats were briefly interrupted by a Yugoslav ultimatum that the Yugoslavs could not wait any longer to begin shooting the Croats.

The first option was that the Croats could surrender to the Yugoslavs and the British would try to ensure they were treated correctly. Secondly another option was that the Croats could keep their arms and stay there which would result in an attack by the Yugoslavs. The third option was that if the Croats tried to move across British lines they would be probably be attacked by the British to prevent this. The first option was accepted by the Croatian representatives resulting in the Croatian surrender to Yugoslavs, whose final ultimatum was that they would begin shooting the Croats anyways after one hour if they did not surrender to them. The Yugoslav Commissar threatened to destroy the Croats if they did not surrender to them.

The Yugoslav Commissar promised that the Croats would be treated fairly according to the stipulations of international laws. Civilians would be guaranteed a safe return home and could keep their belongings. Upon an unconditional surrender others would be escorted to P.O.W. camps and the generals could retain valets and weapons. Resistance would be dealt with. The problem with this surrender according to both the British and the Croats was the short time limit given for the capitulation.

Eye-witness reports concur that a small number of Croats were killed at the Bleiburg field but that the vast majority were marched across country back to Yugoslavia and sent on "Death Marches". Reliable sources and documents suggest that most of the main columns of 200,000 Croatian soldiers and 500,000 Croatian civilians had already been split and blocked before Dravograd and turned back on "Death Marches". In this way most Croats never crossed the Austrian/Yugoslav border or arrived at Bleiburg.

The British in Carinthia had no foreknowledge that the Yugoslavs were planning massacres of Croats, massacres that happened over the months following 15th May 1945, organized massacres which occurred across a wide front along the Yugoslav/Austrian frontier! Decades later, when the former Yugoslavia began to collapse, the hundreds of mass graves unearthed testify to the Yugoslav post-war massacres of Croats and others that took place from mid May 1945 onwards in Yugoslav territory.

The Bleiburg Field & Repatriation: Basically it happened like this at the Bleiburg castle on 15th May 1945. First separate negotiations took place between a British officer and two Yugoslav officers; and secondly between the British and two representatives of the Croatian Army and civilians; and ultimately the three groups were present together. The testimonies in the book "Operation Slaughterhouse" of the main army representatives present at the Bleiburg castle negotiations basically agree with each other on the order of events and outcome. The interpreter also confirmed the nature of the negotiations. Naturally the three accounts are written from three different perspectives. After all, on the 15th May 1945 the three armies present all had a different mission and orders.

Other **Later Repatriations**: Bleiburg was not the first place where Croats, as well as other ethnic groups, had crossed the Austrian/Yugoslav border. It's important to note also that other Croatian groups had already surrendered behind British lines earlier in May at different locations. Those groups included some of Pavelic's government leaders who had left by different routes earlier. At locations far to the west from Bleiburg other various smaller ethnic refugee groups, including up to 26,000 Croats, were repatriated by the British back to Yugoslavia, where they were secretly massacred by the Yugoslavs. These groups were deceived by the British about the destination of their train, in a scenario quite different to what happened at the Bleiburg field, where large numbers of Croats were force-marched back across the border by Yugoslav troops.

Thus, a clear distinction exists between the nature of the events at Bleiburg, and the surrenders and repatriations from other locations in Carinthia Austria. A widespread intentional and coordinated Yugoslav 'plan' to liquidate Tito's opposition took place and this is indicated by the number of repatriation locations involved and the number of mass graves discovered.

Bleiburg is Distinct and Unique: The Bleiburg Tragedy is a unique Croatian historical event, unique from all other surrenders in post-war Austria. Bleiburg was the first Austrian location where Croats surrendered to Yugoslavs, who then marched the Croats out of Austria back to Yugoslavia. A few days after the Bleiburg incident other ethnic groups, including about 26,000 Croats, were repatriated to Yugoslavia by the British, and this happened far away from Bleiburg. Those other surrenders and British repatriations back to Yugoslavia from Maria Elend and Rosenbach, and from Lavamund, are distinct and separate from Bleiburg. My book briefly presents details of the numbers and ethnicity of other groups, but my focus is on Croats at Bleiburg.

QUESTIONS ANSWERED

My first main question was, "**Who did Croats negotiate with at Bleiburg and who did they surrender to?**" The participants present at negotiations, such as Basta, Crljen and Scott, recorded and agreed with each other, in their separate reports, on the main points. The Croatian representatives chose to surrender to the Yugoslavs.

I was really surprised by the material I was reading. Over the past five decades many Croatian versions about the Bleiburg Tragedy have been inaccurate, misleading, too general, too brief, or written in a confusing or un-chronological order.

Relevant official documents on the other hand as referred to by some British authors, testify to the details of the repatriations, accurately portray events, and they express their regret. Others, in particular Croatian authors, do mention documents but use documents about other events in the context of Bleiburg.

Conclusions

And, seventy years later some authors still allege that Britain has not released documents so that we can finally discover the truth, rather than say that the Yugoslavs should release documents. Some authors inaccurately refer to British deceit at Bleiburg by merging all events into one event, instead of referring to Yugoslav deceit at Bleiburg.

The most inflated versions alleged that over half a million Croats at Bleiburg were disarmed by the British and herded back to the Yugoslavs and Yugoslavia by deceit! Others acknowledge that there was a negotiation at the Bleiburg castle but that it was allegedly the British officer, not the Yugoslav officer, who was threatening to bomb Croats within an hour; or that at Bleiburg the British deceived the Croats and sent them back on trains to Yugoslavia! Others use un-sourced photographs with un-sourced captions to create a false impression about the Croatian surrender to Yugoslavs at Bleiburg!

For most Croatian authors however the Bleiburg Tragedy is a catchphrase to represent all surrenders and all repatriations and all massacres. The problem with this symbolic all-inclusive meaning is that some authors, today's pro-Yugoslavs included, use the Bleiburg Tragedy issue as a soapbox for an anti-western political agenda.

The second important question I posed to myself was, "**whether or not the Bleiburg Tragedy is exclusively Croatian**". I believe that the negotiations and eye-witness testimony about events at Bleiburg point to an exclusively Croatian Tragedy. If other ethnic groups were amongst the Croatian throngs at Bleiburg they were not represented during surrender negotiations. The Croatian soldiers (Ustasha and Croatian Home Guards) at Bleiburg were of both the Christian and Moslem faith, and are represented on the monument to the Croatian army victims at Bleiburg. Only a very few authors recently have tried to suggest otherwise because of the presence of other ethnic groups inside Slovenian territory. For example, because there were some Montenegrin Chetniks were amongst the retreating Croatian columns, a few suggest they were also at the Bleiburg field.

At the extreme end some merge all surrenders and repatriations together under the heading of Bleiburg including the Germans, Cossacks, Hungarians, Croats, Serbs, Slovenes, Montenegrins, etc.

Another relevant question was, "**how many British and Yugoslavs were in post-war Carinthia Austria?**" Documents reveal that the Yugoslavs in Southern Carinthia initially outnumbered the British units. On and around 15th May 1945 the British V Corps, under the British Eighth Army, was over-stretched with about 25,000 troops widely dispersed over all Carinthia. In the area there was only one British Division by 12th May.

In contrast most sources accept that Yugoslavia had about 16,000 troops just in southern Carinthia of First, Second and Third Yugoslav Armies. The Yugoslav Fourth Army south of Venezia Giula had about 60,000 troops. Yugoslav troops also numbered about 25,000 just over the Austrian/Yugoslav border especially in Meza Valley and around Eisenkappel. Just in Volkermarkt were 6,000 Yugoslav troops with a further 2,000 Yugoslavs at Lavamund. Yugoslav troops were also stationed with the Bulgarian units and a Red Army unit. The Bleiburg field, and north at Lippitzbach also, was blocked with several Yugoslav brigades. Other Yugoslav battalions were around Holmec and Poljana. On 13th May 1945 Tito ordered more Yugoslav troops to move towards Dravograd to annihilate the retreating Croatian soldiers and civilians.

Chaos in southern Carinthia was created by Tito's forces trying to occupy the area and claim it for a greater Yugoslavia, just as they had done after the first World War. The tens of kilometres-long retreating columns of Croatian soldiers and civilians were being attacked by the Yugoslavs in eastern Slovenia.

"How many Croats came to the Bleiburg field?" This is a question everyone wants answered. The actual numbers of retreating Croats who arrived at the Bleiburg, or Libuce field (Loibach field) is different to the numbers who were retreating.

I estimate that some tens of thousands of Croatian soldiers and civilians made it as far as the Bleiburg field. In the NDH there were both Catholic and Moslem soldiers, and this is illustrated on the Bleiburg monument. Some say tens of thousands, and others estimate up to around 150,000 thousand. Alternatively, others begin at 20,000 to 30,000 Croats at Bleiburg field. The number is probably somewhere in between.

The remaining Croatian exodus columns had already been re-routed by Bulgarian and Yugoslav troops onto "Death Marches" towards Maribor before reaching the Austrian border.

In contrast at the extreme end the highest number alleged to have reached Bleiburg is 700,000, or we read of multitudes or even the entire Croatian nation being there, but these excessive figures can be ruled out by the facts.

This leads us to the question, **"How many Croats were actually massacred at the Bleiburg field after surrendering to the Yugoslavs?"** Once again the numbers killed at Bleiburg vary according to the author. There is an over-ruling consensus amongst the sources reviewed that not many died at Bleiburg and there was no mass killing there, and this is supported by reliable eye-witness accounts. At the Libuce Cemetary a few Croats are buried.

Some write that the "Death Marches" or mass killings 'began' at Bleiburg and continued once back inside Yugoslavia. Others write that between 1,000 and 3,000 Croats were killed at Bleiburg. Some say that there is a mass grave in nearby Poljana rather than at Bleiburg. Some also say that as few as 60 people were killed at Bleiburg. At the other extreme we read that from tens of thousands to about 600,000 or over were massacred at the Bleiburg field!

Next is the problem to answer the question "**why do many authors integrate all events, facts and numbers into one event, one surrender, and one British repatriation to Yugoslavs**?" Here I will try to summarize this 'integration version'. This emotional fabrication, in its various versions, has permeated the collective memory of Croatian communities. This very confusing integration of events into one is one of the main reasons I decided to write this book!

When we examine the testimony about the fate of Croats at Bleiburg, or at Marie Elend and Rosenbach, the differences are clear. From Bleiburg Croats knew they were returning to Yugoslavia after surrender to the Yugoslavs. Croats were marched on foot across country from Bleiburg towards Yugoslavia and soon robbed of their possessions. From Bleiburg Croats were marched through corn fields, ditches, rivers and over walls. This testimony should clear-up for once and for all time the difference between the repatriations at Bleiburg and at Marie Elend and Rosenbach trains stations where Croats were taken from trucks and put onto train cars towards Yugoslavia, after being told their destination was Italy.

When and how did this fabricated version begin? I believe it began because the focus for Croatian people is on the "Death Marches" rather than on the various events which led to the massacres. Thus Croats abroad created a Resolution that Bleiburg is symbolic of all the "Death Marches" ("Way of the Cross") and of all massacres of Croatian people. Perhaps this is how the confusion began. It is still a mystery to me but when put into the context of the Cold War era it is easier to understand.

However it is difficult to rationalize why the inaccurate Bleiburg narrative has remained intact well into the 21st century.

Perhaps it was believed that by merging all events the huge numbers of victims can be better expressed. Or, when testimony about the British repatriation of 26,000 Croats from Rosenbach and Marie Elend to Jesenice is attributed to events at

Bleiburg, perhaps this is to suggest that the British repatriated 'all' Croats at Bleiburg in a similar way.

But while Croats may believe this merging of events under the heading of British repatriations shows a greater number of victims, the opposite is true for the Yugoslavs who take advantage of the confusion.

The Yugoslavs point to fewer numbers by merging events because the British did not repatriate Croats at Bleiburg. Also if there is just one major event then it is easy to refer to random Yugoslav 'revenge' and hide their mass executions without trial on a planned and intentional basis. In other words, what happened to Croats back inside Yugoslavia was an orchestrated and well-coordinated mass murder. Or perhaps some authors cannot look beyond the British deception at Marie Elend and Rosenbach station where Croats were told they were going to Italy in train cars, instead of Yugoslavia.

Alternatively many of those who merge events into one event are able to take focus away from the separate escape route of the Croatian government members. Also, by being vague about what happened at Bleiburg (read everywhere) the claim that documents are still being kept secret can be given.

I next considered the question, **"what were the contributing factors which led to the crisis in southern Carinthia and at Bleiburg where the biggest Yugoslav deception occurred?**

The British policy to abide by the Yalta Agreement as well as the not to confront the Soviets in Austria or the aggressive Yugoslavs, except in self-defense, is also an important factor. And the fact that Stalin did not support Tito's occupation of southern Carinthia was an equally important factor at the time.

After the war the Bulgarian Army did not allow Croats to pass at Dravograd and re-routed the retreating Croatian columns to Maribor with the help of the Yugoslavs. The Yugoslav had already managed to split and attack the Croatian columns earlier. Thus the "Death Marches" began before other Croatian refugees reached Bleiburg and the Bulgarian refusal came before the British order not to accept refugees.

The Croatian state (NDH) did not change sides to the western allies during WWII and a belated Croatian Memorandum did not reach its destination before the end of the war. The Croatian Army therefore remained under the German Army until Lohr surrendered. This fact reveals the limited independence of the Croatian state to operate outside of their occupiers. The Croatian decision in Zagreb that the main exodus columns form a single retreat route was ill conceived without taking regional history into account.

Of course in the bigger picture the historical creation of Yugoslavia itself, and the unaccountable brutal nature of that regime, was a contributing factor towards the continuation of that brutality.

Another main factor briefly mentioned is the long-term Serbian goal to wipe out their Croatian opposition. The Serbs in the Kingdom of Yugoslavia came to dominate this regime. The assassination by a Serb of five Croatian M.P.s inside a full session of parliament in Belgrade in 1928 made world headlines.

Perhaps the writing was on the wall when Tito refused to allow the Ango/American forces to land on Dalmatian coast. This refusal may reveal a Yugoslav long-term intention to occupy Trieste and Carinthia. A Yugoslav "minor reign of terror" created an east-west epicenter of conflict.

Yugoslavia's existence was ensured by the Tito-Subacic agreement before the end of WWII, and the Serbian king's call for Serbs to join the Partisans paid off with the inflation of the number of Yugoslav troops.

What is the bigger picture? When we examine all the extra circumstances this leads us to look at a bigger picture from different perspectives. Although facts are facts, each side sees and values these facts from a different vantage point.

From the Yugoslav perspective their policy was to carry out their revolution using classic revolutionary tactics which take advantage of an unstable historical time frame. The Bolshevik Yugoslavs created havoc and took advantage of a chaotic and rapidly evolving crisis. Killing everything in the way of their 'brotherhood and unity' was a means to an end.

The British did not want to see another war break out, and this whole Yugoslav affair was referred to by Churchill as the start of the iron curtain and the beginning of the Cold War. Also tension was growing between the Soviet Union and the British and American Allies over eastern Europe.

From a Croatian perspective they were apparently caught unawares, not unlike the British, by an unimagined and unpredicted Yugoslav threat. The British weren't the only ones who seemed to have forgotten post-WWI history. For Croats this was the worst tragedy in their long history.

How do we know that a genocide against Croats took place? We have the admission of the Serbian Milovan Djilas who said that Croats "had to die" that Yugoslavia could live; and, of the Serbian Alexandar Rankovic of Tito's Central Committee who reported, in a parliamentary session in 1952, that up until 1952 we (Yugoslavia) have liquidated 586,000 "enemies of the people". But quotations are not enough. In the context of the Bleiburg Tragedy narrative it is important to provide evidence that the Yugoslav crime of genocide did take place across a wide front inside Slovenia, Croatia, and Bosnia-Hercegovina and all the former Yugoslavia as far as Romania or Macedonia. The Yugoslav authorities had carried out by various means the concealment of these graves although the locals always knew of their existence. Some politicians in both Slovenia and Croatia have been less than cooperative to this day about the post-war mass graves.

The written material I have reviewed in this book reports on the mass graves as they are revealed to the world media over a period of years.

Critics and unbelievers may allege that the remains were from the wartime period, but it has been shown that the bigger mass graves recently unearthed date from the post-war period. These were the mass killings of targeted ethnic groups or political 'class enemies' of the communist Yugoslav revolution.

It is known that Tito killed over half a million of his political opponents after the war but until now we did not have the evidence or ethnicity of his victims. Sources reviewed have alleged that from 300,000 victims over 200,000 of them are Croats. The Croatian Home Guards were hugely represented amongst the victims, as were civilians. Apart from the mass graves, Croats in particular more than others, simply perished or starved on long "Death Marches" throughout Yugoslavia. Their bodies were thrown aside or into rivers along these grueling marches as they died from starvation or exhaustion.

The skeletons and remains being unearthed in up to 700 mass graves belong mostly to post-WWII unarmed Croatian civilians and disarmed Croatian soldiers. There were more Croats in the area than other ethnic groups, and they were returned before other groups also, from more than one location. Evidence of the type of killing, and the DNA and types of evidence, confirms the Croatian identity of the majority of victims unearthed to date.

Over 700 mass grave sites have been investigated or unearthed by the Commission on Concealed Mass Graves in Slovenia. So that readers can imagine the horrible unearthed discoveries, the scale of the Serbian genocide of Moslems at Srebrenica pales in comparison.

The process of opening and unearthing post-war mass graves was publicized first around the world regarding a mass grave in Croatia. In Croatia in the Jazovka Pit (karst sink hole) at Sosice in underground caverns are interred the skeletons of Croats who were clearly unarmed victims shot execution style. Even old rusty hospital equipment was found amongst the skeletons. Numbers of victims written about vary from hundreds to tens of thousands at Jazovka.

In Kocevje Rog, Slovenia up to 40,000 victims have been discovered with the majority being Croats who were the first extradited to the Yugoslavs. The remains of Slovenian, German, or Serbian post-war victims can also be found at Kocevje Rog.

At Maribor in eastern Slovenia there are up to 70,000 victims especially in anti-tank trench next to the Slivnica-Pesnica Highway, or at Pohorje. At Maribor at a new cemetery "Dobrava" is a monument to all victims. At Slovenia Bistrica are 4,000 Croatian skeletons. There is a mass grave of Croats near Poljana and at Maceljska Forest there are 20,000 victims. At Tezno Forest there lies up to 20,000 Croatian soldiers and civilians. At Hrastnik (Trbovlje) 7,000 perished, and at Kosice (Teharje) near Celje (Camp Stental) lay more than a thousand. Hundreds more smaller mass graves are known of but yet to be forensically investigated.

At Huda Mine at Lasko (known also as Barbara Trench), in eastern Central Slovenia, the skeletal remains of hundreds of Croatians have been dug out after opening a disused mine where refugees were concealed inside with cement after being gassed.

Finally we come to the question of responsibility and accountability. "Who is responsible for such mass atrocities on a genocidal scale?" Thousands of people filled a hall in Zagreb Croatia on 31st October 2015 for an Ethical Tribunal and conviction against Tito. This unofficial Tribunal has drawn large crowds since 1990. Clearly Tito and Communist Yugoslavia is to blame for the genocide amongst this Croatian group.

It was Yugoslavia's Tito and/or Central Committee which organized these killings at various locations. We know of Tito's order of 13th May 1945 to liquidate the Croats on retreat towards Dravograd via Celje. It was the Yugoslavs at Bleiburg who controlled the location militarily and who were threatening both the Croats and the British that they would begin shooting within 15 minutes. Fifteen minutes was later extended to one hour.

At Bleiburg the Yugoslav (Serbian) Commissar used bullying and threats to convince the British he meant what he said. It was a Yugoslav goal to create a greater Yugoslavia in Carinthia up to the Drava River.

Some authors directly blame the Serbs within the Yugoslav Armies, especially around the area concerned near Bleiburg. Indeed Yugoslavs such as Tito or Djilas both later admitted that there were mass killings, or insinuated that Croats deserved to die, or had to die for the cause of the revolution. Still, some allege that the British should have protected Croats from Yugoslav vengeance, but even Tito himself had said to Ivan Mestrovic that even he could not have protected the Croats from Serbian vengeance.

Interestingly, Tito himself blames the Serbs for their revenge-taking or attributes all responsibility to the high ranking Rankovic. Which ever Yugoslav operative it was, it was the Yugoslav Army which directly turned Croats on "Death Marches", committed mass executions, and then concealed the mass graves with dynamite or cement or waste products, etc. Local people were afraid for their lives or the lives of their families to speak of the genocide they witnessed, for decades, until the collapse of Yugoslavia.

But I have reviewed another theme in my book reviews about responsibility for genocide. A select group of authors continue to blame some British orders for Tito's crimes against humanity, alleging that it could all have been prevented! Even Djilas uses this theme, that the British were wrong to hand over Croats and the Yugoslavs were wrong to kill them. Given the number of locations, the differences in what actually happened, and the fact that most Croats never even crossed the Austrian border, this is a unfortunate and fictitious interpretation of events. These misleading interpretations of events in effect sabotage the victims' chance for justice.

It is a tragedy that 26,000 Croats were turned back by the British on trains at Marie Elend and Rosenbach stations but they had no real foreknowledge of what happened later. Indeed no one would imagine such a horror! Days before at Bleiburg the British had no foreknowledge of the genocide which was to take place once out of sight, and even the interpreter at the Bleiburg castle verified that. Also no massacre actually occurred on Bleiburg field. It took a number of days or weeks before information about the massacres or bad treatment filtered up the British chain-of-command after which the repatriations were halted immediately.

And if the British do bear any moral responsibility, what of the Bulgarians who also turned Croats back? Do not the Bulgarians, or Yugoslavs bear moral responsibility too?

Britain is even blamed by some authors for creating both Yugoslav states, or for recognizing Tito's state. It's as if the loyal Croatian members of the Tito-Subacic Yugoslav coalition government had no part in it. At the time the Allies were trying to defeat Hitler with the help of the Partisans. Had the Croatian state changed sides perhaps there could have been a different outcome. Some authors even allege that documents are not yet declassified, a claim that looks weak when many authors since the 1970s or earlier have been quoting western documents, newspapers and documentaries.

A third group of authors attribute some blame to the Croatian Ustasha Army for the tragedy, for the Croatian government decision to retreat instead of disperse, and for the Croatian failure to change sides during the war. After all the Croatian government leadership was well out of the region before the Croatian Army and civilians could reach safety. But in a court of law it is not permissible to blame the victim for being in the wrong place at the wrong time.

The Legacy Of The Bleiburg Tragedy

For Croatian people the Croatian granite monument at the Bleiburg field has become a national icon for the "Death Marches" (also known as "Way of the Cross") and all post-war massacres. Speaking in symbolic terms, the legacy of the "Bleiburg Tragedy" has been profound -- almost every Croatian family has its "Bleiburg" victim. An entire generation of Croatian people disappeared and were buried due to Tito's post-WWII massacres, a genocide which instilled fear into the population.

The territorial and demographic balance between Croats and Serbs in the Kingdom of Yugoslavia was also irreparably altered under Tito in favour of the Serbs. The apparent peace under Tito was in fact the peace of the grave! The irony is however that for the Yugoslav regime 'Bleiburg' was the beginning of the end.

Post-Yugoslav forensic investigations are taking place as over 700 post-war mass graves have been discovered across a wide front. The tens of thousands of skeletal remains unearthed, which have been identified to date, have been mostly Croatian in origin. Ultimately the number of victims to be forensically investigated could reach the hundreds of thousands. The unimaginable scale of mass graves found in several locations, and their deliberate concealment, also points to the planned and executed Yugoslav intention to commit genocide.

Some media reports reviewed reveal that the unpunished perpetrators and their diehard supporters deem that the national mourning of a massacred generation is 'controversial'! The whole scenario is so scandalous that it's a tragedy in itself!

Tito's post-war Croatian victims remain unidentified in the outside world, except when they are stigmatized or dishonoured, in spite of several books written about the "Bleiburg Tragedy" and the annual Bleiburg commemorations over the decades.

I have posed another question to myself. What is the Value of a Croatian Life? How is it that unarmed, disarmed, post-war, post-surrender, post-disarmament -- let's be clear – victims, can be force-marched, methodically executed without trial, thrown into mass graves over the entire former Yugoslav territory, covered and censored for decades, and then be unearthed, identified forensically and scientifically, and then insulted without accountability?

The fact is that Croatian annual commemorations were held at Bleiburg in Austria because such commemorations were forbidden inside the former Communist Yugoslavia. Even today, as this book goes to print, the annual Bleiburg commemorations still attract controversy from pro-Tito diehards who have outlived the former Yugoslavia! It is normal and appropriate that the Croatian government is once again supporting the commemoration at Bleiburg. However, I do not believe that it is appropriate to suggest reconciliation with the unpunished perpetrators of genocide!

Of course this manufactured 'controversy' is the result of Yugoslav anti-Croatian propaganda. However I believe that justice remains illusive due to the many vague, erroneous, and conflicting interpretations about the Bleiburg Tragedy and the issue of blame, in print, online, and in film. Perhaps the symbolic meaning of Bleiburg has also led to a lot of misunderstanding. A single truthful description about the unique events at Bleiburg is important and non-negotiable and should be put into the context of the post-war Yugoslav occupation of southern Carinthia, and Tito's blatant betrayal of his wartime Allies.

Bleiburg can be a 'symbol' for all massacres but the facts should be clarified and the actual perpetrators who ordered and carried out the massacres singled out.

Total blame for the intentional coordinated execution of mass slaughter and the "Death Marches" should clearly be placed onto the Yugoslav perpetrators for their secretive post-war mass murders, carried out over a wide front, inside Yugoslavia. Unarmed victims are innocent victims and they cannot be blamed for being in the wrong place no matter what the circumstances. The Allies who fulfilled the terms of the Yalta agreement, in particular the British in Carinthia, cannot be blamed for having no foreknowledge of the genocidal scale of atrocities carried out secretly inside Communist Yugoslavia. History records that the British repatriations to Yugoslavia were stopped just weeks later, once news of the atrocities reached the British. In contrast to the British, the Yugoslavs continued to slaughter unarmed victims for the next few years!

A permanent and dedicated "Bleiburg Tragedy" exhibit or museum needs to be located in central Zagreb, Croatia's capital, where visitors to Croatia, and school children, can learn their history. After all it is from Zagreb that the mass of retreating Croatian columns began their perilous unfortunate exodus. There should also be an annual dedicated public holiday set as a national day of mourning. In this way the historical magnitude of the Croatian tragedy can be remembered by generations to come.

"…Bleiburskim – Zrtvama …" ("…Bleiburg – Victims …") Part of a Wreath at Bleiburg Field several months after an annual commemoration, 2014

"Croatian soldiers must die in order that Yugoslavia may live."

Milovan Djilas, in book
'Operation Slaughterhouse'
American Croatian 1960 Resolution
about Bleiburg Tragedy

APPENDIX I

THE CREATION OF FIRST YUGOSLAV DICTATORSHIP

In Belgrade on 6th January 1929 the constitution of the Kingdom of Serbs, Croats, and Slovenes was abolished and a Yugoslav dictatorship was declared. The Kingdom of Yugoslavia came into being following the assassination, during a Belgrade parliamentary session, of Croatian front-bench MPs by a Serbian Deputy in 1928. Five Croatian MPs were shot and three ultimately died. This type of political assassination during a session of parliament has not been repeated to this day anywhere in the world. More than an assassination, more than a coup, this cowardly murder of unarmed Croatian deputies in a parliamentary session is a barbaric stain in the history of parliamentary democracy.

Why were five Croatian front-bench Members of Parliament shot during a parliamentary session by a member of the Serbian People's Radical Party, Punica Racic, on 20th June, 1928? The Croatian MP Stjepan Radic and his party members had been against the parliamentary ratification of the Nettuno Convention with Italy. The Croatian leadership was destroyed and, along with it, opposition to Mussolini was silenced in a hail of bullets. The Serbian assassin, with a few bullets, had catapulted the European region into despotism, fascism, Nazism, and war.

The Serbian MP from Montenegro opened fire in the Parliament Assembly (Skuptchina), in Belgrade, the capital of the Kingdom of Serbs Croats & Slovenes. The Serbian gunman Racic deliberately shot directly at those Croats who were just a couple of metres away, in the front benches, or at those Croatian MPs coming to their rescue. A diagram (not shown here)in a book entitled, 'Atentat na Stjepana Radica' by Kulundzic, Zagreb 1967, illustrates where the Serbian gunman was standing at the front and centre, and where the Croatian deputies were positioned in the front benches.

The premeditated murders occurred on the morning of 20 June 1928. But, in weeks preceding there had been demonstrations in Croatian cities regarding the tyrannical Serbian police, and regarding Mussolini's pressure to have the Nettuno Treaty (an article of the Rapallo Treaty) ratified in the Belgrade parliament, which was being obstructed by Croatian MPs within the Opposition Coalition bloc.

In 1927 the Croatian Leadership had formed the 'Opposition Coalition' together with Svetozar Pribichevic, President of the Independent Democratic Party of Serbs in Croatia. Debates in parliament had occurred amidst mounting tension within a kingdom which came into power under an undemocratic feudal parliamentary system when voting rights were restricted to those above an unattainable financial threshold.

Five bullets fired at close range found their target killing or wounding the Croatian deputies. Besides Punisa Racic, another Serbian MP, Lune Jovanovic, had a revolver drawn out, as reported in local newspapers which pointed to an alleged conspiracy. The dead and wounded in order of the shots fired were:

CROAT: IVAN PERNAR, MEMBER OF PARLIAMENT, CROATIAN PEASANT PARTY SECRETARY.

Wounded: Shot first, and after an operation, Mr. Pernar lived out the remainder of his life, partly as a political prisoner, partly in exile, with the Racic bullet embedded in his heart.

CROAT: DJURO BASARICEK, MEMBER OF PARLIAMENT, CROATIAN PEASANT PARTY VICE-PRESIDENT, LAWYER, ACTIVIST AND WRITER.

Died: Instantly. He received the bullet intended for Stjepan Radic by heroically running between Radic and the gunman. During his career he had been collecting data together with Pavle Radic, in particular, documenting the deliberate Serbian colonization of Croatia.

CROAT: IVAN GRANDJA, MEMBER OF PARLIAMENT, CROATIAN PEASANT PARTY DEPUTY.

Wounded: Heroically, he stepped in front of Stjepan Radic as he sat next to him in the front bench, realizing who the next intended target was, as he witnessed the shooting of Basaricek. He took the next bullet aimed for the Croatian President which struck his watch in the pocket of his vest, saving them both from instant death.

CROAT: STJEPAN RADIC, MEMBER OF PARLIAMENT, CROATIAN PEASANT PARTY PRESIDENT, AND FOUNDER IN 1904 (WITH HIS BROTHER ANTE RADIC), FOUNDER OF 'DOM' NEWSPAPER, AND POLITICAL PRISONER.

Died: after a few weeks, on 8 August 1928, in hospital from bullet wound in abdomen. Stjepan Radic had entered parliament that day in spite of rumours and published threats against his life in a Serbian newspaper, 'Jedinstvo' on 14 June 1928'. (Today Stjepan Radic appears on the 200 Kuna currency of Croatia.)

CROAT: PAVLE RADIC, MEMBER OF PARLIAMENT, CROATIAN PEASANT PARTY DEPUTY, AND NEPHEW OF STJEPAN RADIC.

Died: one hour after being deliberately shot whilst running towards his uncle Stjepan Radic who had just been shot. The gunman, aimed his revolver at Pavle and said, "I have been looking for you" (no doubt because of his active role in collecting data together with Djuro Basaricek regarding the Serbian colonization of Croatia).

Newspapers, around the world such as the London Times or the American Time magazine, reported on the Serbian assassination of Croatian MPs and its political consequences. The main concern of most of these journalists is for the life of the "kingdom". In date order some of those articles are listed here:

"Down With Mussolini", Time, 11 June 1928

"Deputies Shot in Belgrade—Wild Scene in Chamber—Raditch badly wounded", London Times, 21 June 1928

"The Belgrade Shootings—Croat Anger", London Times, 22 June 1928

"Tragedy in Belgrade", London Times, 22 June 1928

> page 17: "... it would be tactless, for foreigners to express any opinion as to these charges (re Serbian monopoly of the State). But all good Europeans will hope that the very dismay caused by the tragedy in the Skupshtina, and the dangers that may well arise from it, will compel the political leaders on each side to take a broad view and to subordinate party passion and "tribal" advantage to the benefit of the kingdom as a whole..."

"Throwback to Assassination", Time, 2 July 1928

"Death of Radic", Time, 20 August 1928

In this article the Croatian MP Radich is referred to as the son of gypsies whose death

> "may yet prove to have been for the eventual good of the whole kingdom"

"Ratification After Assassination", Time, 27 August 1928

The grave consequences of the assassination are illustrated in a David Low cartoon, one of many featured by the British Cartoon Archive on their website. The captions refer to a "Chorus of European Dictators" welcoming the new regime of King Alexander, who is depicted sitting on top of his "bound and gagged" 'Jugoslav' people.

The British Cartoon Archive website also notes below the cartoon that the Croatian politician Stjepan Radic was shot in a meeting of Parliament in June 1928, and that he died soon after. Also the same website notes add the following:

> "As a result of this assassination ethnic tensions in the region increased. In January 1929 King Alexander dissolved Parliament, abolished the Constitution and established a dictatorship. He re-named the Kingdom of Serbs, Croats and Slovenes 'Yugoslavia'..."

The consequences of the assassination of the Croatian leadership were immediate. Opposition to dictatorship and fascism in Europe was silenced as the Nettuno Treaty was ratified in Belgrade. Political opposition to the despotic Serbian Kingdom was silenced. 'Jugoslavia' became a cruel dictatorship in January 1929 with the subsequent dissolution of the parliament, the end of the constitution, and all Orthodox believers were declared to be Serbian Orthodox no matter what their ethnicity!

APPENDIX II

WHO CREATED THE FIRST YUGOSLAV STATE?

ONCE THE WHOLE WORLD KNEW OF THE CROATS

Historical evidence of Croatia, Croatian people, and the Croatian language are scattered throughout the pages and maps of both ancient and recent history.

- The French king, for example, created an elite Croatian regiment, "Le Royal Croate", and from "les cravates" neckties came to be known as 'cravats' in the 18th century.

- European cartographers recorded Bosnia as "Turkish Croatia" up until the 19th century.

- In Istanbul the Croatian language was the 'second' language and language of 'diplomacy' for centuries.

- In America, Nikola Tesla recorded his birthplace as Croatia, as did tens of thousands of others in 19th century.

While the word Croat or Croatia was engraved in history all around the globe, the opposite was occurring in the once great Croatian kingdom itself. Since the 19th century in occupied Croatia the educated classes were gradually replacing the Croatian culture and identity with artificial descriptions such as Slav, Slavic or Illyrian.

HOW DID THE CROATS BECOME KNOWN AS 'SOUTH-SLAVS'?

Pan-slavism gradually spread into Croatia as a legacy of Saints Cyril & Metodius, and Illyrianism from the previous Greek, and then Roman name given to the Croatian region. According to the late Prof. B. Franolic, in "An Historical Survey of Literary Croatian" (1984) during the counter-reformation period in Croatia,

> Franolic: "...Guided by the work of Jesuits both at home and abroad, literary creation expressed broad doctrines advocating unification of the South Slavs and reunion of the Eastern Christians with Rome".

In addition, for most of its history the Pontifical College of St. Gerome in Rome was known as the Pontifical Illyrian College of St. Gerome, until the recent recognition of Croatia in the late 20th century. This institution had a great influence on Jesuits such as Bartol Kasic who published the book "The Structure of the Illyrian language in Two Books", in the 17th century, although today, ironically, amongst Croats he is known as the "father of Croatian linguistics".

The Franciscan Andrija Kacic-Miosic also produced a 'best seller' book in 1756 entitled "Pleasant Conversation of Slavic Peoples". These authors and others played a key role in the development of the shokavian dialect and they were true believers in the concept of 'slavic' peoples. Croatian clerics such as B. Kasic, and J. Krizanic who had traveled to Russia, were followed in later centuries by the powerful Illyrian and south-slav political activism of the Bishops Vrhovac, Racki and Strossmayer, within the Hapsburg empire, to unite so-called 'south slavs'.

POLITICALIZATION OF SOUTH-SLAVISM

During the last half of the 19th century pan-slavists were able to take power because the majority of rural Croatian people were ineligible to vote in the feudal system. Professor Margaret Macmillan who lectures at the University of Toronto, in her book "Peacemakers: The Paris Conference of 1919 and Its Attempt to End War" is the granddaughter of former 1918 British Prime Minister Lloyd George.

> Macmillan: "The Peace Conference, contrary to what many people have believed since, did not create Yugoslavia; that was done by the time it met ... The creation of Yugoslavia was primarily a byproduct of domestic politics which already existed before the Paris Peace Conference ... Seventy years later the powers were equally unable to prevent its disintegration."

The so-called 'first' Yugoslavia was eventually recognized internationally in 1919, with England being one of the last powers to recognize it in June 1919.

Russia was also a factor in Croatian 'south slav' politics as noted in "The Rough (travel) Guide to Croatia".

> "Strossmayer ...(concluded)... that an independent Yugoslav (which literally means 'South Slav' in Croatian and Serbian) state including all Croats and Serbs and supported by Russia, would be the best solution. ... exiles formed the 'Yugoslav Committee' in Paris in order to lobby foreign governments ... the political leaders of Austria-Hungary's Serbs, Croats and Slovenes formed the National Council in Zagreb ... declared their independence from Budapest and Vienna."

In the same theme, the life of Bishop J. G. Strossmayer is described in detail by I. Sivric. This book describes Strossmayer's correspondence with the 19th century Russian idealist, philosopher and Christian slavophile, V. S. Soloviev.

> Sivric: "Regardless of how ardently he (Strossmayer) loved his nation and what sacrifices he performed for it, the welfare of the Church and the realization of her mission in the world had the priority over that of his nation ... the main goal of the life of the Bishop was to reconcile the Eastern and Western Church ... His diocese, one of the richest in Europe ... All this wealth ... extended as far as Paris, France, ...(where)... unlimited funds (given) by Strossmayer for his (Louis Leger, professor at the Sorbonne) ... publications dealing with South Slav problems."

The problem, for Strossmayer, with Ante Starcevic was that Starcevic stood in the way of 'south slav' unity because he did not accept the invented Serbian claims to all the pre-existing Croatian Orthodox churches and peoples in Croatia. Sivric describes Strossmayer's shocking reaction to the illness of Starcevic as recorded in his correspondence to Racki.

> Strossmayer: "I do not know if one should wish him (Starcevic) to be dead because he poisoned our youth".

But it wasn't only Starcevic, now known as the 'Father of the Croatian Nation' who was criticized.

Macek describes the opposition to Stjepan Radic in detail in his book "In the Struggle For Freedom" (1957) as follows.

> Macek: "In its persecution of the Croatian Peasant Party, the government had the strong support of the great majority of the intelligentsia, the middle classes, and above all, of the Catholic clergy. ... Why... The answer is that it was the instinctive defense of the educated classes who could not and would not accept the despised peasants as their equals, let alone permit them a decisive role in national politics. Before long, the priests were denouncing the party from their pulpits ..."

THE ILLYRIAN KINGDOM & FIRST SOUTH-SLAV STATE

Croatian south-slav politicians in the former Austro-Hungarian empire stigmatized political alternatives for Croatian independence, such as Starcevic's Party of Rights, or Radic's Peasant Party -- and they left nothing to chance, working to build a south-slav foundation by creating the following institutions.

- (Illyrian) 'People's Party' (the legacy of the Illyrian Movement: Narodna Stranka, 1841)

- 'Illyrian' literary society (Matica Illyrska, 1842)

- standardized Serbo-Croat language (Vienna Agreement 1850)

- 'Yugoslav Academy of Arts & Sciences' (1866)

- Constituent status for Serb immigrants to Croatia (1867)

Croatian politicians such as Supilo, Smodlaka, Trumbic and other 'Yugoslav' true believers such as the sculptor Ivan Mestrovic, and all of the upper class, did not support the idea of a Croatian independent state. Thus a 'Croato-Serbian' political coalition took power, the forerunner to the 'National Council of the Slovenes, Croats and Serbs' in Zagreb and the declaration of the first south-slav state there.

As for the 'Yugoslav Committee' in London in exile, its mission was to lobby for support abroad, and to unite with independent Serbia, resulting in the Corfu Declaration. The Yugoslav Committee ultimately worked as representatives of the 'National Council' in the creation of the 'Kingdom of the Serbs, Croats and Slovenes'.

THE FOREIGN SCAPEGOATS

Many Croatian authors have minimized the role of Croats and magnified the role of foreigners, mainly the British, in the creation of the first Yugoslav state, citing British 'writers' such as Evans, Gladstone or Seton-Watson. However I have shown that this south-slav state was the product of influences closer to home, from the Italian peninsula or from France or Russia.

If not for Napoleon there would have been no 'enlightenment' in any newly created Illyrian provinces, or Illyrian Kingdom, and considering the lethal legacy of this Illyrianism, namely Yugoslavia, it would seem that the British did not defeat the French soon enough!

Who Created The First Yugoslav State?

Croatian authors such as Percela & Guldescu, Omrcanin, Grubusic, Vitez, Cic and others, who have self-censored part of Croatian history, have had a strong influence on some authors of non-Croatian origin. The late American M. McAdams and the Australian L. Shaw, and others are just two examples who took Croatian authors at face value, myself included.

In their "Operation Slaughterhouse" (1995) Percela and Guldescu briefly describe the "romantic nationalism" of Liudevit Gaj, Racki or Strossmajer, or the "romanticist nationalism" of the Yugoslav "Exile Committee" as if these factors were of minor significance.

Omrcanin, in "Diplomatic & Political History of Croatia" (1972) presents a chronology of key events and documents in Croatia's centuries-long history, but he omits 50 years of history between the Hungarian Nagodba in 1868, and the already created Kingdom of Yugoslavia in 1918.

In "Years of Terror" (1976) Grubusic Ed., omits 19th century political activity in Croatia, the Serbian-Croatian Coalition, or the "Yugoslav Committee". Instead, in "Years of Terror" it is alleged that,

> "all the various peoples making up this great power (Austrian empire) proclaimed their own independent states ... Versailles peace did not bring about justice for all nations ... they (Paris and London) assisted the Serbs in the annihilation of the young Croat state, in the occupation of Croatia and Slovenia and in setting up a kingdom ... on 1.12.1918. In this way the independence of the Croat people was crushed ..."

In "Adriatic Coast of Croatia and the Mediterranean" (1971) V. Vitez discusses the 19th century out of chronological sequence without mentioning Strossmayer or others. In the immediate pre-WWI period a Yugoslav-slavistic struggle is described.

> Vitez: "rised by a part of the Croatian clergy and some members of the Croatian parliament ...(and how)... "Supilo, together with his colleagues, Dr A Trumbic and sculptor I. Mestrovic, created an idea about the unity of the South Slavic nations into a common state ...(a)... funny Croat-Serbian coalition inside the Croatian Parliament ...(led by)... Svetozar Pribicevic".

In the book "In the Defence of Justice" V. Vitez explains that the Italian's alleged "inherited right" contributed to the censoring of Croatian identity.

> " ... Frequently in Italy is used the name Illyrians to designate the Croats."

and that it is in this way that Croats came to be known as Slavs from Illyria rather than Croats from Croatia—Italian influence on one hand, together with the so-called Slavic creation of Cyril & Methodius. Other sources have argued that the word "Illyrian" in Rome was supported and encouraged by the Croatian elite.

In "How Yugoslavia was created" online in Chapter 4 "Summary of A History of Croatian Enemies", E. Cic concludes that the British founded Yugoslavia from the writings of pro-Serbian English writers such as Arthur John Evans in his book 'Illyrian Letters'(1877).

> Cic: "... that the British had conceived this plan hundreds of years earlier ..."

Unlike many Croatian authors M. McAdams does not shy away from offering some details about the creation of the first Yugoslav state, even though he is not completely accurate. This book was welcomed by those interested in justice for Croatian people when it first appeared during the Serbian siege on Croatia in the early 1990s.

> McAdams: "The Yugoslav National Council of Slovenes, Croats and Serbs was organized in Zagreb on October 15, 1918. This twenty-eight member Council was self-appointed, not elected. ... This is the body so often cited as having 'asked' to join Yugoslavia."

McAdams then later does correctly acknowledge that it was at the 'Congress of the Croatian Peasant Party' and not at the Zagreb parliament ('Sabor') where Peasant Party representatives voted for a "Neutral and Peasant Republic of Croatia".

In 1973 another book appeared in the English language which, it cannot be stressed enough, had a great influence on those of us who relied on information in English at the time. The Australian reporter L. Shaw in 'Trial by Slander' (1973) gives some details about the activities of the Croatian Peasant Party, but Shaw also left-out many important pieces of the puzzle. In this way I believe that readers could be forgiven for thinking that the proclamation of the 'Peasant Party' in Croatia was the official parliamentary position at the Sabor, and that the proclamation of the 'National Council' was the un-elected position!

Many took Croatian authors at face value, myself included. Although I majored in Communist political systems including communist Yugoslavia at university it was a long time before I questioned the origins of the first south-slav state. In fact, before Croatian independence, it was deemed by supporters of a free Croatia that anything written against Croats was false Yugoslav propaganda.

Who Created The First Yugoslav State?

Vesna Drapac in "Constructing Yugoslavia A Transnational History" (2010) in 335 pages has done little to enlighten readers about the Croatian pan-slav politicians' contribution to Yugoslavism other than to briefly acknowledge the following.

> Drapac: "Discussions about South Slav unity (as opposed to the independence of, for example, the Serbs or Montenegrins) were Croatian in origin. Ljudevit Gaj ... was a leading proponent of the Illyrian movement ... Illyrianism, influenced by Pan-slavism, also sought greater understanding between South Slavs on cultural and linguistic grounds. The Croatian liberal Bishop of Djakovo, Josip Juraj Strossmayer (1815-1095) ... became one of the South Slav ideal's most illustrious advocates. He was known as a founding father of Yugoslavia. ..."

In her book "Constructing Yugoslavia" Drapac instead focuses on quotations of British travel writers in Croatia in the 19th century who she alleges,

> Drapac: "informed the creation of Yugoslavia ...(that Yugoslavia) ...became what outsiders willed it to be, from its foundation ... was constructed, promoted and sustained by a combination of international and transnational forces." ... (and she argues that) ... "the history of Yugoslavia is inherently transnational in the sense that it cannot be understood in isolation ... (that Yugoslavia's) ... actual form was profoundly shaped by what outsiders had imagined it should be from at least the second half of the nineteenth century ... that the story of Yugoslavia is not a story about Europe's backyard but about Europe itself".

Gradually the hidden chapter of Croatian history is coming to light, although in hindsight, Macek's "In the Struggle for Freedom" sheds some light on the era; as did Katicic and Novak in "Two Thousand Years of Writing in Croatia" (1987).

Also, M. Kovacevic writes in "My Croatia the Land & Its History" (1994) that,

> Kovacevic " ... the Croatian-Serbian coalition was founded in 1905, which fought for the union of Croatian lands, ... the political independence of Croatia and the union of South Slavic nations, after their candidates won a majority in the Parliament in 1906 (and kept the situation unchanged until 1918) ..."

L. Boban in "Croatian Borders—1918 to 1993" gives a detailed chronology and maps of how Croatian politicians, along with some Slovenes or Serbs, formed the first south-slav state.

Conclusions

Throughout history, until recently, Croatia and the Croats were once known around the world. But 19th and 20th century Croatian political history almost disappeared into a black hole partly maybe because Croats have been self-censoring it, rather than because foreigners were responsible for it. Using the quotations above I have argued that foreigners, in particular the British, did not 'create' south-slav nationalism — their travel writers, journalists, and politicians 'described' it. In the absence of a strong alternative national political culture in Croatia, foreigners described the domestic south-slav movement they witnessed during a period of political change and violent upheaval in European history.

Bibliography & Further Reading

Books

Applebaum, Anne, 'Iron Curtain The Crushing of Eastern Europe 1944—1956', Penguin Books, London, 2013

Baletic, M., Ed., 'Croatia 1994', INA-Konzalting, Zagreb, 1994

Basta, Milan, 'Rat Posle rata' (The war after the war), Stvarnost, Zagreb, 1963

Batty, Peter, 'Hoodwinking Churchill: Tito's Great Confidence Trick', Shepheard-Welwyn Publishing, London, 2011

Bethell, Nicholas, "The Croats and the Cossacks" in 'The Last Secret: The Delivery to Stalin of Over Two Million Russians by Britain and the United States', Basic Books Inc., New York, 1974

Blaskovich, Jerry, 'Anatomy of Deceit: An American Physician's First-hand Encounter with the Realities of the War in Croatia', Dunhill Publishing Company, New York, 1997

Boban, L., 'Croatian Borders: 1918-1993', Skolska Knjiga, Zagreb, 1993

Booker, Christopher, 'A Looking-Glass Tragedy: The controversy over the repatriations from Austria in 1945', Gerald Duckworth & Co. Ltd., London, 1997

Bousfield, J., 'The Rough Guide to Croatia', Penguin Group, London, Fifth Edition, 2010

Brooks-Pincevic, Suzanne, 'Britain and the Bleiburg Tragedy', Leon Publications Ltd., Auckland, 1998

Cerovac, Ivan, 'Hrvatski Politicki Leksikon', Worldwide, London 1988

Cohen, Philip J., "The Metamorphosis of Chetniks into Partisans", in 'The World War II and contemporary Chetniks: Their historico-political continuity and implications for stability in the Balkans', CERES, Zagreb, 1997

Cowgill, Brig. Anthony, Lord Brimelow, Christopher Booker, Chapter Five "Bleiburg: The End of the Croat Incursion–15 May" in 'The Repatriations from Austria in 1945: The Report of an Inquiry', Sinclair--Stevenson Ltd., 1990

Dizdar, Zdravko, Grcic, Marko, Ravlic, Slaven, Darko Stuparic, Darko, Editors, 'Tko je Tko u NDH: Hrvatska 1941—1945', Minerva, Zagreb, 1997

Djilas, Milovan 'The New Class: An Analysis of the Communist System', Harcourt Brace Jovanovich, San Diego, 1983

Drapac, Vesna, 'Constructing Yugoslavia, a Transnational History', Palgrave Macmillan, NY, 2010

Dujmovic, Franjo, 'Hrvatska na putu k Oslobodjenju: Uspomene i Prosudbe', ZIRAL (Zajednica Izdanja Ranjeni Labud), Roma-Chicago, 1976

Franolic, B., 'An Historical Survey of Literary Croatian', Nouvelles Editions Latines, Paris, 1984

Gaddis, John Lewis, 'Strategies of Containment: A Critical Appraisal of American National Security Policy during the Cold War', Oxford University Press, New York City, 1982

Grcic, Marko, Ed., 'Otvoreni dossier Bleiburg', START magazine, Zagreb, 1990

Grubisic, Slavko, Biosic, Josip, 'Years of Terror', Hrvatski Radnicki-Savez (HRS), Silverdalen, Sweden, 1976

Guldescu, Stanko, Prcela, John, Editors, 'Operation Slaughterhouse: Eyewitness Accounts of Post-War Massacres in Yugoslavia', Pittsburg, First Edition, 1970; Second` Edition, Dorrance Publishing Co., Pittsburg, 1995

Hefer, Stjepan, 'Croatian Struggle for Freedom and Statehood', Croatian Liberation Movement (HOP), Buenos Aires, 1959

Jareb, Jerome, Mirth, Karlo, Managing Editors, 'Ivan Mestrovic Centennial', Journal of Croatian Studies – Annual Review of the Croatian Academy of America, Inc.), New York, Volume XXIV 1983

Jupp, James, General Editor, "Croatians" in 'The Australian People: An Encyclopedia of the Nation, Its People and their Origins', Angus & Robertson, North Ryde, 1988

Jurcevic, Josip, 'The Black Book of Communism in Croatia: The Crimes of Yugoslav Communists in Croatia in 1945', Croatian Herald--Melbourne, Zagreb, 2006

Jurcevic, Josip, 'Bleiburg: Jugoslavenski poratni zlocini nad Hrvatima' Dokumentacijsko informacijsko srediste (DIS), Zagreb, 200

Katicic, R. & Novak S.P., 'Two Thousand Years of Writing in Croatia', Sveucilisna Naklada Liber, Zagreb, 1987

Klemencic, Mladen, 'A Concise Atlas of the Republic of Croatia & of the Republic of Bosnia and Hercegovina', Miroslav Krleza Lexicographical Institute, Zagreb, 1993

Kovacevic, Mate, "History" in 'My Croatia The Land and its History', Garvran, Zdravko, Editor, DMD, Zagreb, 1994

Kramer, Mark, Consulting Editor, 'The Black Book of Communism: Crimes, Terror, Repression', ebook, Harvard University Press, Cambridge, 1999

Lindsay, Franklin, 'Beacons in the Night: With the OSS and Tito's Partisans in Wartime Yugoslavia', Stanford University Press, Stanford, 1993

Loftus, John, Aarons, Mark, 'Ratlines: How the Vatican's Nazi Networks Betrayed Western Intelligence to the Soviets', William Heinemann Ltd., London, 1991

Bibliography & Further Reading

Macek, Vladko, 'In the Struggle for Freedom', Pennsylvania State University Press, University Park and London, 1957

MacMillan, Margaret, 'Peacemakers: The Paris Conference of 1919 and Its Attempt to End War', John Murray Publishers, London, 2001

Marevic, Jozo, 'Fifty Godina Bleiburga: Zbornik radova o Bleiburgu i kriznim putovima s treceg medunarodnog znanstvenog simpozija u Bleiburgu 14. i 15. svibnja 1995', Croatiaprojekt, Zagreb, 1995

Marjanovic, Jovan, Stanisic, Mihailo, 'The collaboration of D. Mihailovic's Chetniks with the Enemy Forces of Occupation: 1941—1944', Archivski pregled, Beograd, 1976

McAdams, C. Michael, 'Croatia Myth and Reality', Croatian Information Service (CIS), Arcadia, 1992

Moore, Michael, "The Former Yugoslavia" in 'Stupid White Men', Penguin Books Australia, Camberwell, 2001

Nikolic, Vinko, 'Tragedija se Dogodila u Svibnju--I & II', Knjiznica Hrvatske Revije', Barcelona, 1984 & 1985

Omrcanin, Ivo, 'Seed of Blood', self-published, Sydney, 1961

Omrcanin, Ivo, 'Diplomatic & Political History of Croatia', Dorrance & Company, Philadelphia, 1972

Omrcanin, Ivo, 'The pro-allied putsch in Croatia in 1944 and the Massacre of Croatians by Tito Communists in 1945', Dorrance & Company, Philadelphia, 1975

Omrcanin, Ivo, 'Dramatis Personae and Finis of the Independent State of Croatia in American and British Documents', Dorrance & Company, Inc. Philadelphia, 1983

Omrcanin, Ivo, "Military History of Croatia", Dorrance & Company Inc., Bryn Mawr, 1984

Omrcanin, Ivo, 'Enigma Tito: Documentary Expose of SOE and OSS Agents in Yugo-Communist State', Samizdat, Washington, 1984

Omrcanin, Ivo, 'Holocaust of Croatians', Samizdat, Washington, 1986

Omrcanin, Ivo, 'Croatia 1941—1945: Before and After', Samizdat, Washington, 1988

Orsag, Vladimir, 'The Balkans Conspiracy', Ginninderra Press, Charnwood ACT, 2002

Orwell, George, Nineteen Eighty Four, Secker & Warburg, London, 1949

Pozzi, Henri, 'Black Hand over Europe', Croatian Information Centre (CIS), This edition edited by Ante Beljo, Zagreb, 1994 (originally published in 1935)

Rude, George, 'Revolutionary Europe 1783-1815', Fontana Press, London, 1964

Rulitz, F. T., 'The Tragedy of Bleiburg and Viktring, 1945', Northern Illinois University Press, USA, 2016

Sanader, Mirjana, "Ancient Greek and Roman Cities in Croatia", Skolska Knjiga (SK), Zagreb, 2004

Shaw, Les, "Bleiburg 1945" in 'Trial By Slander', Harp Books, Canberra, 1973

Sivric, Ivo, 'Bishop J. G. Strossmayer: New Light on Vatican I', Ziral--Rome (Franciscan Herald Press), Chicago, 1975.

Stedul, N. & S.H., 'Krizar – The Soul of Freedom', self-published, Washington, 1980

Schneid, Frederick C., 'Soldiers of Napoleon's Kingdom of Italy: Army, State and Society, 1800—1815', Westview Press, Boulder, 1995

Tolstoy, Nikolai, 'The Minister and the Massacres', Century Hutchinson Ltd., London, 1986

Vitez, Vladimir, sen., 'In the Defence of Justice – An Answer to Dr. J. Cairns – History and Life 1', self-published, Melbourne, 1970

Vitez, Vladimir, sen., 'Adriatic Coast of Croatia and the Mediterranean – History and Life 4', self-published, Melbourne, 1971.

Vitez, Vladimir, sen., 'Rise and Fall of Tito – History and Life Publication, Melbourne, 1972

Vukusic, Bozo, 'Bleiburg Memento: fotomonografija', Croatian Calvary Association, Zagreb, 2005

West, Richard, 'Tito and the Rise and Fall of Yugoslavia', Faber & Faber Ltd., London, 2009

Westwood, J. N., 'Endurance and Endeavour: Russian History 1812—1980', Oxford University Press, London, Second Edition 1981

Wilton, Janis & Bosworth, Richard, 'Old Worlds and New Australia The post-war migrant experience', Penguin Books Australia, Ringwood, 1984

Zanko, Zelimir, Solic, Nikola, Editors, 'Jazovka', Vjesnik, Zagreb, 1990

Walters, Eric, 'Camp X', Puffin Group, Toronto, 2002

Wolff, Larry, 'Venice and the Slavs – The Discovery of Dalmatia in the Age of Enlightenment', Stanford University Press, Stanford, 2001

Articles & Journals, Etc.

Advocate, "Yugoslavs Forming Own Military Government in Conflict With Allies—British Ignored", Advocate (Trove), Burnie, 17 May 1945

Applebaum, Anne, "The Holocaust that no one cares about", in 'The Spectator', re-published in The Age (in Opinion Analysis), Melbourne, 10 March 1994

Asic, Stjepan, "Obljetnica 70. godina Bleiburske tragedije "Kriznog puta" u Hrvatskom centru u North Fremantlu", Hrvatski Vjesnik, Melbourne, 20 May 2015

Associated Press (AP), "Mussolini's son dead", page 20, Herald Sun, Melbourne, 14 June 1997

Bakovic, Don Anto, Editor, "Kako Je u Posljednjih 60 Godina Nestalo 2.5 milijuna Hrvata", pages 12—13 Narod, Zagreb, 15 February 2003

Barbic, F., "Visiting Historian (M. McAdams) Reveals Facts on the Bleiburg Massacres: Expert reveals unrecorded horror", page 4, Hrvatski Vjesnik, Melbourne, 21 May 1985

Bibliography & Further Reading

Barilar, Suzana, Turcin, Kristina, "Pokraj tvornice Impol 1948. spaljena trupla 4000 Hrvata", page 8, Hrvatski Vjesnik, Melbourne, 2001

Barisic, M., "Bleiburg i Krizni put kao opomena", page 12, Vjesnik, Zagreb, 15-21 May 2001

Barisic, Marko, "70th Commemoration of Bleiburg: More than 60,000 gather from all over the world to remember victims of Bleiburg", 'New Generation'in Hrvatski Vjesnik, Melbourne, 20 May 2015

Barisic, Marko, "Sjecanje na mnostvo je zadnji put vidjeno na Bleiburskom polju", Hrvatski Vjesnik, Melbourne, 20 May 2015

Basta, Milan Lt. Col., Commissar 51st Vojvodina Division, "The Bleiburg talks are described by a high-ranking Serbian Commissar", in 'Operation Slaughterhouse', page 136—147, Dorrance Publishing Co., Inc., Pittsburg, 1995

Baxter, David M., "The Serbo-Croatian Antagonism", in 'Operation Slaughterhouse: Eyewitness Accounts of Post-War Masacres in Yugoslavia', Dorrance Publishing Co., Pittsburg, 1995

Beljo, Ante, Editor, "Greater Serbia from Ideology to Aggression", a Supplement: Croatia in Yugoslavia 1918 – 1991, second edition, Croatian Information Centre (CIS), Zagreb, 1993

Beram, Tomislav, "Bleiburg 2015, Sydney--Svecana Komemorativna Akademija Odrzana u Hrvatskom Drustvu Sydney", Boka Cropress, Sydney, 27 May 2015

Boka Cropress, "Hrvatska Drustva, Udruge, Kao i sve Hrvatske Organizacije Prireduju Komemorativnu Akademiju u cast 70 Godina Blajburske Tragedije Kriznog Puta", Advertisement in Boka Cropress, Sydney, 29 April 2015

Boka Cropress, "Komemoracija Za Svibanjske Zrtve: 70 Obljetnica Bleburske Tragedije", Advertisement in Boka Cropresss, Sydney, 13 May 2015

Boka Cropress, "odlaskom na Bleiburg je poslana poruka vladajucima", heading and photograph on front page, Boka CroPress, Sydney, (Vol. 3, No. 135) 20 May 2015

Boka Cropress, "Povjesnicar u Emisiji 'Bujica': Broj Ljudi Na Komemoraciji je Velika Politicka Poruka", Boka Cropress, Sydney, 20 May 2015

Boka Cropress, "Bleiburg--istina koja nas sve oslobadja", Editorial, Boka Cropress, Sydney, 20 May 2015

Borovcak, Damitr, "Medju nama:...Bleiburg, Bleiburg...", page 8, Spremnost Hrvatski Tjednik, Sydney, 29 May 2001

Bosnjak, Marjan, "Englezi, Bleiburg i Stjepan Mesic!", page 12, Hrvatski Vjesnik, Melbourne, 18 May 2001

Budak, Luka, "Post-War Croatian Settlement", in 'The Australian People: An Encyclopaedia of the Nation, Its People, and Their Origins', Angus & Robertson Publishers, North Ryde, 1988

Butkovic, Ivo, "Svehrvatsko zajednistvo na Bleiburskom polju—1945—Bleiburg—2015", Hrvatski Vjesnik, Melbourne, 20 May 2015

Brooks-Pincevic, Suzanne, "Britain and the Bleiburg Tragedy: An artist's impression", (book review) in 'New Generation English Supplement', in Hrvatski Vjesnik, Melbourne, 21 August 1998

Brooks-Pincevic, Suzanne, "Do Not Bury Bleiburg", page 11, Nova Hrvatska (New Croatia), Sydney, 25-31 January 2000; Also: page 2, 'New Generation English Supplement' in Hrvatski Vjesnik, Melbourne, 28 January 2000

Brooks-Pincevic, Suzanne, "Commemoration of 'Bleiburg': Croatia's Reason To Be...", page 4, 'New Generation English Supplement' in Hrvatski Vjesnik, Melbourne, 13 June 2003

Coslovich, Gabriella, "A tragic history that brought thousands of Triestini to Australia", The Age, Melbourne, 26 March 2012

Crljen, Danijel, "The Bleiburg talks and the beginning of the Bleiburg Tragedy are described by a Croatian negotiator who is now living in Buenos Aires", pages 147—155, in 'Operation Slaughterhouse', Dorrance Publishing Co., Inc., Pittsburg, 1995

D'Ancona, Matthew, "Macmillan papers give Major touch of EC déjà vu", page 11, The Times, London, 1993

Davorin, Josip, "Kako je 1945 Izrucena Hrvatska Drzavna Vlada", article republished in three parts from 'Godisnjak' (Argentina) 1954, in Spremnost Hrvatski Tjednik, Sydney, page 7--15 May 2001; page 12--22 May 2001; page 5--29 May 2001

Dedic, Dinko, Editor, "Tihi Krivci", Hrvatski Tjednik, Melbourne, 29 Sept 1981

Dedic, Dinko, Editor, "Od Bleiburga do pobjede" (headline on front page), Hrvatski Tjednik, Melbourne, 14 May 1985

Dedic, Dinko, "Bleiburg--Istina i Samo Istina ce Osloboditi Hrvatsku", Boka Cropress, Sydney, 20 May 2015

Dedic, Dinko, "Sramota Hrvatska! Sramota!", Boka Cropress, Sydney 27 May 2015

Franovic, Marko, Milinovic, Ante, "Dvostruki odnos titoista prema Jasenovcu i Bleiburgu pokazuje njihovo antihrvatstvo", Boka Cropress, Sydney, 20 May 2015

Freytag & Berndt, 'Karnten Carinthia' (map & information booklet), Freytag-Berndt u. Artaria KG, 1230 Wien (Vienna)

Gelo, Petar, "Sunshine Odrzana Komemoracija uz 70. Obljetnicu Strasne Bleiburske Tragedije", Hrvatski Vjesnik, Melbourne, 27 May 2015

Gladovic, Mira, "Croatian Tragedy: Croatian Genocide--Lest We Forget", pages 17-19, Klokan, Sydney, May 1991

Glamatovic, Ivica, (tajnik HKD "Bosna" Sydney), "Komemorativna akademija Bleiburske tragedije u hrvatskom klubu "Bosna" un Sydneyu", Boka Cropress, Sydney, 27 May 2015

Gwyn, Richard, editor International Affairs, "Yugoslavia the next hot spot", The Toronto Star (4 July 1986), re-published in Hrvatski Tjednik, Melbourne 29 July 1986

Hennessy, Peter, "Harold Macmillan: Roll up, ladies and gentlemen, you never had it so good", pages 19—22, The Economist, London, 20 April 1991

Bibliography & Further Reading

Hodak, Zvonimir, "Tko studentima u Lijepoj nasoj predaje noviju hrvatsku povijest?", page 27, Hrvatski Vjesnik, Melbourne, 4 March 2014

Hout, H., "Letter to Editor", The European newspaper, Sydney, 29 April 1994

Hrvatin, Hrvoje, "Kako su nas Ubijali", page 3, Spremnost Hrvatski Tjednik, Sydney, 15 May 2007

Hrvatska izvjestajna novinska agencija (Hina), "Slovenija: U jami Konfin pronadjeni posmrtni ostaci 26 Hrvata surovo ubijenih po svrsetku Drugoga svjetskoga rata: 60 Slovenaca, 26 Hrvata, i 2 Srba", re-published in Hrvatski Vjesnik, Melbourne, 29 September 2006

Hrvatski Vjesnik, "Hrvatska Drustva, Udruge, Kao i sve Hrvatske Organizacije Prireduju Komemorativnu Akademiju u cast 70 Godina Blajburske Tragedije Kriznog Puta", Advertisement in Hrvatski Vjesnik, Melbourne, 29 April 2015

Hrvatski Vjesnik, "I ove godine hodocasce od Zagreba do Bleiburga", Hrvatski Vjesnik, Melbourne, 13 May 2015

Hrvatski Vjesnik, "Bleiburg i Krizni put bili su masakr nad nevinim civilima", Hrvatski Vjesnik, Melbourne, 13 May 2015

Hrvatski Vjesnik, "Svibanj '45. pamtimo po strasnim pokoljima pocinjenima pod znakom zvijezde petkorake", Hrvatski Vjesnik, Melbourne, 20 May 2015

Hrvatski Vjesnik, "Bleiburg 70 Years on: Our wounds will never heal, nor will we ever forget!", (heading) in 'The New Generation English Supplement', Hrvatski Vjesnik, Melbourne, 20 May 2015

Hrvatski Vjesnik, "Kolinda in Bleiburg on Thursday", (heading) in 'The New Generation English supplement', Hrvatski Vjesnik, Melbourne, 20 May 2015

Hrvatski Vjesnik, "Htjeli su zrtvama zatrti svaki spomen i trag groba--Vise od Sezdeset tisuca ljudi u Bleiburgu" (headline front page), Hrvatski Vjesnik, Melbourne, 20 May 2015.

Hrvatski Vjesnik, "Pocast Vise od Sezdeset Tisuca Ljudi Na Komemoracij Nevinim Zrtvama na Bleiburskom Polju: Deseci tisuca ljudi dosli su odati pocast nevinim zrtvama" (heading), Hrvatski Vjesnik, Melbourne, 20 May 2015

Hrvatski Vjesnik, "Svibanj '45. pamtimo po strasnim pokoljima pocinjenima pod znakom zvijezde petkorake, Hrvatski Vjesnik, Melbourne, 20 May 2015

Hrvatski Vjesnik, "Vratio sam se sa 36 kilograma, ni majka me nije prepoznala", Hrvatski Vjesnik, Melbourne, 20 May 2015

Hurford, Chris, "Hurford: Yalta Tragic Error Enslaved Millions", (speech by Mr Chris Hurford to a Meeting organized by the Renounce Yalta Committee held at the Polski Centre in Adelaide), published as 'Yalta Condemned', Page 12, Hrvatski Vjesnik, Melbourne, 21 May 1985

Ivankovic, Davor, "Tajni Britanski Dokumenti Potvrduju: Bleiburg: Hrvati su bili zrtvovani", Spremnost Hrvatski Tjednik, Sydney, 29 May 2007 (This article appears today online on Vecernji.hr, 19 May 2007, and was published in Spremnost Hrvatski Tjednik, Sydney on 29 May 2007

Jesser, John, "Visitor recalls 'slaughter great powers would prefer forgotten'", in 'The Canberra Times' (9 May 1985), re-published (front page), Hrvatski Vjesnik, Melbourne, 21 May 1985

Jones, Nigel, "Daily Mail Lista Najgorih Masovni Ubojica 20. Stoljeca – Komunisti daleko najgori masovni ubojice, Hitler treci, Tito trinaesti", in DailyMailOnline, UK (8 October 2014) under heading "From Stalin to Hitler, the most murderous regimes in the world", re-published in Hrvatski Vjesnik, 4 March 2015

Jurcevic, Josip, Fish, Bruno, Vukusic, Bozo, "Cuvari Bleiburske Uspomene", Klub hrvatskih povratnika, Zagreb, 2003

Knight, Robert, "Ethnicity and Identity in the Cold War: The Carinthian Border Dispute, 1945-1949", pages 274—303 in 'The International History Review', University of Toronto Press, Downsview, Volume 22 Number 2, 2000

Kruselj, Zeljko, "Testimony of an Officer Who 'Led 900 Croats to their Death", page 13, Croatia Weekly, Zagreb, Number, 5 March 1998

Kruselj, Zeljko, "Apel saveznickoj vojsci da sprijeci krvoprolice", (re book 'Vatre u noci' and visit of Robert Plan) in Vecernji list (Zagreb), re-published (page 14) in Nova Hrvatska (New Croatia), Sydney, 21-27 July 1998

Kruselj, Zeljko, "Prodajcom Obale Pavelic je Prigrabio Vlast", Hrvatski Vjesnik, Melbourne,19 October 2001

Kruselj, Zeljko, "Dr Jere Jareb Komentira Izjavu Ljubljanske Drzavne Tuziteljice Grobistu Kraj Radovljice: Ministri NDH Nisu Pokopani u Sloveniji", page 8, Hrvatski Vjesnik, Melbourne, 2 November 2001

Kynaston, Edward, "Djilas: a moral man in an amoral age", (book review about 'Rise and Fall'), The Weekend Australian Magazine, page 14, Canberra, January 4-5 1986

Kynaston, Edward, "Harold Macmillan as the villan" (book review in 'Books' Sandra Hall, Editor), page 14, 'The Weekend Australian Magazine' (26-27 July 1986), re-published in Hrvatski Tjednik, Melbourne, 19 August 1986

Lasic, Jure, "How Tito put down the Croatian Spring", page 13, Hrvatski Tjednik, Melbourne, 10 April 1984

Latkovic, Radovan, "Thoughts on a Commemoration: Our Debt to the Victims of Bleiburg", pages 16—18, Klokan, Sydney, Winter 1995

Leko, Mladen, "Two Commemorations" (heading in broadsheet) 'The New Generation English supplement', Hrvatski Vjesnik, Melbourne, 20 May 2015

Lewis, Jonathon E., "Balkan Warfare",(book review of Franklin Lindsay's 'Beacons in the Night: With the OSS And Tito's Partisans In Wartime Yugoslavia') in "Reviews and Commentary" pages 245—248, 'International Journal of Intelligence and Counterintelligence', Volume 7 Number 2, Stanford University Press, Stanford, 1994

Luburic, Vlekoslav, "The End of the Croatian Army" (Spain 1967), in 'Operation Slaughterhouse', Dorrance Publishing Co., Pittsburg, 1995

Bibliography & Further Reading

Lunt Marinovic, Jean (under name: Jean Marinovic) "The Bleiburg Connection", Hrvatski Tjednik, Melbourne, 22 May 1984

Lunt Marinovic,(under name: Jean Marinovic) "The 40th Anniversary of the Ambush at Bleiburg", Hrvatski Tjednik, Melbourne, 21 May 1985

Lunt Marinovic, Jean, "Hiding Bleiburg Won't Lessen the Guilt", Hrvatski Vjesnik, Melbourne, 29 May 1987

Lunt Marinovic, Jean (under name: J. Marinovic), "We Will Not be Fooled Anymore", Hrvatski Tjednik, Melbourne, 24 November 1987

Lunt Marinovic, Jean (under name: Jean W. Marinovic), "Preserve Maribor World War II Genocide Evidence", Hrvatski Vjesnik, Melbourne, 23 July 1999

Lunt Marinovic, Jean, "Bleiburg in today's 'anti-fascist' political culture", page 17, Spremnost Hrvatski Tjednik, Sydney, 25 July 2000

Lunt Marinovic, Jean, "Lessons from Bleiburg", page 10, Nova Hrvatska, Sydney, 22—28 May 2001; also: page 15, Spremnost Hrvatski Tjednik, Sydney, 29 May 2001

Lunt Marinovic, Jean, "The Hague Court and the Bleiburg Genocide", page 10, Nova Hrvatska, Sydney, 20—26 November 2007

Lunt Marinovic, Jean, "Why Croats Commemorate the Bleiburg Genocide at Bleiburg: The Bleiburg Genocide – Croatian Tragedy!", page 10, Nova Hrvatska (New Croatia), Sydney, 1-7 May 2012; also in www.croatia.org (Croatian World Network Discussion Forum),23 April 2012

Manne, Robert, "We Must Rescue Croatia", Herald Sun, Melbourne, 13 December 1991

Marinovic, Ante, "Podignimo do Zvijezda Prah Heroja", Poličnik, 1998

Marinovic, Ante, "Bleibursko Polje Crvene i Bijele Boje", Melbourne, 2005

Northern Star, "Stand by Tito Forces New World Crisis", Northern Star (Trove), Lismore, 17 May 1945

Obrknezevic, Milos, "Development of Orthodoxy in Croatia and the Croatian Orthodox Church" (English translation) pages 229-262, in 'Croatian Review' Munich-Barcelona, June 1979

Ozich, Davorin, "Britain and the Bleiburg Tragedy sells out at New Zealand preview within minutes", 'New Generation English supplement' in Hrvatski Vjesnik, Melbourne, 21 August 1998

Petricevic, Juraj, "The Systematic Oppression of Croats in the First and Second Yugoslavia through Economic Abuse and Hegemony", page 7, History' in CX (Croatian newspaper), Sydney, 19 February 2009

Queensland Times, "Marshall Tito repeats his Trieste tactics in Klagenfurt", Queensland Times (Trove), Ipswich, 17 May 1945

Richards, Christopher, "The basics on the Balkans" (re BBC documentary "Tito: Churchill's Man"), page 3, The Age, Melbourne, 23 July 1992

Riverine Herald, "Tito Flouting Allies—Seeking Control in Austria", Riverine Herald (Trove), Echuca, 17 May 1945

Rora, Ivana, "Cuvari Bleiburske Uspomene", 'Matica Casopis Hrvatske matice iseljenika', number 5, Zagreb, May 2003

Roscic, Fr N. M., "Govor Fra Nikola Mate Roscic" (speech), page 7-8, Spremnost Hrvatski Tjednik, Sydney, 29 May 2001

Rullman, Hanz P., "The Death of a Greengrocer", article in 'Assassinations Commissioned by Belgrade: Documentation about the Yugoslav Murder Machine', published in 'That's Yugoslavia', Ost-Dienst, Hamburg, 1981

Sare, Tom, "Iseljenici Osigurali 12 Besplatnih Autobusa Za Bleiburg" Boka Cropress, Sydney 20 May 2015

Saric, Paul, "Croatian Community sponsors buses for 70th Bleiburg Commemoration", (heading) in 'The New Generation English supplement', Hrvatski Vjesnik, Melbourne, 20 May 2015

Saric, Paul, "Obiljezavanje 70. Godisnjice Bleiburske Tragedije: Hrvatska zajednica sponzorirala autobuse za odlazak u Bleiburg", Hrvatski Vjesnik, Melbourne, 20 May 2015

Schwartz, Mladen, "Prijegor Bleiburga", about book, 'Bleiburg: Uzroci i posljedice', page 18, published in Hrvatski Tjednik, Melbourne, 30 August 1988

Shaw, Terence, Legal Correspondent, "Tolstoy takes libel appeal to Europe", page 4, Weekly Telegraph, London, Issue 143, April 1994

Simonic, Ante, "52 Obiljetnica Bleiburga, Austria", page 7, Spremnost Hrvatski Tjednik, Sydney, 29 May 2001

Skrobica, Marina, "Bleiburg i BBC", page 7, Spremnost Hrvatski Tjednik, Sydney, 22 May 2001

Sopta, Marin, "Nikolaj Tolstoj u Toronto", Hrvatski Tjednik, Melbourne, 29 July 1986

Spremnost Hrvatski Tjednik, "Britain and the Bleiburg Tragedy: Radio Interview with Suzanne Brooks Pincevic", pages 13--14, Spremnost Hrvatski Tjednik, Sydney, 6 February 2007

Stedul, Shirley, "Letter to the Weekend Australian", published in Hrvatski Tjednik, Melbourne, 19 August 1986

Stedul, Shirley H., "How many names on the Obelisk", Hrvatski Tjednik, page 7-8, Melbourne, 1986

Stenhouse, Paul, "He Who Pays the Danegeld Never Gets Rid of the Dane", Klokan: (The Australian-Croatian Magazine), Sydney, Volume 6, Number 4, Summer edition 1995/96

The Advertiser, "Growing Crisis Over Trieste – Tito's Reply To Note Not Acceptable", Australian Associated Press (Trove), Adelaide, 20 May 1945

The Advertiser, "Marshall Tito's Men To Leave Carinthia", The Advertiser, Adelaide, 21 May 1945

The Age, "Trieste Not the Biggest Problem", The Age (Trove), Melbourne, 17 May 1945

Bibliography & Further Reading

The Australian, "Macmillan: scholar, super-statesman", in 'The Times', re-published on page 7 in The Australian (newspaper), Canberra, 31 December 1986

The Australian, "Slavs find mass grave", The Australian, Canberra, 2 July 1990

The Canberra Times, "Tito Defying Allied Request—Yugoslav Troops in Klagenfurt, The Canberra Times (Trove), ACT, 17 May 1945

The Daily News, "Tito Grabs in Austria", page 13, The Daily News (Trove), Perth (WA), 16 May 1945

The West Australian, "Storm Centres--Tito Makes New One—-Moves in Austria—Land-grabbing Elseshere", The West Australian (Trove), Perth (WA), 17 May 1945

Tito, Josip Broz, "The Commander-in-Chief praises the Third Army and its leading officers", in 'Operation Slaughterhouse: Eyewitness Accounts of Post-War Massacres in Yugoslavia', page 135, Dorrance Publishing Co., Pittsburg, Second Edition 1995

Tolstoy, Nikolai, "The Klagenfurt Conspiracy", The Weekend Australian, Canberra, 9—10 July 1983

Topic, L., "McAdams at Melb. Uni.: The Truth Emerges", 'Croatian Students Association of Victoria Page', page 11, Hrvatski Vjesnik, Melbourne, 28 May 1985

Townsville Daily Bulletin, "Tito's Forces Encroach in Austria—Klagenfurt Entered—British Troops Ignored by Partisans", Townsville Daily Bulletin, Townsville (Qld), 17 May 1945

Vetma, Marin, "The Fall of Yugoslavia and The Italian Occupation", in 'The South Slav Journal: Volume 24 No. 3—4 (93—94) Autumn--Winter 2003

Vukic Ina, "Croatia: Bleiburg Massacres of Victims still Hostages of Communist Ideology", Boka Cropress, Sydney, 20 May 2015

Vukic, Ina, "Croatia: Stjepan Mesic And The Scourge of Communist Past", Boka Cropress, Sydney, 27 May 2015

Vukic, Ina, "Purging Croatia of Darkness of Tito and Communism" Za Dom Press, Sydney, 11 November 2015

Ward, Olivia, "Harold Macmillan linked to wartime slaughter", in Toronto Star (Toronto), re-published page 13, 'Hrvatski Tjednik, Melbourne, 29 July 1986

Ward, Olivia, "Survivor recalls praying for a quick death", in Toronto Star (Toronto), re-published page 11, Hrvatski Tjednik, Melbourne, 5 August 1986

Audio/Visual Media, YouTube, DVDs & Documentaries

BBC, 'Betrayal', in 'True Stories', documentary by Laurence Rees, Producer, London, 1991

BBC, 'Tito: Churchill's Man?', documentary, advertised in Herald-Sun and reviewed in The Age Green Guide, Melbourne, 1992 (also on You Tube, 2013), London, 1992

BBC, 'The Secret War -- The Aristocrat and the Balkan Communists', documentary, TV History Channel, London, 2000

Palaich, Michael, Producer, 'British intelligence officer with 1st Guards Bde, 6th Armoured Div south Austria May-June 1945: organisation of transportation for repatriated Croatians from Austria to Yugoslavia', audio interview with Nigel Nicholson, British Imperial War Museum Archives, London, 1988

Majic, Goran, "An Exclusive Interview with Michael Palaich, Producer of the Video Documentary Bleiburg Tragedy: Great Britain Shares Responsibility for Post-World War II Mass Executions of Croatians by Tito's Communist Forces", (Interview focuses on edited YouTube interviews by Palaich of British officers and others), www.HRsvijet.net (Croatian Information Portal), 2011

Sedlar, Jakov, Producer, 'Cetverored Prica o Bleiburgu', documentary film on VHS, Croatia Film, 1999

Sedlar, Jakov, Producer, 'Pavelic bez Maske', documentary film on DVD, Zagreb, 2009

Sedlar, Jakov, 'The Croats and the Serbs: A History of an Aversion', documentary film, Panorama 360, Zagreb, 2011 (also on You Tube)

Thompson, J. Lee, Director, Sinclair, Andrew, Screenplay, 'Before Winter Comes', full-length movie, London, 1969

Internet References

Axis History Forum, "Forced Repatriation, Operation KeelHaul and Bleiburg Tragedy", internet, 2005

Axis History Forum, "Bleiburg Memorial", internet, 2009

Axis History Forum, "Bleiburg Memorial", internet, 2012

Baric, Ivana, "Post-War Execution Site 'Core' of Croatian Army Buried Near Maribor?", www.javno.com, 2007

Barker, Thomas M., "Partisan Warfare in the Bilingual Region of Carinthia", http://www.slovenestudies.com/, 1989

Beljo, Ante, "The Bleiburg Massacres" in 'An International Symposium Southeastern Europe 1918-1995', Croatian Heritage Foundation & Croatian Information Centre, http://www.hic.hr/, 1998

Brooks-Pincevic, Suzanne, "The Truth about the NDH and the effect on the Hague Court", Hrvati AMAC Forum, 2006

Brstovsek, Andrej, "Slovenia & Italy: Moving On?", www.Croatia.org, (Croatian World Network), 2005

Canada.com, "Worse than Srebrenica? MARIBOR, Slovenia--Officials are exhuming a mass grave in the Tezno Forest of northeastern Slovenia, thought to hold the remains of more than 15,000 people in The Vancouver Province", www.canada.com, 10 August 2007

Bibliography & Further Reading

Crawford, Charles, "Regret is Not Enough in Slovenian Tragedy", RadioFreeEurope/RadioLiberty, 2010

Cic, Emil, "The History of Croatian Enemies", http://emilcic.exactpages.com/chapter4.html

Corriere della Sera, "Croatians in Italian Concentration Camps", www.Croatia.org (Croatian World Network) 2004

Danas, "Barbara Pit: two pits are hiding thousands of victims--witnesses and after 54 years in fear", www.Danas.hr, 2009

Delic, Ante, "On the Concealment of Ante Pavelic in Austria in 1945-1946", www.hrcak.srce.hr/file/29126627, 2011

Department of Munitions & Supply, "The Canadian War Industry World War 2", www.wwii.ca/content-17/ , 2010

Direktno.hr, "Na Bleiburgu--Bozanic: Ponovno se namecu podjele, Hrvaska je dobila novi totalitarizam" in Boka Cropress, Sydney, 20 May 2015

Direktno.hr, "Miro Kovac: Milanovic radi na podjelama, on je zabranio pokroviteljstvo Bleiburga", in Boka Cropress, Sydney, 20 May 2015

Direktno.hr, "Na Bleiburgu--Bozanic: Ponovno se namecu podjele, Hrvaska je dobila novi totalitarizam", www.Direktno.hr , 20 May 2015

Direktno.hr, "Skupina hodocasnika krenula je pjesice na Bleiburg za 70 gosisnjicu", in Boka Cropress, Sydney, 6 May 2015

Gallagher, Brian, "The biggest known post-WWII execution site in Europe: Tezno Forest, Slovenia, holds remains of more than 15,000 post-WWII victims", www.Croatia.org , (Croatian World Network), 17 August 2007

Gavranavic, Zvonimir, "Remember Bleiburg",'Annals Australasia' on Sean O Lachtnain Homepage, April/May 2005---2005: "History of World War II: Remember Bleiburg The Massacre the world chose to forget", www.jloughnan.tripod.com/bleiburgh.htm, April/May 2005

Grahek-Ravancic, Martina, "The Handing over of Prisoners from Bleiburg Field and its Surroundings in May 1945" (summary) in 'Controversies about the Croatian Victims at Bleiburg and in "Death Marches"', Portal of Scientific Journals of Croatia (Hrcak), http://hrcak.srce.hr, 2007

Gurrin, Graham, "Gassed to death: 300 victims of Yugoslavia's communist regime found in mass grave", http://www.dailymail.co.uk/news/article-1160708/ 11 March 2009

HRT Vijesti, "Predsjednica će ići na Bleiburg, ali neće držati govor", http://vijesti.hrt.hr/, 28 April 2015

Informativna Katolicka Agencija, "Commemoration of the 63rd Anniversary of the Bleiburg Tragedy", www.ika.hr (Catholic Press Agency), 18 May 2008

Ivankovic, Davor, "Tajni Britanski Dokumenti Potvrduju: Bleiburg: Hrvati su bili zrtvovani", www.Vecernji.hr ; also in: Spremnost Hrvatski Tjednik, Sydney, 29 May 2007

Jackson, General Sir William, Gleve, Group Captain T. P., "The Mediterranean & Middle East", Volume 6, 'Victory in the Mediterranean Part III: November 1944 to May 1945 (iv): Trieste and Austrian Crises', (UK Official History, Naval War College Library, Newport RI, on 'Military History Network', HMSO, pages 1--8, London 1988) www.milhist.net/history

Josipovic, Ivo, "Ustaska obiljezja na Bleiburgu nisu u duhu Ustava, to ne treba financirati", www.Vjesnik.hr, 17 April 2012

Karamarko, Tomislav, "Vodio sina na Bleiburg, da vidi gdje je bio i njegov djed", www.index.hr, 16 May 2015

Kluckhorn, Frank, "Heidelberg to Madrid--The Story of General Willoughby" in 'The Reporter' (N Y Journal), 19 August 1952, on www.maebrussell.com/Articles%20and%20Notes/Charles%20Willoughb

Knezevic, Ivana, "Sabor ukinuo pokroviteljstvo, ali zasad ne i financiranje komemoracije u Bleiburgu", www.Vjesnik.hr, 17 April 2012

Lijepa Nasa Domovina website, "Bleiburg Massacres: Untold Holocaust--the Shame of the British Army and Yugoslav communists". Http://www.lijepanasadomovina.hr, 2004

Lovric, Jelena, "Decoration that Conveys a Message", www.aimpress.org, 29 October 2001

Lunt Marinovic, "The Croatian Surrender to Yugoslavs at Bleiburg", www.croatia.org, (Croatian World Network Forum), 2013

Lunt Marinovic, Jean, "Bleiburg Anthology", www.croatia.org,(Croatian World Network) May 2006

Marinovic, Ante, Lunt Marinovic Jean, "Bleiburg Anthology", www.croatianviewpoint.com,(Croatian Viewpoint), 2006

McAdams,C. Michael, "Yalta and the Bleiburg Tragedy", in 'Od Bleiburga do Nasih Dana', from Skolska Kniga, 1995, on www.Dalmatia.net, 1999

Mijatovic, Andjelko, "Bleiburska Tragedija i krizni put Hrvatskoga Naroda Godine 1945", published by S. Coric, www.hsk.hr (Hrvatski Svjetski Kongres(HSK), 2007

Northerntruthseeker, "More Hidden History Revealed: The Bleiburg Massacre", www.northerntruthseeker.com, 2012

Pavlakovic, Vjeran, "Red Stars, Black Shirts: Symbols, Commemorations, and Contested Histories of World War Two in Croatia", in National Council for Eurasian and East European Research, University of Washington, www.ucis.pitt.edu/nceeer/2008_822-16h_Pavlakovic.pdf, 2008

Pavletic, Ivan, "Why are we Croatians so afraid of the Bleiburg truth?", Croatian World Network, www.croatia.org, 2006

Scott, TPD, Brigadier, "Balkan Troubles' (narratives, May 1945), in 'The Story of the 38th (Irish) Brigade in the Second World War', http://www.irishbrigade.co.uk/ as printed 2014

Bibliography & Further Reading

Spolar, Christine, "Slovene mass graves reopen historic wounds: A WWII historian has unearthed 570 hidden sites, Few want to deal with the finding, and revisionists want to blame the communists", The Chicago Tribune, www.chicagotribune.com, 2008

Springer, Zvonko Z., "Outcast Without Guilt or My Way of the Cross: Four Months of a Young Home Guard Alias Hrvatski Domobran" (1985), www.cosy.sbg.ac.at/~zzspri/index.html, 1999

Springer, Zvonko Z., "Croatian Army's Withdrawal Route Westward in 1945",(1985) http://www.cosy.sbg.ac.at/~zzspri/, Salzburg, 1999

Stanton, Gregory H., President, "Genocide Watch--The crime of genocide is defined in international law in the Convention on the Prevention and Punishment of Genocide", http://www.genocidewatch.org/genocide/whatisit.html , 9 December 1948

Studia Croatica, "The Bleiburg Tragedy" (1963), http://www.studiacroatica.com.libros/tragedia/tb080401.htm, as printed in year 2000

Studijski center za narodno spravo, "Invitation to the Symposium, 'The Massacres of Bleiburg and the tragedy of Viktring field: The fate of the military and civilian refugees in the area of Austrian-Yugoslav border in May and June 1845" (a crossborder and multidimensional project for contemporary history) on 11-12 May 2013 in Viktring Austria, http://www.scnr.si/sl/wp-content/uploads/vabilo-simpVetrinj1.pdf (Študijski center za narodno spravo (Slovenia)--Study centre for national reconciliation), 2013

The Economist, "Britains ancient shame in Slovenia", www.theeconomist.com.uk, 30 October 2010

The Telegraph, "Brigadier Anthony Cowgill, MBE," www.telegraph.co.uk/news/obituaries/, London, 2009

Trifkovi, Srdja, "Lord Aldington: Dead, but no R.I.P.", www.serendipity.li/hr/trifkovic.htm , 19 December 2000

Wikipedia, "Bleiburg Massacre", (on Wikipedia as printed 21 January 2006--now discontinued), see: http://abuse.wikia.com/wiki/Bleiburg_massacr e

Wikipedia, "Bleiburg repatriations", https://en.wikipedia.org/wiki/Bleiburg_repatriations , as printed May 2013

Wikipedia, "East Africa Campaign (World War II)", https://en.wikipedia.org/wiki/East_African_Campaign_(World_War_II) as printed 2013

Wikipedia, "Operation Keelhaul", https://en.wikipedia.org/wiki/Operation_Keelha ul ,as printed in 2012

Yahoo News, "Croatian leader pays tribute to killed pro-Nazi collaborators" https://www.yahoo.com/news/croatian-leader-pays-tribute-killed-, pro-nazi-collaborators-192309877.html?ref=gs, 15 May 2015

Memorials, Monuments & Museums

'Camp X Memorial Park', Canada, http://www.camp-x.com/; and http://www.thecanadianencyclopedia.ca/en/article/camp-x/, and http://www.cbc.ca/xcompany/dispatches/the-real-camp-x-10-facts-about-canadas-elite-spy-school, Ontario, Canada

'Carinthian Regional Museum', Slovenia, "And What is the Price of Freedom: End of World War II in Carinthia", permanent outdoor Exhibit: M. Linasi, Design: E. Koraca, Review: M. Osojnik, Translation: E. Kozar, maps: T. Ferenca, Photographs: from museum, Poljana, 10 May 2010

'Genocide Memorial', Australia, Irwin, Julia, "Genocide Memorial: Sculpture Destined for Preston Reserve", Preston Leader, Preston (Vic), September 15, 2015; refer also to :Tippet, Harrison, "Genocide memorial on hold after complaints received", Preston Leader, Preston (Vic), December 15, 2015

'Maribor Monument', Slovenia, "Maribor Building Monument to Post-WWII Victims", Vlado Zagorac, "Croatia Weekly", Zagreb, No. 71, 10 June 1999

'Mirogoj Cemetery Monument', Croatia, Inscription: "Victims of Bleiburg and the Way of the Cross", https://www.tripadvisor.com/LocationPhotoDirectLink-g294454-d316812-i100391417-Mirogoj_Cemetery-Zagreb_Central_Croatia.html

'The Yalta Memorial', UK, Wikipedia, "Twelve Responses to Tragedy" (The Yalta Memorial), https://en.wikipedia.org/wiki/Twelve_Responses_to_Tragedy

INDEX

A

Addis, Sir J. M. 65, 76
Adriatic Croatian coast 34
after the war 192. *See also* post-war
Aldington, Lord 94, 113, 117, 120. *See also* Toby Low
Alexander, Field Marshall 14, 18, 33, 36, 38, 43, 72, 78, 90, 96, 112, 127, 130, 150, 155, 162, 172, 195, 201, 207, 229, 280
alleged agreement 57. *See also* Willoughby
alleged "trade-off" 90. *See also* McAdams
Anglo-American Mission 200
annex 35. *See also* Trieste
annexation policies 111. *See also* Tito
annihilation 48, 119. *See also* liquidation
anti-Anglo/American 57
anti-Bolshevism 68
anti-facist 228, 239
    banning investigation 239
    new antifascist ideology 242
    revisionist anti-Fascist pro-Communist 246
anti-Nazi mutiny at Villefranche-de-Rouergue 205
Appelbaum, Anne 130, 235, 236
approaching 49, 61. *See also* Croatian retreat
Aralica, Ivan 161
Arip, Dr 122
Armenian
    victims 250
arms embargo 152
Auschwitz 174
Austria
    decision to retreat to 76
    share post-war occupation 112
    Austrian border 165
Avenue of the Croats 205
Axis forces 33
Axis states 188

B

Barker, Thomas M 110
Barnard, Michael 93
Bartosek, Karel 160
Basta, Commissar Milan 63, 64, 80, 251. *See also* Yugoslav Army
Basta 92, 161, 195
    belligerent behaviour 156
    losing his patience 126
Basta, Colonel Milan 172
Basta, Milan 134
Basta's Report 7, 8, 9, 10
battle of Krbava Field 175
Battle of Stalingrad 91
Baxter, Dr David M 55
BBC 37, 90, 169
    BBC2 174
    "Betrayal" documentary 149, 151, 180
    Klagenfurt Affair 77
    Timewatch 77
Beacons in the Night 226
Beehive 143
Belgrade 112, 133
    Assassinations 29
Berlin Wall 170
Bethell, Nicholas 6, 60, 134, 149
    The Last Secret 75
Bjelovar 62
Black Book of Communism 197
blame 74, 76, 133, 173, 194, 203, 235. *See also* Responsibility
Bleiburg 140
    castle xv, 1, 5, 7, 10, 13, 16, 18, 20, 23, 30, 40, 44, 49, 55, 58, 61, 71, 92, 94, 95, 104, 120, 121, 122, 127, 129, 133, 135, 147, 148, 149, 150, 152, 156, 161, 162, 164, 176, 189, 190, 195, 196, 200, 201, 207, 208, 209, 222, 259, 261, 263, 270
    meeting at 126
    Thurn-Valsassina castle 30, 200
    evacuation 62
    extradited from 109
    marched 142

negotiations 1, 5, 17, 18, 20, 21, 22, 23, 45, 46, 47, 49, 51, 55, 56, 58, 59, 60, 61, 64, 71, 74, 75, 78, 81, 82, 92, 122, 123, 127, 129, 133, 135, 137, 140, 151, 152, 156, 161, 162, 164, 165, 171, 189, 191, 193, 195, 197, 200, 201, 203, 207, 208, 209, 224, 225, 226, 230, 259, 260, 261, 262, 263
    surrender negotiation at 104
Bleiburg field 141, 144, 185, 200
    massacre at 92
    mass executions 145
    mass murders 146
Bleiburg Field
    encircled 39
    memorial 190
    monument 233
        star and crescent 215
    tragedy of the innocent 241
        symbolic 1, 81, 90, 133, 146, 180, 189, 202, 229, 230, 233, 238, 249, 263, 265, 271, 272
            of Croatian national suffering 175
Bleiburg Honorary Guard 188, 189, 196
Bleiburg Honorary Platoon 216
Bleiburg Honor Guard 214
Bleiburg-Maribor Massacres 56, 128
Bleiburg-Maribor genocide 68
Bleiburg memorial 250
    controversy 216
Bleiburg Memorial
    Zrtvama, Nevinim 241, 273
Bleiburg Monument
    Nevinim Zrtvama 241
Blue Helmets 210
Boban, L 287
Bogdan, Ivo 67
Boka CroPress 244
Bolshevik 1, 5, 14, 177, 181, 185, 260. *See also* Yugoslavia
Booker, Christopher 24, 35, 37, 92, 95, 111, 125, 138, 139,

305

140, 141, 142, 143, 144, 149, 190
Borovlje 223
Bosnia 44. *See also* Meshihat of the Islamic Community
  Hercegovina 39
  Herzegovina 242
Bosnian
  Muslim soldiers 215
Bozanic
  platform of 'equal guilt' 247
Bozanic, Archbishop 244
Bozanic, Archbishop Josip 237
  Bishops' Conferences 214
Bozanic, Cardinal 214, 240, 245, 247
Bozanic, Cardinal Josip 242
bratstvo i jedinstvo 173
British
  betrayal 150
  deceived Croats 184
  extraditions 36, 200
    ghastly mistake 64, 74, 76
  hand-over by 189
  handover of Croats at Rosenbach 143
  handover to Tito's Partisans 237
  Johnson, Sgt W.G. 138
  not to shoot except self-defense 98
  out-numbered 23
  policy of non-confrontation 98
  POW camps 49
  Prisoners of War 202
  refusal of their surrender 238
  Spitfire planes 208
  trial 93
  use deceit 60
  V Corps
    weakness of 112
  War Diaries 13, 20, 38, 46, 59, 60, 124
British Army
  13 Battery 12, 13
  British V Corps 49
  Durham Light Infantry 122, 142
  Eighth Army 36
  Keightley, General 98
  Keightley's Fifth Corps 111
  Keightley's order 60
  Keightly at Klagenfurt 91
  Keightly's V Corps 37
  McCreery, General 37
  Mitchell, Brig 123
  Moore, P M N 111
  Murray, Officer 18
  O'Sullivan, Bernard 146
  Paul Lunn-Rockcliffe's Battery 12
  repatriations 74
  Sixth Armoured Division 35
  V Corps 31, 94, 97, 120
  Welsh Guards 146
  Welsh Regt 121
  Worral, Lt. Col. D.M.C. 122, 142
British Eighth Army 13, 119, 123, 130, 132, 138, 231
  1st Guards Bde 123
  1st Irish Brigade 143
  6th Armoured Division 12, 99, 136
  16 Durham Light Infantry Division 13
  17th Field Regiment 12
  27 Lancers 12
  38th Irish Brigade 1, 12, 35, 37, 93, 112, 210
  38th (Irish) Infantry Brigade tripartite discussions 121
  38th Irish Infantry Brigade 208
  45 Recce Regiment 122
  46th Division 12, 98
  46th Division headquarters 98
  46th Recce Reg 142
  Faughs 12
  Fifth Corps 104
  First Royal Irish Fusiliers 231
  Grenadier Guards 152
  Hogan, Lieutenant 92, 124
  lack of available forces 36
  London Irish 12
  Low, Brigadier Toby 94, 120, 154, 177
British Imperial War Museum 99, 118, 138, 231
British officers
  testimony of 231
British policy
  changed 120
  KP 115 120
  KP 128 121
  KP 143a 123
  KPs 89 and 105 121
British repatriations 147
British Slovene Society 228
buffer zone 193. *See also* Yugoslavia
Bulgarian 21, 22, 23, 47, 111, 124, 200, 223
  Army 17, 35, 45
    1st Bulgarian Army 12
  blockade 11, 48
  near Dravograd 92
  options 48
  outposts 13
  refusal 39, 140
  refused to accept 46
Bulgarians 91, 124, 128, 139, 152, 188
  cut off by 140
    blockade 199
  blocked 47
burial of the victims 212
Butmir 62

C

camp Stental 193
capitulation 8, 118, 136, 145, 261
  conditions of 10
capitulatons
  conditions of. *See also* Croatia
Carinthia 57
  goals to annex 130
  occupying 48
  Tito's occupation of 133
Carinthian Regional Museum of Revolution 191, 221
Carnaro 98
Caserta 70
Cecelja, Vilim 11
Celje 39, 44, 47, 58, 62, 94, 119, 139, 155, 166, 187, 188, 193, 218, 224, 242
Celovec 223
Chetnik 256
Chetniks 22, 90, 94, 119, 132, 134, 227. *See also* Yugoslavia
Chicago Tribune 213
Churchill, Winston 34, 76, 78, 82, 144, 150, 155, 172, 235
CNN 169
Cold War 34, 48, 56, 68, 74, 84, 142, 153, 181
Conquest, Robert 131
conspiracy 64, 93, 101, 104, 109, 156, 235
Cossack Calvary Corps 223
Cossacks 12, 33, 38, 46, 60, 87, 91, 101, 102, 216, 223

INDEX

15th Cossack Cavalry Corps 138
Covic, Dragan 242
Cowgill, Lord 24, 94, 99, 117, 118, 119, 120, 121, 122, 123, 125, 139, 144, 149, 176, 178, 195, 201
Crawford, Charles 228
Crljen, Colonel Daniel 17, 21, 48, 64, 71, 75, 80, 135, 146, 148, 156, 171, 188, 208
   atrocity 20
   testimony of 195
Croatia
   decision to evacuate 71
Croatian
   13th May 1945
      appeal written 148
   14 May 122
   1960 Resolution 55
   1973 Resolution 56
   collective memory 142
   columns 207
   decision to surrender 127
   Defence Ministry 17
   Emissary's journey 127
   French resistance in Aveyron 205
   "government" extradition 175
   government group 46, 58
   government leaders 70
      government leadership 76
   government ministers 12, 45, 70, 165, 178, 179
   Holmec Pass 223
   Home Guards 166, 199, 215
   mass emigration 108
   memorandum of 3-4 May 1945 199
   officials 164
   retreat 160
   retreat towards Dravograd 130
   state authorities 63
   surrender to Yugoslavs 63, 233, 235
   Ustasha 23. *See also* Ustachi
Croatian Armed Forces
   Boban, General 21, 22, 48
   Gustovic, General 21, 48
   Herencic, General 17, 18, 19, 20, 21, 22, 23, 44, 48, 71, 75, 80, 92, 142, 145, 146, 148, 151, 156, 157, 162, 163, 171, 188, 189, 208, 209

   deception 22
   Hrvatska Legija Stalingrad 205
   Kvaternik, General Eugen (Dido) 29
   Luburic, General Vjekoslav 'Maks' 33, 43, 55
   Metikos, General 17, 19, 21, 22, 48, 208
   Metzger, General 21, 48
   Moskov, General Ante 44
   Sertic, Tomislav 9
   Servatski, General 17, 18, 19, 21, 22, 43, 48
   Servatzy 75, 171, 208
   Stancer, Colonel General Slavko 10, 20, 21, 48, 145, 209
   Sudar, General 19, 22, 48
   Tomasevic, General 10, 21, 48
Croatian Army 9, 82, 209, 212
   12th Croat Division 123
   Croatian Home Guard (Domobrani) 212
   Croatian Home Guards 249
      Homeguard 198
      Home Guards 166, 215
Croatian Commission for War and Post-war Victims 207
Croatian government 80, 119, 139
   Croatian Parliament 214
   Croatian state
      defeat of 144
      decision of the 68
Croatian Government
   Memorandum 188
   peace emissary 164
Croatian government members 207
Croatian government ('sabor') 43
Croatian National Ethical Tribunal 254
Croatian Officials
   Vrancic, Minister 164
Croatian Retreat 160
   mistake 39
   multitude 11
   withdrawal 36, 38
   withdrawal route 166
   withdrawal routes 57
Croatian Retreat Route
   different route 45, 128
   different routes 44
   Hanzic and Kotije 166
   Smartno 166

Straze 166
Sustriji 145
Trieben 45
Turiska Vas 166
Turracher Hohe 46
Varazdin 44, 57
Velenje 166
Zidani, Most 44, 57
Croats
   approach of 151
   Austrian frontier 62
   cut off to the 199
   did not cross the border 23
   lured into trap 68
   surrendered 23

D

Dalmatian coast 82
Davorin, Josip 175
D.C. Owena 117
Deakin, Sir W 111
Death March
   routes 57, 150
Death Marches xviii, xix, 1, 23, 41, 45, 48, 49, 54, 55, 62, 79, 90, 105, 127, 135, 145, 146, 153, 154, 160, 165, 166, 172, 175, 176, 183, 185, 186, 187, 189, 232, 236, 237, 242, 248, 253, 261, 264, 265, 270. *See also* Way of The Cross
demographic 193
Denny, Maj. J.G. 122, 142
Deutsch-Maceljski 48
Deutsch-Maceljski, Liaison Officer 37
Dezman, Joze 192
Diaspora 188
discrepancies in the media 248
Djilas 175, 202
Djilas, Milovan 56, 67, 79, 82, 101, 133, 173, 180
Dobja Vas 118, 191
Dobrava 212
Dobroj Vas
   Dobroj Vasi 191
Dolensko 62
Dolic 166
Dolič 223
Domobran 22, 165, 204, 209
   Croatian and Slovenian Home Guards 134
   Domobrani 151, 215

307

Domobrani Croatian Home Guards 194
Domobran Officers 242 Klub of Zagreb 204
Domobranski Slovenian Homeguard 33, 223
doublespeak 141
Draper, Gerald 231
Drava River 13, 17, 21, 22, 23, 45, 46, 47, 48, 57, 73, 92, 93, 98, 124, 126, 143, 151, 155, 166, 223, 224, 225, 229, 270
Drau 92
Dravograd 8, 17, 21, 22, 23, 35, 39, 44, 45, 46, 47, 48, 88, 92, 94, 118, 119, 130, 138, 139, 147, 149, 152, 178, 188, 194, 199, 200, 208, 223, 224, 227, 229, 261, 264, 266, 269
Dubajic, Major 120, 154
Dubocac 62

E

East-West conflict 169
ecumenical Mass of Reparation 228
eight-mile long tunnel 101
Eisenhower 38
Eisenkappel 111, 123, 187
   Eisenkappel (Zelezna Kapla) 224
end of hostilities 251. See also Geneva Convention
Engels, Friedrich 136
English Army
   handed over by 138. See also British Eight Army
English commanders
   alleged agreement 57. See also British
English policy 173. See also British policy
Enns River 45
entrapment of the NDH columns 225
Epstein 127
equal guilt 186, 210
Esih, Bruna 187
   Esih, Bruno 219
EU 166, 216, 249, 252
   European anti-Communist political culture 228
   European Parliament 197

Europe's communist regimes 228
evacuation 16, 62
   of Zagreb 17, 18
evidence
   covering up 128
evils of Fascism, Nazism and Communism 247
Exhibit in Poljana 111
   freedom 49, 144
   Koroska 222
   Koruska Provincial Museum of the Revolution 117
   Memorial Region of 'Freedom and Peace' 221, 256
exodus 38, 40, 44. See also Croatian Government

F

Ference, Dr Mitja 212, 213
Ferlach 28, 36, 112
Fisher, OSS and Captain Charles 20
founders of Yugoslavia 81. See also Strossmayer
Fucek, Vladimir 242

G

Gaj 81
Geneva Convention 63, 74, 150, 152, 177, 202
   1929 Geneva Convention 183, 251
   Article 75 251
genocide 41, 79, 160, 233, 250, 254
   Bleiburg-Maribor 68
German Army
   Topolsica 97
German Army Group E 97, 111, 120, 223
   Army Group E 33
   Germans 216
Gleve, Capt. T P 97
Glibota, Ante 255
Goldstein, Slavko 246
Goli Otok 236
Gorizia 98
Grabar-Kitarovic 237, 238, 239, 242, 244
Gray, QC Mr Charles 141. See also Tolstoy
Grcic, Marko 117, 145, 197
Great Britain

limit German influence in Balkans 137. See also British
Griffen 12, 36, 52, 62, 92, 138, 184, 190
Gunner, Captain Colin 123, 231
   Gunner's Brigade. See also British 8th Army
   Gunner's Brigade 124
   testimony 92
Gvozd Mountain 175

H

Hague
   International War Crimes Tribunal 185
Hague Court 210
   ICTY Hague Court 79
hand-over 38. See also Yalta
handover 53. See also Cossacks
handover of Slovenian civilian refugees 194. See also Viktring Camp
Hecimovic 127
Hefer, Stjepan 202
Hintersee 45. See also Croatian - retreat route
Hitler 203
"Hitman" 105
Honorary Bleiburg Guard 212. See also Bleiburg
   Honorary Bleiburg Leader 242
   Honorary Bleiburg Platoon 244
Horne, Sir Alistair Allan 101
how Yugoslavia was created 107. See also Strossmayer
Hrust 8, 11, 58, 73, 150, 208, 257
Hugarians 175
   Hungary 30

I

Idealogy
   Marxist 18
   menacing communist 37
ideological 29, 245
   divisions 247
   ideological position 228
   ideology 170
ideology
   new antifascist ideology 242. See also Revolution
Ideology

Index

liberation 29, 34
"Il Giorno" 116
Illyrian 28
"Independent on Sunday" 116
Independent State of Croatia (NDH) 10, 145, 179. *See also* NDH
indicted for libel 91. *See also* Tolstoy
innocent victims 241. *See also* Bleiburg Memorial
in rapid pace 226. *See also* Exhibit
Institutum Historicum Croaticum 196
international law 9, 10, 11, 47, 64, 74, 81, 101, 164, 172, 183, 196, 210. *See also* Geneva
interpreter 5, 6, 7, 9, 14, 15, 18, 19, 20, 23, 72, 101, 118, 129, 140, 141, 147, 156, 162, 163, 171, 208, 209, 260, 261, 270. *See also* Robert Plan
Irish officer 59. *See also* Gunner, Colin
Iron Curtain 30, 38, 235. *See also* Cold War
Islamic Community in Croatia 243. *See also* Bosnia
Istria 98
Italy 164, 227
    transferred to 151

J

Jackson, Gen. Sir William 97
Jansa, Prime Minister Janez 212
Jareb, Dr Jere 178
Jasenovac 215, 246
    anti-Fascists 239
    Jasenovac memorial 216
Jesenice 57, 175, 178
Jezersko pass 225
Jones, Nigel 107
Josic, Tomislav 255
Josipovic, Ivo 255
Judenburg 45, 58. *See also* Croats - Retreat Routes
Julian Region 199
Jurcevic, Josip 205, 219, 255

K

Karamarko, Tomislav 248
Karavenken Mountains 30, 223
Karawanken 44
Karlovac 17, 44
Katalinic, Kazimir 135
Katyn 131
    Katyn Forest 176
Kingdom of Serbs Croats and Slovenes 28, 198. *See also* Yugoslavia
Kirk, Ambassador 70
Klagenfurt 5, 18, 27, 28, 29, 35, 36, 37, 38, 39, 46, 49, 57, 58, 67, 70, 72, 74, 77, 78, 86, 87, 91, 92, 99, 100, 104, 109, 111, 112, 120, 133, 140, 148, 151, 154, 169, 171, 174, 175, 185, 187, 189, 195, 196, 200, 204, 208, 223, 259
Knight, Robert 95, 96, 169
Koraca, E. 221
Kovacevic, Anto 255
Kozlic, John 255
Kranj 225
Krapina 166
Krizni Put 230. *See also* Death Marches
Kruselj 45
    Kruselj, Zeljko 140
Kulundzic, Zvonimir 135

L

Lasko 154, 243
Laugham, Major J. 122, 142
Lausic, Dr. Ante 134
Lavamund 12, 13, 38, 58, 59, 60, 92, 112, 122, 124, 125, 139, 140, 142, 231, 232, 242, 262, 264
    Lawamauend 184
    Lawamund 62
Leko, Josip 241
Lester Pearson 210
Lewis, Jonathan E. 34, 132
Libuce 95, 223, 225. *See also* Loibach
Lidington, David 229. *See also* EU
Life magazine 147
Lilik, Miroslav 21, 117, 191
Lindsay 198
    Lindsay, Franklin 20, 31, 34, 38, 106, 129
    Lindsay's 118

Lippitzbach 225
Ljeljak, Roman 255
Ljubljana 28, 57, 178, 192, 199, 217, 223, 228
Lohr, General Alexander 12, 33, 97, 111, 120, 199, 224, 266. *See also* German Army
Loibach 30, 58, 207
    cemetery "Unter-Loibach" 214
    field 39
    Loibach field 208. *See also* Libuce
Loncar, Budimir 255
London Observer 77
London Times 74, 77, 136
Lorkovic-Vokic Coup d'etat 197
    Lorkovic-Vokic Plot 44. *See also* Croatian Government
"Los Angeles Times" 116
Lunt Marinovic, Jean 210. *See also* Marinovic

M

Macek 119, 139
Maclean, Fitzroy 34, 132
Macmillan 120, 150, 155
    Macmillan and Alexander—liaison 90
    Macmillan, Harold 38, 49, 90, 91, 96, 101, 102, 105, 112, 185
    documents 70
Maksimir 175, 191, 197
    Maksimir Park 153, 154
Mandic, President Nikola 127
Manne, Robert 179
Maria Elend 100, 175. *See also* British - exhibitions
Maribor 19, 39, 40, 45, 47, 48, 56, 57, 59, 62, 65, 68, 80, 83, 84, 122, 125, 128, 130, 138, 154, 164, 166, 167, 171, 172, 186, 188, 193, 199, 208, 211, 212, 223, 226, 228, 229, 241, 246, 260, 264, 266, 269
Marinovic, Jean 6, 83, 85, 107, 108, 109, 159, 167, 170, 177, 196, 210, 233, 234, 235
Martinovic, N
    Martinovic, Nikica 190
    Martinovic, Nikola 67
Meily, John J 29, 69
Meshihat of the Islamic

Community 190. *See also* Islamic
Mesic, President Stjepan 250, 253, 255
Mestrovic, Ivan 81, 203
Mestrovic, Mate 202, 203, 204
Meza River 17, 39, 45, 46, 48, 128, 140, 191. { Miess River}
Meza Valley 111, 112, 223
Mezica 39, 48, 97, 118, 140
Milanovic, Prime Minister Zoran 241, 248, 254
Mirogoj 187
   Mirogoj Cemetery 153, 154
Mladen Leko 239
Montenegrin 216
   Chetnik representative 256
   Krivokapic, Dr Dusan 148, 256
   Montenegrin chetniks 142, 223, 225, 226
   Montenegrins 21, 22, 33, 75, 142, 206, 207, 209, 227, 263, 287. *See also* Chetniks
Morgan Line 37
Moscow Declaration of 1943 130
Moslem victims 243. *See also* Bosnia - Islamic
Mufti Aziz Hasanovic 243. *See also* Islamic
munitions 21, 35. *See also* Bleiburg Field
Mussolini 33, 39, 46, 203

N

Nadj, Kosta 48, 134
National Council 28, 215, 283, 284, 286
NATO 249
Nazi collaborators 238
nazifascists 250. *See also* Idealogy
NDH 46, 215
   NDH government 188. *See also* Croatian Government
new government (1944) 188. *See also* Yugoslavia
Nicholson, Nigel 99, 100, 141, 152, 157, 176, 185, 231, 232, 233
Nikolic, Vinko 87, 117, 127
Nobilo, Mario 117
'no' British deception 101. *See also* Bleiburg - negotiations
no "conspiracy" 196
'no' mass slaughter 140. *See also* Bleiburg field
non-cooperation 34. *See also* Yugoslav Army
non-Partisan Yugoslavs 70
not to accept 13, 14, 23, 38, 49. *See also* British Policy
numbers on retreat 248. *See also* Croatian Retreat
Nuremberg
   trials 68
Nuremburg 230, 231

O

occupation 12, 29, 30, 34, 35
occupying 23, 48. *See also* Yugoslavs, Bulgarians
occupy part of Austria 178
Omrcanin, Ivo 128, 181, 285
Operation Keelhaul 64, 176, 193
Operation Slaughterhouse 1, 7, 17, 19, 21, 30, 35, 36, 37, 43, 44, 45, 46, 47, 48, 49, 55, 56, 57, 58, 59, 62, 68, 71, 73, 74, 80, 84, 92, 108, 118, 119, 121, 127, 135, 140, 141, 149, 150, 152, 153, 157, 162, 167, 180, 186, 190, 227, 232, 261, 285
Operation Storm 185
options 15, 20, 23, 47, 48, 49, 126, 196. *See also* British policy
Orsag 202
Orthodox 92. *See also* Tolstoy
Orwell 109
OSS 20, 118, 132
Otiski Vrh 166
Ottomans 175
Owen, OSS Captain Douglas 20, 21

P

Paka River 166
Palaich, Michael 123, 124, 125, 154, 182, 230, 231
Panne, J. 160
Partisan 189
   alleged agreement 57
   bands 22
   Fourth Zone 20
   Headquarters 20. *See also* Hrust
   mass executions 145
   procrastination 110
   soldiers 21
   Southern Carinthia 223
   WWII 101
Partisans 15, 20, 34, 36, 61, 82, 92, 104, 111, 125, 126, 150, 164, 194, 197, 199, 208, 242. *See also* Yugoslav Army
   16th Voyvodina Partisan Division 23
   17th Partisan Assault Division 62
   Allied and Partisan objectives 130
   already occupying 119
   camouflaging 151
   communist 61
   deportation 56
   handed over to 138
   intention 178
   intention to annex southern Austria 129
   lack of cooperation 132
   obstructing Allied efforts 130
   political interests of 138
   Prekmurje Brigade 223
   sabotage and stockpiling 129
   surrendered to 251
   well-armed 47
   Wilkinson's goals 111
   withdraw 78
Partisan vengeance 74
Pavelic, Dr Ante 29, 45, 76, 111, 119, 139
   absence of the government 23
   domestic politics 63
   elite group 43, 45
   Pavelic group 207
   regime 23
   soldiers 8, 134
Peace Conference 100
Peric, Blago 204
Permanent Exhibit in Poljana 207. *See also* Exhibit
Petzen Mountain 30
Plan, Robert 20, 118, 121, 122, 129, 148, 208. *See also* Interpretor
Plebiscite 28, 30
Pliberk 112, 223. *See also* Bleiburg
Pohorje 193, 226
politically correct 235
Poljana 39, 45, 48, 122, 128, 140

Index

Battle of 49
Polygraph 248
Pope John Paul II 247
post-war massacre 144
   massacred 138
   massacre of Croats 133
   massacres 41, 154, 202
   mass executions 145
   mass slaughters 62
   slaughtered 205
post-war mass graves 218
   Dogoze 226
   Hrastnik 155
   Huda Jama 218
   Huda mine 243, 246
   Jazovka 115, 185
   Kasindol 62
   Koceve 243, 246
      Kocevje 160, 194
      Kocevje forest 185
      Kocevski 102
      Kocevski Rog 62, 154, 187
   Kocevski Rog 192
   Konfin 192
   Kosice 155
   Krsko 62
   Macelj 239, 245
   Maceljska
      Maceljska forest 138
   mass grave 55, 94, 116, 122, 173, 187, 192, 221, 241, 246
   mass graves 49, 62, 81, 84, 102, 144, 154, 176, 193, 206, 214, 226, 228, 229, 237
   mausoleum in Slovenia 212
   Podgraci 62
   Podravski Klostar 62
   Ptuj 62
   Sestine 62
   sink hole 115
   Sisak 44, 62
   Slivnica – Pesnica 167
      highway 166
   Slovenia pit 96
   Sosice 62, 115
      ghosts of 116
   Tezno 187, 239, 243, 245
      mass grave 241
   Tezno Forest 211
   Teznot 226
   Trbovlje-Hrastnik 218
   Virovitica 62
   Vrgn-Most 62
post-war mass grave sites 189

post-WWII massacres 166
Po Valley 199
POW camp
   Toschling 36
POW camps 49
   Krumpendorf 36, 62, 184
   Maria Saal 36
   Tamsweg 36, 92
   Teharje camp 218
   Wolfsberg 12, 36, 45, 58, 73, 92, 124, 232
POW Camps
   Grafenstein 36
   Viktring 36, 57, 77, 96, 100, 201
   Viktring Camp 70, 99, 101, 142
   Villach 35, 37, 57, 62, 78, 79, 97, 146, 147, 160, 175, 184
Prcela & Guldescu 149
Prcela, John 157
Prevalje 221
prisoners of war
   15,000 Hungarians 36
   24,000 Slovenes 36
   25,000 Croats 36
   46,000 Cossacks 36
   100,000 Germans 36
   prisoners-of-war, 220,000 36
   treatment of 63
propaganda 198, 238. *See also* Ideology
Pupovac, Milorad 255
Pusic, Vesna 255

R

Racki 81
Radovljice 178
Radstadt 45
reconciliation 210
   agenda of 247
repatriation 183, 251. *See also* Geveva Convention
repatriations 101, 235. *See also* Nicholson
responsibility 11, 22, 73, 74, 170. *See also* blame
retreat routes 193. *See also* Croatian Army from NDH 187
Reuters 95
"revanchism" (no revenge) 117
revisionism 213, 253
   revisionist anti-Fascist pro-

Communist 246
revolution 5, 131, 164, 267, 268, 270
   revolutionary 31. *See also* Idealogy
River Drava 123
   objective to occupy 98
Rogaska Slatina 45, 166
Roosevelt 235
Rosegg 28, 36, 92. *See also* POW camps
Rosenbach 100, 146, 194, 230
routes 207. *See also* Croatian Retreat
Royalist Serbs 33. *See also* Chetniks
Rullman, Hanz P 67
Russians 12
   did not support Tito 133. *See also* Sovients

S

sabotage the Allies 178. *See also* Partisans
Salzburg 45, 58
Sankt Andra (Saint Andra) 37, 58
Sankt Andrea
   St. Andre 12
Scott, Brigadier Patrick 1, 7, 10, 12, 13, 14, 15, 16, 18, 20, 35, 38, 60, 98, 121, 132, 140, 141, 143, 149, 151, 161, 163, 171, 176, 189, 195, 196, 200, 206, 208, 209, 256
   Balkan Troubles 210
   conditions 16
   order to surrender 75
   Scott's Report 11, 93, 140, 151, 210
   three alternatives 140. *See also* British Army - 38th Brigade
   War Diaries 124
SDP (Social Democrat Party) 248
self-defence 36. *See also* British Policy
Sentvid 118
Separovic, Dr Zvonimir 255
Serbs 100, 116
   Serb Chetnik Royalists 99
   Serbia 28
   Serbian and Slovenian Yugoslav negotiators 126

Serbian Cetniks 216
Serbian Chetnik Royalists 227
Serbian rule 133
Serbians 75, 257, 270
signpost 88, 177, 190, 197, 205, 236
 "Griffen" 243
Simo Dubajic 154
Sittersdorf 123. *See also* Eisenkappel
sketched maps 207
Sklopan, Vladimir 135
Slovene and Serb repatriation 102
Slovene Gradec 17, 117, 166, 191, 224
Slovenia
 commission for hidden mass grave sites 212
 Commission on Concealed Mass Graves in Slovenia 167, 228
Slovenian
 claims to region 111
Slovenian Partisans 130. *See also* Partisans
Slovenian post-war victims 238. *See also* post-war mass graves
Social Democratic Party (SDP) 246
SOE 111
south-Slav 28. *See also* National Council
Soviet
 Soviet Union 235
 Soviet Union and the Western Allies
  war 203
Soviet pressure 96
Soviets 193
 Red Army 223, 224
Spalatin, Christopher 81
Springer, Zvonko 190
Srebrenica 233
Srem Front 222. *See also* Exhibit
Stalin 155
 Stalinist 177
 Stalin-Tito split 38, 153
 Stalin-type mass murder 194
Stambuk, Bishop Slobodan 214
St. Ana church 166
State of Slovenes Croats and Serbs 28. *See also* Yugoslavia

status quo 36. *See also* British Policy
Stedul
 "Crime Story" 105
Stedul, Nikola 255
Stedul, Shirley and Nilola 105
Stepinac
 Metropolitan Aloysius Stepinac 164
 Stepinac, Archbishop Aloysius 44
 Stepinac, Cardinal 82
Strossmayer, Bishop 81, 136
Styria 70, 112
Subasic, Ivan 82
Sunic, Tomislav 255
surrender 30
 of Croats to Yugoslavs 143
 to the Communist troops 80
 to Yugoslavs 20, 23, 34, 46, 49, 54
Svijet, Hrvatski 124
Symposium, Resolution of 56

T

Tehran Conference 34
Terselic, Vesna 255
"The Times" 90
three options 72, 156, 162, 163. *See also* Bleiburg negotiations
Thurn-Valsassina, Dr 121, 122
"Times Literary Supplement" 96
Tito xv, xvi, xvii, xviii, 1, 20, 22, 27, 28, 30, 37, 38, 40, 51, 59, 62, 63, 67, 68, 74, 76, 77, 90, 96, 97, 98, 101, 108, 112, 113, 119, 121, 122, 123, 127, 129, 131, 132, 133, 139, 143, 144, 146, 148, 151, 153, 154, 155, 160, 161, 169, 172, 180, 181, 184, 186, 194, 197, 199, 201, 202, 204, 206, 213, 226, 227, 229, 230, 232, 233, 234, 236, 237, 240, 242, 246, 250, 253, 255, 259, 260, 262, 264, 266, 268, 269, 270, 271, 272
 alleged conspiracy 180
 blames Serbs 82
 border dispute with 201
 causing Allies trouble 60
 confrontation 178
 consolidation of power 131
 crimes 246

 crimes against humanity 250
 forces 94
 intention to commit genocide 119
 message of 139
 Partisans 184
 refusal to take responsibility 82
 responsible 73
 return of anti-Tito groups 100
 Stalinist 177
 surrendered to 72
 Tito's Partisans 78
 under Western and Soviet pressure 169
 withdraw his army 100
Tito, Josip Broz 133, 254
Tito's
 intention to commit genocide 232
Tito's forces
 aggressive behaviour 206
 surrender to 121
Tito's occupation
 Moscow did not support 112
Tito-Subasic Agreement 34
Tito-Subasic union 181
Tito, Walter
 post-war crimes 252
Tolbukhin, Marshal 73
Tolstoy, Nikolai 24, 36, 38, 40, 47, 60, 95, 96, 99, 100, 101, 102, 104, 105, 108, 110, 113, 117, 118, 121, 123, 124, 126, 127, 131, 135, 138, 139, 140, 141, 142, 143, 144, 147, 149, 150, 152, 154, 155, 156, 157, 158, 175, 176, 177, 178, 191, 193, 194, 201, 207, 227, 229, 231, 232, 237, 250
 incorrect allegations 121
 libel trial 138, 141
 libel trial under oath 152
Tomac, Zdravko 255
Trieste 5, 17, 27, 34, 35, 36, 37, 76, 97, 98, 99, 130, 199, 201, 206, 223, 228, 235, 259, 267
 Crisis 132
Tripartite
 negotiations 23. *See also* Bleiburg negotiations
Truman, President 144
Tudjman, Franjo 117, 175

Index

U

Ukraine 131
Ukrainians 87
ultimatum 9, 172, 196, 260. *See also* Yugoslav
United Nations 235
   Peacekeeping monument 210
   UNHCR political refugee 68
   UNPROFOR 177
unsuccessful negotiations 224. *See also* Bulgarians
Unterdrauburg 88. *See also* Dravograd
Unter-Loiback 187, 242. *See also* Loiback
Urban, George 131, 180. *See also* Djilas
Ursic, J 21
USSR
   lack of support from 112. *See also* Soviets
Ustasha 7, 10, 22, 23, 44, 45, 115, 116, 124, 134, 139, 149, 166, 171, 186, 194, 199, 208, 215, 218, 224, 227, 238, 249, 263, 271
   elite group of Generals 45
   escaped execution 194
   Ustachi 123, 232
      Ustaša 223
      Ustase 29, 215
   Ustase
      coup d'etat 29
   Ustashe 43
   Ustashis 94, 119. *See also* Croatian Armed Forces

V

VE Day 88
Venezia Giulia 35, 70, 97, 98, 143
Versailles 28, 34, 198, 203, 285
Veselica, Dr Marko 136, 255
Victoria and Albert Museum
   memorial 152. *See also* Yalta memorial
Villiers, Charles 151
Vitez 62
Vladanovic, Zdravko 255
Vokic, General Ante 44. *See also* Lorkovic
Volkermarkt 12, 28, 36, 58, 88, 112, 190
Volkermarkt-Dravograd junction 118
Vranyczany Dobrinovic, Janko 197
Vucic, Petar 137
Vukusic, Bozo 88, 118, 175, 181, 205, 212, 219

W

Way of the Cross xvi, 133, 144, 146, 165, 166, 175, 176, 194, 207, 230, 236, 237, 239, 242, 243, 245, 247, 248, 250, 252, 265, 271. *See also* Death Marches
West German compensation after WWII 219. *See also* Yugoslavia
White Russians 33
Wikipedia 95, 194
Williams, Carol J 116
Willoughby, Major General Charles 55, 56, 57, 62, 73, 74, 127, 150, 180

Y

Yalta 38, 64, 87, 89, 152, 153, 155, 161, 196, 235, 251
   Agreement 38, 49, 60, 63, 96
   Conference 34, 35, 89
   Memorial 105
   Treaty 133
   Victims Memorial 180
Yugo-Communists
   surrender to 73, 76
Yugo-communist Walter Tito
   post-war crimes of 252
Yugoslav
   1990s aggression 177
   admission of guilt 133
   "atrocious" and "inflammatory" behaviour 156
   belligerent behaviour 196
   claim to Carinthia 120
   deception 101
   government denied 128
   occupation 201
   threats and impatience 140
   threats to attack 61
   vengeance 186, 189
   war prisoners 113
   withdrawal 36, 39
Yugoslav Army 29
   3rd Yugoslav division 72
   5th Yugoslav division 72
   11th Dalmatian Brigade 62
   12th Proletarian Brigade 8
   12th Slavonian Proletarian Division 10
   14th Slovenian Division 208
   15th Majevac Brigade 243
   51st Division 63, 208
   51st Vojvodina Division 7, 225
   51st Yugoslav Division 72, 200
   arrival of in Zagreb 145
   cannons and bazookas 48
   communist 30
   Communists 23
   concealment 45
   Fourteenth Shock Division 112
   Fourth Army 37, 112
   Fourth Yugoslav Army 97, 120, 199
   four Yugoslav armies 9, 223
   Hocevar 120, 133, 154
   intransigence 35
   Kovacic, Ivan 172
   liquidate 30, 153, 226
   liquidated 63, 73, 128, 199, 221
   liquidation 9, 10, 61, 89, 128, 172, 184, 202, 255
   liquidations 197
   non-cooperation 34
   Third Army 40, 243
   Third Battalion (Tomsic Brigade) 225
   Third Yugoslav Army 35, 48, 63, 207, 222
   used deceit 60
   Weitzendorf 72
   YNLA's Fourth Army 112
   Yugoslav 12th Brigade 9
   Yugoslav 14th Division 123
   Yugoslav Third Army 243
Yugoslav-Bolshevik crimes against humanity 181
Yugoslav Commissar 61, 101. *See also* Basta
Yugoslav Committee 203
Yugoslav Communists
   surrender to 64
Yugoslavia
   control of a postwar 132
   coup d'etat 29
   Greater Yugoslavia 100
   monopoly on power 160
   proclamation 37

refugees from 108
responsible for genocide 250
Yugoslav Killing Fields 116
Yugoslav-occupied zone 76
Yugoslav Partisans
   continuing attacks by 126
Yugoslavs
   continuing battles with 130
   covering-up 74
   deceived the British at Bleiburg 89
   guarantee of 172. *See also* Beliburg negotiations
   intended genocide 79
   outnumbered the British 112
   pressure from 127
   surrender to 64, 81. *See also* Bleiburg negotiations
   threatened 23
   withdraw 98

Z

Zadar 57, 98
Zagreb 63, 153, 242
   evacuate 43
   exodus 44
Zdenka Cerar 178
Zumberek mountains. 115

www.ingramcontent.com/pod-product-compliance
Lightning Source LLC
Chambersburg PA
CBHW081157230426
43666CB00016B/2845